Growing up in a Shrinking World

GROWING UP IN A SHRINKING WORLD:
How politics, culture and the nuclear age defined the biography of Ali A. Mazrui

Edited by
D. Ndirangu Wachanga

AFRICA WORLD PRESS
Trenton | London | Cape Town | Nairobi | Addis Ababa | Asmara | Ibadan | New Delhi

AFRICA WORLD PRESS
541 West Ingham Avenue | Suite B
Trenton, New Jersey 08638

Copyright © 2017

All rights reserved. No part of this publication may be reproduced, stored in a retrieval system or transmitted in any form or by any means electronic, mechanical, photocopying, recording or otherwise without the prior written permission of the publisher.

Book design: Dawid Kahts
Cover design: Ashraful Haq

Cataloging-in-Publication Data may be obtained from the Library of Congress.

ISBN: 978-1-56902-559-8 (HB)
      978-1-56902-560-4 (PB)

TABLE OF CONTENTS

Foreword – Willy Mutunga   vii

Introduction – D. Ndirangu Wachanga   ix

Chapter 1: Ali A. Mazrui
Growing Up in a Shrinking World: From a Kenyan Childhood to the
Cuban Missile Crisis   1

Chapter 2: Ngũgĩ wa Thiong'o (Tribute)
A Tribute to Ali Mazrui, the Global Kenya   21

Chapter 3: Henry Chakava
Publishing Ali A. Mazrui: An eloquent Debater   25

Chapter 4: Mĩcere Gĩthae Mũgo
Orature Poems of Celebration and Healing in Honor
of Mwalimu Ali Mazrui   29

Chapter 5: Ngũgĩ wa Thiong'o
Mazrui and Achebe:
The Literary Artist and the Political Scientist   39

Chapter 6: D. Ndirangu Wachanga
Recording Ali Mazrui Documentary Biography:
Lessons and Challenges   45

Chapter 7: Macharia Munene
Recasting Ali Mazrui   65

Chapter 8: Adekeye Adebajo
Who Killed Pax Africana?   109

Chapter 9: Michael O. West
Kwame Nkrumah and Ali Mazrui:
An Analysis of the 1967 *Transition* Debate   117

Chapter 10: Wanjala S. Nasong'o
Global Citizen, Dialectical Thinker: Ali Mazrui and the Analytical
Potency of Mazruiana   137

Chapter 11: Alamin M. Mazrui
The African Impact on American Higher Education:
Ali Mazrui's Contribution   155

**Chapter 12: N'Dri T. Assié-Lumumba &
Tukumbi Lumumba-Kasongo**
Salient Features in Mazrui's Thought on Education in Africa:
Critical Reflections   169

Chapter 13: Maurice N. Amutabi
The Trial of Ali Mazrui's Trilogy, Scholarship and
the Making of a Public Intellectual in Africa:
Revisiting His Legacy in the World of Knowledge   183

Chapter 14: Oscar Mwangi
Terrorism and Counterterrorism in
Ali Mazrui's Political Thought   201

Chapter 15: Etin Anwar
Paradox of Gender in Mazrui's Triple Heritage   219

Chapter 16: Abdul Karim Bangura
Pan-Blackist Conceptualizations of the Black Power Paradigm:
From Cheikh Anta Diop to Ali Al'amin Mazrui   233

Chapter 17: Darryl C. Thomas
Ali A. Mazrui's meditation about Global Africa:
From Otto Von Bismarck to Barack Obama   295

Notes on Contributors   311

FOREWORD

I first met Ali A. Mazrui at Dar es Salaam Univeristy in 1969. He was already a respected scholar and public intellectual. From Makerere University College, he was assiduously stirring debates, which reverberated across the entire continent. Across the border, he praised Julius K. Nyerere as a philosopher king with original ideas in the same measure he criticized his Ujamaa policies. In one of his controversial articles in Transition, he referred to Kwame Nkrumah of Ghana as a Leninist Czar, praising him for being a great African, but criticizing him for not being a great Ghanaian.

To say that Mazrui's public lectures at Makerere University College were popular is an understatement. Not many intellectuals have had a sitting head of state respond to them when delivering a speech in parliament. But Milton Obote responded to Mazrui's criticism of Uganda's failure to ensure equal distribution of resources.

In those days, we had regular academic conferences under the auspices of the University of East Africa, and Mazrui was a frequent presenter, rousing controversies in ways that irritated some and inspired others. I was witness to the great debates by this pioneering East African intellectual at his brilliant best. These are the debates that shaped the idea of a university, an idea, which was destroyed when we allowed oppressive forces to destroy the university as a self-directed space for free thinking. When scholars like Mazrui left, others like Ngũgĩ wa Thiong'o and Mĩcere Gĩthae Mugo were exiled, the university – as an institution – suffered and our collective progress stunted. The tragedy of losing our best minds when the country was still very young continues to haunt us and to destroy our country and our continent. A critical reflection of Mazrui's legacy should allow us to evaluate those losses, and provoke genuine commitments toward building institutions that would prevent such a tragedy to ever visit our country.

Alamin Mazrui and I wanted to write Mazrui's biography after reflecting deeply about his role as a scholar and as a public intellectual. When we approached Mwalimu Mazrui, he suggested we edit some of his major debates.

We have edited three major volumes around some of his major debates. In retrospect, it is clear that writing a biography of a colossal intellectual who was constantly giving talks across the globe, publishing new material, addressing emerging global issues and tirelessly debating, would have been incomplete.

As Chief Justice and President of the Supreme Court of the Republic of Kenya, I hosted Mazrui at the Judiciary. He spoke to judges about law and politics under the 2010 Constitution of Kenya. His speech was judicious, particularly for judges who still professed the dishonorable idea that "the law is the law is the law." Mazrui historicized the transformation of the Kenyan Judiciary in subtle ways that offered discernments to a complex interplay between law and politics, maintaining the importance of judicial freedom.

In his peerless way, Mazrui reminded us of the importance of intellectual debates on good governance and public policy issues between academics and leaders, suggesting that the culture, which interfaces public service (of which judges and magistrates are part), and academy, should be revived for the sake of our grandchildren and the future of our nation.

Mazrui was a champion of justice and good governance. Yet, he believed that good governance is impossible without giving people voice. It is only when multiplicity of voices compete that knowledge is generated.

This volume of essays in honor of Mazrui leads us to examine his numerous suggestions on ways to expand discursive spaces in order for those voice to thrive.

Dr. Willy Mutunga, D. Jur, SC. EGH
Chief Justice/President, Supreme Court of Kenya
May 2016
Nairobi

INTRODUCTION

I had the privilege of serving as Ali Mazrui's authorized documentary biographer, tracing his life from his birthplace in the East African coast, to his residence in Binghamton, New York. I travelled with him in three continents – Africa, Europe, and United States - for seven years. When I first asked him about his legacy in 2009, he requested me to pose that question to other scholars who know about Africa. This collection of essays seeks to respond to that request.

In 2012, I listened to the renowned African historian, Toyin Falola, describe Mazrui as a great scholar, particularly because his work offers powerful insights to three fundamental aspects that concern humanity: Religion – whether one is a believer or not is irrelevant – politics, and love. He was speaking at a reception organized to celebrate Mazrui's 80th birthday. The event had been put together by the International Institute of Islamic Thought at the annual African Studies Association (ASA) conference in Philadelphia.

This was to be Mazrui's last ASA meeting. That evening, Mazrui sat pensively in his wheelchair. He wore his trademark blue blazer, spotted a beard, held his walking stick, and with a contemplative posture of a philosopher, he curiously looked around the room, exchanging nods here and waving his hand there. But there was something portentous and sad, which hang and haunted the room with palpable density.

His health had been failing. For a year or so, he had to be accompanied by a health escort in all his travels. His voice was becoming less resonant. But he maintained his sangfroid and his speeches remained poetic and captivating, pulsating with his usual unbridled creativity, but delivered with carefully measured combat. Even the most controversial, he once confided in me, become mellow with age.

What struck me that evening was Mazrui's switch from English to Swahili as he concluded his short speech. I had never heard him address a gathering in Swahili in my seven years of travelling with him. The tone was deliberately unhurried. The content was weighty. The reception hall was quiet.

Even when the attentive audience cheered him on, it was clearly expressing its gratitude to him for something than the brief speech he delivered that evening; something bigger than the 80th birthday celebration; something no one seemed to be able to define, but one which we knew was bigger than the event that brought us together that evening. Maybe that was Mazrui's project: A project that he could not define; one that therefore, demanded relentless pursuit.

In a classic convergence of his triple heritage model – a reception in a Western capital (Philadelphia) during the African Studies Conference, and at an event organized by an Islamic Institute – he ended his speech in his native tongue, Swahili:

Nataka dua zenu, muendelee kuniombea Mungu, na tutaonana tena wakati mwingine, tukijaaliwa.

Please continue praying for me, and we will meet again, if that is the will of God.

He was biding us, and ASA farewell.

Mazrui was a common presence at ASA for more than four decades, and one often found him surrounded by scholars, critics, publishers, and graduate students at the conference hotel's lobby. Dressed modestly, he would have an equally modest bag. From this simple bag, he would reach out for some of the most recently published reflections on the most complex issues. He generously shared his copies after a hearty conversation, pushing those around him to reflect on both irritating and inspiring views as one way of questioning the thought of thought itself. His modesty never betrayed his sophistication and intellectual wealth. When you couple that with his charming smile, one encountered a complex scholar whose charisma was always inviting without intimidating.

Such is the presence that we now miss with his absence. As the world mourned his death, it confronted the absence of the central and colossus figure he was; reminding us that death is the only rite of passage where the main subject is absent.

"The colossus with the feet of steel joined his ancestors in the early hours of October 13, 2014," is the way Toyin Falola introduced his eloquent obituary on his longtime friend, Ali Mazrui. For someone who traversed all corners of the globe for close to half a century, it is apt to describe him as having feet of steel. At one point, Mazrui joked that he exercised when walking between airport terminals. Yet, Mazrui's presence resides in those prints his feet of steel left behind: an extensive body of work, which was appropriately christened Mazruiana, and one that he assiduously nurtured for more than half a century.

Introduction

It is precisely the absence of his voice and the presence of his writing that makes a reflection of his legacy both liberating and apprehending. It is liberating because we are no longer tied to the authority of the author. Reflecting on his legacy therefore, enables us to examine the beginning of his writings and the contexts within which he produced his work, especially because we now know where the writing ended. Still, he offered his work as a gift without asking for anything in return. For that reason, we must be apprehended in our acceptance of a gift where nothing is asked for in return. Essays in this volume will hopefully serve as a guide to a new epistemological space where Mazrui's work and life lessons can be re-read and re-interpreted outside the limitations assumed previously.

His death attracted numerous commentaries across the globe, which examined his legacy. There were several newspaper articles about his legacy, which were published across the globe. Putting together various reflections about his work and legacy in form of a book is a challenging undertaking. However, chapters in this volume are by some of the powerful voices about Africa and African scholarship: from the renowned novelist Ngũgĩ wa Thiong'o to the legendary poet and oraturist, Mĩcere Gĩthae Mugo. TThe contents are also diverse: ranging from terrorism and counter-terrorism efforts to the politics of international peace; from Mazrui's role as an Islamic scholar to his contributions in global education.

In my last interview with him in his office in Binghamton, New York, in March 2013, he made an intriguing request:

> You will let me know when we meet in AfterAfrica if other scholars continued to use my triple heritage model after I am gone.

In this volume, Mazrui's triangulated model is discussed, contested, redefined and challenged by some of the powerful and leading voices in African scholarship. The voices contained in this book touch on diverse topics just as they are from scholars from diverse backgrounds, making the book an interdisciplinary examination of Mazrui's legacy. It contains three orature poems of celebration and healing in honor of Mwalimu Ali Mazrui by the iconic poet, Mĩcere Gĩthae Mũgo. Her first poem, *Leo ni Shangwe, Mwalimu Ali*, was delivered at Mazrui birthday banquet during the 38th annual conference of the New York African Studies Association in April 2013. When Mazrui was admitted in hospital for the last time, Mĩcere Mũgo would send flowers to him and his family. One day as she inquired from Pauline, Mazrui's wife, whether to send flowers to the hospital or at home, Pauline replied that Mazrui had requested for a poem instead of flowers. Included in this volume are two of those 'flower' poems.

In a tribute to Mazrui, written just a few days after his death, Ngũgĩ wa

Thiong'o suggests we leave it to political scientists to evaluate Mazrui's legacy. However, he strongly acknowledges Mazrui's role in making Kenya and Africa visible in the highest ranks of intellectual production.

Looking at Mazrui's biography, it is increasingly clear that it is a story of the becoming of the Kenyan nation. It is, therefore, fitting that the volume starts with an autobiographical chapter by Mazrui, *Growing up in a shrinking world: From a Kenyan childhood to the Cuban missile crisis*. In this autobiographical essay, Mazrui traces his growing up in Mombasa and delineates his early influences, which gives us clear insights into his formulation of the triple heritage model that he developed later in his academic life.

This chapter is important because Mazrui introduces us to his mother and his relationship to her, describing her as a conciliator and a disciplinarian. In his numerous writings, Mazrui did not write a lot about his mother, but he often acknowledged the impact his father- who served as a Chief Kadhi in colonial Kenya- had on him although he died when Mazrui was only fourteen years old. Yet, the death of his father changed Mazrui's intellectual destiny. His father wanted him to study Islam. But there was no one to promote that alternative after his father's death.

Through his interactions with his father, Mazrui drew his oratory interest from listening to the theological and juridical conversations his father was having with other adults. Those childhood experiences exposed him to the aesthetics of debating and to the importance of creative use of language.

In his chapter titled, *Mazrui and Achebe: The Literary Artist and the Political Scientist*, Ngũgĩ wa Thiong'o alludes to Mazrui's creativity, describing him as a political scientist with a literary bent. This chapter is derived from Ngũgĩ wa Thiong'o's presentation at the 38th Annual Conference of the New York African Studies Association (NYASA). This lecture was given as part of a plenary conversation in memory of Chinua Achebe. NYASA had organized this conference in honor of Mazrui's 80th birthday. This session had been devoted to a discussion about Africa at fifty, featuring Chinua Achebe, Ali Mazrui and Ngũgĩ wa Thiong'o. But Achebe died a few months before the conference. Ngũgĩ's presentation therefore, was a reflection of Achebe's legacy while at the same time celebrating Mazrui's 80th birthday. As Ngũgĩ demonstrates in his piece, discussing Mazrui and Achebe is an inevitable invitation to examine the complex relationship between art and politics. "Politics is about the organization and management of power in society; art, literature in particular, is part of the organization and management of values in society. The way power is organized, who or what social groups control it, the ends to which it is put, impacts the entire realm of the human, and ultimately the quality of human life. And ultimately, this is what the work of both Achebe and Mazrui is all about," Ngũgĩ notes in his chapter.

In my chapter, *Recording Ali Mazrui Documentary Biography: Lessons and challenges*, I describe Mazrui's eminence in the debates, which were taking place in East Africa after independence. This was a period when new post-colonial states had not delineated the line between politicians and intellectuals. There was a misunderstanding by politicians about the role of intellectuals in politics. It was erroneously assumed that intellectuals who spoke about politics were interested in political power. Therefore, when Mazrui spoke about political institutions and political processes such as democratization, equality, and representation, he was not interested in political position; rather, he was playing the role of a public intellectual, serving as a model in defining the role of intellectuals in societies. It is not surprising that one of Mazrui's most controversial essays was when he described Kwame Nkrumah as the Leninist czar.

In *Kwame Nkrumah and Ali Mazrui: An analysis of the 1967 Transition debate*, Michael West provides the foundations for Mazrui's decades-long engagement with Nkrumah's ideas. In course of his wrestling with these ideas, Mazrui acquired a greater intellectual appreciation of Ghana's founding father.[2] As West notes, this controversy set in motion by Mazrui's article was one of the outstanding Pan-African debates of the postcolonial era.

Describing his life as one long debate, Mazrui often attracted debates because of his numerous controversial ideas. Maurice Amutabi provides a catalogue of some of Mazrui's controversies, including his proposal that certain politically stable countries in Africa should colonize the less stable ones. In his chapter, *The trial of Ali Mazrui's trilogy, scholarship, and the making of a public intellectual in Africa: Revisiting his legacy in the world of knowledge*, Amutabi draws our attention to Mazrui's vulnerabilities, especially his casting of Islam as an African religion and his attempts to sanitize the East African Arab slave trade.

Etin Anwar adds another element in the catalogue of Mazrui's vulnerabilities: gender. In her chapter, *Paradox of Gender in Mazrui's Triple Heritage*, Anwar argues that Mazrui's triple heritage model is a paradox, especially in ways that it converges and diverges from dominant feminism theories. Drawing from Mazrui's theory of the paradox of gender, Anwar demonstrates the convergent sexual reciprocity among men and women regardless of racial, cultural, religious, and civilizational boundaries.

And Mazrui did not shy away from crossing academic boundaries, quoting from poets and philosphers, in ways that powerfully redefined Africanity across geographical spaces, time, and cultures, as Abdul Karim Bangura demonstrates in his chapter, *Pan-Blackist Conceptualizations of the Black*

Power Paradigm: From Cheikh Anta Diop to Ali Al'amin Mazrui. Bangura invites us to re-think Africanity as a complex idea rather than as a point of origin. Such an orientation, Bangura suggests, should strengthen our perspective in the debate about the place of Africa in global cultures and civilizations. Let us remember that when Mazrui started to write, there existed a long and established European tradition that denigrated Africans as a people who had neither histories nor means of self understanding. Mazrui challenged those narratives, serving not only as an interpreter of history but also as one of the leading African intellectuals who shaped that history.

His unique analytical style has as its central feature the notion of opposites, of reconcilable contradictions, of paradoxes. In his chapter, *Global citizen, dialectical thinker: Ali Mazrui and the analytical potency of Mazruiana*, Wanjala S. Nasong'o underscores Mazrui's analytical prowess as a dialectical thinker. According to Nasong'o, Mazrui's ability to masterfully use the dialectical method strengthened his analytical potency as well as his explanatory clarity.

In his chapter, *Recasting Ali Mazrui*, Macharia Munene guides us in re-examining Mazrui's biography, identifying in details some of the qualities that allowed Mazrui to function as a global Kenyan while belonging to a category of people who suffer from delayed display of brilliance. Munene is referring to Mazrui's mediocre high school performance, which denied him enrollment at Makerere University College. For a period of five years after his high school performance, Mazrui felt humiliated by this failure. It was only after reciting a poem in the presence of the then Kenya's colonial governor that he received a scholarship to join a community college in England to boost his grades before joining the University of Manchester in 1957. Mazrui considered that poetry recital as one of the most important lectures he ever gave because it gave him a second chance in life; rising to the highest echelons in the academy to bear the title *mwalimu*, teacher. It is important therefore, to examine his contributions to the education system in Africa and globally.

N'Dri Assié-Lumumba and Tukumbi Lumumba-Kasongo's chapter is a critical reflection of salient features in Mazrui's thought on education in Africa. As a strong believer in the power of education to transform the world, Mazrui's contribution to education in Africa is predicated on his interrogating the "kind of education that can contribute to the progressive reconstruction of the African societies, states, and their political economies."[1]

But it is also important to examine Mazrui's influence on the American higher education system because he spent most of his academic life teaching in the United States. To this end, Alamin Mazrui's chapter, *The impact*

Introduction

of American higher education: Ali Mazrui's contribution, identifies various key areas in which Mazrui's ideas have made fundamental contributions in shaping academic discourses as well as educational policies both at home and abroad.

Mazrui's interest in peace and conflict resolution can be traced from his 1967 publication, *Towards a Pax-Africana: A study of ideology and ambition*,[2] where he wondered who was to keep the peace in Africa with the withdrawal of Pax Britannica. As discussed by Adekeye Adebajo in his chapter, *Who killed Pax-Africana*, Mazrui was calling on Africans to create and consolidate peace on the continent. Adebajo adopts a Mazruiana approach reminiscent of Mazrui's article *Who killed democracy in Africa*. But in his chapter, Adebajo identifies and discusses five villains that are responsible for the death of Pax-Africana, or as he calls it "the epic murder mystery."

But the post 9/11 world is facing different questions regarding peace, especially after the declaration of war against terror by the US government. Mazrui died at a time when acts of terror are ravaging part of Africa, including his own country, Kenya, and that of his wife Pauline, Nigeria. In his chapter, *terrorism and counterterrorism in Ali Mazrui's political thought*, Oscar Mwangi uses social constructivism as a framework of analysis to examine the relationship between Mazrui's social milieu and his construction of terrorism and counterterrorism as a reality in the political world. According to Mwangi, Mazrui's approach is a function of his social milieu at two levels: the normative and the empirical. In other words, Mazrui constructs terrorism and counterterrorism in his political thought in such a way that they deconstruct the often-held negative perceptions of Islamism.

Although he remained critical of the American international policy, especially towards Islam, he wrote in grandiosely glowing terms about the rise of the first Black President of the United States, Barack Obama, describing him as the most powerful Black man to have ever walked planet earth. Darryl Thomas analyzes how this power has been used to foster Pax-Africana. In his chapter, *Ali Mazrui's meditations about Global Africa: From Otto von Bismarck to Barack Obama*, Thomas discusses Mazrui's analysis of the impact of Global Africa on world's socio-economic, political, religious and cultural systems by invoking biographical experiences of some of the major black figures in world history.

What made Ali Mazrui an exceptional scholar was his active participation in producing and enriching a form of scholarship that provided a global view of Africa, especially at a time when it was very tempting to retreat to parochialism. He ably connected that scholarship to other places because he understood that Africa is not isolated.

African intellectuals in the diaspora often grapple with the challenge of repatriating the knowledge they produce away from home. Mazrui struggled with this question for more than three decades. I hope the conversations contained in these chapters will start a dialogue around that question.

Mazrui's intellectual biography will continue to challenge us to look at Africa in the world, and the world in Africa. The sheer quantity of his work, its wide range and diversity of ideas, significantly explains why he will continue to attract keen admirers and harsh critics even in death.

Ndirangu Wachanga
Madison, Wisconsin
February 2017

---

[1] N'drie Assie-Lumumba and Tukumbi Lumumba-Kasongo, "Salient features in Mazrui's thought on education in Africa: Critical reflections," in *Public Intellectuals and the Politics of Global Africa: Essays in Honor of Ali A. Mazrui*, ed. Seifudein Adem (London: Adonis & Abbey Publishers Ltd), 173 – 186.

[2] Ali A. Mazrui, *Towards a Pax-Africana: A Study of Ideology and Ambition* (Chicago: The university of Chicago Press, 1967).

1

Growing Up in a Shrinking World:
From a Kenyan Childhood to the Cuban Missile Crisis[1]*

Ali A. Mazrui

What is a political scientist? In my own view, a political scientist combines the personal experience of political consciousness, the general ethos of scholarship, and the specialized skills of interpreting political phenomena. Political consciousness is sensitivity to issues of public concern and to the policy implications of private interests. The ethos of scholarship is rooted in adherence to the rules of evidence, documentation, and logic. But the discipline of political science itself requires additional specialized skills concerned with handling data or effectively using the discipline's conceptual tools.

If a political scientist is a fusion of political consciousness, scholarship, and the skills of political analysis, then what is the relationship among these three elements? It is difficult to say which of the three is the most important, but easy to determine which comes first. Political consciousness must come before the acquisition of either the ethos of scholarship or the specialized skills of the discipline. A political scientist has first to be a politically conscious animal before he or she can move in the direction of acquiring the

---

* This chapter, "Growing up in a shrinking world: From a Kenyan childhood to the Cuban missile crisis" by Ali A. Mazrui was originally published in Public intellectuals and the politics of global Africa: Essays in honour of Ali A. Mazrui." edited by Seifudein Adem 2011 pp. 1-20, and published by Adonis & Abbey publishers Ltd, and is printed here with the permission of the editor, and the publisher.

necessary equipment from the discipline. Political consciousness must therefore be seen ultimately as the most deeply personal, in some ways the most subjective, of the three elements that add up to that breed of scholar we call a "political scientist."

Because political consciousness is so intricately bound up with the growth of a person's general awareness, political scientists should perhaps devote more time to using their own lives as data for the study of the growth of political consciousness. This autobiographical essay is an exercise in that direction. It is the story of the growth of political consciousness in a single individual, inevitably bound up with his expanding world of awareness as he grew up in a shrinking world. Some of the elements acquired extra meaning only in retrospect: a scholar, like a poet, must stop at times and "recollect in tranquility." Little incidents, like having to rebuke a student for throwing a bed down the steps, could constitute milestones in a person's discovery of the phenomenon of authority. This essay also refers to a little incident in Zanzibar, of one child chasing another, and of the resultant confrontation between two families – all adding up to the discovery of the wider meanings of simple things. As an African philosopher has put it in revising Descartes, "I *feel*, therefore I *am*!"

This essay therefore begins with that first stage in development of a political scientist – the stage of acquiring general political consciousness.

Early Influences

A number of interrelated process helped to initiate me into the study of international relations. First was my gradual *politicization* as an observer-culminating in my choice of political science as a field of study. Second was my discovery of the world as a *cross-cultural* or *multicultural* reality. This realization was through both my upbringing and my involvement in the mass media. Third was my discovery of the *nuclear age* as the temporal context in which I lived.

We are dealing here with politics, culture, and science. Politically I grew up in a colonial situation that was inherently *international*. One country (Great Britain) was dominating another (Kenya). The city in which I grew up was *multicultural*. For centuries Mombasa, a seaport, had experienced the winds and smells of other civilizations – initially from Africa, Arabia, and Asia, and later from the West. My politics were therefore partly internationalized from the outset; so were my cultural experiences. I *experienced* international relations as a person before I studied it professionally.

As for my initiation into the nuclear age, at first this was through socialization about life and death, and about creation and destruction. In my case part of the background was Islamic attitudes toward creative art.

It is ironic that my socialization into issues of life and death should have been connected with the divide between ethics and aesthetics. It is a double irony that this particular artistic dialectic should later condition my attitude to science, including the social significance of nuclear physics.

It all began with the distrust of idolatry in fundamentalist Islam. Pre-Islamic Arabia had worshiped idols in precisely the place were Muslims today circumambulate the Kaaba in Mecca. The Prophet Muhammad destroyed some of those idols with his own hands. They were the "graven images." To ensure that they did not return, Islam discouraged such art forms as sculpture and painting if the images took the form of God's creatures and plants. In time, to paint an animal was regarded in Islam as an attempt to imitate God. Organic art (in the sense of making art recreate living natural organisms) became increasingly taboo to fundamentalist Islam. Mosques were decorated with *letters* of the *Qur'an* rather than with creatures.

Many centuries after the entry of Islam into Africa a Kenyan boy was caught up in this tradition. My father caught me drawing human figure in pencil. I was doodling. "If you were called upon to make the human figure live on the Day of Judgment, would you be able to do so?" That was the question my father posed to me. Would I be able to give my doodle a *soul*? I confessed my impotence in this regard. To my father, the conclusion was clear – I was not to paint or draw living beings from then on.

I could draw the fruit of a living organism, but no the organism itself. I could draw a mango but not a mango tree. I could draw a shoe but not the shoemaker. Islamic fundamentalism seemed to curtail the culture of pictures more decisively than the culture of letters.

I do not know whether I would have developed into a great artist or not. It is true that if there was an artistic talent in me, my father might have killed it in the name of Islam. It is as if my father were formulating an imperative:

"DO NOT CREATE AND DO NOT KILL – *both* are prerogatives of God."

The lesson was completed on another occasion. We were in our country home in the outskirts of Mombasa, which at the time had no electricity. We were using lanterns and other kerosene lamps. There were insects around, and as a cruel little child I caught one of these insects and brought it closer and closer to the flame of one of the lamps. My father caught sight of me and stopped me saying in the Arabic language: "Only God punishes with fire."

Alienation from Science

These two incidents – the day my father stopped my "creating" and the day he stopped my "destroying" – had a profound effect on my future attitudes to life and death, art and science. I felt a neo-phenomenological impact.

Perhaps my father distrusted in art what he should have distrusted in science. When the artist tries to imitate God with paint or clay, the product (even at its most successful) is unlikely to be dangerous to God's design on earth. But when a scientist tries to imitate God either by genetic engineering or by splitting the atom, the results are incalculable. Imitating God through art could be a salute to the Almighty. Imitating God through science could be a venture into nuclear blasphemy.

My more sensitive teachers at school drew certain conclusions from my declining interest in the natural sciences. My waning appetite for these scientific studies was attributed to the special nature of my Islamic upbringing.

The nuclear age was dramatically announced while I was still at secondary school with the U.S. atomic bombing of Hiroshima and Nagasaki. There were school debates as to whether or not this was the birth of a new dark age. We even staged a one-act play about whether science was a blessing or a curse. Because it was a school play in the mainstream of Western tradition, the basic message was in favor of science. I was less sure. My father's condemnation of art as an imitation of God was being hesitantly applied to science in my young mind.

And yet whatever reservations I might have had about science, I was clearly getting increasingly interested in society. I was shrinking away from the natural and physical sciences. Was I beginning to be captivated by the social sciences? Were there early indications that I would evolve into a political scientist?

A Tradition of Debate

I came to political science partly through a childhood interest in law and journalism. And I came to these twin interests partly though my family background. As I was growing up my father was already the chief kadhi of Kenya. And because Islamic law had full status in Kenya, the chief kadhi was not merely a religious leader but a senior judge in the national judicial system. I realized that my father was one of the two or three leading experts on Islamic law in East Africa. He took a considerable interest in Islamic jurisprudence, and as I stood around serving coffee to guests or bringing the trays for lunch, the background conversation among the adults was often a sustained discourse on an issue in jurisprudence or theology.

Although my father did have this solemn side to his career and temperament, it was a solemnity that was often animated by intellectual liveliness. He was a gifted polemicist in the Ki-Swahili language and great public debater in his day. In the 1930s he established a kind of newspaper, *Al-Islah*, of his own, at first written by hand, then duplicated by a rather imperfect method of the time, and later printed. He had inherited some property, and used much of the income from his coconut plantation running this small-circulation Swahili paper as a medium of polemics and social reform. My father had a puritanical side to his convictions, and was greatly disturbed, for example, by the waste and extravagance that went into weddings in our region. One major social reform he envisioned was the restoration of marriage to its original religious simplicity, without the parents of both the bride and the bridegroom going heavily into debt. He was also profoundly disturbed by elaborate mourning ceremonies, and considered them all to be quite incompatible with his vision of true Islam. The dead needed our prayers, but in as simple a form as possible. It was not necessary to prolong the collective chanting of the *Qur'an*, or to have three days of crowded, enclosed mourning by the women, with all the ritualistic wailing.

I used to listen to all these cross-cultural discussions as a child, often admiring the passion that underlay my father's reforming zeal. Sometimes he used his "newspaper" for more ad hoc issues, often coming into conflict with the local colonial officials of the day.

My father also had a great sense of family. Among his family heroes was Sheikh Mbaruk Mazrui, the nineteenth-century coastal rebel who defied both the British and the Sultan of Zanzibar. I used to hear romanticized stories about Sheikh Mbaruk, his courage, and his defiance of the grand alliance between the Britons and the Barghash Dynasty, between *Pax Britannica* and the Sultan's claim to sovereignty over the coast of mainland East Africa. I was learning about the interplay between diplomacy and warfare.

As I went through school in Mombasa, I also developed a special interest in the English language, initially as a medium of debate. Perhaps my family's legal background and my father's polemical side influenced this initial interest in language as a tool of verbal combat. I took part in almost every school debate that was organized and for which I was eligible. I wrote short articles for student magazines. I even won an essay competition or two. My mother tongue was Ki-Swahili, but my new obsession was English. My cross-cultural preoccupations were maturing. I began to sense that fulfillment for me would not lie in Islamic jurisprudence and theology, but in more secular forms of intellectual endeavor. Becoming a writer and a journalist were at the time intricately intertwined in my vision of my own future. I saw both the novel and the newspaper as great media of "stories of social meaning." I saw in Charles Dickens a little of my father – the social reformer commanding a pen. That my father was primarily a pamphleteer, whereas Dickens was primarily a novelist, was to me a distinction without significance. They both used words for great public causes.

I dreamt about going to Makerere University College in Uganda. They did not teach law then at Makerere University College, nor did they teach journalism. But they did teach English. I reasoned, in my simple way, that with a greater command of English I could enter the world of public issues. Colonies used the language of their master for public purposes.

Then the shock came. My father died in 1947, a year before I was due to complete school. I was deeply shaken; but more important than the bereavement was the increased stature that the old man assumed in my vision. I was fourteen years old then. His passion for public involvement became even more heroic in its dimensions. My father's world had been, I now realized, relatively small. He was best known in the Swahili world, especially along the coast of Tanganyika, Kenya, and in Zanzibar. But within that world and in his field he had been a man not only of stature, but more important, of clear commitment. As was customary among my people, questions were being asked whether I, as a son, would follow in his footsteps. I already knew I could not do to so in the theological field. The question was – could I excel in a secular professional field? Would I switch cultures?

My Years as a School "Dropout"

In 1948 I sat for the Cambridge school certificate examinations. In a sense this British examination was a test of cultural assimilation. At the end of the period I was disturbed. I sensed that I had not done well. I even feared that I might have failed altogether.

The results came; I had not failed, but I had obtained a mere third-class grade in the school certificate. I saw my ambition to go to Makerere University College crumble before me. There was no question of being admitted to Makerere with such a certificate. The college, understandably in the circumstances, would not touch me with the proverbial barge pole. My bright dream of Western-style higher education seemed extinguished.

I saw old classmates making their way to Makerere, while I looked around Mombasa for a job as a clerk. I was what in East Africa is called a "school leaver" – someone who had failed to get beyond secondary education, I saw myself as a school "dropout."

I was fifteen at the time. I had taken my school certificate rather early, partly because I had previously shown evidence of precociousness and had been permitted to jump classes. My problem in life had not been that of a late developer; it might have been that of an overestimated precocity.

I first staggered into a Dutch trading firm with a branch in Mombasa. It turned out that I was not precocious enough for the job they had in mind – they wanted to train a, fifteen-year-old to become an assistant manager very quickly. Alas, I could not rise quickly enough, and had therefore to be dismissed after two months. The firm was apologetic and gave me an excellent reference. But they had made a mistake in employing one so young for the job they had in mind.

On leaving the trading company, I idled around for a while, and then a relative telephoned a European acquaintance of his, Lt. Col, H. W. Newell, to inquire if there was a vacancy for a junior clerk in the new project known by the name of the Mombasa Institute of Muslim Education. This institute was the brainchild of Sir Philip Mitchell, then governor of Kenya, who had felt that the Muslims were being left behind in East Africa, and needed a new mechanical institute to equip them with modern skills.

When my relative telephoned Colonel Newell for a job for me, the institute had not as yet acquired its own buildings. There were only offices, provided by the generosity of Sir Philip Mitchell, in Government House, his own residence in Mombasa. Colonel Newell told my relative that there was no job at the particular time, but that if I was prepared to go and work without pay for a while, I would have priority once a vacancy opened. I was encouraged to accept this offer. I was now close to the imperial order.

My work at the institute was an important experience in my maturation as an observer of social and imperial issues. For one thing I was involved in a project that was just beginning, and saw it grow to fruition until the day when students were admitted. At the time I joined the project we were in the north wing of Government House, overlooking the Indian Ocean in an elegant area of the town near the golf course. Later we moved to the site where the construction of the institute was taking place. Our office was temporary – a wooden *banda*, with palm thatching. I observed a new aspect of colonial Kenya. My immediate superiors were Europeans, around every day interacting and joking with each other, and participating in seeing the project through. They were all from the armed forces, and therefore represented a distinct sector of the British imperial presence, though they had all retired from military service by then. Visitors came through now and again, a parade of history in its own way. I remember Prince Aly Khan and his wife Rita Haworth, arriving on the site, and my helping to show them around. I remember the Sultan of Zanzibar coming to open the institute at last, welcomed by Sir Philip Mitchell amidst pomp and splendor. More than one British governor of Kenya came visiting. Here was a vantage point to imperial pomp.

The most important aspect of my experience politically at the institute was not in this parade of imperial history, but my appointment as boarding supervisor. In this role I began to grapple with problems of authority in an institution that was both multiracial and Pan-East African. Virtually all the teachers at the institute were Europeans. All the students were Muslims by religious affiliation, but drawn from different races: Africans, South Asians, and Arabs. There were students from Uganda, Tanganyika, Zanzibar, Somalia, as well as from Kenya itself. The Mombasa Institute of Muslim Education was virtually the first Pan-East African educational institution of its kind, and the different governments of East Africa made an annual grant-in-aid to the institute precisely because it was Pan-East African. In some important way the institute was my first experience of East Africa as a wider *region*, my first awareness of myself as an East African and not merely a Kenyan from Mombasa.

My Discovery of Authority

My first problem was that of being accepted as someone with authority. I was barely eighteen when I was appointed boarding supervisor. The majority of students were about my own age, and one or two were older than I. The hall of residence became in an important sense a political community. I was all too aware that my two boarding supervisor predecessors had failed in ignominy. The beginning of my reflections on authority goes back to this period.

I also trace my concept of social distance as a precondition for political legitimacy partly to my experience as boarding supervisor. Later on, as a trained political scientist observing African nations at the macro level, I began to sense that part of the problem of the legitimacy of African governments lay in the fact that they were too close to the people, and not that they were out of touch with the people. In situations where the leaders are readily identified as people who have risen from the ranks, it is easier for those who remain in the ranks to become envious of the privileges enjoyed by their former peers. Long established elites are sometimes forgiven luxurious living more easily by the "lower classes" than newly arrived members of the privileged classes. Those who have been rich for generations have consolidated their social distance and made it appear natural, if not deserved. The newly opulent are more easily accused of "giving themselves airs" – and are more easily resented as a result. Resentment arises not from a clearly defined social distance, but from the persistent residual social *nearness* between these newly opulent and the poor folk from whom they spring. The Africa of the first generation of independence was an Africa bedeviled by precisely this close interpenetration between the elites and the masses.

In the case of my first exposure to this predicament, the age factor was also important. A teenager entrusted with authority over other teenagers suffers the handicap of social nearness of a special kind. Among children especially, age becomes an important basis for determining the peer group. My authority as a teenager was difficult to assert precisely because of the danger that I might be taken as too much of a peer. I was afraid of any major incident that would require an assertion of authority. I retreated before the Theater of the Absurd.

And then one evening it happened. My apartment was centrally placed between the two wings of the hall of residence so that I could hear any great commotion that might take place in either of the wings. On this particular evening the shouting was boisterous, with two or three people quarreling and a sizeable number of onlookers joining in and contributing to the din. I waited for a little while, hoping that the row would quickly subside, and that I would not have to go and see what was happening. But the shouting got louder, and there was also the noise of furniture being pulled apart. I swallowed hard, put on my *kofia* (local cap), and found my way to the student dormitories. Before long I saw a bed being pushed down the steps. Two of the students were still shouting at each other; clearly, one of them, in a fit of anger, had dragged out the other's bed and flung it down the staircase.

Within me a miracle happened. My timidity was overcome by rising indignation. Before I knew what I was doing I demanded to be told promptly who was responsible for flinging the bed down those steps. One of the angry students confessed he had done it. He and I stared at each other, then his eyes fell. In that dramatic move I ordered him promptly to go and pick up the bed and return it. The other students waited to see if he would do so; I myself had forgotten to allow for the possibility of a defiant refusal.

Then the offending student grunted, seeming to curse under his breath, and went down the steps to retrieve the bed. He staggered back with it. The crowd watched, and as he got nearer the top I lent him a hand. Then other members of the crowd joined in to help him put it back. As the student straightened his back after replacing the bed I looked at him and said, "Thank you. Don't do it again."

I then turned around and left. What sticks in my mind is a simple problem of authority among peers – and how spontaneous anger came to the rescue of someone still unsure of himself, and lent him a voice of authority in a tense situation.

The Tensions of Transcultural Integration

In that small social community, I soon discovered that there were horizontal problems of relationships as well as vertical ones. The problem of horizontal relationships concerned the interaction among groups of students, be the groups racial, regional, or "tribal." The initial problem of the two boarding supervisors who were dismissed and the young successor who was unsure about his position was a problem of authority; the problem of inter-student relations emerged in my mind as the problem of amity.

The worst problems did not concern issues of interaction between Africans and Indians. Between these groups there was sufficient social distance to make interaction minimal, though cordial. The worst tensions I had to deal with were in fact between the highly Swahilized Arabs of Zanzibar, on one side, and the highly Arabized Waswahili of Zanzibar on the other. These two groups, on categorized as Arab and the other as Swahili, each partaking considerably of Swahili culture, turned out to have the worst problems of getting on with each other. Words like "national integration" were still unknown to me, but I understood that Zanzibar was an island of considerable racial and cultural intermingling.

In fact, I knew Zanzibar quite well. I first visited the island when I was only a few years old. My second visit to Zanzibar confirmed my image of an isle of peace. World War II had broken out, and although the Germans seemed remote, the Italians and Mussolini appeared too near for comfort, for Ethiopia was still under Italian occupation, and the desire to liberate it was already a war aim of the British in my part of the continent. Mombasa, my hometown, was the most important port on the eastern seaboard of the continent, and was therefore an attractive target for enemy attacks.

One day an Italian bomb fell on Malindi, less than eighty miles north of Mombasa. The bomb did little damage, but it was enough to create a scare all along the coast. A feeling rapidly spread that the war had come to our part of the continent. My horizons were expanding to encompass global conflict.

Many families in Mombasa began to wonder whether it might not be a good idea to evacuate women and children from Mombasa itself, and send them to a less vulnerable part of East Africa. My own family was among those that decided to send women and children to Zanzibar. There had once been a time when Zanzibar was indeed a major metropolis in East Africa, and would have been among the first targets of enemy attacks. But by 1939 Zanzibar was certainly a less strategic center than Mombasa.

The fact that as a child I had scrambled for safety to Zanzibar, and had spent there memorable months of peaceful excitement, gave me an image of the island closely associated with tranquility, with escape from the clouds of a global war. That image was later to have a compulsive contradiction in the entire experience of the bloody local revolution that convulsed the island twenty years later.

My first encounter of the potential racial tensions concerned a little incident. Some mattresses of ours were put outside in the sun to dry, and to enable the heat of the day to frighten away bedbugs. I was playing on my own not very far from the mattresses. The little boy was evidently a stranger, and I calculated, had no business playing on our mattresses with his dirty feet. There was a small and thin fragment of a branch nearby, with a few leaves on it, which I grabbed; I gave a war cry, and made for the little intruder. My little branch was raised high, a menacing weapon in the tropical sun, as I chased away an intruder.

Panting, and a little frustrated, and yet still congratulating myself for having chased him away from our mattresses, I resumed my quiet game a little longer before I heard voices. When I turned around I saw a crowd of women, shouting and complaining in anger, coming towards our house. My mother appeared in the doorway and gave a shout of desperation, asking me to run back to our house. My mother and the other women from our own house then stood across the doorway, while someone else took me away to hide in a room inside. The women who had just come shouted and ranted in violent indignation. They said I had chased their little boy like a dog and was going to whip him like a slave. Indeed, some of them claimed that I had already started this humiliating exercise. I heard some of these accusations, and was bitter at the inaccuracy of some of them, though also very bewildered and frightened by it all. Some of the Zanzibari women of our own household were arguing back, but my mother was the supreme conciliator. She appealed to the maternal instincts of the invading women, as against what turned out to be their wounded racial pride. My mother argued that it had been a quarrel between children, but she would have felt the same way if it as her child on the run threatened by a stranger. She conceded that her own son was guilty, and she promised with Allah as a witness that she would herself thrash her son for his aggressive games. Gradually the visiting women were mollified, and departed with a sense of satisfaction that justice was going to be done.

Inside the house I had heard it all. I continued to be both angry and threatened. My mother came in, caught hold of me, equipped herself with a thin broom of palm sticks, and proceeded to thrash me. She was soon stopped by the other women in the house, while I ran into a corner, rubbing my sore bottom, and shouting angrily at the injustice of it all. Wiping my eyes curiously, and asserting that the other little boy had been spoiling our mattresses and all I had done was to chase him away, I shouted that I had been beaten only because another little boy was a liar. If my family wanted to slaughter me or kill me, that was all right; but it was not all right to do so on the basis of a lie. High honor at the Theater of the Absurd.

The importance of the incident as a factor in my evolution as a political and cross-cultural observer lay in what, at the time I only imperfectly understood, but which later assumed more meaning when I was boarding supervisor at the Mombasa Institute of Muslim Education. I came to learn later that the family I was living with in Zanzibar was a family of Swahilized Arabs; the child I chased from our mattresses was a child of the Arabized Waswahili. The indignation of the invading women did not lie in a simple case of one child fighting another, or chasing another with a branch of a tree. The fundamental tension lay in this clash, incredible in many ways, between an Arab population in Zanzibar that had acquired Ki-Swahili as its mother tongue and become substantially Africanized in certain aspects of culture, and the Africans of Zanzibar who also spoke Ki-Swahili as their mother tongue, who also accepted Islam as their religion, who had acquired certain aspects of the Arab lifestyle, but who nonetheless still considered themselves a group apart. Behind this entire phenomenon was the historical fact of the Arab slave system, once accepted as a matter of course on that island, but now a memory of bitterness and humiliation.

Yet these two peoples had experienced considerable biological and cultural interpenetration. Intermarriage between the Arabs and the Africans was part of the very fabric Zanzibari society. These people had the same type of staple diet, the same language, many of the same jokes, and they prayed at the same mosques. If countries become more peaceful as cultural integration becomes more complete, Zanzibar should have lived up to that old image I had of it – as the isle of peace.

As boarding supervisor of the Mombasa Institute of Muslim Education I encountered afresh this paradox of integrated cleavage; this disturbing anomaly concerning the tensions of social nearness in horizontal relationships, I still remember a series of meetings I had with Zanzibari students at the Mombasa Institute of Muslim Education. Some of these meetings were held at night, as we sought to avoid onlookers from other communities and other regions of East Africa. I remember finding quotations from commentators on Zanzibar, who had paid tribute to the remarkable race relations of that island. I read these quotations at the beginning of the meeting. The acrimony between the Swahilized Arabs and the Arabized Waswahili was quite intense, but my technique of appealing to their shared Zanzihariness did have some temporary success. Those opposite quotes I had read, paying tribute to race relations in Zanzibar, made the students suddenly self-conscious about their own failure to live up to such observations. This embarrassment was not a very solid basis on which to build continuing amity, but it did carry us beyond the immediate disputes of the day between two very culturally similar groups, who were nevertheless the most mutually hostile of all the groups in my little society with the walls of the halls of residence.

Between Education and Journalism

Yet another avenue of my internationalization was through involvement in the media, and part of that experience was again multicultural. There was a newspaper in my hometown of Mombasa, owned and edited by British people. The newspaper decided to devote a page fortnightly to news about the Swahili people of the coast of Kenya. These were a people who at the time were often referred to as "Arabs" because most of them claimed (not always justifiably) descent from Arab immigrants into East Africa generation or even centuries earlier. The special page of the *Mombasa Times* was often referred to as "the Arab page." I became the sole writer of the page – and sometimes the sole collector of the news that went into it.

The news was mainly local, but it was of a culturally distinct group that claimed international origins. It also appeared in a basically British-style colonial newspaper, owned and edited by British people. I was constantly forced into culturally comparative perspectives, either consciously or unconsciously. The "Arab page" was one of my first sustained experiences in printed journalism.

My involvement with electronic media goes back to radio broadcasting in Mombasa, also in the early 1950s. The British colonial authorities in Kenya had initiated radio broadcasting in the colony before World War II, and strengthened the local Nairobi broadcasting during the war as part of the propaganda effort. But in my hometown of Mombasa (Kenya's second city) there was no broadcasting station.

My uncle (Abu Suleiman) a few friends, and I inaugurated Mombasa's first radio station. The station was called in Kiswahili *Sauti ya Mvita*, Voice of Mvita, our island's ancient name. The British colonial authorities in the 1950s gave us technological help for the radio, but the rest was all volunteer work from the old families of Mombasa, including my own family. My own role on the radio was that of a cross-cultural storyteller – narrating in careful installments stories made up by me or others in our narrow circle of ancient families of Mombasa. The storytelling was an important cultural and theatrical experience for me. I remember pretending to sob on the microphone as part of the story I was telling. I also remember having to bark as a dog of a

Western couple. I am not sure if either the sobbing or the barking was successful or convincing – but my critical audience was limited to the Coast of Province of Kenya confronted with a relatively new medium. The audience seemed prepared to suspend its disbelief at that stage. I was given polite applause all over the coast of Kenya as a storyteller.

Suddenly my radio career seemed to come to an abrupt end. Quite unexpectedly after many years of futile applications I was awarded a scholarship by the Kenyan government. I was to leave Mombasa for Huddersfield in England to complete my secondary education and then, if successful, to proceed to university in Britain. Was this a new phase in my internationalization; a new stage in my cross-cultural experience.

When the colonial authorities in Kenya asked me what I was interested in, I mentioned *law* and *journalism*. The British authorities in Nairobi told me that law was out of the question. Colonial lawyers tended to be political agitators and Great Britain was not about to subsidize the training of more colonial lawyers.

What about journalism? Those who had interviewed me in Nairobi believed that great journalists were not products of schools of journalism but products of a solid liberal education with experience on the job. The British officials in Nairobi were prepared to afford me a general liberal education in Huddersfield and beyond. I packed my bags and left for the Western world. I seemed to be turning my back on both my Africa's oral tradition and my Islamic literary legacy, just as I had once rejected the sciences.

But what liberal education could Huddersfield afford? I had been given two years in Huddersfield to complete a minimum of two subjects at the advanced level of the British General Certificate of Education (the minimum for entry to a British university). I decided to enroll for five subjects at the advanced-level history (European and British); economic history (Western); geography (global); the British Constitution; and English literature and two subjects at the ordinary level of the examination-mathematics and Arabic. I passed all seven subjects, but wondered whether I was receiving the liberal education that a journalist needed.

My next move was to the University of Manchester. I was able to choose the institution but not the degree for which I was to be enrolled. The colonial authorities wanted me to pursue studies that would qualify me to teach in a secondary school in Kenya. After teaching for five years, I could then aim for a journalistic career. The degree the colonial authorities had in mind was a broad general degree in what Americans would call "liberal arts."

I did not mind doing a broad general education, provided there were opportunities for working towards an exceptional performance. I was carefully informed by the University of Manchester of what would be the requirements for getting a General Bachelor's Degree with Distinction, equivalent to a B.A. with Honors First Class. But I decided that equivalence had to be really credible to the observer, and not merely to university authorities. I made up my mind to *double* the minimum requirements for a General Degree with distinction, and I succeeded in meeting the requirements for a distinction twice over.

I emerged from my undergraduate training with a type of broad liberal education that could fulfill my early journalist promise. But was that the direction I wanted to take? Was I about to become a journalist at long last? I later went to Columbia University in New York for my master's degree and to Oxford University in England for my doctorate.

By this time my central focus was *political science*. The training in the discipline would still be relevant for journalism. I was still on the road toward further involvement in the media. Destiny was helping to shape for me a role of some relevance to both African studies and journalism. But there was still a range of missing links on the way.

Electronic Internationalism

Every year the British Broadcasting Corporation invites a major figure from the world culture, politics, or education, gives the person up to twelve months in which to prepare six lectures on a subject within his or her area of competence, and then gives this Reith Lecturer a microphone from which to address the British people and the world. The lectures are named after the BBC's founder Director-General Lord Reith. Nineteen seventy-nine was my year as a Reith Lecturer. Even before delivering the lectures, my radio producer, Michael Greene, was already raising the possibility of a major television assignment.

He told me that the question of my "playing Africa's Alastair Cooke" had been raised in BBC television circles. Indeed, he said, a BBC woman was before long going to talk to me about it in a very preliminary way.

The woman did turn up and talked about this "germ of an idea" We had lunch together. She then walked out of my life never to reappear. I began to wonder if the BBC had changed its mind. I even wondered if my Reith Lectures on BBC had caused so much offense politically that the television side of the BBC had been scared away. My views conditionally in favor of nuclear proliferation had been particularly controversial. Had BBC television in England decided that Ali Mazrui was too "radical" to be an African Alastair Cooke?

Then came 1980 and two new BBC characters briefly entered my life.

They phoned from London and asked to see me in Ann Arbor, Michigan. I wondered if they were going to ask me to play the Alastair Cooke of Africa. Tony Isaacs and Ann Webber were indeed from the television side of BBC but their idea sounded different. There were looking for Third World personalities who would talk about issues from the inside. Indeed, the working title of the proposed series at the stage was, I believe, "The Eye Within," They were going to ask Mrs. Anwar Sadat of Egypt to present a film about women in the Third World, Benigno S. Aquino, Jr., of the Philippines to present a program on repression in the Third World, and they wanted me to present a program about the intellectual elite in the Third World.

Shortly thereafter Anwar Sadat was killed and this presumably changed the status of his wife in television terms. Benigno Aquino was also killed. I was not killed-just crossed off Tony Isaac's list! Instead, he invited a former student of mine, Hussein Adem, to present a program about his own country, Somalia. The whole concept of the series had changed. "The Eye Within" had become "The Third Eye."

But my own sense of deprivation did not last long. In 1981 came a letter from John Reynolds, a new BBC name for me. Reynolds explicitly used the analogy of Alastair Cooke's *America, as* well as the analogy of Kenneth Clarke's *Civilisation* and Jacob Bronowski's *Ascent of Man*. Would I consider presenting a series on Africa in the same tradition as those other series?

The television project *The Africans* was at last truly in the making. The BBC and later the Public Broadcasting System in the United States became partners in a nine-part T.V. series with myself as the author and narrator. Channel WETA in Washington, D.C., was the PBS member that became co-producer with the BCC. I decided to make the story truly cross-cultural. Africa was to be viewed through its own *triple heritage*, the heritage of indigenous, Islamic, and Western civilizations.

My role in *The Africans: A Triple Heritage* was the highest point in my lifelong flirtation with the media. The series was shown in Britain and the United States in a blaze of controversy and publicity. Within the year it had also been bought by some twenty other countries, ranging from Australia to Jordan, from Finland to Zimbabwe. My political, trans-cultural, and international socialization had found a new theater of fulfillment on television screens across the world.

But perhaps the most personal link of all between me and international relations concerns my marriage. On that issue politics, culture, and science had once again converged. Religion, race, and the threat of nuclear war were jointly at stake in one man's matrimonial fate,

Religion, Race, and a Nuclear Marriage

"Let's get married before these lunatics blow us up!" It must have been one of the most symbolic proposals of marriage of the atomic age. The world hovered over the brink of a thermonuclear catastrophe. Eyeball to eyeball John F. Kennedy and Nikita S. Khrushchev were still considering whether or not to unleash a nuclear holocaust upon the human race. And yet, here was a young African Muslim making a decision on a chance of fate. He was making up his mind to die married to a young Westerner if the nuclear worst came to the worst.

"Come on, let's get married", repeated the young Kenyan to the young English woman. His primeval distrust of science had awakened a new faith in matrimony. His nuclear existentialism had come full circle, from father figure to mother refuge. Love is the other face of motherhood.

For nearly seven years Molly and I had agonized over whether or not to get married. For her the issues were more clear-cut than for me. I was more confused than she was about the politics of culture and the culture of politics for her, all that mattered was basically the two of us. For me the two of us was a part of wider social forces.

I had expected that two issues would be of concern to either or both sides of the extended family if we got married: race and religion. But response to those issues differed significantly. For Molly's side of the family the most serious problem in the early days of our courtship had been race (the idea of a black son-in-law was at one time uncomfortable to contemplate). For my side of the family, the most serious challenge was religion (she was a Christian and I was a Muslim). I could not change my race and become white. But would it be fair to make Molly change her religion and become Muslim? We hesitated on the idea of religious conversion. In any case, her side of the family had been expecting me to propose for years (the courtship was long), whereas my side of the family was new to the idea of Molly as a relative. Her side of the family had in time transcended racism, whereas my side of the family had not had long enough to transcend sectarianism.

Could a Muslim marry a Christian (or Jew) without conversion? It is one of the principles of Islam to identify with "the people of the Book" (Jews and Christians). But my Shafi denomination of Islam insists that a Muslim can only marry a Christian without conversion to Islam if the Christian's own people or society were already Christian before the Prophet Muhammed began to preach Islam in the seventh century of the Christian era. It turned out that the English were first converted to Christianity quite early, but then relapsed into heathenism. By the time St. Augustine of Canterbury was re-converting them, it seemed as if it was after the Prophet of Islam was born but before he began to preach (Muhammed started preaching at the age of forty); at any rate the dates were so close that Molly and I decided to honor the Shafiite dictum of conversion. Had Molly been an Amhara from Ethiopia (the Amhara were converted to Christianity at least two centuries before Islam was born) she would never have had to be converted to Islam.

And then, out of the blue, came the Cuban missile crisis of October 1962. It was the closest the human race had ever been to global nuclear conflagration. All of a sudden issues of who was converted when to which religion diminished in importance. We seemed to be on the verge of the worst of all holocausts, greater than any of the ancient Biblical scourges, more ominous than the plagues of God's anger.

Could it be, 0 tell me Lord, that radioactive sectarianism was not "worth the candle"? It was not art that was a dangerous imitation of God; it was indeed science!

Had we not arrived at a situation when, in the nuclear age, we could afford neither racism nor religious exclusivity? I could hear my father's voice when I was trying to burn insects in a colonial village, "Only God punishes with fire!" And Jean-Paul Sartre added: "Hell is other people."

So long as the nuclear threat persisted, all cultural details seemed minor to Molly and me. But the wider forces of society were making their own demands, and we were being influenced by a thousand years of cultural expectations.

Molly and I got married at Woking Mosque near London in October 1962. The imam at the mosque made us agree on a suitable "brideprice" (bride-wealth) before the ceremony could start. Molly acquired the Islamic first name of *Muna*. In Western terms she also acquired her husband's surname of *Mazrui*. Sexism and culture were still transcending the nuclear age.

I was indeed already converted to the proposition that in the nuclear age we could afford neither blatant racism nor overt sectarianism. That is why I decided to get married in the midst of the Cuban missile crisis. What I had yet to learn was that *sexism* was the most obstinate of all forces in the nuclear age. The masculinity of war was part and parcel of the dangerous *macho* game between Kennedy and Khrushchev in October 1962 in the Cuban missile crisis. I thought they were lunatics in their confrontation. That is why I popped the question of marriage to Molly. I forgot that Kennedy and Khrushchev were also merely males in a war game.

Conclusion

As I grew up in a shrinking world, three forces shaped my perspective on world affairs, politics, culture, and the arrival of the nuclear age. These three forces were sometimes distinct and sometimes mutually reinforcing. Under the influence of those forces I became a cross-cultural and cross-national observer.

At the center of the *political* force was the very fact that my country Kenya was a British colony. After all, imperialism was itself inherently international. But my politicization as an observer had other causes as well. My father, a pamphleteer played his part in my own politicization. There was also my cumulative discovery of the nature of political authority as I was put in charge of a hall of residence at the Mombasa Institute of Muslim Education. Anger taught me authority. As Leopold Senghor once put it: "I *feel*, therefore *am*!"

My cross-cultural socialization was rooted in Africa's triple heritage-indigenous, Islamic, and Western legacies interacting in Mombasa. My father's distrust of figurative art became a warning that art was dangerously an imitation of God. But in my mind that was transformed into a warning that science could be a dangerous approximation of a holy design. My father's distrust of it became my own distrust of science at almost exactly the same time when the nuclear age declared its ominous entry in the 1940s.

My additional avenue of internationalization came through a sustained love affair with the mass media beginning with "the Arab page" in the *Mombasa Times* in the 1950s, through the local radio broadcast of *Sauti ya Mvita*, and onwards to the global broadcasting of the BBC Reith Lectures in 1979. My higher education began with the dream of journalism and was consummated in the class of political science. But even in the awesome precincts of the academy, journalism for me was only partly a dream deferred. A semblance of fulfillment came with the BBC/WETA television series, *The Africans: A Triple Heritage*, aired in Britain and the United States in 1986.

But the most personalized interaction between my private life and public concerns was in relation to my marriage. For years I had hesitated about marrying an English woman friend notwithstanding her own readiness to take the plunge. The racial divide and my own denomination of Islam played a part in the complications of the love affair. It took the Cuban missile crisis of 1962 to push aside all hesitations about marriage. Religion, race, and my old distrust of science had a last converged on the highly personal level of love and matrimony. Neo-existentialism taught me global affairs from immediate experience before I learnt from books. As Samuel Johnson put it:

> Deign on the passing world to turn thine eyes,
> And pause a while from learning to be wise.

What all these factors amounted to was the remarkable story of one African child growing up in a world that was rapidly shrinking around him. The horizons were expanding precisely as the globe was becoming a village in stark cosmic isolation. Politics, culture, and the nuclear age were redefining the human condition in terms of its most dangerous contradiction; man, the new master of the universe, was still not master of himself.

Note

[1] See Ali A. Mazrui, "The Making of an African Political Scientist," *International Social Science Journal* (Paris) 25, no. 1 – 2 (1973): 101 – 10, Consult also Sulayman Nyang, "The Scholar's Mansions," *Africa Events* (London) 2, no. 7 – 8 (July-August 1982):39 – 43; and Muhammad Hyder, "Mazrui: Showman or Showpiece?" *Africa Events* (London) 2, no.10 (October 1986):45 – 47.

2

A Tribute to Ali Mazrui, the Global Kenyan

Ngũgĩ wa Thiong'o

Ali Mazrui and I were not social friends; and we did not always see eye to eye on politics and art. In the analysis of African politics, he emphasized ethnic conflicts where I saw class conflicts as the prime mover. But our lives interacted in the most amazing of ways. In a documentary that Ndirangu Wachanga has made of the life of the late Ali Mazrui, he asked me what I thought of my fellow countryman. Mazrui, I said, is primarily a political scientist with a literary bent; and I, primarily a literary artist with a political bent. I knew he had this bent because, way back in the early sixties, as a guest editor of a special issue of *Ghala*, then the literary arm of *The East African Journal*, I had published one of his short stories. Later he would write the novel, *The Trial of Christopher Okigbo* that would confirm this bent.

Our first international conference together was at the 1969 International Congress of Africanists in Dakar, Senegal, where, on the eve of the conference, President Sedar Senghor received us in his Palace and who, on shaking my hands, told me proudly that he knew Jomo Kenyatta. The conference was attended by the leading Africanists of the time. When it was the turn of Ali Mazrui to speak a day later, the hall was already packed, standing room only, with intellectuals from all over the world, pushing and shoving each other for space. I had seen similar crowds at his lectures in Makerere where he was the Professor of Political Science, the new wonder kid newly crowned with a PhD from Oxford, towering over a campus that once rejected his application for admission. I had just resigned over issues of Academic Freedom from the

University of Nairobi in the English Department; and it was Mazrui together with David Cook who came up with a rescue package that enabled me to teach creative writing in the English Department and a class on Pan-Africanism in the Political Science department. It was from Makerere that Mazrui and I had jetted to Dakar for the Congress of Africanists. It was on the way to Dakar that he came up with the possibility of both of us, a creative artist and the political scientist, writing a biography of Jomo Kenyatta. The plan would later be shot down by those around the State House Nairobi but the idea was intriguing: he the first African Professor of political science and I the first published African novelist writing about the First President of an Independent Kenya.

It was in dark alone in my hotel room that I had my first serious attack of asthma. I had no idea that I had this ailment; it was just that, one night, alone in my room at the hotel, I found myself unable to breathe. I remember crawling on all fours from my room down the stairs to seek help at the lobby. It was dawn. I hardly knew French and they were equally deficient in English, but somehow I managed to scribble down Mazrui's name. It worked. They tracked him to his hotel and in no time he was with me, now a prostrate figure on the ground, fighting for every breath. Kenya had no mission in Dakar; so it was finally the British Embassy who represented Kenya's interests who promptly managed to get me a doctor. It was magical: one moment I was literally dying for lack of air, and the next minute, I was breathing freely, normally. I was really grateful but vaguely disappointed that we had sought the offices of our former colonizer for my rescue, the way the newly independent East African states in 1964 had sought help from the same quarters to quell the African military mutinies.

After my one-year stint as a Makerere Fellow in creative writing, Mazrui, through his good contacts with the late Gwendolen Carter of Northwestern University in the USA, enabled my invitation as Visiting Associate Professor of English and African Studies, there, from 1970 to 1971. It was there where I began writing my third novel, *Petals of Blood*. It was this novel together with the play, *I Will Marry When I Want*, that would in 1978 have me sent to Kamiti Maximum Security Prison and later forced into exile. In the course of it, somehow, Mazrui and I had earned the wrath of the Moi regime. I worked with the London-based Committee for the Release of Political Prisoners and Mazrui was very outspoken on human rights abuses.

Years later he and I would return to Dakar Senegal as special guests of the CODESRIA, Council for the Development of Social Research in Africa, at their 30th conference, where we were made life members. My Honorary Doctorate from Walter Sisulu University in 2004 became special to me because Mazrui and Mandela received theirs on the same occasion. Two Kenyan intellectuals being honored at the same time once by the prestigious research institution in West Africa, and by an African university in South Africa.

We leave it to political scientists to assess his legacy. But for me, taking his intellectual output as a whole, he more than lived up to the description of the global African. He made Kenya and Africa visible in the highest echelons of intellectual production. To see him on the platform quoting from poets and philosophers alike in support of his arguments was to witness a master intellectual performer. He dined and wined and argued with kings, presidents, and generals but he never lost his common touch, attentive to the voice of the student with the same respect that he gave to the mighty. He belonged to generations; they saw themselves in him.

I witnessed this at close quarters at the 2013 New York African Studies Conference in Binghamton to celebrate Mazrui's 80th Birthday. Intellectuals of his generation and others who could as easily have been his grandchildren gathered and read papers in his honor. Among these "grandchildren" was my 20-year-old Mũmbi W. Ngũgĩ from Harriet Wilkes Honors College of Florida Atlantic University, who gave a paper on the Politics of Silence and Agency. She opened the address by saying that there was no way she could have been left behind when it came to the celebration of a Kenyan legend and global African. Ali Mazrui sat through most of these, listening keenly to what the young had to say.

Mazrui was very fond of a Wordsworth poem welcoming the French revolution, particularly the lines:

> Bliss was it in that dawn to be alive,
> But to be young was very heaven!

I may not talk about Heaven but it was truly bliss to have witnessed Ali Mazrui intellectual performance at the height of his powers. He shone: he dazzled; he enlightened. Some of that bliss can be found in his numerous publications that keep his spirit alive for generations to come.

3

Publishing Ali A. Mazrui:
A Lover of Knowledge and an Eloquent Debater

Henry Chakava

The death of Ali Mazrui has not only snatched away an invaluable author, but also made me lose a friend I first met way back in 1974. It's rather interesting, almost bizarre, the way death creates fresh and fond memories of days gone by, making one to nostalgically reminisce about the happy times one shared with the deceased. This is the state I found myself in, on receiving the sad news of Mazrui's demise.

In 1974, I had the pleasure of receiving him at the Heinemann Educational Publishers offices at the International House, Nairobi, when he paid us a visit on arrival from Kampala, Uganda. Mazrui was accompanied by his wife at the time, Molly, and two children.

Although I cannot clearly recollect the circumstances leading to his travel from Uganda, I can guess that it was the time he realized that he was exposing himself to serious danger lecturing at Makerere University during the murderous regime of Idi Amin Dada.

Since he was a close friend and guest of my Managing Director Bob Markham, we took good care of him and his family, including doing some shopping for them to ensure they were as comfortable as possible.

Mazrui later travelled to the US where he ended up teaching for many years until his death. I later had the privilege of publishing him and, therefore, personally interacting with him at the East African Educational Publishers (EAEP) — the company I set up after acquiring Heinemann in the early 1990s.

We first worked on his volume, *Swahili, State and Society: The Political Economy of an African Language*, which he co-authored with his nephew and linguistics scholar, Alamin Mazrui. After that we published his most referenced work to-date, *Nationalism and New States in Africa: From 1935 to the Present*, co-authored with Michael Tidy.

Others were *General History of Africa Vol. VIII: Africa Since 1935*; and the famous Reith Lectures published in the volume, The African Condition: A Political Diagnosis.

I need to mention that before these works, at Heinemann we had already published his The Trial of Christopher Okigbo under the African Writers Series, a work that drew sharp criticism from literary enthusiasts.

It's unfortunate that I did not get the chance to publish *The Africans: A Triple Heritage*, which is perhaps Mazrui's magnum opus, and which firmly placed his global intellectual stature at a higher pedestal. Publishing Mazrui was both intellectually fulfilling and stimulating. He had the rare gift of engaging in a lot of interesting wordplay in speech and in his writing, which made his work to read rather well. He loved engaging in debates and discussions, and would draw examples from a wide range of subjects to support his arguments.

Combine this with his gripping stature, which made him inspire many people, young and old alike, and actually become a mentor to many. At times as he spoke passionately and eloquently on a subject, his audience would be spellbound, as if he was a form of a deity. Yet he was also humble and would not shy away from interacting and chatting with people of all walks of life, sometimes even inviting some to his hotel room for a chat.

I must also say that professor was a generous man — not just in sharing his knowledge — but also his resources. I recall that in the 1980s we had a telephone conversation during which he informed me that he would be presenting a paper at the African Studies Association (ASA) seminar in the US.

I indicated that I would love to listen to him, and he immediately offered me a return ticket and promised to take care of my upkeep during my stay there. Unfortunately, I was unable to take up the offer due to other engagements, but he assured me that the offer was still open any time I was ready to travel.

His life was a kind of an open book, so to speak. He annually released a newsletter through which he shared his accomplishments in the past year, as well as key developments at a personal and family level. He would then circulate the newsletter to as wide an audience as possible. With this kind of information, I have no doubt his biographer will have more than enough resources to put together a credible work on the life and times of Mazrui. That was vintage Mazrui — a lover of knowledge; an eloquent debater; a mentor to many; and also a connoisseur of top-class restaurants and good food.

Although he is gone, we are lucky that he has left us with enormous knowledge in the form of the books we published at EAEP; and we are therefore glad that future generations will continue to benefit from his wide knowledge and wisdom. This volume by Ndirangu Wachanga contains powerful essays about an intellectual who loved his country and his continent, and who belonged to the world.

4

Orature Poems of Celebration and Healing in Honor of Mwalimu Ali Mazrui

Mĩcere Gĩthae Mũgo

"Leo ni Shangwe, Mwalimu Ali!"

(This is an African orature-inspired epic poem in commemoration of Professor Ali Mazrui's 80th Birthday, delivered at the Mazrui Birthday Banquet during the 38th Annual Conference of the New York African Studies Association (NYASA), Binghamton University, April 6, 2013.)

Call response/Refrain:
Poet: *Leo ni shangwe!*
Audience: *Leo ni shangwe!*

Poet: *Leo ni shangwe, Mwalimu Ali!*
    Shikamoo, Mwalimu Mkuu!
    Shikamoo, Mzee Maalum!
    Shikamoo, Mheshimiwa!
    This is celebration day
    A day bubbling with jubilation
    A day giddy with happiness
    in commemoration
    of a beauty-full elder
    born in Mombasa

on the twenty fourth day of February
the month of the dry season
when torrents of rain
drenched the parched soil
showering blessings upon
the Mazrui homestead
the Mazrui family
epic breed of the uprising tradition
The day was clothed in splendor
as the sun shone brightly
upon the land of Kenya

Poet: *Leo ni shangwe!*
Audience: *Leo ni shangwe!*
Poet: *Leo ni shangwe, Mwalimu Ali!*
Leo ni shangwe, NYASA!
On that day of the dry month
on that day of the rain of blessings
the expansive waters of the African ocean
they call the Indian Ocean
seemed to swell with forceful fullness
then suddenly, the waters stood still
no more lapping the shore
but holding back
their aggressive surge
to greet the child
The waters sat peacefully
in spectacular expansive blueness
the ancient ocean splendidly calm
absorbing the news of the day
welcoming the new "arrivant"
Then, as suddenly, they broke into a dance
of twirling ripple rhythm
wildly dancing, dancing, dancing
in circular formations of royal blue splendor
embracing the brand new "arrivant."
Poet: *Leo ni shangwe!*
Audience: *Leo ni shangwe!*
Poet: *Leo ni shangwe, Mwalimu Ali!*
Leo ni shangwe, wenzangu!

Orature Poems of Celebration and Healing

> For, that night
> after showers of rain
> had blessed the earth
> on the month of the dry season
> above, multitudinous stars
> lit the expansive sky
> till it shone with stardom
> bright stars lit the expansive sky
> winking knowingly to each other
> before darting wildly
> as if tipsy with happiness
> In approval, the moon smiled back
> with a wide enchanting grin
> laying a spell on the marveling sky
> The day after, dawn broke
> with a softness never witnessed
> in Mombasa, *mji wa pwani,*
> gently touching the eyes
> of the awaking town
> with a caressing tenderness
> that whispered: embrace this birth!

Poet: *Leo ni shangwe!*
Audience: *Leo ni shangwe!*
Poet: *Leo ni shangwe, Mwalimu Ali!*
Leo ni shangwe, Binghamton!

> As we remember how the sun
> burst through the clouds
> adorned with dazzling rays
> that struck Fort Jesus
> with the force of their brightness
> as if to warn
> the colonial fortress that
> Another Mazrui
> of the uprising epic dynasty
> had been born
> The branches of the trees in the hinterland
> trembled
> But the palm trees along the coastal line

stood erect
their leaves swaying in rhythmic harmony
ready to bid the sun good morning
and to greet the child
Ali Alamin Mazrui
declaring: arrive well!
Then all the baby palm trees
from Mombasa to Malindi
from Mombasa to Zanzibar
woke up chuckling and giggling
in childish merriment
their little ukuti leaves
whispering to each other
from branch to branch
spreading the fiery news
that another Mazrui
of the uprising epic dynasty
had been born.

Poet: *Leo ni shangwe!*
Audience: *Leo ni shangwe!*
Poet: *Leo ni shangwe, Mwalimu Ali!*
But where shall I find the words
to narrate the epic?
The artist in me had prayed
for possession
  by the spirit of eloquence
but the words shriveled like mushrooms in the desert
The word crafter in me had begged the ancestors
to fan the imagination with creative genius
to power Nommo, the breath of utterance,
with such forceful eloquence
that the poem would
never be forgotten
  This orature artist had wanted
to weave bouquets
of words, and thoughts, and feeling, and love
and place them before you:
one, at the banquet's high table
and the other, a garland

to decorate the scholar
of the orate and written word
This singer of songs had planned
to compose a song
so captivating and luring that it would
make our orate-literate scholar
intoxicated with sober pride
But my tongue is shorn of words
like the lizard born without hair
The voice that used to sing praise songs
has cracked with age and become frog-like
Yet, the poet in me
must find the voice
to ululate this birth

Poet: *Leo ni shangwe!*
Audience: *Leo ni shangwe!*
Poet: *Leo ni shangwe, Mwalimu Ali*
Five trills of ululation to you
Mwalimu Ali Alamin, son of Mazrui
as the croaking poet implores
the ancestors to oil them
with the balm of soothing beauty
voice bouquets
to lay on your feast table
for I will not wait till you have
crossed the border of life
to tell you this:
In Mombasa, mji wa pwani,
 eighty years ago
'the beauty-full one was born'
and now sits on the golden stool
of an Africana elders' authority
occupying the stool splendidly:
Mazruically.

Poet: *Leo ni shangwe!*
Audience: *Leo ni shangwe!*
Poet: *Leo ni shangwe, Mwalimu Ali!*
Mungu akulinde, uwe na maisha marefu!

Growing up in a Shrinking World

During Mwalimu Mazrui's final illness, I would send floral arrangements and fruit bouquets as expressions of solidarity with him; Pauline, his wife and the family. One day as I was preparing to send some flowers, I called Pauline to find out whether to send them to the hospital or home. I believe she asked me to send the arrangement to the hospital, but I remember clearly what she went on to say. "You know what he said he would really like you to send?" she asked. I scratched my head for a moment and then admitted ignorance. "A poem," Pauline said. She further suggested that I record the poem on her cell phone's voice mail so that she could play it for Mwalimu. "Done," I said.

"Bouquet of Healing Words."

Shikamoo, Mwalimu Mkuu Ali!
Shikamoo, Mzee Mheshimiwa!
Tafadhali accept this belated
but artistically belabored intricate
bouquet of healing words
words of love from the heart
of my poet's mind
that have been simmering in
my imaginative creativity
patiently waiting for the flavors to
season to the right consistency
worthy of your elder's taste buds.

        At last, breaking free of Central New York's
        mind-freezing twenty fourteen winter
        my imagination has taken wings
        wings of love to Mombasa
        in search of the choicest of flowers
        to bring to your hospital bed-side
        I have found them in such staggering bounty
        that the bouquet will be an enduring statement
        fusing metaphors of nature with flowers of the mind
        all worthy of your elder's eagle sharp inner and outer eyes.

Mwalimu Mkuu Ali! Mzee Mheshimiwa!
to your winter-bound hospital room

Orature Poems of Celebration and Healing

I bring roses: white, red, pink, purple, yellow and gold
roses beaming with joy, laughter, happiness and love
matching them are domes of orange-red blood lilies
brilliant lilies anchored in obstinate hope, affirming life!
Betwixt the glamorous roses and glowing blood lilies in the vase
I have planted gracious water lilies standing tall and sure
breathing calm, peacefully whispering: all is well
into your fine-tuned, channel-clear elder's inner and outer ears.

> ***Mwalimu Mkuu Ali, Mzee Mheshimiwa***
> close your outer eyes and rest for now
> rest well for now surrounded by these
> metaphors of natural and poetic beauty.
> When you awake I will have returned from
> the coastal countryside bringing floral plants

floral plants with herbal cure
healing plants medically chosen by
the finest of *pwani*'s indigenous healers
keepers of ancient *zamani*-tested wisdom
limitless like the horizon; deeper than the deepest of oceans.

> Pauline will massage your tired elder's muscles
> with their embalming, healing juices
> and the healing juices will stir back
> the rhythm of your blood flow
> as we who love you surround her, chanting in chorus
> the mantra:
> **Heal, Mwalimu, heal!**
> **Heal, Mwalimu, heal!**
> **Heal, Mwalimu, heal!**
> **Heal, Mwalimu, Heal!**
> **Heal, Mwalimu, Heeeeeaaaaal**

Syracuse, March 16, 2014.

About two weeks after sending "Bouquet of Healing Words" for Mwalimu Ali, Pauline and I were having a conversation about his progress towards recovery when she shared with me that he was increasingly finding it more and more difficult to communicate verbally, but that he had asked her when I would be sending him another poem. Apparently, Mwalimu would

wear a big smile as he listened to "Bouquet of Healing Words" with a twinkle in his eyes.
I set to work immediately.

"A Herbal Floral Arrangement for Mwalimu Ali"

Shikamoo, Mwalimu Mpendwa, Ali Mazrui!
Shikamoo, Mzee Maalum, Ali Mazrui!

The wind of urgency has given my legs wings
and I have flown back to your bedside
bringing bundles of indigenous herbs
from Mombasa and Miji Kenda
We are together now in room 308 Kindred Hospital
where your kindred gather daily pouring balms of love…
So, get up and swim in these oceans of love
Get up, Mwalimu Mpendwa, Ali Mazrui
Get up, Mzee Maalum, Ali Mazrui

Wake up and see these succulent aloe leaves I have brought
picked from resistant plants still growing strong in the
compound of your legendary Mazrui family-dynasty home,
Mazruis, strong breed that resists colonial and neo-colonial
desertification of historical legacies of resistance.
We will heat the leaves and massage your body
freeing it from the pinning grip of pangs of illness:
feeding it with the juices of healing herbal fullness

Sit up now, Mwalimu Mpendwa Ali of the Mazruianas
Sit up now, Mzee Maalum of the Omari-Arab clan
Wake up and see the African juniper, aromatic herb
collected while journeying across the land of the Giriama…
(searching for Mijikenda *waganga,* trusted medicine *gurus*
to school me, a novice, in the art of herb-gathering)…
my spiritual homage touching the borders of Kaya Fungo,
the *zamani* sacred shrine and political capital of the Giriama
Sit up, Mwalimu and see the graceful grass-like sedge plant
adorned with green flowers that speak of rejuvenation.
Alongside the greens are shoots of deep cream sedge
and shoots of decorative yellow star grass flowers

all in celebration of your dignified golden presence…
An African elder seated on the golden stool of authority.
Sit up and admire the irresistible tufted ferns sprinkled
all over your herbal bouquet, crowning its healing beauty…
From the hinterland of Miji Kenda
To the borders of Kaya Fungo
From the homeland of Mekatilili wa Menza,
Mother of the art of healing
inherited from *zamani* healers…
accept this herbal floral arrangement
Mwalimu Mpendwa, Ali Mazrui!
Accept this herbal floral arrangement
Mzee Maalum, Ali Mazrui!

Pauline will massage your tired elder's muscles
with their embalming, healing juices
and the healing juices will stir back
the rhythm of your blood flow
as we who love you surround her, chanting in chorus
the mantra:
Heal, Mwalimu, heal!
Heal, Mwalimu, heal!
Heal, Mwalimu, heal!
Heal, Mwalimu, Heal!
Heal, Mwalimu, Heeeeeaaaaal!

Ashe! Afya! Moyo! Amen! Amin!

Syracuse, March 30, 2014.

5

Mazrui and Achebe:
The Literary Artist and the Political Scientist[1]

By Ngũgĩ wa Thiong'o

I was coming here to praise my fellow countryman, Mwalimu Ali Mazrui, but the passing on of my fellow writer, Chinua Achebe, who was supposed to be here in dialogue with us, changed the focus. I had to scramble to find ways of talking about them both and thus continue the dialogue. I have personally known Achebe longer having first met him in 1962. In fact, I did not realize how interactive my family and Achebe had been until he passed on. Quite unknown to each other, two of my sons, Tee Ngũgĩ, Mũkoma Ngũgĩ, and I wrote lengthy responses for three different news venues, each piece citing anecdotes of personal encounters.

There could have been more. When I skyped my daughter in Florida that Achebe had passed on, Mũmbi, closed her eyes, and then reminded me of their only encounter at Bard College during the celebrations of Achebe's birthday. She was then about six and she drew a birthday cake on piece of paper and presented it to him.

Thiong'o, her younger brother by a year, remembers reacting very differently to the same Achebe event. It was all on account of my introducing him to Achebe's publisher, James Currey. The five-year-old asked his mother for a piece paper. He jotted some marks, folded it, and took it to James Currey. Here, I have just written a book, will you please publish it? James took the piece of paper and of course promised to publish it. Thiong'o rushed back to our table, asked for another piece of paper, wrote another novel, and took it back to James Currey. James would publish it. Thiong'o was back for

---
1   Presented at the 38th Annual Conference of the New York African Studies Association, Binghamton University, in a plenary conversation in memory of Chinua Achebe.

a third piece of paper. By the time he wrote his seventh novel, in just under ten minutes, surely a Guinness book of records, James Currey had resorted to avoiding the young writer. I think he left the party earlier than he intended. Being stalked by a five-year-old novelist was the price an Achebe publisher had to pay.

Ali Mazrui was not at the birthday celebrations but there was a Mazrui, his nephew, Alamin Mazrui. Though I cannot relate similar dramatic family interactions in the case of Mazrui, I have known the Mazrui's longest, though in an abstract kind of way, because the Mazrui family history is synonymous with that of Kenya. I mean, I cannot think of another such prominent family, with an unbroken history all the way back to the encounter between East Africa and Europe in 16th and 17th centuries. They have been active makers of the history of which I am a part. There has been a prominent Mazrui intervening in the moment for each of the last four centuries. And yet I have never been mistaken for Mazrui, my countryman, the way I have been mistaken for Chinua Achebe, the West African. In truth, I have never once been mistaken for Mazrui. So I can't use mistaken identity as a common point of departure in talking about the two.

Achebe and Mazrui were not intellectually or politically conjoined in the same way that Mazrui and Wole Soyinka were; first through their contribution to the Rajat Neogy edited *Transition*, contributions that made the journal one of the liveliest intellectual fora for political scientists and artists alike; and secondly, through their famous polemics in the same journal. I stand to be corrected, but I am not aware of any polemics between Mazrui and Achebe. The Mazrui-Soyinka rivalry has not been paralleled with a Mazrui-Achebe rivalry.

But what does a devout Muslim scholar, a scion of an intellectual and political family in East Africa have in common with a devout Anglican, a second generation African Christian family in West Africa? Both are steeped in the finest western intellectual tradition as likely to quote from Yeats and Wordsworth as from sages of the indigenous religious and intellectual systems. Both are known for their measured responses to current events via the media and for their general adherence to the middle between extremes. Both would share the view of Africa contemporary culture as a triple heritage of the indigenous, the Muslim and the Christian, or a variation of the three. So on a closer look we may find that they are branches from the same literary and political tree.

Ndirangu Wachanga, the maker of the Mazrui documentary, *A Walking Triple Heritage*, once asked me to assess Professor Mazrui in relations to me. I did not hesitate. Mazrui, I said, is a political scientist with a literary bent; and I, a literary artist with a political bent. The same division can apply equally to Mazrui and the late Chinua Achebe. Achebe has published many novels but also analytical texts with incredible political insight. He once wrote about bad governance and leadership in *Trouble with Nigeria*. And of course the last book, *There Was a Country,* is an obvious reference to Biafra. Biafra made Achebe turn to politics to understand it: Biafra made Mazrui turn to literature to understand it.

I regret that I once stifled what would have shaped as incredible debate between Mazrui and Achebe on Biafra. Achebe was a kind of roving ambassador for the Biafran cause, and in 1969, he came to Makerere to deliver a lecture, 'Biafra and the African writer,' to which I would respond. I was in Makerere on a one year writing fellowship, following my resignation from the University of Nairobi in disagreement about the University's stance on the government's direct infringement on academic freedom. His delivery was measured but it did not delve into the detailed politics of the Biafra. It seemed to me that there was nothing to add to what came across, to me at least, as a personal testament. Mazrui came to the rescue. He was then the dashing young professor of political science known to dazzle audiences with his incredible ability to yoke two or three apparently incompatible histories and somehow make them yield fire and light. Such was his famous description of Nkrumah as a Leninist Czar or his linkage of Julius Nyerere and Milton Obote to Shakespeare and Milton. Mazrui asked Achebe several questions; the debate became of the two giants. Achebe ended his lecture with a reference to Albert Schweitzer who talked of the African as a brother with Schweitzer as the elder to make the point that Biafra was somehow fighting to get away from under the shadow of the Western brother; Mazrui would end up holding the Albert Schweitzer Professorship in the Humanities at Binghamton University, and in one of his lectures, explained why he accepted it, later describing Albert Schweitzer as benevolent racist, the conclusion Achebe had arrived at minus the benevolence part.

Makerere and Biafra tie Mazrui and Achebe in a different way. The college was the site of the now famous 1962 African writers of English expression. It was attended by virtually every African writer of the time including Es'kia Mphahlele, Lewis Nkosi, Bloke Modisane, from South Africa; and John Nagenda, Jonathan Kariara and I represented East Africa. West Africa, Nigeria in particular, had the largest contingent that included Wole Soyinka, Chinua Achebe and Christopher Okigbo. The attendance of Langston Hughes and Saunders Redding from the USA and Arthur Drayton from the Caribbean gave it a Pan-Africanist air. Achebe's *Things Fall Apart* was the model text against which other writings of the time were measured. But stealing the drama was the brilliant poet Christopher Okigbo, then working for the Cambridge University Press. Asked about the influence of T. S. Eliot, Ezra Pound and Gerald Manley Hopkins which made his work difficult to access, he retorted that he wrote his poetry for poets, a view he later reiterated and elaborated upon in an interview with Lewis Nkosi: "I am writing for other poets in the world to read and see whether they share in my experience."

Ali Mazrui was not at the conference. But when Okigbo who had joined the Biafran War died at the front, Mazrui wrote *The Trial of Christopher Okigbo*, in which he raised issues of literary and political commitment. Had Okigbo, the poet, betrayed the pen of a writer by taking up the sword of a soldier? By writing the novel, Mazrui had inserted himself right in the middle of the Biafran war. The creative invention was pure Mazruiana. Drawing on his triple heritage, Mazrui made Hamisi, a Muslim lawyer, defend Christopher Okigbo, the Christian but also in line for Yoruba priestly succession. In the trial, the triple heritage of Christian, Muslim and African indigenous systems meet in a most Western type legal battle over a question that has been a central theme in the Western aesthetic debates over arts and politics. Whatever, Okigbo, publisher, poet and soldier, linked Mazrui forever in the Nigerian, and by extension, African literary tradition.

Achebe was close to Okigbo as were all the major Nigerian writers of the time. In a story in the 25 March 2013 issue of *Daily Times*, the President of Christopher Okigbo Poetry Society, Mr. Patrick Oguejiofor, was quoted as saying that with the passing on of Achebe, the heavens will bubble because of the reunion with Okigbo. Achebe regarded his friend as the finest poet of his generation; he not only dedicated books to Okigbo but also wrote elegy for the poet:

For whom are we searching?
For whom are we searching?
For Okigbo we are searching

He described Okigbo as "owner of the riches in the dwelling place of the spirit", a phrase that could equally apply to the departed Chinua Achebe.

But it is an accolade that Mazrui assumes in putting Okigbo on trial in an AfterAfrica charged with the offence of putting society before art in his scale of values. No artist had the right to carry his patriotism to the extent of destroying his creative potential. Mazrui saw the Biafra war being compressed in the single poetic tragedy of the death of Christopher Okigbo. The novel was published by the Heinemann *African Writers Series* of which Chinua Achebe was the editorial adviser.

Through his position in the series, the Achebe of the Makerere event went on to nurture and inspire a whole generation of African writers as the editorial adviser of the Heinemann *African Writers Series*. I have written of him as synonymous with the series and African writing in English. But his influence has been reborn in a new generation of Nigerian writers, notably in the work of Chimamanda Adichie and Helon Habila.

Interestingly in the works of these writers, in which the Biafran war takes center stage, Christopher Okigbo has been reborn as among the group of Nigerian intellectuals in and around the University Nssuka who gather to argue and read poetry in Adichie's novel *Half of a Yellow Sun* and among the soldiers in Habila's *Measuring Time*. In *Measuring Time*, Okigbo does appear. Uncle Haruna who returns from the front talks of his friend Chris with whom they traveled together. There is a kind of afterlife of Christopher Okigbo anticipated in Mazrui's novel.

So while the storyteller, launched new writers who dabble in politics and history, the political scientist, launched an African literary tradition of the fictional afterlife of artists.

Mazrui has written short stories. I published one in *Ghala* magazine way back in the sixties, and I am sure he must have many more in store, poetry as well; and Achebe has published political pieces, poetry in Igbo as well, and there may well be many more that he has left behind him.

But any discussion about them raises the larger question of the relationship between art and politics. Politics is about the organization and management of power in society; art, literature in particular, is part of the organisation and management of values in society. The way power is organized, who or what social groups control it, the ends to which it is put, it impacts the entire realm of the human, and ultimately the quality of human life. And ultimately, this is what the work of both Achebe and Mazrui is all about. One iroko tree has fallen but the other still stands strong among us.

The work of two of Africa's finest public intellectuals will always live and it is only fitting that it is at Mazrui's event, that we remember, this son of Africa, who now dwells in AfterAfrica.

6

Recording Ali Mazrui Documentary Biography:
Lessons and challenges

D. Ndirangu Wachanga

Ali A. Mazrui entered intellectual history following his death on October 12, 2014. The physical absence of this eloquent intellectual reminds the reader of his books, listener of his radio broadcasts, and viewer of his electronic visual productions, of the effects of severing the voice from the body, especially because Mazrui spent more than half a century writing, teaching, giving public lectures and debating. There is a vivid imprint of him in especially the film archives, including my 2015 biographical documentary on his life and work, "Ali Mazrui: A Walking Triple Heritage." Even more striking is the way new communication technologies, including YouTube, have created him for us, as well as commemorated and preserved his memory. Following his death, numerous conferences and symposiums were organized across the globe in his memory. Moving obituaries appeared in major newspapers around the world. But one of the most profound essays in memory of Mazrui was by Wole Soyinka, who reminisced not only about their "unflagging"[1] adversarial relationship, but also highlighted how Mazrui, on his seventieth birthday, pursued a path that led to their reconciliation:

> The ranks keep thinning, bringing both sadness for the individual loss and for the inevitable receding of an era whose seizure owed so much to the intellectual industry of such scholars such as Ali Mazrui. Ali and I were unflagging adversaries. Indeed, it is only by dint of a hard effort of recollection that I find myself able to cite a few areas of absolute concordance on any critical issue that concerned the "African Project"! Fortunately, I

was able to participate – at his touching insistence! – in the colloquium at Binghamton Univeristy to mark his seventienth birthday. He was the perfect host, presiding affably over the multidisciplinary motley of African scholars and Africanists, including statemen and – women that he had labored very hard to bring together. [H]is passing is a great loss to us all. I already feel his absence, and miss him.[2]

Like many readers of Mazrui and Soyinka, I followed their debate, which degenerated into a heated diatribe, in the media, and grew up with an abstract notion of who they are. But my first meeting with Mazrui was in 2008, at the annual African Studies Association Conference in Chicago. At the time, I was designing a model, which examined ways in which information in politically and socially restrictive environments is sanctioned and controlled; how such information flows and how it is propagated in ways that give salience to certain elements and deny significance to others; how information is translated in such environments and what happens to that which resists translation. More important was the need to understand the effect of such restrictive information environment on a nation's collective memory, especially when documents containing a country's past are destroyed, distorted and/or inaccessible. I telephoned Ali Mazrui's hotel room from the front desk. He was not in his room. I left him a voice message and my cellular phone number. Later that evening, he returned my call and we arranged to meet the day that followed. Suddenly, I became anxious about my encounter with the renowned scholar, partly because of an awe-inspiring sentience: Although I was going to meet Ali Mazrui the person, I had been living with the idea of him through his books, book chapters, journal articles, newspaper articles, TV and radio broadcasts, as well as in his encyclopedic 9-hour TV series, *The Africans: A Triple Heritage*.

Inside his hotel room, I noted copies of several bookmarked texts on his desk. There were brown envelopes containing manuscripts he was editing laying on a small coffee table. On his bed lay a small radio, which as I later found out, he never left behind. In fact, on his 33rd birthday, he received a radio as a gift, and as he listened to the midday news bulletin, he heard that Kwame Nkrumah had been overthrown. "Osagyefo was overthrown on my birthday," he said, as he turned off the radio.[3]

His level of preparedness for our meeting continues to be a source of humility. Here was an internationally recognized scholar, meticulously taking notes during our first conversation. We talked for more than one hour. And as I listened to him narrate his experiences growing up as well as the intellectual trajectory of his legendary contributions, reflected in the apparently inexhaustible passion for the controversial, it became clear that his life and work, if documented, would offer an insightful sociology of East Africa. Two months after our meeting, he authorized me to be his documentary biographer.

What I remember from our first meeting is Mazrui's ability to listen and his capacity to hear what was being said. As a good listener, he possessed a capacity to see the undercurrent of what was being said. In him one finds the combination of being a particularly astute listener, coupled with an exceptional gift of language, making him a formidable intellectual able to articulate what has been said with exceptional clarity. Over the years, I came to appreciate his genuine curiosity whether he was engaging with undergraduate students in his classroom, young scholars at conferences, and with policy makers and heads of states in boardrooms.

Documenting Mazrui's life and work has been part of my bigger project in which I seek to preserve African memory through conversations with thinkers and thought leaders. Including Mazrui's biography in this project was motivated by the fact that his own personal biography and intellectual experiences are invaluable in offering insights about the biography of East Africa in particular and Africa in general.

Mazrui leaves behind an extensive oeuvre: diverse ideas contained in more than three dozen books, hundreds of book chapters and journal articles, TV series and radio broadcasts, and controversial lectures he generously gave across the globe. The relentlessness with which he pursued difficult ideas, and did so over such a long period of time, demands recognition, and more importantly demands of students and scholars of African studies to pause to reflect on his legacy as one way of honoring this public intellectual who was popularly referred to as a global African.

Mourning his passing, the editors of *Transition*, (a magazine that Mazrui edited during his days at Makerere University, serving not only as one of *Transition's* frequent contributors but also one of the most controversial writers), recognized his unique contributions as a "fearless, fiery and intellectually curious" political theorist.[4]

To meaningfully honor him requires a reflective recognition and an acceptance of the intellectual gift he left behind. But readers must at the same time be apprehended in the acceptance of that gift as one way of searching for the meaning of receiving a gift where nothing is asked in return. But the archive that is Mazrui extends beyond the footprints in writing, and perhaps it is this more powerful embodiment and auditory archive that gives us a better understanding of his roles.

One way to appreciate his intellectual gift should be by recognizing the significance of the questions he raised in his work, especially because those questions continue to haunt us even after his transition to AfterAfrica. With his passing, the reader is liberated from the authority of the author, creating a space to reflect on Mazrui's legacy differently, and in an edified approach. It is now possible to trace the beginning of his writings as well as the circumstances under which the work was produced, especially because it is now clear where his writing ended.

The centrality of Mazrui in African scholarship is premised on his ability to use his writings and lectures to make African debates relevant and essential in global discourses. Popularly known as a gifted debater and orator extraordinaire; a powerful teacher who was intellectually sophisticated and exceptionally erudite; an iconoclast who helped non-African audience to realize that Africa needs to be understood and not to be feared; perhaps less well-known is Mazrui's early childhood dream to become a taxi driver. His desire to be a taxi driver was a yearning to travel to different places and meet different people from different cultures. Ironically, Mazrui never learned how to drive a car. But he realized his dream to travel, traversing the globe giving numerous and controversial lectures; meeting iconic legends such as Nelson Mandela and Martin Luther King, Jr.; debating founding fathers such as Kwame Nkrumah and Julius Nyerere; controversial figures such as Muammar Gaddafi and Louis Farrakhan; athletic legends such as Mohammed Ali; political activists such as Malcolm X; and political dictators such as Idi Amin.

Born February 24, 1933 in Mombasa, Mazrui was raised in a family with a long and distinguished history of political participation along the East Africa coast. The conflict between his family and the Portuguese settlers is a part of a long history that goes back to the 16th century. Mazrui, therefore, served as a legend because he connected us to that history by being part of it and through analysis of it. Most East Africans only encountered this history in books. It is the history of East Africa's contact with the outside world; of conflict and resilience; of enslavement, emancipation, loss, and emergence of a multicultural society along the coast. He wrote: "The city in which I grew up was multicultural. For centuries, Mombasa, a seaport had experienced the winds and smells of other civilizations – initially from Africa, Arabia, and Asia, and later from the West."[5]

Mazrui's father, Sheikh Al-Amin A. Mazrui, served as Kenya's Chief Kadhi, and wanted the young Mazrui to pursue Islamic studies at Al-Azhar University in Egypt. But Sheikh Al-Amin Mazrui died in 1947 when young Mazrui was only 14 years old, and was only one year away from completing his high school education. On the impact of his father's death, Mazrui wrote:

I was deeply shaken; but more importantly than the bereavement was the increased stature that the old man assumed in my vision. His passion for public involvement became even more heroic in its dimensions. My father's world had been, I now realized, relatively small. He was best known in the Swahili world, especially along the coast of Tanganyika, Kenya, and in Zanzibar. But within that world and in his field he had been a man not only of stature, but more important of clear commitment. As was customary among my people, questions were being asked whether I, as a son, would follow in his footsteps. I already knew I could not do so in the theological field.[6]

Mazrui's high school performance was modest, a mere third class grade, which was not good enough for university admission. His failure to join Makerere University College, weighed heavily on him, and this near-failure became a source of motivation as he sought ways to redeem himself. For a period of five years after his high school education, Mazrui was carrying an overwhelming personal burden of wanting to prove to his family and friends that he was capable of excelling academically, more than his high school exam records indicated. Whenever he saw his former classmates coming back from Makerere University College over the holidays, Mazrui would be disturbed and humiliated by his mediocre high school performance. All the while, he was working as a boarding master at the Mombasa Institute of Muslim Education (MIOME), which is now one of the campuses of Jomo Kenyatta University of Agriculture and Technology. Half a century later, Mazrui would return to this campus not as a boarding supervisor but as the Chancellor of JKUAT.

Concerned as he was with his near-failure, this also was the period when he began his writing career, serving as the youngest editor of the *Arab Guardian*, an opinion monthly publication of the Swahili community. Between 1953 and 1955, Mazrui served as the sub-editor for *Mombasa Times*, a fortnightly news outlet for the local Arab and Swahili news. He also served as a storyteller on *Sauti ya Mvita,* Mombasa's first radio station in the early 1950s.

It was after reciting a poem on the birthday of the Prophet Mohammed (PBUH) in the presence of Sir Phillip Mitchell, the then governor of colonial Kenya, that Mazrui was, shortly thereafter, awarded a scholarship to attend Huddersfield Technical College, where he took various bridging courses before joining the University of Manchester for his bachelor of arts degree. In his long intellectual career, Mazrui always considered his encounter with Sir Mitchell as a "second chance in life," and his poetry recital as "the most important brief lecture I have ever given, especially because it turned my life around. It gave me a second chance."[7]

His confession about his mediocre high school performance and his ascent to prominence as a global intellectual serves as an important message, especially to those who don't make it the first time. His view that we do not have to be excellent at the beginning, and neither should such failure stop us from achieving our goals, acted as an inspiration to his readers and students.

As he left for England in 1955, members of his family jokingly warned him not to return with a white woman. Although these statements were made tongue in cheek, there was an undercurrent of fear of racial tension if he indeed did came back with a white woman because Kenya was still a British colony at the time.[8] But this came to pass. At Huddersfield Technical College, he met Molly Vickerman, and although they didn't start dating until they went to Manchester, Mazrui married Molly and they had three sons: Jamal, Al'Amin, and Kim. Although Molly's father was uncomfortable with Mazrui's race in the beginning of their marriage, race was not as major a concern as was religion with the Mazrui family because Molly was not a Muslim.

While in England, Mazrui's impressive academic performance in the fields of politics and philosophy earned him a Fulbright fellowship, allowing him to pursue a master's degree at Columbia University. He later attended Oxford University for his doctoral studies, spending three years under the guidance of Dame Margery Pelham, a Nigerianist and the biographer of Lord Lugard; and John Plamenatz, a political scientist, from the then Yugoslavia. He was lucky to be "guided both by an Africanist and a political theorist."[9]

As he finished his doctoral work at Nuffield College in Oxford in 1963, Mazrui's ambition was to become an international civil servant, and he was highly attracted to United Nation positions and ambassadorial appointments, especially because this was a period when most African countries were becoming independent. But it is Collin Leys, a British scholar based at Makerere University at the time, who convinced him to take an academic position at Makerere University College, which he joined in 1963 and where he rose to full professorship in less than two years. The year he turned 30, in 1963, was also one of his most productive intellectually. He published five journal articles in some of the leading international journals in the English language, including *International Affairs*[10], *The American Political Science Review*[11], and *International Organization,* where his article, "The United Nations and Some Political Attitudes"[12], was the Prize Award Essay. According to his childhood friend, Prof. Mohammed Hyder, the significance of Mazrui's position at Makerere could be seen in contrast to his previous failure "to make it to Makerere as a student, but he joined that institution as one of its most powerful figures: a teacher."[13]

During his tenure at Makerere University, Mazrui became one of the leading voices in the discourses that were taking place in East Africa at the time. According to Apolo Nsibambi, the former Premier of Uganda, who once taught with Mazrui, "When people say that Makerere has declined, it is because they are comparing the institution's vibrancy to the 1960s when Mazrui was around."[14]

Mazrui's classes were popular and his public lectures overflowed with an attentive audience, who also included government informers. One of the most memorable and extraordinary public debates Mazrui had in Uganda was with the Head of Intelligence of the Ugandan government, Mr. Akena Adoko, which was held in and televised from the Town Hall of Kampala in 1968. The debate revolved around the role of an intellectual in the post-colonial "African revolution," and had been prompted by Mazrui's definition of an intellectual as "a person who has the capacity to be fascinated by ideas and has acquired the skills to handle some of these ideas effectively."[15] During the debate, Mazrui insisted that the three most important resources in Uganda were its people, land, and Makerere. Although Makerere was meant to refer to Uganda's intellectual resources, his critics interpreted it as an indicator of an unacceptable arrogance of the academics and the detachment of the academy from the ordinary Ugandan. The following day, Ugandan newspapers headlines screamed in their verdict: "The People, The Land and Makerere."[16]

After giving a talk at Makerere University on another occasion, a student newspaper reporter asked Mazrui for a copy of his speech. Although he only had one copy of this speech, he gave it to the student reporter and requested him to return it after compiling his story. In a few days, the copy mysteriously made it back to Mazrui with remarks in the margin made by President Milton Obote. The speech had been delivered to Obote!

Mazrui had several encounters with President Obote. One of the memorable meetings was when President Obote summoned him to Parliament and as Mazrui told it, "admonished me as I pensively sat in the public gallery."[17] Obote also warned: "We don't know if Ali Mazrui will be picked up tonight, but he should consider going to teach elsewhere. We thought they would come for us that night. We waited nervously. Nothing happened."[18] But the then Chief Justice of Uganda, Sir Egbert Udo Udoma, confided in Mazrui that Obote was under intense pressure to either imprison or expel Mazrui. Interpreting Obote, Sir Udoma advised Mazrui that: "This idea of inviting you to parliament was President Obote's substitute. He would rather shame you in public rather than physically hurt you."[19]

Despite his regular verbal harassments, Mazrui remained absolutely fearless in talking truth to power; pursuing tyrannical leaders whenever he could find them; and challenging misguided policies whether they were African, European or American.[20] But it is his debate with Akena Adoko, which affirmed that gown, town, and government were capable of entering into meaningful if contentious conversations in pursuit of national goals.

At Makerere, Mazrui wrote some of his most controversial articles. "Nkrumah: The Leninist Czar," is often cited as the most controversial.[21] In this essay, Mazrui concluded that Kwame Nkrumah was a great African but not a great Ghanaian, a paradoxical assessment, which speaks to Mazrui's "brilliant dialectical mind," with a "capacity to discern the unity of opposites."[22] The article was a diagnosis of Kwame Nkrumah's failed leadership just months after he had been forced to exile. A detailed analysis of this debate is contained in Michael West's chapter in this volume.

His intellectual interests were diverse, ranging from international politics to interracial heart transplants, from religious crisis to regional conflicts, and from the ethics of migration to ethnic marginalization. In one of his fiercest battles, which played out in the pages of *Transition*, and which degenerated into a personal diatribe, he attempted to demonstrate "why Wole Soyinka was wrong about nearly everything."[23]

Most of his articles failed to follow traditional scholarly guidelines, and he is one of the few political scientists who included poetry in his articles. Such an approach has not passed without criticism. Mazrui's response was that he had already demonstrated his ability to "use footnotes" and conduct empirical research during his "Nuffield phase." According to Mazrui, the intention of adopting this writing style was an intellectual experiment, which sought to interrogate other ways of being persuasive, especially in the absence of evidence.[24] It is during this phase when he wrote such articles as "Political Sex, The Poetics of Transplanted Heart,"[25] and "Sacred Suicide," among others. Although this *Transition* phase liberated him from the "Nuffield documentation phase", it was heavily criticized because of its textual analysis approach. In "Sacred Suicide,"[26] Mazrui wondered whether Dag Hammarskjöld committed suicide. Hammarskjöld was one of the most brilliant Secretary Generals of the United Nations who died in a plane crash near Ndola in Zambia when he was trying to solve the problem in the Congo. Mazrui weaved the suicide narrative about Hammarskjöld's death by analyzing notes complied by the deceased. The evidence in this article is textual because, according to Mazrui, Hammarskjöld was a worried, unhappy, and disturbed man who felt enormous world pressures. Hammarskjöld wrote what he called jottings, which were subsequently then published after his death. They were very moving but they betrayed suicidal elements. In one of his jottings, he wrote, "Do I fear a compassion in me to be so destroyed... Tired and lonely, so tired the heart aches."

Most of Mazrui's admirers praise his eloquence of the pen, his ability to combine prose and rhythm, often choosing the right word to describe the phenomenon or the problem in front of him. This eloquence allowed him to combine different variables in his construction of paradoxes, inviting his audience to think about new ideas outside the existing epistemological structures.

He credits *Transition* for "liberating" him from a struggle to find a style that was both artistic and convincing; a style that allowed his mind to roam. His writing is epigrammatic, and flourishes in the use of paradoxes as is exhibited in some of the titles of his prestigious 1979 BBC Reith Lectures "The Garden of Eden in Decay," paradox of "The Cross of Humiliation (an Africa humiliated but not brutalized), and "The Burden of Underdevelopment" (Africa's underdevelopment as a paradox of poverty-stricken millions in the golden continent).[27] These six paradoxes, he argued were a prognosis of "Africa's state of health after a hundred years of intense interaction with Europe" as one way of "measuring the state of the world" because "Africa is in part a mirror of the human condition."[28]

In "The Garden of Eden in Decay," for instance, he wondered why a continent that is considered to be the cradle of humankind was the "last one to be made habitable."[29] He traced that decay to centuries of humiliation and brutalization, an analysis, which offers insights into the contradiction of a continent that is now ruled by westernized Africans; and a continent that is resource-rich yet remains underdeveloped, and is "physically central but strategically and politically peripheral and weak."[30] With the rise of Anthropocene and the raging climate crisis, one wonders whether African will be the fist continent to be destroyed.

Still, owing to the wide range of Mazrui's intellectual interests and artistic writing style, he became regarded more as an essayist than a traditional scholar, and as an intellectual maverick who resisted following any tradition. And if the young Mazrui was steeped in political philosophy and political sociology, we see Mazrui the elder gravitating toward sociological and cultural approaches.

As Seifudein Adem notes in his article, "Ali Mazrui and The Study of International Relations," it was often difficult to pigeonhole Mazrui:

> [W]ith his emphasis on deconstructing Euro-centrism, with his deep interest in the study of languages and their role in the - construction of subjects,- with his special attention to inter-subjectively shared ideas, norms and values, with his longstanding fascination about the issues of culture

and identity formation, and with his preference for transactional methodology, including the reliance on semi-autobiography, Mazrui's scholarship rhymes more naturally with (post-positivist) social constructivism than any other "ism" in the mainstream discipline.[31]

His penchant for using paradox as a form of analysis was predicated on an acceptance that contradictions are not necessarily irreconcilable; and that paradox can be illuminating of reality. He tied that acceptance of reconcilable contradictions to his growing up in a multicultural society in Mombasa where he used Swahili as his mother tongue, was called to prayer in Arabic, and was educated in English. His African identity was, therefore, global in character, and was shaped by diverse influences including indigenous cultures, European capitalism, and western education and heritage. Islam also had a significant influence on him, just as it has had an impact on the African continent, irrespective of whether it was introduced through jihad or evangelism.

If Mazrui's ability to put Africa at the center of global understanding is a unique intellectual contribution, his scholarly work written while at Makerere University is important in the biography of East Africa because it coincided with a time when the line between politicians and intellectuals was not as clearly marked as it might seem today. There were politicians who also wanted to become intellectuals, and they entered into conversations with intellectuals. It was a moment in the history of the idea of the university in Africa when univeristies were seen as laboratories for training civil servant and government officials. Much of the conflict within universities revolved around this tension, of whether the university was a space for nationalist improvement, or more neutral and autonomous spaces of scholarly inquiry.

President Julius Nyerere in Tanzania and President Milton Obote in Uganda often had arguments with Ali Mazrui, and these arguments would be published in journals such as *Transition* as well as in daily newspapers. Mazrui therefore, became a model of what intellectuals should do: that intellectuals should be influential in shaping national and public debates. This role was particularly important at the time when East African countries were newly independent and many of those who were to later occupy important political and academic positions were students at Makerere.

Mazrui was clear about his role as an intellectual and this required rigorous interrogation as well as fearless protection of intellectual materials through debates. He effectively performed this task, and he did so with a sense of humor. He enjoyed debates, often irritating his compatriots because he seemed to be having a good time in the midst of a heated debate. He never shouted, and because of his creative use of language, he was able to use tightly knit-phrases that made his fellow debaters sound silly. This humor seems a crucial part of his philosophical approach, too: ironic, political-motivated and paradox-driven. He belongs to a genre of intellectuals who resist bending to and being shaped by a narrow "nationalist" understanding of knowledge.[32]

The importance of his scholarly work while at Makerere becomes evident when we examine his active participation in producing and enriching a form of scholarship that provided a global view of Africa, especially at a time when it was very tempting to retreat. Although the late 1960s and 1970s was characterized with great centers of intellectual production in Africa, it was also the case that most discussions ran the risk of being inward looking given the comforts of being in the nationally recognized and supported institutions. These institutions were seen as instruments of nationalism. Mazrui constantly opened up debates about Africa to other influences, not only to the relationship between Africa and the West, but also the place of Islam in African societies. Indeed, if there have been questions about his triangulated theory of the convergence of three heritages – African, Islam, and Western – it is increasingly being appreciated that the question of Islam and its place in Africa cannot be ignored, and if it is ignored, it will return to haunt us. He was among the earliest critics of African communalism, which emerged with the unfinished project of decolonization. He saw it as yet another form of Western influence, especially when its economic conception was not rooted in the histories and experiences of Africans.

By opening African discourses to other influences, Mazrui made African debates key and pertinent to global debates: about politics, about religion, about culture, and about change. By connecting his scholarship to other places, Mazrui was reminding us that the best scholarship about Africa is a scholarship that connects it to global debates because Africa is not and has never been isolated.

Equally important was Mazrui's success at entering dominant academic and cultural institutions. He taught at some of the best universities in North America, and gave lectures in academically revered institutions of higher learning across the globe. The lesson from his presence in these institutions was that as long as African knowledge is produced on the margins or in marginal institutions, its global influence and significance would remain unrecognized or minimal. Owing to his reputation and personality, Mazrui was able to become an influential player in major institutions across the globe.[31] It is from such visible intellectual and academic spaces that he was able to provide counter narratives to discourses – both within and from without - that have caricatured Africa, its peoples and their cultures and histories for centuries.

His philosophical approach to African liberalism was two-pronged: a) rejection of dogma, especially his criticism of Marxism and Western capitalism, both of which he delineated as an unsuitable remedies for Africa's economic ills. He rejected their ideological and practical applications and wrote extensively to contest their theorization. b) Commitment to pragmatism, which required committed reflection on and analysis of the reality of the continent and using that reflection in defining its global outlook.

These elements, today still, serve as the guiding principles of the African Union, – its power and value notwithstanding – and how it is fashioned. Mazrui therefore, provided, without intending to do so, the philosophical foundation from which the current AU operates, his insights still guiding its member countries on how to reject dogma and cultivate pragmatism.

As a product of colonialism, its cultural, and its educational institutions, Mazrui understood Europe very well, and was able to articulate issues rooted in Africanity in a language and grammar that is comprehensible to the West. His role, therefore, was that of a translator of Africa to Europe; more of a cultural broker than a bridge-builder because of inequalities inherent in translation, but a tireless debater who consistently challenged dominant European ideas and images of Africa in very powerful ways. Permeating his body of work is the triple heritage model, a convergence of African, Western, and Islamic heritages, which is also an insistence of the heterogeneous nature of Africa. With all its shortcomings, this model serves as a counter to the condescending, stereotypical and warped western narratives that portray Africa as a monolith. Acknowledging that slavery and colonialism have shaped African history, Mazrui added other factors, including the classical Mediterranean, Africa's experience with the Semitic peoples, and the consequences of Islam and the Indian Ocean networks.

One of the forceful messages in his work was that African voices are not marginal. If they are not heard loud enough, it is because they have been denied legitimacy by institutions of interpretation. Mazrui argued that whenever Africans are framed as incapable and unable to speak for themselves, the world is reminded that Africans must be represented. Such are the narratives he strove to debunk while providing alternative viewpoints from the very start of his intellectual career at Makerere University. But things changed when Idi Amin came to power in Uganda in January 1971, since Amin had a wavering relationship with Mazrui.

Following Mazrui's criticism of Obote's leadership, Idi Amin surprisingly considered Mazrui both as a political asset and an intellectual resource. At one point, Idi Amin proposed that Mazrui should lead a "delegation of black thinkers to apartheid South Africa for the purpose of convincing white racists that Blacks could be highly intelligent and capable of being rational."[32] But this odd relationship disintegrated, especially when Idi Amin's dictatorial regime deployed repressive mechanisms, targeting communities such as Acholi and Lango and individuals such as Chief Justice Benedicto Kiwanuka and Makerere's Vice-Chancellor, Frank Kalimuzo; and exiled Asians, giving them a 90-day-notice to leave Uganda. The murderous regime destroyed every fabric of Uganda, including the university. Fearing that Mazrui would speak up following numerous mysterious disappearances and deaths of university professors, his colleagues at Makerere advised him to "shut-up" to avoid endangering their safety.[33]

Rather than shut up, he decided to move to Kenya, and twice applied for a position at the University of Nairobi. The then Vice Chancellor, Dr. Josephat Karanja, took Mazrui for lunch at the Norfolk hotel, where he informed him that the Kenyan government could not give him a job because he was too outspoken. It was only after President Mwai Kibaki appointed Mazrui to serve as the Chancellor of the Jomo Kenyatta University of Agriculture and Technology in 2003 that he was able to be of service to Kenya.

As his life continued to disintegrate in Uganda in the early 1970s, he spent one year (1972-3) at the Centre for Advanced Study in Behavioral Sciences, in Palo Alto, California, and the following year, as a senior fellow at the Hoover Institute on War, Revolution, and Peace, at Stanford University. He joined the University of Michigan in 1974, and rose to be the Director of the Centre for Afro-American and African Studies. While at the University of Michigan, he got another joint appointment with the University of Jos in Nigeria. This happened when his marriage with Molly was falling apart, eventually ending in divorce. It was during his summer trips to Jos University that he met Pauline Uti, whom he later married and with whom he had two sons: Harith and Farid.

While at the University of Michigan, he was selected to give the prestigious BBC Reith Lectures in 1979 and a decade on, he produced a 9-hour TV series, *The Africans: A Triple Heritage*, a project jointly produced by the British Broadcasting Corporation and WETA (Public Broadcasting Service). "In the television series, I was to look at Africa – and the BBC and WETA were supposed to translate my ideas into lively television."[34] But the series, like its narrator, was provocative. In its November 1986 edition, *People Magazine* described the series as one of the most controversial series ever seen on American television.[35] Writing for *The New York Times* on October 26, 1986, John Corry accused Prof Mazrui of using "facts and statistics like an ideologist and not as a historian;" for locating and weaving the narrative only within "moralistic and political ordinates, rather than the historical records." For Corry, *The Africans* is so clamorous "on its moral equations that we lose what may be its most serious message: Africa needs assistance; millions of lives are being lost to famine and disease."[36]

But that was not the purpose of the series according to Mazrui. The series was meant to provide a human context when reading, discussing, and interpreting Africa. In an interview with the *New York Times*, Mazrui said both PBS and BBC had invited him to "tell the American and British people about the African people, a view from the inside. I am surprised, then, that people are disappointed not to get an American view. An effort was made to be fair but not to sound attractive to Americans."[37]

Although the National Endowment for the Humanities spent $600, 000 in endowment grants on the series, the then Chairperson, Lynne Cheney, dismissed *The Africans* as an anti-Western diatribe that blamed "all the moral, economic and technological problems of Africa on the West."[38] Cheney demanded the removal of the NEH's name from the series' credits.

But there are others who celebrated the series, including mayoral recognition in Detroit and Chicago. The renowned South African writer, J.M. Coetzee, noted in 1987 how the series was destined to be the "standard audiovisual introduction to the continent in schools and colleges for years to come, or at least till the phalanx of tin-pot dictators who parade across the screen have vanished into oblivion and an update is needed."[39]

Another appreciative assessment, came from Ward B. Chamberlin Jr., the president of WETA, who argued that the TV series was ''an African's view of Africa," comparable to a "PBS series that presented the history of the Jews as seen by Abba Eban, the Israeli scholar and diplomat." According to Chamberlin, Mazrui's TV series was "strong stuff," especially because the "the Western world doesn't come out very well in the series, but the Western world shouldn't come out well regarding its role in Africa."[40]

Writing for the *Chicago Tribune*, Clifford Terry described the series as "a curious piece – a provocative, exhaustive, highly selective potpourri that is enlightening and irritating, informative and intriguing, petulant and polemical. By no means the traditional down-the-middle PBS documentary, it is a self-styled "commentary" – a sort of "One Man`s Continent."[41]

In 2011, for the 25th anniversary of the TV series, I asked Mazrui what changes he would make if he were to do the series a quarter century later. He said his product would reflect changes that have taken place on the continent since 1986, including the implications of the collapse of the Berlin Wall; the consequences of the end of apartheid in South Africa; considerably larger democratic spaces in most African countries; and the rising usage of new communication technologies and a more pluralistic media. However, he said he would not change the tone he adopted in the series, especially because the TV series was about the place of Africa in relation to global economic distribution, world history, international politics, social justice and human rights. He was grateful to the University of Michigan for allowing him time and space to work on the series.

After a very productive tenure at the University of Michigan, he created the Institute of Global Cultural Studies at the State University of New York-Binghamton, in 1991. Mazrui served as the Founding Director of the institute until his death in 2014. During his directorship, he guided the institute towards developing multidisciplinary approaches to the study of culture and cultural influences across societies in the contemporary world.

His death took me back to November 2009 in his hotel room in New Orleans, Louisiana. I was recording my first interview with him for a documentary on his life and work. It was 9 a.m. He had drafted ten possible titles for the documentary. His room was neatly arranged. He sat near a coffee table, with some of his books carefully propped to appear in the camera frame. Mazrui was photogenic, and he was always conscious of the presence of a camera. This morning, he was re-reading John Mbiti's *African Religions and Philosophy*. The interview ran for close to two hours. At the end, I asked him: "How would you like to be remembered?" He chuckled, thumbing his eyeglasses strap. "I will leave that to other scholars who study Africa," he said.[42]

Nearly five years later, April 2013, in what became my last interview with him, I asked him the same question in his office in Binghamton. He was more forthcoming with details this time; his response was more reflective, weaving together his experiences as a scholar, personal beliefs and fears, his sense of mission, and his philosophy of life. It was clear during this interview that he was already thinking about his end. But it was also a reflection of the "deep hanging out" of my methodology in reecording his documentary biography, and the increasing intimacy in our bond, and his opening up to personal and sensitive questions. As he leaned forward from his swivel chair, he started with a sense of finality:

> If, at the end of time, I will be asked what I did with my life, I hope I will have spent most of it creating a rainbow world or making contributions towards it; a world guided by considerable acceptance of multiculturalism, tolerance of differences and dissent, and acceptance of diversity. I have tried to minimize wasting the life that God has permitted me to have.[43]

The first answer to this question five years before was polite, academic, and ironic. The later answer is more revealing and intimate, sharing more and showing more. I believe he had become more trusting of me, the affective bonds we nurtured, encouraged and allowed beyond the camera. "If there is anything I did not share with you, it is because you did not ask. I did not deliberately conceal anything from you," was his final statement in my last interview.[44]

But he had one regret: "I am a frustrated novelist, who would have wanted to write more novels and poetry both in English and Kiswahili. I have always wanted to write a novel where the head of the Catholic Church, Pope, is a Kenyan Maasai."[45] He only wrote one novel, *The Trial of Christopher Okigbo*, in which he raised questions of both literary and political commitment. Drawing from the creative invention of his triple heritage, Mazrui made Hamisi, a Muslim attorney, defend Christopher Okigbo, a Christian, and one who was also in line for Yoruba priestly succession.[45] In this trial, we find three heritages – Islam, Christianity, and African indigenous cultures – converging in the most veritable Western-type legal battle, around a question that has been a central leitmotif in literary aesthetic debates about art, the role of artists, and their politics and commitment. According to Ngũgĩ wa Thiong'o, Mazrui was a "political scientist with a literary bent, and I am a literary artist with a political bent."[46] For Ngũgĩ, the Biafran War was so complex that Mazrui had to "turn to literature to understand it. Biafra made Achebe turn to politics to understand it."[47]

But given his prominence in global circle, critics felt that Mazrui should have intervened more forcefully when the repressive mechanisms were being deployed in Kenya beginning from the mid-1970s and onwards. According to Simon Gikandi, Mazrui should have been more equivocal in opposing what was going on but he adopted a gentleman approach, a liberal approach in a situation, which was illiberal.[48]

Based on his intellectual approach and writing style, Mazrui was seen as more of an essayist than a systematic social scientist who should gather evidence rigorously. He was accused of dancing with words and texts and for making generalized conclusions that were not backed by empirical data. Still, other critics raised questions about his ability to speak authoritatively on such a huge range of issues – from nuclear enriched weaponry to constitutional power, and from Islamophobia in the United States to xenophobia in South Africa. While he was commended for generating new ideas, it was observed that he fell short of intellectually advancing them, and he was likened to a parent who bears many children but is not present to raise them. According to his nephew, Alamin Mazrui, when Mwalimu prevails as a man of ideas, the scientist in him is devoid of meticulousness. "But it is his originality of many ideas that has made his reputation internationally." Alamin

Mazrui and Dr. Willy Mutunga have co-edited three volumes on Mazrui's debates with his critics.[49]

One of the poignant questions about African scholarship revolves around authenticity. Who speaks authentically for Africa? Mazrui did not escape this question, and critics wondered whether he was capable of speaking for the subaltern, women or other disadvantaged groups, especially given his privileged and elitist background. When Wole Soyinka dismissed Mazrui's TV series as one produced by an Arab, he was raising the question of African authenticity.

Although Mazrui made his name as a scholar of Islam after his TV series in 1986, he became increasingly vocal about the subject following the events of September 11, 2001. But he had spoken on the intersection of Islam and politics before and, not surprisingly, had attracted fierce criticism. In Kenya, for example, when the authoritarian regime of Daniel arap Moi refused to register the Islamic People's Party (IPK), Mazrui argued for the Party to be registered as long as its manifesto demonstrated democratic values. His position was criticized, with the suggestion that he should do "more work to harmonize his liberal democratic conscience and his Islamic conscience."[50] But Mazrui argued that Pan-Africanism and Pan-Islamicism are not mutually exclusive. Two years later, he penned a newspaper article in which he expounded on this point in details: "Pan-Africanism is as much a matter of conversion as Islam. Your anti-Muslim readers cannot be at the same time Pan-African. What are they going to do with the 60 million African Muslims in neighboring countries? Put them in Noah's ark? Is that the measure of their Pan-Africanism?"[51]

Regarding his position on the Israel-Palestine crisis, critics accused Mazrui of being reckless in his criticism of Israel, especially in what they regarded as his lack of clarity in separating the Zionist project from the Jewish project.[52] But he was among the first public intellectuals who compared the occupation of Palestine by Israel to the South African apartheid system, and he spoke strongly against the exploitative mechanisms of racial discrimination. In his intellectual biography, Mazrui was very committed to the ideals of liberation and global understanding. This commitment is visible in his eloquence about the need for peaceful co-existence between Israel and Palestine. Yet, this message of co-existence is applicable to any society and any community, the need to peacefully co-exist both within and between communities. His idea of tolerance and co-existence despite differences was important in his work, which is what he saw as the true meaning of African liberalism. He was also very clear in his rejection of violence no matter where it was coming from. He spoke strongly against US and European military interventions, and was a harsh critic of the war in Iraq and Afghanistan, just as he was against Western interventions in the global south.

Taking stock of his legacy, we must strive to understand what he has left behind and what it means to us. Importantly, there is a need to pause and to recognize the contributions made by Mazrui's generation of intellectuals; a generation that emerged from the worst excesses of colonialism but who never even for a moment gave up their right to 'modernity.' What did it mean to grow up in a colonized society? What did that generation make of colonial education? What was the responsibility of radical transformation? What was the meaning and intentions of the decolonization project? Mazrui's generation did not let these questions pass, and they responded to them often under very oppressive conditions, while working and living with contradictions but not disabled by them.

There seems to have been an environment Mazrui and his generation of thinkers and writers realized that they had to preserve. They feared that if that environment were destroyed, it would do untold damage. In a sense, Mazrui's generation was involved in a kind of environmental politics- environment as cultural and intellectual milieu. His survival was dependent on the survival of that environment, and he protected it to his last days, travelling across the globe even when his health was failing. He continued to engage in dialogue across the world about the destiny of Africa and its peoples in a globalized world. To his last days, he was clear that abandoning the continent is similar to neglecting one's parents, and it should be considered a form of abuse.

He was committed to excellence and was able to carefully express that commitment with humility. A cursory overview of his academic vitae is clearly intimidating. Yet, his humble demeanor was inviting, allowing him to interact with members of our society regardless of their political status, academic background, race, religion or sexual orientation. Still, his ability to clearly and methodically explain complex ideas in simple ways, made him the model teacher that he was – Mwalimu.

April 2013: This was my last interview with Mwalimu Mazrui. We spent two hours in his office. As he strained to rise from his swivel chair to shake my hand, the usual smile planted across his face, he made a request: "When we meet in AfterAfrica, you will let me know if other scholars continued to use the triple heritage model after I am gone."[53] This collection of essays is a clear statement that his legacy is alive and well even after the passing of the body.

He taught me many things, but the most important was how to conduct oneself as a human being, the ability to only be well when the other is well.

This characteristic is most important because it is through this kindness that we aspire to the higher angels of ourselves.

Mwalimu Mazrui's legacy is uniquely African and it should be celebrated. He was a global figure who never tired of sharpening his tools in order to deal with the world's demanding and complicated issues. The continent has not produced many such dedicated and brave intellectuals who care so much.

Notes

1. Wole Soyinka, "Remembering Ali Mazrui," *Transition* no. 117 (2015): 193.
2. Ibid.
3. Ali Mazrui, interview with the author, San Francisco, CA, November 2010.
4. *Transition* Magazine.
5. Ali Mazrui, "Growing up in a shrinking world," in *Public Intellectuals and the Politics of Global Africa: Essays in Honor of Ali A. Mazrui*, ed. Seifudein Adem (London: Adonis & Abbey Publishers Ltd), 1 – 20.
6. Ibid., 5 – 6.
7. Ali Mazrui, interview with the author, New Orleans, LA, November 2009.
8. Ali Mazrui, interview with the author, San Francisco, CA, November 2010.
9. Ali Mazrui, interview with the author, Oxford, UK, July 2010.
10. Ali A. Mazrui, "African Attitudes to the European Economic Community," *International Affairs (Royal Institute of International Affairs 1944-)* 38, no. 1 (Jan., 1963): 24 – 36, doi: 10.2307/2610502.
11. Ali A. Mazrui, "On the Concept of 'We are All Africans'," *American Political Science Review* 57 no. 1, (Mar., 1963): 88 – 97, doi: 10.2307/1952721.
12. Ali A. Mazrui, "The United Nations and Some African Political Attitudes," *International Organization* 18, no. 3 (Summer, 1964): 499 – 520. This article was also reprinted in full in *East African Journal*, 1, no. 6 (October).
13. Mohammed Hyder, interview with the author, Mombasa, Kenya, January 2010.
14. Apolo Nsibambi, interview with the author, Kampala, Uganda, January 2013.
15. Ali Mazrui, "A Confluence of Three Cultures," in *The Scholar Between Thought and Experience*, ed. Parviz Morewedge (Institute of Global Cultural Studies, Binghamton University, Binghamton, NY 2001): 103 – 117.
16. Sam Makinda, "Leadership in Africa: A Contextual Essay," in *Governance and Leadership: Debating the African Condition*, eds. Alamin Mazrui and Willy Mutunga (Africa World Press, Inc., New Jersey, 2003), 8.
17. Ali Mazrui, interview with the author, Binghamton, NY, April 2010.
18. Ibid.
19. Ibid.
20. Ricardo Laremont, interview with the author, Binghamton, NY, May 2012.
21. Ali Mazrui, "Nkrumah: The Leninist Czar," *Transition* 6, no. 26, (1966): 8 – 17, doi: 10.2307/2934320.
22. Ibid.
23. *Transition* Magazine.
24. Ali Mazrui, interview with the author, Washington, DC, November 2012.
25. Ali. A. Mazrui, "Political Sex, The Poetics of Transplanted," *Transitions* 4, no. 17 (1964): 19-23.
26. Ali A. Mazrui, "Sacred Suicide," *Transitions* 5, no. 21 (1965): 10-15, doi:

10.2307/2934092

27 Mazrui's 1979 BBC Reith Lectures, The African Condition, were later published in a book form by Cambridge University Press in 1980 under the same title.
28 Ali Mazrui, *The African Condition: A Political Diagnosis*, (Cambridge: Cambridge University Press, 1980), 2.
29 Ibid.
30 Ibid., 3.
31 Seifudein Adem, "Ali Mazrui and the Study of International Relations," *IGCS Newsletter* 8 no. 1, (Fall, 2010): pp 8, http://binghamton.edu/igcs/docs/News8.pdf .
32 Simon Gikandi, interview with the author, Philadelphia, PA, November 2012.
33 Molly Mazrui, interview with the author, Binghamton, NY, May 2011.
34 Ali A. Mazrui, *The Africans: A Triple Heritage* (Greater Educational Telecommunications Association, 1986), 7.
35 Jane Hall, "The Gospel According to Mazrui-PBS Broadcasts One Scholar's Startling View of African History," *People Magazine* (Nov. 24, 1986), http://www.people.com/people/article/0,,20095092,00.html .
36 John Corry, "TV Reviews; 'Africans,' A series on 13," *New York Times*, Oct. 9, 1986, http://www.nytimes.com/1986/10/09/arts/tv-reviews-africans-a-series-on-13.html .
37 Irvin Molotsky, "US Aide Assails TV Series on Africa," *New York Times*, Sept. 5, 1986, http://www.nytimes.com/1986/09/05/movies/us-aide-assails-tv-series-on-africa.html .
38 Ibid.
39 J.M. Coetzee, "Out of Africa!" *American Film* 12 (March, 1987): 19-22.
40 Irvin Molotsky, "US Aide Assails TV Series on Africa," *New York Times*, Sept. 5, 1986, http://www.nytimes.com/1986/09/05/movies/us-aide-assails-tv-series-on-africa.html .
41 Clifford Terry, "PBS 'Maddening, Moving "Africans" Deserves To Be Seen," *Chicago Tribune*, Oct. 9, 1986, http://articles.chicagotribune.com/1986-10-09/features/8603160130_1_africans-pbs-ali-mazrui .
42 Ali Mazrui, interview with the author, New Orleans, LA, November, 2009.
43 Ali Mazrui, interview with the author, Binghamton, NY, April 2013.
44 Ibid.
45 Ali A. Mazrui, *The Trial of Christopher Okigbo* (London: Heinemann ,1971).
46 Ngũgĩ wa Thiong'o, interview with the author, Irvine, CA, July, 2010.
47 Ngũgĩ wa Thiong'o, Speech given at the 38th New York African Studies Association, April 2013, in Binghamton, NY. The event was organized as part of honoring Mazrui's 80th birthday. Achebe was expected to attend the conference but he died March 21, 2013
48 Simon Gikandi, interview with the author, Philadelphia, PA, November 2012.
49 Wachanga Ndirangu, "Mazrui at 80," *Daily Nation,* September 3, 2013, http://www.nation.co.ke/news/Mazrui-at-80/-/1056/1714790/-/view/printVersion/-/dcy3e3z/-/index.html
50 Joseph Irungu Simon, *Daily Nation,* June 29, 1992.
51 Ali Mazrui, *Sunday Nation,* January 30, 1994.
52 Ricaredo Laremont, interview with the author, Binghamton, NY, May 2012.
53 Ali Mazrui, interview with the author, Binghamton, NY, April 2013.

7

Recasting Ali Mazrui

Macharia Munene

Introduction

Ali Mazrui died in 2014 a revered man of intellect but he died in a foreign land, the United States of America, and had to be transported back to Mombasa to be laid next to his ancestors. What was more, a special prayer held for him in a Binghamton Mosque where three women, and they were not Muslims, broke tradition and spoke in the Mosque, in the praise of Mazrui.[1] It was a rare honour for a Muslim because the tradition is for a dead person to be buried within 24 hours at the place of his death. But then Mazrui was not an ordinary Muslim because he was beyond being just a Muslim, he was either a Kenyan who became global or he was a global who happened to be Kenyan. That paradox of being either global Kenyan or Kenyan global, was the hallmark of Mazrui's life. Mazrui, noted the BBC, "was a household name in Kenya and beyond."[2] Few people enjoy that privilege.

He also enjoyed the privilege of being among people who suffer mixed beginnings. They display brilliance either early or late; Mazrui did both. The early display of brilliance enabled him to jump classes in school, got stunted temporarily, and then bloomed. Because of the stunted period, he was always among the first to admit his limited intellectual beginnings.[3] In this he was in the good company of Albert Einstein, the physicist whose relativity upset the

---

[1] Horace Campbell, "The Humanism of Ali Mazrui: His Journey to the Vision of Openness," Counterpunch, Weekend Edition, October 17-19, 2014.
[2] BBC NEWS Africa, "Kenya's Ali Mazrui: Death of a towering intellectual," BBC NEWS Africa, October 13, 2014.
[3] Ali A. Mazrui, "The Making of an African Political Scientist," International Social Science Journal, Volume XXV, Number 12, 1973, pp.103-104.

certainty of Newtonian logic. Not qualified to enter universities of choice, Einstein had ended up in a polytechnic and was lucky to find a clerk's job in a patent office. On seeing what people were patenting, and probably influenced by French scientist Henri Poincaré,[4] he believed he could do better and so he started doing experiments at night and the result was his theory of relativity. Mazrui was also in the good company of Winston Churchill, the naughty son of British aristocracy who barely scraped through Harrow and Sandhurst to become the greatest defender of the British Empire in the 20th Century. Churchill was like Mandela, Mazrui wrote, "an interpreter of history and a maker of it."[5] And so was Mazrui who, like Abdal-Rahman b. Muhammad Ibn Khaldūn roughly 600 years before,[6] made and wrote history.

Although his intellectual beginnings appeared shaky, he proved he was not mediocre once he got his second chance. He wanted to surpass his father in scholarly output[7] and he succeeded so much that he, according to Ngũgĩ wa Thiong'o, "more than lived up to the description of the global African. He made Kenya and Africa visible in the highest echelons of intellectual production."[8] With his adulthood being global rather than Kenyan, he twice married outside Kenya, to a British protestant whom he met at Manchester, Molly Vickerman, and they had three children.[9] The two divorced amicably in 1982, Molly got married to an American, Jim Walker, and Mazrui then married a Nigerian catholic, Pauline Ejimah Uti, that he met at Jos. Despite being a practicing Muslim, his British and Nigerian wives continued to practice their respective versions of Christianity.[10] He taught in Uganda, Nigeria, and the United States but never in Kenya.

He did not start that way, given that his performance at Cambridge School Certificate in 1948 was wanting. He had then worked for the Dutch Trading Company before becoming a clerk at the Mombasa Institute of Mus-

---

4 Francis Kwarteng, "A Tribute: Ali Mazrui, Ghana, & The World (3)", Thursday, 23 October 2014, http://www.ghanaweb.com/GhanaHomePage/features/artikel.php?I...
5 Ali Mazrui, "Africa, Mandela and the Centennial Muse," in <u>Mazrui Newsletter</u> Number 27, early 2003, p. 6.
6 Seifudein Adem Hussein, "Ali. A. Mazrui: A Postmodern Ibn Khaldūn?" <u>Journal of Muslim Minority Affairs</u>, Volume 23, Number 1, April 2003, p. 127.
7 Okello Oculi, "Mazrui's Culture of intellectual tolerance" <u>Daily Nation</u>, Tuesday, October 14, 2014.
8 Ngũgĩ wa Thiong'o, "How Ali Mazrui, the global Kenyan, charted my path," <u>The Standard Digital News,</u> Thursday, October 23, 2014, http://www.standardmedia.co.ke/article/2000139170/Ngũgĩ-wa-thio...
9 Ali Mazrui, "The British Connection: Manchester and Oxford," <u>Mazrui Newsletter,</u> Number 27, early 2003, pp. 17-18.
10 Mobile telephone discussions with William Mayaka, a close friend of Mazrui, in the Sunday afternoon of June 21, 2015, from around 2.10 pm.

lim Education.[11] Mazrui, however, was not of humble lineage being scion of the ruling Mazrui dynasty in Mombasa that was also scholarly. The father, and the grandfather, had distinguished themselves in Islamic scholarship and Mazrui had thus probably inherited a craving for intellectual pursuits. The father, Chief Kadhi Al'Amin had written <u>The History of the Mazrui Dynasty of Mombasa</u> in Arabic that was later translated into English by the Oxford University Press in 1995 for the British Academy. Mazrui was very close to his father with whom he used to walk almost everywhere "since my Dad wanted me to be around him most of the time."[12] The Chief Kadhi had dreams of the son attending the Al Azar University in Cairo to become an Islamic scholar. But then the father died in April 1947 when the son was fourteen, "rather pre-maturely".[13] This affected his school work. "After my old man died," Mazrui wrote in his 2002 Annual Newsletter Number 26, "my school work took a nosedive. It was the crucial year of my taking the Cambridge School Certificate."[14]

Besides accompanying his father almost everywhere, Mazrui's childhood was that of a British colonial subject of the coastal type. As a child, he played football in Mombasa around Fort Jesus along with Ahmed Idha Salim,[15] the historian of the Waswahili.[16] In the 1930s and 1940s, Salim wrote, the debate among the coastal people was on whether to be identified as a native or not.[17] Ordinances, he noted, "removed the Arabs, and also as much members of the 12 tribes as could establish some 'non-native' descent on either side, from the operation of certain ordinances affecting 'natives.'"[18] Most people preferred not to be "native" because being "native" meant exorbitant taxation; those who could became "non-native". In Lamu, among the

---

11   Ambassador Juma V. Mwapachu, "A rich legacy: The life and times of Ali Mazrui," October 16, 2014 http://mobile.thecitizen.co.tz/opinion/A-rich-legacy--The-life-and-ti... Accessed June 20, 2015.

12   Ali Mazrui, "Death, Destiny and Coincidence," <u>Mazrui Newsletter</u> Number 27, early 2003, pp.34-35.

13   Ali Mazrui, <u>Annual Mazrui Newsletter: Between Global Africa and the World of Islam</u>, No. 22, Early 1998, pp.2-3, 21-22; Mazrui, "Death, Destiny and Coincidences," pp. 36-37; Mwapachu, "A Rich Legacy."

14   Ali Mazrui, "Legal Dreams and Colonial Nightmares," <u>Annual Mazrui Newsletter</u>, Number 26, Early 2002, p. 8.

15   Author Oral Discussions with Ahmed Idha Salim when Salim was Chairman, Department of History, University of Nairobi in the late 1980s.

16   Ahmed Idha Salim, <u>The Swahili Speaking Peoples of Kenya's Coast, 1895-1965.</u> (Nairobi: East African Publishing House, 1973).

17   Ahmed Idha Salim, "'Native or Non-Native?': The Problem of Identity and the Social Stratification of the Arab-Swahili of Kenya," in B.A. Ogot, editor, <u>History and Social Change in East Africa: Proceedings of the 1974 Conference on the Historical Association of Kenya</u> (Nairobi: East African Literature Bureau, 1976), pp. 65-85.

18   Ibid., p. 76.

Bajuni for instance, it became necessary to create a committee of "elders of good repute and standing" to advise the DC on "who was a *Muungwana* or 'free man' and who was of slave descent"[19] This way, the Mazruis escaped the pain of colonial over taxation because members were not "natives."

Burjor Avari, Mazrui's friend at Manchester who also grew up in Mombasa remembers Mazrui as bright, articulate, and "hilariously naughty". In Manchester, he saw Ali pee in "a milk bottle."[20] The "naughtiness" started in his childhood and was enough to attract parental bottom thrashing. During World War II in Zanzibar, where the family had taken refuge to escape likely Italian bombing of Malindi extending southwards to Mombasa, he saw a boy jumping up and down a family bedbug ridden mattress. The family had taken the mattress out to dry in the sun. Not amused, Mazrui took a branch and "gave a war-cry and made for the little intruder" to scare and chase the "invader". The boy returned accompanied by irate women who wanted to inflict their form of revenge justice on Mazrui. After Ali's mother received the unpleasant news, and despite Mazrui's protests that the other boy was a liar, and to reconcile angry women, she administered corrective pain on her son's rear anatomy.[21]

In school, he was fascinated by the English language as "a medium of debate," and dreamt of going to Makerere College to study English "as a tool of verbal combat." He early showed an argumentative trait and impressed teachers with his debating and writing of short stories. This early display of "precociousness," led the school to promote him to upper classes probably before his time. The school "overestimated precocity" and this would probably, besides the trauma of his father's death, partly account for his poor performance in Cambridge School Certificate. The poor performance, however, could not take away his gift of the garb of the English language "as a tool of verbal combat" and slightly more. The more was his ability to weave ideas and articulately convey them to other people. This ability was probably inherited, given that his immediate forefathers had been men of the pen, and they liked debating. They had probably passed the genes for being articulate to the young man.[22]

---

19   Ibid., p. 82.
20   Burjor Avari, "Recollections of Ali Mazrui as an Undergraduate," in Omari H. Kokole, editor, The Global African: A Portrait of Ali A. Mazrui (Trenton, NJ: Africa World Press, 1996), p. 295.
21   Mazrui, "The Making of an African Political Scientist," pp. 108-109.
22   Ibid., pp.102-104.

The Second Chance

It was that garb of language that attracted Sir Philip Mitchell, governor of Colony and Protectorate of Kenya. Mitchell, an unfortunate governor who ignored signs of danger to the colony that would culminate in the Mau Mau War,[23] was at least successful in founding Mombasa Institute of Education to enable, wrote close Mazrui friend William Mayaka, "African Muslims catch up with twentieth century through technology."[24] He was also successful in launching Mazrui's academic career by deciding to help Mazrui recover from his academic deficit. This was after Mazrui told him that he wanted the opportunity to go to study law in India and since Mitchell had little respect for India, he organized for Mazrui to go for remedial tuition or "pre-university qualifying education" in England at "Huddersfield Institute of Technology which served as springboard into the world of academia."[25] Mazrui remained grateful to Mitchell and other colonial authorities for giving him a second chance. "I received a letter from the Department of Education confirming that I had been awarded a scholarship, first to complete my secondary education at a college in Huddersfield, England, and later to a British University … In spite of the third class Cambridge School Certificate results, Ali Mazrui had been given a second chance."[26] And they did, at the height of the Mau Mau War, as they sought to groom new leaders for Africans.

In the effort to groom new leaders, the British were also reacting to a perceived threat emanating from American influence through the offering of educational opportunities to "natives" who then seemed to turn anti-colonialist. Among such "natives" was Harry Thuku whose teachers were American missionaries of the Gospel Missionary Society led by Knapp.[27] After the Great War or World War I, Thuku had become an anti-colonial agitator that in part led to the need to reassess the type of education that should be offered to "natives." He ridiculed colonial officials by showing that they were illogical and also called on African Americans to help in setting up anti-colonial

---

23   Keith Kyle, The Politics of the Independence of Kenya (London: Macmillan Press, 1999), p. 45; Caroline Elkins, Britain's Gulag: The Brutal End of Empire in Kenya (London: PIMLICO, 2005), pp. 29;-30.

24   William Mayaka, "Ali. A. Mazrui: Profile of a Scholar," in Seifudein Adem, editor, Public Intellectuals and the Politics of Global Africa: Essays in Honour of Ali A. Mazrui (London: Adonis, 2011), p. 123.

25   Ibid., pp. 124-125, 128.

26   Ali Mazrui, "From MIOME to Huddersfield," Annual Mazrui Newsletter, Number 26, Early 2002, p. 12.

27   Francis Kimani Githieya, The Freedom of the Spirit: African Indigenous Churches in Kenya (Atlanta: Scholars Press, 1997), pp.31-32, 67-68.

schools.²⁸ He wrote to the secretary of the Tuskegee Institute on September 8, 1921 complaining of oppression as he asked black Americans to set up an educational institution in Kenya to fight white rule because "the children of the soil have been ceaselessly exploited under the pretext of civilizing them and the country is governed primarily not for the aboriginal races but, for all interests and purposes, for the governing race."²⁹ It was to deal with the consequences of Thuku agitations that the British consulted the Phelps Stoke Foundation in New York that, besides recommending a Tuskegee type of technical education, also had James Aggrey of the Gold Coast as a commissioner.

Aggrey's symbolic impact was contrary to British expectation. It inspired natives to go to America, among them being the son of colonial chief Koinange wa Mbiyu. The chief organized, with the help of the Phelps-Stokes Fund in New York for his son, Peter Mbiyu, to go to the Hampton Institute in Virginia in 1927. After acquiring degrees from Ohio, Wesleyan, and Columbia Universities, Mbiyu spent two years at Cambridge and London to pocket British teaching certification.³⁰ Most important, he became close to another Kenyan African, Jomo Kenyatta, who had been sent there by the Kikuyu Central Association to agitate for African rights. He returned to Kenya in 1938.

Upon his return to Kenya, Mbiyu engaged in activities that had long range political impact. Offered a teaching job at Alliance High School, Mbiyu rejected the offer because the salary was "at one half the pay that its former occupant, a white man, had been getting. Pointing out the fact that the money he had to pay for his education had not been halved because he was black, he refused to accept the post."³¹ He had then founded Githunguri Teachers College whose undeclared aim was to educate people politically while training teachers for independent schools. He also hosted an African-American academic, Ralph Bunche, who was then nicknamed *Kariuki*, and became involved in the founding of Teachers College at Githunguri. In 1944, he enjoyed hosting more than 200 American black and white soldiers who were then stationed in Kenya.³² Mbiyu's objective was to prepare Africans for the independence

---

28   Macharia Munene, "The United States and Anti-colonialism in Kenya," <u>African Review of Foreign Policy</u>, March 1999, Volume 1 Number 1, pp. 5-6.
29   H. Thuku to the Secretary, Tuskegee Institute Alabama, USA, September 8, 1921, in G.H. Mungeam, editor, <u>Kenya: Select Historical Documents, 1884-1923</u> (Nairobi: East African Publishing House, 1978), pp. 495-497.
30   Robert F. Stephens, <u>Kenyan Student Airlift to America, 1959-1961: An Educational Odyssey</u>, pp 4-5.
31   Negley Farson, <u>Last Chance in Africa</u> (New York: Harcourt, Brace and Company, 1950), p. 119.
32   R. Mugo Gatheru, <u>Child of Two Worlds</u> (London: Routledge and Kegan, 1964), pp. 207-208; Mbiyu Koinange, <u>The People of Kenya Speak for Themselves</u> (Detroit, Michigan: Kenya Publication Fund, 1955), pp. 42-43; Oral Interview with Mwangi Karangu, Baltimore, Maryland, April 27-28, 1996.

that, in 1948, he was sure was coming.[33] This would explain his desire to have as many Africans as possible acquire an American education and return to help prepare for independence.

Mbiyu's big headedness was in comparison to Eliud Mathu who had stayed put at Alliance, had gone to Fort Hare in South Africa, and had ended up at Oxford as a protégé of Margery Perham. Mathu played colonial good boy, agreeing to teach at Alliance at a lower salary than less qualified white teachers. Mathu, however, paled before Mbiyu in terms of political renown for Africans. Probably for that reason, colonial authorities decided to appoint Mathu the first African to the Legislative Council, LegCo, instead of Mbiyu who had been campaigning for it, and old Chief Koinange was not amused by the colonial snub to his son.[34] Once in LegCo, however, Mathu championed education or the acquisition of "those letters that appear after other people's names."[35] Nicknamed "Mathu B.A", because of those letters, he became close to Mbiyu and the other Kenyan political adventurer, Kenyatta, in their anti-colonial activities.

In their different ways, all three were inspirational to Kenyan youth but it was mostly Mbiyu who catalyzed and helped other natives to emulate him in terms of educational achievements. He actively encouraged others to go to America and tried to contact his friends for help who included Ralph Bunch at the United Nations and St. Clare Drake at Roosevelt University in Chicago. Among the inspired was Kariuki Njiiri, son of another colonial chief, Njiiri, as well as political activist R. Mugo Gatheru. Most annoying to Carey Francis of Alliance High School, was the decision by Alliance educated boy, Julius Gikonyo Kiano, to follow Mbiyu's footsteps into America. Mbiyu had virtually ordered Kiano to surpass him academically by returning from the United States with a doctorate.[36] Kiano, fumed Francis in 1953, was a bright boy who went to America to get fourth rate degrees from third rate universities. "If you want a good education," he advised, "go to a British university. Don't run all over the world going to India and America and come back with a

---

33   St. Clair Drake, "Mbiyu Koinange and the Pan-African Movement", in Robert A. Hill, editor, Pan-African Biography (Los Angeles, African Studies Center, University of California, 1987), pp. 182-183; Mbiyu Koinange, The People of Kenya Speak for Themselves, (Detroit: Kenya Publication Fund, 1955).

34   John Spencer, The Kenya African Union (London: KPI, 1985), pp. 124-125; Kyle, The Politics of the Independence of Kenya, p.38.

35   Eliud Mathu's Contribution in the Legislative Council debates, 16th February, 1956, Colony and Protectorate of Kenya: Legislative Debates, Tenth Council Fifth Session Second Meeting, p. 111.

36   O.I. Njiiri.Oral; Interview with J. Gikonyo Kiano, KBC Chairman's Office, June 21, 1996; Irunguh Thatiah and Jane Kiano, Gikonyo Kiano: Quest for Liberty (Nairobi: Longhorn, 2013), pp. 33-34.

fourth grade degree from a fifth grade university."'³⁷

In Kiano's mischief, Francis sensed failure of his mission to mold Africans to imbibe British mannerisms and values. The government did not want any more Koinanges because those who went to America, British officials argued, received substandard education and returned to the colonies to create political problems.³⁸ Alliance student Ngũgĩ wa Thiong'o, wrote that "Francis saw Alliance as a grand opportunity to morally and intellectually mold a future leadership that could navigate among contending extremes." Instead, it "birthed a radical anticolonial nationalist fever. Ironically, in its very structure, Alliance actually subverted the colonial system it was meant to serve."³⁹ Among those birthed into "anticolonial nationalist fever" was Kiano who had manifested some rebelliousness by founding a newsletter that dared to challenge school policy. He had joined Mbiyu at Githunguri and quit Makerere in order to go to America.⁴⁰

Francis, still smarting from Kiano's "mischief," was part of that British officialdom and he disliked American education so deeply that he drilled others around him to have the same attitude. One mathematics teacher at Alliance, Bethwell Allan Ogot, remembered that Francis was "particularly opposed to Indian and American degrees.... So when I informed him that I was likely to secure an American scholarship, he reacted so violently that I never raised the issue with him again."⁴¹ And Benjamin Kipkorir, a pupil at Alliance, observed that Francis "had very strong views on such an important matter and never hid his disdain for 'foreign' education, especially that of American and Indian universities. He strongly advised us to proceed to Makerere where 'excellent education' was offered to those who 'deserved and needed it'. He constantly warned … that we should be aware of the dangers of trying to go beyond what we were capable of, for we would come unstack."⁴²

Subsequently, in a way to counter growing American infiltration into British educational preserve, Francis was involved in creating opportunities,

---

37   Oral Interview with Shadrack Kwasa, August 30, 1995, University of Nairobi.

38   J. Pifer, Forecasts of the Fulbright Program in British Africa: A Report to The United States Education Commission in the United Kingdom (London: The United States Education Commission in the United Kingdom, 1953), p. 11.

39   Ngũgĩ wa Thiong'o, In the House of the Interpreter (Nairobi: East African Educational Publishers, 2013), pp.6, 7.

40   Interview with J. Gikonyo Kiano, KBC Chairman's Office, June 21, 1996; Irunguh Thatiah and Jane Kiano, Gikonyo Kiano: Quest for Liberty (Nairobi: Longhorn, 2013), pp. 33-34.

41   Bethwell A. Ogot, My Footprints on the Sands of Time: An Autobiography (Kisumu: Anyange Press, 2003), p. 70.

42   B.E. Kipkorir, Descent From Chereg'any Hills: Memoirs of a Reluctant Academic (Nairobi: Macmillan, 2009), p. 153.

at the height of the Mau Mau War, for select "natives" to attend British universities. Knowing of "the tremendous influence that Carey Francis wielded in the Department of Education in particular and government circles generally,"[43] Ogot steered clear of the American subject and was one of several young men who got the opportunity to partake of the new British educational generosity. The others included Munyua Waiyaki, Duncan Ndegwa, Kitili Mwendwa, Morris Alala, Timothy Riungu, Dunstan Mlamba, Munene Kibuga, James Mbotela, Taaita Toweett, Ephraim Andere, Cherop arap Murgor, and Ali Mazrui.[44]

Although Mazrui's grades were probably the poorest in that group, he seemingly was the most famous, at least at the Kenyan coast. He had spent his time gaining experience and sharpening skills in the use of spoken and written language. He was a journalist, serving as the "Arab Correspondent" for the Mombasa Times and a contributing editor for the Arab Guardian. In addition, he became a local celebrity for his weekly half-hour as a Kiswahili radio story teller in Sauti Ya Mvita or ("The Voice of the Isles of War") radio station in Mombasa. On top of that, he was in high demand as an after dinner speaker in English in Mombasa clubs.[45]

The other person who came close to Mazrui in terms of public renown was Ogot, a more established student who had even been to Makerere and had taught at Kagumo and Alliance High school. The two were in the same plane, BOAC flight BA 176 from Nairobi to London on 5th September 1955. Mazrui was, wrote Ogot, going "for his high school education"[46] at Huddersfield Technical College, a kind of pre-university program, before being admitted to Manchester University.[47] In contrast, Ogot went to a prestigious Scottish university, St. Andrews University, and switched to study history.[48]

Despite such British effort, and given that the offers were limited to only a select few, American educational opportunities still bested the English and had far reaching effects on the colony. When Britain started the Nairobi Royal Technical College, mainly for European and Asian students, its first African instructor was the same Kiano, now called "Dr. Kiano", who had

---

43   Ogot, My Footprints on the Sands of Time, p. 71.
44   Duncan Ndegwa, Walking in Kenyatta's Struggles: My Story, New Edition (Nairobi: Kenya Leadership Institute, 2011), pp. 141, 151; Ogot, My Footprints on the Sands of Time, pp.74-76.
45   Ali A. Mazrui, "From MIOME to Huddersfield," Annual Mazrui Newsletter, Number 26, Early 2002, p. 12.
46   Ogot, My Footprints on the Sands of Time, pp.74.
47   Mayaka, "Ali. A. Mazrui: Profile of a Scholar," pp. 124, 128; Chaly Sawere, "Scholar, Ideologue, Philosopher, Artist" in Omari Kokole, editor, The Global African: A Portrait of Ali Mazrui (Trenton, NJ: Africa World Press, 1998), p. 270.
48   Ogot, My Footprints on the Sands of Time, pp.75-77.

annoyed Francis so much. The first in the region to obtain any doctorate, he was fresh from the University of California at Berkeley. Since the Royal Technical College was reluctant to hire him and so Mucohi Gikonyo, then a member of the LegCO, complained to Governor Evelyn Baring: "My brother is the most educated African and he is going to sell oil?" There after the governor intervened for Kiano to be appointed a lecturer.[49] In 1956, therefore, Kiano paved the way for others who included Josphat Karanja with his 1958 history doctorate from Princeton University in New Jersey. Karanja became the first African historian at the University of Nairobi. Those who followed Karanja included Simeon Ominde, the geographer, and Ogot in 1964.[50]

And what was more, the number of Africans going to the United States in the 1950s rose tremendously, with American encouragement driven by desire to win Africans to its side of the Cold War. The American point man became Tom Mboya who initially was guided by James Bury, a Canadian trade union expert.[51] Mboya was tailor made for British interests and so, wrote newsman Smith Hempstone, later American ambassador to Kenya, the British built up Mboya in order "to create a new and, hopefully, more pliant leader".[52] They sponsored him to Oxford University where Dame Margery Perham, the leading advocate of identifying and grooming potential African leaders took interest in him. Having concluded that Eliud Mathu, her former protégé, had some Mau Mau connection,[53] she adopted and promoted Mboya as the African spokesman on Kenyan issues, advised him to write a pamphlet on Kenya, and then arranged for the Fabian Colonial Bureau to publish it, The Kenya Question: An African Answer.[54] She wrote a "Foreword" to the booklet pointing out that Mboya was "not a Kikuyu" and praised him for having "a clear head and a quiet restrained manner."[55] To her, Mboya was the new, young, and educated leader that Kenya Africans "desperately" needed.[56]

---

49   Macharia Munene Discussions with J.Gikonyo Kiano, KBC Chairman's Office, June 25, 1996.
50   Ogot, My Footprints on the Sands of Time, pp. 130, 132-134.
51   James Bury, "Trade Union Movement in Kenya", Africa Today, May-June 1955, p. 16.
52   Hempstone newsletters to Rogers, SH-25 and SH 26, June 23 and June 26, 1957; George Bennett, Kenya A Political History: The Colonial Period (London: Oxford University Press, 1963), p. 141.
53   Jack R. Roelker, Mathu of Kenya: A Political Study (Stanford: Hoover Institution Press, 1976), p. 112.
54   Tom Mboya, Freedom and After (London: Andre Deutsch, 1963), pp. 50-51; David Goldsworthy, Tom Mboya: The Man Kenya Wanted to Forget (Nairobi: Heinemann, 1982), pp. 57-60.
55   Mergery Perham, "Foreword", in Tom Mboya, The Kenya Question: An African Answer (London: Fabian Colonial Bureau, 1956), pp. 1-2.
56   Ibid., pp. 2-3.

Mboya attracted the attention of the American Committee on Africa and it "stole" him from the British. It arranged for Mboya's tour of the United States to mingle with American liberal and labor union circles.[57] Having been promoted as a "soft-spoken smiling man" who brought to the American people "a message for African freedom and democracy,"[58] he returned to Kenya having established himself as an African spokesman to the American people and, to the chagrin of the British who first groomed him, an American protégé. He also had, according to Smith Hempstone, a lot of money from the AFL-CIO.[59] The Americans were to promote and defend Mboya as "basically a product of the democratic upsurge in Africa today."[60] And often through a man called Irving Brown, Mboya's later cabinet colleague Joseph Murumbi noted, the Americans flooded Mboya with money, which he used to silence people by telling them that he owed them nothing because he had paid them. "I've heard Mboya tell people," Murumbi stated, "'Well, I owe you nothing, I paid you for what you did for me and that is the end of it.'"[61]

This British groomed Mboya, turned American point-man, linked up with American trained people like Kiano and Njiiri to inspire the "airlifts" to North America. There was, wrote Kipkorir, "rush for study abroad that hit Kenya in the years 1959-62. The most celebrated was 'The Airlift' that Tom Mboya arranged for several hundred Kenyans to study in the United States…. It was a time of opportunity with many attractive offerings and one had to stay focused."[62] The rush made it appear as if Britain was under siege in its colonies as American educated returnees started taking top positions in the fast changing political Kenya. This worried Britain and it had to do something to up its educational game for Africans.

For the British, thereafter, as Kayode Soremken argued, "the game plan was this: since independence was inevitable, what they simply did, by way of cutting their loss was to hand over power to … pliant domestic elite."[63] To do that, Britain seemingly adopted two strategies that would ensure contin-

---

57　Sally H. Jacobs, The Other Obama: The Bold and Reckless Life of President Obama's Father (New York: Public Affairs, 2011), pp. pp. 65-66; Goldsworthy, Tom Mboya, p. 60-62.
58　The New York Times, August 19, 1956, p. 9.
59　Smith Hempstone newsletters to Walter S. Rogers, SH 26, June 26, 1957, p. 4.
60　George M. Houser, Letter to the Editor on "Mboya's Politics", The New York Times, May 11, 1958.
61　Anne Thurston Interviews with Murumbi, A Path Not Taken: The Story of Joseph Murumbi (Nairobi: The Murumbi Trust, 2015), pp.229, 231.
62　Kipkorir, Descent, p. 154.
63　Kayode Soremkun, "Tentative Reflections on Literature and Governance in the Kenyan and Nigerian Social Formations," in Gbemisola Adeoti and Mabel Evwierhoma, editors, After the Nobel Prize: Reflections on African Literature, Governance and development (Lagos: Association of Nigerian Authors, 2006), p. 184.

ued influence. First, it recruited bright young men into provincial administration and sent them to premier British universities for short term courses on leadership and administration, not for degrees, that enabled them to say they were at Oxford or Cambridge. At independence, these short course trainees took over administrative positions as District Officers and Commissioners.[64] Second was to produce "academics" who would man the new universities that it was creating. And the training included "how to sit at a table and how to utilize the various cutlery items arrayed at the table" Alliance student Kipkorir wrote, "… it was those introductory cultural exposures, re-enforced soon after at Makerere, which helped prepare us, an emerging elite, to acquire some of the … airs which made it so easy to rise so fast from African DC's to become independent Kenya's rulers not many years after they left school or college."[65] After Alliance, Kipkorir went to Makerere where he found Ogot lecturing.

Makerere had offered Ogot a post of tutorial fellow in 1959 on graduating and he remembers that "in the world of academia, bright prospects were beginning to loom in the horizon. Posts … were advertised in African history, and there appeared to be very few people" who qualified.[66] He registered for doctoral research on the Luo under Roland Oliver in London University. Wrote Oliver, "I felt enough confidence in Ogot to support him in his desire to work entirely in oral evidence concerning the migration settlement of the Luo peoples…. This, if successful, would be a methodological breakthrough."[67] While Ogot, as Oliver hoped, made methodological breakthrough in studying history, Mazrui overcame his supposed intellectual mediocrity.

Re-bloomed Mazrui

The two, Ogot and Mazrui, had unique sense of self-awareness, complained about people in their biological neck of the woods being neglected or marginalized by post-colonial African governments, and inadvertently engaged in subtle competition for intellectual renown. Mazrui complained about the Coast in his 1996 "Paradox of the jewel that never shone" article and Ogot complained about the Luo in his 1998 "Siege of Ramogi" lecture that he

---

64   Simeon Nyachae, Walking Through the Corridors of Service: An Autobiography (Nairobi: MvuleAfrica, 2010), pp, 59-60
65   Kikorir, Descent, p. 146.
66   Ogot, My Footprints on the Sands of Time, pp.74-76.
67   Roland Oliver, In the Realms of Gold: Pioneering in African History (Madison: University of Wisconsin Press, 1997) p. 127.

republished as a chapter in a book. In their zonal grumblings, both sounded as if they were romanticizing colonialism.[68]

They had good reason given that both had benefitted from colonial desires in the 1950s to groom the acceptable among the Africans. Both knew of, and could not resist trumpeting, their brilliance. Ogot did not shy from pronouncing his brilliance, mainly in his writings where he pointed out his achievements and the shortcomings of the others.[69] Mazrui, though he refrained from passing intellectual judgements on others, was also good at blowing his trumpet and he did it in three ways. First he declared his initial *Cambridge* deficit, second he expressed gratitude to the British for giving him a second chance, and third he tended to discuss his rare achievements in rising to the top of the intellectual world.

It was Huddersfield and Manchester that opened Mazrui's social, leadership, and intellectual doors. Socially he was easy to get along with and so he made friends with lasting impact. Huddersfield in Yorkshire, Mazrui asserted in 1986, "was a turning point in my life", private and intellectual, and became a place of pilgrim and nostalgia. He acquired a job "as a bus- conductor on a trolley bus" and more importantly he met Molly Vickerman, the English woman who later became his wife. In addition, Huddersfield "was the place of my academic re-vindication in secondary education after doing poorly in high school in Mombasa. At Huddersfield College I had my second chance – a turning point in my academic career!"[70]

While Huddersfield gave him a wife, he linked with fellow Mombasa boys at Manchester and they became close. There was the Indian called Burjor Avari who noticed Mazrui's "hilarious naughtiness." And there was his college room-mate nicknamed "Panya" by close friends. "Panya", whose actual name was Muhammad Ali Abdulrahamn grew up with Mazrui in Mombasa but had migrated to Oman and then later returned to Mombasa.[71] Mazrui also showed his leadership skills when African students at Manchester elected him "President of the African Students' Association."[72]

---

68 Ali A. Mazrui, "Paradox of the jewel that never shone," Sunday Nation, July 7, 1996, p. 7; B.A. Ogot, "The Siege of Ramogi: From National Coalition to Ethnic Coalition, 1960-1998," in Bethwell A. Ogot, Building On the Indigenous: Selected Essays, 1981-1998 (Kisumu: Anyange Press, 1999), pp.277-288.
69 Ogot, My Footprints on the Sands of Time, passim.
70 Ali A. Mazrui, "A Triple Heritage: The Finale," Mazrui Newsletter, Eve of 1987, p.1.
71 Ali Mazrui, "The Bonds of Friendship and the Menace of Time," Annual Mazrui Newsletter, Number 22, Early 1998, p. 19; ------------"The British Connection: Manchester and Oxford," Annual Mazrui Newsletter, Number 27, early 2003, p. 11.
72 Ali Mazrui, "Politics of Ancestry," in McGregory Gripen Blog, "Majuto ni mjukuu@ Kenya, "Exciting intellectual exchange between Mazrui, Soyinka, Gates et al," Sunday March 19, 2006.

Most important, it was at Manchester that Mazrui re-bloomed intellectually so much that he jumped over all the others academically and became what his colleague Horace Campbell termed "the darling of western liberals."[73] He was determined to exorcise the ghost of Cambridge and he did. "I entered the Western game with such gusto," he wrote, "that I did it brilliantly at Manchester emerging with a bachelor's degree with Distinction."[74] He thus worked for and obtained a First Class and then went to Columbia, New York, where he again distinguished himself. He thereafter became an object of competition for Britons and Americans. At the time, there was intense competition between the United States and Britain on recruiting bright students or offering educational opportunities to potential players in decolonizing countries. He therefore received competing doctoral scholarships from Princeton University in the United States and University of Oxford in England.[75]

Mazrui and Oxford had mutually attractive interest in each other. For Mazrui, Oxford would expunge the ghost of *Cambridge*[76] and for Oxford, ensuring that Mazrui remained in the British camp would redeem some pride. Princeton had produced Karanja, a student rebel at Makerere who had become the first African historian at the University of Nairobi. Expelled from Makerere in 1952 because of leading a food strike, Karanja had gone to New Delhi, and wound up at Princeton to obtain a 1958 doctorate.[77] For Britain, Mazrui going to Princeton would have been to add intellectual insult to injuries inflicted by American universities which, Francis believed, were inferior. It was thus seemingly in British interests to ensure that Mazrui received a "good" British doctorate instead of what Kiano and Karanja had obtained at Berkeley and Princeton. Subsequently Oxford, the citadel of the British Empire, won the bout against the American Ivy League in the battle for Mazrui.

With Oxford's success, at least four people helped to mold and launch Mazrui's academic career and intellectual pro-Westernism. They were Margery Perham, John Plamenatz, Kenneth Kirkwood, and Colin Leys. Perham, the first director of the Oxford Institute of Colonial Studies, had long worried about the vigor of American anti-colonialism and on occasion had to

---

73   Campbell, "The Humanism of Ali Mazrui."
74   Mazrui, "The Bonds of Friendship," p. 38.
75   Sawere, "Scholar, Ideologue, Philosopher, Artist,", p. 271.
76   Ibid.
77   Ogot, My Footprints on the Sands of Time, p.56.

"correct the distorted view of the character of the British Empire."[78] She also became, in 1961, the first woman to give the BBC Reith lectures. In six lectures, she talked of "Colonial Reckoning", advised Britons to prepare for losing colonies and also to groom potential African leaders.[79] She had done that since the 1930s and, disappointed with Mathu because of the Mau Mau War, wanted leaders for Africa that were not Kikuyu. Mboya came in handy only to be "stolen" by the Americans.

Not willing to watch the Americans "steal" another brilliant mind, she and Plamenatz, a native of Yugoslavia who was also a leading political philosopher at Nuffield, acted to ensure that Mazrui landed at Oxford in 1961.[80] Plamenatz was one of those scholars that were, as Jan Vansina put it, "retooling".[81] He had argued in his 1960 On Alien Rule and Self Government that non-Europeans resented the Europeans because they had accepted European values and were simply imitating the Europeans.[82] Plamenatz became Mazrui's mentor and his intellectual and ideological influence was so deep that Mazrui seemed like some kind of intellectual implant of Plamenatz in Africa. Among the things that the Yugoslav mentor taught the Kenyan student was that "the sins of the powerful acquire some of the prestige of power."[83]

Oxford was a place of brilliance, whether students or teaching staff. Among the students from East Africa were Okot p'Bitek who entered Oxford in 1960, a year before Mazrui, to study social anthropology[84] and Yash Pal Ghai studying law.[85] In the teaching staff were such other brilliant minds as that of Isaiah Berlin. "We were all intellectually influenced," Mazrui wrote of Berlin's lecture on "'Two Concepts of Liberty'-but I was ideologically to

---

78 Roger Owen, "The Dark Continent: The Colonial Reckoning, by Margery Perham; and Africa for Beginners, by Melvin J. Lasky," Commentary, July 1, 1963 https://www.commentarymagazine.com/article/the-colonial-reckoni.... accessed June 21, 2015.
79 Ibid.
80 Sawere," Scholar, Ideologue," p. 270
81 Jan Vansina; Living With Africa (Madison, Wisconsin, 1994), p. 117; Macharia Munene, Historical Reflections on Kenya: Intellectual Adventurism, Politics& International Relations (Nairobi: University of Nairobi, Press, 2012), p. 37.
82 John Butler, Book Review Book Review of John Plamenatz, On Alien Rule and Self-Government, in Canadian Journal of Economics and Political Science, Volume 27, Issue 04, 1961, pp. 560561; A.A. Castagno, Book Review of John Plamenatz, On Alien Rule and Self-Government, in Political Science Quarterly, Volume 76, Number 1, March 1961, pp. 113-115.
83 Ali Mazrui, "Pretender to Universalism: Western Culture in the Globalising Age," BBC WORLD LECTURES, BBC ONLINE NETWORK, www.bbc.co.uk/worldservice/people/features/world-lectures/mazrui/lect.shtml.
84 Okot p'Bitek, African Religions in Western Scholarship (Nairobi: Kenya Literature Bureau, 1970), p. vii.
85 Ali Mazrui, "Between Campus and Career" Annual Mazrui Newsletter No. 19 Early 1996, p.9.

his left on the kind of liberty worth pursuing."[86] His other teacher, Kenneth Kirkwood was the Rhodes Professor of Race Relations[87] one of whose big contributions to African studies was his 1965 Britain and Africa in which he argued that on balance British colonialism was positive for Africans. He warned against "precipitate, even hysterical, severing of links, including those which allow most hope for the future," and added that "the fomenting of negative action such as destructive revolution by pen, speech, or sword are equally to be condemned." Although there were many debits, he argued that "the total balance sheet is plainly one of credit, and of further opportunity, for both Africans and Britons after their three and more centuries of increasingly close contact."[88]

Kirkwood, with a lot of intellectual influence on Mazrui, went on to prescribe future British-Africa relations. He called for Britain to develop a Lugardian "dual partnership" with independent African countries to be "located between *apartheid*-governed South Africa and Mau Mau stricken Kenya." Britain was to use "bridgeheads available to Britain in Commonwealth African states" through which "Britain can continue to offer her special 'gifts'. If accepted," he added, there can be confident expectation of mutual reward both in the long term and the short term, though the proper emphasis should perhaps be on generations rather than decades, on decades rather than years."[89] Kirkwood participated in Mazrui's doctoral examination. The two, Kirkwood and Mazrui, became and remained close until Kirkwood's death in 1997.[90]

And there was also Colin Leys who initially distinguished himself by helping to establish departments of political science at Makerere and Nairobi where he introduced courses on Marxism and Development.[91] Leys, the author of a well-received 1959 book titled European Politics in Southern Rhodesia, had examined the voting structure in Southern Rhodesia and had noted that it was designed to de-franchise Africans.[92] It was at Oxford that

86 Ali Mazrui, "The Bonds of Friendship and the Menace of Time," Annual Mazrui Newsletter, Number 22, Early 1998, p. 37.
87 Ibid., p. 36; Ali Mazrui, "The British Connection," p. 21.
88 Kenneth Kirkwood, Britain and Africa (Baltimore: Johns Hopkins Press, 1965), pp. 13-14.
89 Ibid., pp. 204, 208.
90 Ali Mazrui, "The Bonds of Friendship and the Menace of Time," Annual Mazrui Newsletter, Number 22, Early 1998, p. 3; Ali Mazrui, "The British Connection," p. 21.
91 Walter O. Oyugi, "Teaching of Political Science in East Africa: A Narrative," Paper presented at the International Political Science Conference on International Political Science: New Theories and Regional Perspectives, Montreal, Canada, April 30-2nd May, 2008, p.9.
92 Colin Leys, European Politics in Southern Rhodesia (Oxford: Oxford University Press, 1959), passim.

Leys probably met Mazrui and the two seemingly struck a relationship. Leys was impressed enough to prepare the way for Mazrui at Makerere.

Mazrui's early display of "precociousness" in schools that had enabled him to jump classes reappeared at Oxford and Makerere. He subsequently had meteoric rise, jumping stages in academic ranks. Using language as a tool of verbal combat, he published a series of articles in 1963 that established his scholarly credentials. Among them were "On the Concept of 'we are all Africans,'" and "Consent, Colonialism and Sovereignty".[93] The publications prepared the way for Mazrui's entrance into Makerere which was also under pressure from the few African lecturers to Africanise the entire university. Among the agitators for increased Africanisation was Ogot who had joined Makerere's History Department in 1962 and, along with Ominde, plunged into the successful campaign to hire Africans in senior positions.[94] In this sense, Ogot helped to prepare the way for Mazrui to join Makerere in 1963.

Uganda, which attained independence in 1962, was thus under pressure to build institutions and Africanise them. To beef up the political science program, Makerere had in 1963 hired Leys from Oxford as professor and chairman of department who in turn went back to Oxford to hunt for Mazrui. Britain then waived a bond requirement that Mazrui return and work in Kenya for five years. Makerere, London argued, was the equivalent of Nairobi, being part of the University of East Africa and Mazrui would be teaching Kenyans.[95] Within two years, in 1965, Leys left the professorship and the chairmanship to Mazrui who was yet to get his PhD. For Mazrui, Oxford was expunging the ghost of *Cambridge*.[96] Mazrui's doctorate and professorial progress, noted critic Taban Lo Liyong, "were extremely accelerated."[97]

This development fitted British strategy of establishing colleges and universities and recruiting instructors. Among the recruited was another "retooling" person, Italian Political Economist Giovanni Arrighi, who was then looking for a job in British universities. He had reviewed Leys' book and had ended up at the University of Rhodesia and Nyasaland, UCRN, in 1963 because, he observed, "I learnt that British universities were actually paying people to teach and do research." What was more, he added, "in the early 1960s the British were setting up universities throughout their former

---

93   Sawere, "Scholar, Ideologue," p. 271.
94   Ogot, My Footprints on the Sands of Time, pp. 116-123.
95   Sawere, "Scholar, Ideologue," p. 272
96   Ibid, p. 271; Mazrui, "The Making of a Political Scientist."
97   Taban Lo Liyong, "Let the Intellectualism of Ali Mazrui Die," Daily Nation, February 14, 2006 as reproduced in https://natna.wordpress.com/2014/10/14/let-the-intellectualism-of-a.... Accessed June 18, 2015.

colonial empire, as colleges of British ones."[98] These included the Royal Technical College, Nairobi.

Nairobi was an interesting place, initially meant for European and Asian students. Its first African instructor was Kiano in 1956, followed by Karanja in 1958. After Karanja was appointed High Commissioner to London, the university recruited and rapidly promoted three London trained lecturers from Makerere. These were David Wasawo in zoology, Simeon Ominde in geography, and Ogot in history. While the three recruits became instant stars, Nairobi did not attract as much attention as Makerere which had a special place of pride for the nascent African elite as the oldest institution of higher learning in East Africa. And although Mazrui was not one of them as a student, he became one of them as an instructor.

Mazrui, like the other budding elite in East Africa, was thus a beneficiary of decolonisation trends and British and American neo-colonial strategies to control post-colonial thinking through universities. "They provided funds for creating fora for such magazines, unions, conferences, and scholarships," asserted Lo Liyong, and which the West used to "capture the academic princes" like Mazrui.[99] In the planned academic decolonization, Mazrui was slated to become the first African professor of political science, he later wrote, in the same way that Mwai Kibaki was slated to become the first African professor of economics. Kibaki deviated into other pursuits, mainly practical politics, thereby leaving Mazrui to become Makerere's first African professor of political science in East Africa.[100]

That achievement was partly due to the other development that was taking place in decolonizing colonial states; this was Africanisation. He got along with, and was influenced by, Apollo Milton Obote, the Ugandan executive prime minister. Obote, wrote Mazrui, "had considerable political influence on my life in my Uganda past."[101] Obote was also consolidating power and developed a growing belief in the political value of brutality, with General Idi Amin Dada, as his student. With Amin's help, Obote overthrew President Kabaka Muteesa in 1966, made himself an executive president, and systematically increased his authoritarianism. It was then that Mazrui started questioning Obote's policies so much that Obote wondered whether

---

98 David Harvey Interview with Giovanni Arrighi, "The Winding Paths of Capital," New Left Review, Volume 56, March-April 2009, p. 62.
99 Taban Lo Liyong, "Let the Intellectualism of Ali Mazrui Die," Daily Nation, February 14, 2006 as reproduced in https://natna.wordpress.com/2014/10/14/let-the-intellectualism-of-a.... Accessed June 18, 2015.
100 Ali Mazrui, "Mazuriana Africana," Newsletter, Number 27, Early 2003, pp. 7-8.
101 Ali Mazrui, "Conclusion: From Obote to Obama," Annual Mazrui Newsletter, No. 32, Spring 2008, p. 28.

Mazrui knew the differences between a political scientist and a politician.[102] The implication was that Obote, the politician knew but Mazrui, the political scientist, did not.

In the process, the politician in Obote seems to have developed an anti-Kenyan itch. In the on-going politics of Kenyatta's death in Kenya between capitalistic trade unionist Tom Mboya and socialistic Jaramogi Oginga Odinga, Obote preferred Jaramogi over Mboya and his trade unions. In 1965, wrote Phares Mukasa Mutibwa, Obote's government "barred militant Kenyans from leadership positions" in labour movements.[103] In 1966, even as he was deposing the Kabaka, Obote seemingly helped Jaramogi to create his own "socialistic" Kenya Peoples Union, KPU.[104] In 1969, Obote "proceeded to expel Kenyan workers *en masse* from Uganda 'on grounds of improving the conditions of national labour.'" It was part of Obote's move to the left and as he issued his own "socialistic" Common Man's Charter in 1969, he expelled a lot of Kenyan workers. This was the first mass expulsion in Ugandan history"[105] but it was dwarfed in the media by Amin's expelling of Indians three years later in 1972. Amin probably learned the art of cruelty from Obote's brutal expulsion of "about thirty thousand Kenyan workers. They constituted some ten percent of Uganda's urban work force." [106]

Enjoyment of Intellectual Controversy

As Obote was Africanising and increasing his capacity for atrocities, Mazrui was intellectually sky rocketing. At Makerere, commented Mahmood Mamdani, Mazrui was "catapulted" from lecturer to professorship because of Africanisation and because he was "among the best of homegrown timber."[107] Mazrui used to joke that while he could not get into Makerere through the front door of the student route, he ended there through the back door of the lecturer's route. He surpassed other Africans teaching at Makerere who included John Mbiti, the Anglican pastor who is also an expert on African religions and concepts of God and as well as Ogot, the historian of Luo migrations. Mazrui was in a class of his own as an intellectual. An intellectual,

---

102   Sawere, "The Multiple Mazrui," p. 271.
103   Phares Mukasa Mutibwa, Uganda Since Independence: A Story of Unfulfilled Hopes (Trenton, NJ: Africa World Press, 1992), p. 67.
104   Charles Hornsby, Kenya: A History Since Independence (London: I.B. Taurus, 2012), p.178.
105   Mutibwa, Uganda Since Independence, p. 67.
106   A. Kasozi, Social Origins of Violence in Uganda, 1964-1985 (McGill-Queens Press, 1994), p. 120.
107   Mahmood Mamdani, "Ali Mazrui defined the terms of political debate for his generation," Daily Monitor, October 2014.

he argued, was a person who enjoyed playing games with ideas effectively.[108] He certainly did and ended up as an intellectual giant.[109]

That enjoyment in playing games with ideas distinguished Mazrui as a controversial man of the establishment, some kind of radical of the right when "socialism" was the ideological in thing in progressive African intellectual circles. One of the critics, Taban Lo Liyong, however, was not impressed and dismissed Mazrui's "intellectualism" as "sterility" and failure "to grapple with issues."[110] Mazrui commanded the respect of the *mzungu* by waxing Western ideas into an African context to suit certain situations. He was, Lo Liyong insisted, one of the "captured academic princes" by the West.[111]

He enjoyed the attention. At one time he traced the Greek roots to African political thinking and at another, after Kwameh Nkrumah was overthrown in Ghana, he termed Nkrumah a Leninist Czar. Given that both Lenin and the Czar were synonymous with epithets in Western circles, the reference to Lenin and Czar was effectively to portray Nkrumah as a confused man who happened to have been an African leader.[112] Nkrumah was overthrown in the month of February 1966 and noting that a lot of coups in Africa tended to take place in the months of January and February, Mazrui suggested that the two months be abolished. He did it in such a way that it was entertaining and thought provoking.[113] Irrespective of the position that he took, it was his clarity that impressed the readers.

At Makerere, however, there was one of the sharpest critics of Western scholarship in the person of a crude Ugandan poet who thrived on causing

---

108   Ali Mazrui, "What is an intellectual? What is his role in the African revolution?" East African Journal, April 1969, p. 11.
109   Macharia Munene, "Why Mazrui was an intellectual giant," Business Daily, October 21, 2014, p. 10.
110   Taban Lo Liyong, "Let the Intellectualism of Ali Mazrui Die," Daily Nation, February 14, 2006 as reproduced in https://natna.wordpress.com/2014/10/14/let-the-intellectualism-of-a.... Accessed June 18, 2015.
111   Ibid.
112   Macharia Munene, Politics and the African Intellectuals: Perspective from East Africa," in Gbemisola Adeoti and Mabel Evwierhoma, editors, After the Nobel Prize: Reflections on African Literature, Governance and development (Lagos: Association of Nigerian Authors, 2006), pp. 191-192.
113   Ibid.; Ali Mazrui, On Heroes and Uhuru Worship: Essays on Independent Africa (London: Longman, 1967);-----The Africans: A Triple Heritage (London: BBC Publications, 1986); -----Ancient Greece in African Political Thought: An Inaugural Lecture Delivered on 25th August 1966 at Makerere University College (Nairobi: East African Publishing House, 1967); ------ "Thought on Assassination In Africa," printed in Martha Crenshaw, editor, Terrorism in Africa(Aldershot, England: Dartmouth Publishing Company, 1993), pp.5-23; see also Omari H. Kokole, editor, The Global African: A Portrait of Ali A. Mazrui (Trenton, NJ: Africa World Press, 1998)

intellectual consternation; Okot p.'Bitek. In his *African Religions in Western Scholarship*, Okot pierced through the armor that African scholars wore as intellectual warriors by accusing them of smuggling Western concepts into African religions. What seemed to irk him, when Africans tried taking positions, was the reliance on Europeans whose scholarship on Africa, he claimed was "systematic and intensive use of dirty gossip." His attack on Kenyatta, Mbiti, and Mazrui was based on his belief that these men, in attempting to justify an African position, had ended up using Western concepts in order to argue an African case.[114] They had essentially used the wrong weapons to fight an all pervading enemy and instead of winning, they had ended up sounding like the enemy they were supposed to have been fighting. The reaction from the establishment to p'Bitek's writings varied. To Mazrui, p'Bitek was both intellectually "stimulating" as well as "irritating." Bethwell A. Ogot thought that p'Bitek had produced 'thought-provoking,' blasphemous, and 'disturbing' and not wholly convincing, work.[115] While Mazrui found merit, Ogot was not amused.[116]

Like that of Mazrui, Ogot's rise to professorship had been meteoric. The two seemed to switch positions on obtaining doctorates and rapid promotions. While Mazrui attained professorship in 1965 and completed the doctorate in 1966, Ogot completed his PhD in 1965 but attained professorship in 1966. In terms of university achievements, therefore, Mazrui had caught up with and even surpassed Ogot in being renowned. Ogot developed into a man of establishment, holding high positions in the Kenya of Jomo Kenyatta, Daniel Moi, and Mwai Kibaki, but Mazrui remained the intellectual outsider until President Mwai Kibaki rehabilitated him in 2003. Both Ogot and Mazrui benefitted from Kibaki's relinquishing of the title of "Chancellor" in public universities to people he respected and happened to be his age mates. Kibaki appointed Mazrui to be chancellor of Jomo Kenyatta University of Agriculture and Technology in Juja and Ogot to be chancellor of Moi University in Eldoret.

The reason Mazrui was initially an outsider in Kenya was because the British wanted him to be and had placed him at Makerere, rather than Nairobi. At Makerere, besides distinguishing himself, he helped to start <u>Transition</u> and <u>East Africa Journal</u> that became platforms for regional intellectual

---

114   Okot P'Bitek, <u>African Religions in Western Scholarship</u> (Nairobi: Kenya Literature Bureau,1971), passim.
115   Ali A. Mazrui, "Epilogue" to Okot p'Bitek, <u>African Religions, pp.121-134;</u> B.A. Ogot, "Intellectual Smugglers in Africa," reprinted in Bethwell A. Ogot, editor, <u>Reintroducing Man into the African World: Selected Essays, 1961-1980</u> (Kisumu: Anyange Press, 1999), pp.133-138.
116   Munene, "Politics and the African Intellectuals, pp. 192-193.

steam letting. He wrote such provocative articles as "Nkrumah: The Leninist Czar" and "Tanzaphilia: A Diagnosis," in Transition, as well as "The National Language Question in East Africa," and "Political Censorship: Intellectual Creativity and Nation Building," in East Africa Journal. His evaluation of Nkrumah as a Leninist Czar after the 1966 coup in Ghana, Mazrui later wrote, was "the most controversial thing" he had done before his 1979 Reith Lectures.[117] It was his "Tanzaphilia" in 1967, however, that led Leys to declare Mazrui to be above normal as a political scientist. Leys started an article in the Transition by asserting that "Ali Mazrui is incapable of writing a dull paragraph."[118] In itself, the declaration made Leys some kind of authority on Mazrui and thereafter he became a reference point on assessing Mazrui's brilliance.

That Mazrui could write was not the issue that concerned critics, it was the import of what he wrote so well. Among those who took Mazrui on were two African students in North America each calling himself *Young African Activist* who accused Mazrui of displaying Euro-centric "misdirected brilliance" that is dedicated to worshipping "objectivity, but it is ritualistic objectivity out of joint with our *damned* condition" as colonized people.[119] And James Karioki at Howard University argued that while other African intellectuals "may be tickled by Mazrui's skilled linguistic twists, they are profoundly disenchanted by his overall insensitivity to the phenomena that affect Africa... the disagreement is ... largely over a scenical attitude that runs below what on the surface may appear to be logical and true."[120] Mazrui took such criticism in stride, responded to some of them, and continued to raise more issues in Transition and the East African Journal.

Within their pages of East African Journal were by people like Barrack Hussein Obama. One of those who had rushed to America, Obama was similar to Mazrui in that he suffered a delayed display of brilliance. He had no seat in the 1959 flight of 81 students because Robert Stephens cut him off for not having "finished high school and lacked the required Cambridge School

---

117 Ali A. Mazrui, letter to "Friends and Relatives", Ann Arbor, Michigan, the Eve of 1981, p.1.
118 Colin Leys, "Inter Alia- or Tanzaphilia and all that," Transition, No. 34 (December 1967-January 1968), p. 51.
119 O.F. Onoge and K.A. Gaching'a, letter to the editor, "Mazrui's 'Nkrumah': A Case of Neo-Colonial Scholarship," Transition 30, pp.25-26.
120 James N. Karioki, "African Scholars verses Ali Mazrui," as reprinted in Seifudin, Willy Mutunga, and Alamin M. Mazrui, editors, Black Orientalism and Pan-African Thought: Debating the African Condition, Ali A. Mazrui and His Critics, Volume III (Trenton, NJ: Africa World Press, 2013), p. 96.

Certificate."[121] He still found his way to Hawaii, "with the help of an American friend, Elizabeth Mooney."[122] He bloomed at the University of Hawaii where he liked arguing, debating, showing off, and he performed so well that he ended up receiving two doctoral offers, a full scholarship at The New School in New York and partial scholarship at Harvard. He chose Harvard but he never finished because American immigration officials deported him reportedly due to his cultural philandering proclivities. He, however, left living evidence of his presence in Hawaii. He returned home to display his new found brilliance as a member of the growing African elite.[123]

In Kenya, Obama joined Tom Mboya's Ministry of Economic Planning and Development, MEPD, where the chief advisor to the ministry was Ford Foundation seconded Rice University Professor of Economics, Edgar O. Edwards. It was Edwards who hired Obama as a planner in Mboya's planning ministry.[124] Edwards was also largely responsible for helping Mboya to write and conceptualize Kenya's 1965 political blueprint, *Sessional Paper Number 10 on African Socialism and Its Application to Planning in Kenya*. The paper made it clear that there was no room for scientific socialism and that African socialism meant capitalism with an African twist.[125] Edwards later wrote that Mboya was far sighted and determined "to subdue the rapid population growth that characterized Kenya at the time."[126] Obama was thus a ministry insider who turned "enemy."

Obama was backing the political tide. In the raging debate on socialism, President Kenyatta had already, in his first Madaraka Day speech, June 1, 1963, declared that the "Marxist theory of class warfare" was irrelevant to Kenya and had added: "attitudes which were appropriate when we were fighting for independence have to be revised."[127] He wanted to terminate the debate and proceeded to tell those complaining about scientific socialism to

---

121   Robert F. Stephens, Kenya Student Airlifts to America: 1959-1961, An Educational Odyssey (Nairobi: Kenway Publishers, 2013), p.62.
122   Ibid.
123   Jacobs, The Other Obama, pp. 103-161.
124   Jacobs, The Other Obama, p. 179; David Goldsworthy, Tom Mboya: The Man Kenya Wanted to Forget (Nairobi: Heinemann, 1982), p. 251.
125   Colin Leys, Underdevelopment in Kenya: The Political Economy of Neo-Colonialism, 1964-1971 (Berkeley, California: University of California Press, 1974), pp. 220-224.
126   Edgar Edwards, "Development Policies as Reveled in Independent Kenya: An Essay by Edgar O. Edwards", an unpublished and undated document obtained from William Mayaka, a friend of Edgar Edwards.
127   Quotes in G. Macharia Munene, "Constitutional Development in Kenya: A Historical Perspective," in Yash Vyas, Kivutha Kibwana, Okech-Owiti, Smokin Wanjala, editors, Law and Development in the Third World (Nairobi: Faculty of Law, University of Nairobi, 1994), pp. 58-59.

keep quiet because he had answered their concerns.[128] Whether Obama had raised his concerns during the drafting of the paper is not known but it was in attacking this MEPD paper, as if he was an outsider, that he showed his daring brilliance. Obama dismissed the paper as political hot air; it was "capitalism" disguised as "socialism." There was hardly any socialism, Obama stated as he called for the government to limit land sizes, "to force people to do things they would not do otherwise", and to engage in both curative as well as preventive policies.[129] This socialistic argument was not in Mazrui's line of thought.

In contrast, Mazrui distinguished himself as anti-socialist and as an avid advocate of the ability of capitalism to smother socialism.[130] As head of Political Science Department, wrote Walter Oyugi of Nairobi University, Mazrui "had no time for radical approaches to the teaching of the discipline."[131] Being Tom Mboya's "academic friend," he declared his friend to have "an ease of conceptionalization in his analysis and a familiarity with the terrain of developmental argument, which made his speeches impressive." He defensively argued that "Mboya was the most hated politician among radical critics of Kenya's politics… much of the Kenyaphobia outside the country was little more than Mboyaphobia."[132]

Like Mboya, Mazrui was a good debater and also had his radical sharp critics. This was particularly in debates at Makerere and beyond in Dar es Salaam where his intellectual prowess appeared to floor every one. He astounded both students and faculty, pushing the liberal lockean line, mesmerizing people with his command of the Greeks, Romans, and other Euro icons. He taught his students what Plamenatz had taught him on the glories of Western Civilisation. In his class on *History of Western Philosophy*, Mazrui presented his students with the foundation for Western political thought.[133] At Makerere, Ngũgĩ wa Thiong'o remembered, Mazrui attracted crowds as "the new wonder kid newly crowned with a PhD from Oxford, towering over a campus that once rejected his application for admission…. He shone: he dazzled: he enlightened."[134]

---

128 Kenyatta's statement on "African Socialism" in Jomo Kenyatta, <u>Suffering Without Bitterness: The Founding of the Kenya Nation</u> (Nairobi: East African Publishing House, 1968), p.273.
129 Barrack H. Obama, "Problems Facing Our Socialism," <u>East Africa Journal</u>, July 1965, pp. 26-33.
130 Karioki, "African Scholars verses Mazrui," pp. 100-102.
131 Oyugi, "Teaching of Political Science in East Africa," p. 11.
132 Goldsworthy, <u>Tom Mboya</u>, pp. 249, 259.
133 Mwapachu, "A rich legacy".
134 Ngũgĩ wa Thiong'o, "How Ali Mazrui, the global Kenyan, charted my path," <u>The Standard Digital News</u>, Thursday, October 23, 2014, http://www.standardmedia.co.ke/article/2000139170/Ngũgĩ-wa-thio...

This was until Mazrui's intellectual wonder boy balloon was pricked in May 1970 when he met more than his match in what amounted to a debate of the "radicals" that was broadcast live on television and radio in Uganda. It featured Dar es Salaam historian Walter Rodney on the "left" and Makerere's political scientist Mazrui on the "right" and was reportedly organized and moderated by Makerere student leader Peter Anyang Nyong'o. The debate placed Mazrui in the neo-colonial camp.[135] He, Mazrui, sounded as if he was regurgitating Kirkwood's argument about the balance on colonialism being positive.[136] That enabled Rodney to charge: "Professor Mazrui has argued that colonialism was good, that on the one hand this and on the hand that. Colonialism had only one hand: the hand of oppression, the hand of exploitation. Exploitation was mainly a means to oppress and exploit African brothers and sisters." And Mazrui retorted, "Professor Rodney and I are not really in conflict over this issue: it is an issue where I am being faithful to historical facts while Walter is filial to the Marxist interpretation of history." Rodney rebutted, "Professor Mazrui and I are not in conflict: we are not even in contact!"[137] Thereafter, Mazrui acquired the reputation of being a "neo-colonialist" or apologist for Euro exploitation of Africa.[138] In physics and mathematics, parallel lines can never meet and so Rodney and Mazrui could never meet because they held parallel positions. In that sense, both were parallel radicals.

Despite their ideological differences, both men had great respect for each other. It was Mazrui who drifted to Rodney's side and actually made personal and ideological "contact." He did this after both men had left East Africa, Mazrui to the United States and Rodney to Guiana to become a political activist. Mazrui's days at Makerere had become numbered in January 1971 after Amin overthrew Obote and started his own reign of terror. Subsequently, as Amin clamped down on free thinking, Mazrui was no longer tolerated. He fled to the United States but stopped in Nairobi to discuss job prospects and have lunch at the Norfolk Hotel with Vice-Chancellor Josphat Karanja but there were no openings.[139]

Mazrui settled in the United States but since his fame had preceded him, he had no problem landing lucrative fellowships and appointments in various institutions of research and learning.[140] These included the Hoover Insti-

---

135   Peter Anyang Nyong'o, "Appreciating Ali Mazrui," Daily Monitor, October 19, 2014.
136   Kirkwood, Britain and Africa, p. 14.
137   Quotations in Peter Anyang Nyong'o, "Appreciating Ali Mazrui," Daily Monitor, October 19, 2014.
138   Ahmed Rajab, "Ali Mazrui obituary," The Guardian, 20 October, 2014 http://www.theguardian.com/world/2014/oct/20/ali-mazrui.
139   Ali Mazrui, Mazrui Newsletter, Number 27, early 2003, pp. 10-11.
140   Ibid., pp. 11-12.

tute at Stanford University, the University of Michigan, and SUNY at Binghampton in addition to side appointments at Cornell and Jos in Nigeria. He kept contact with East Africa through newspaper articles in the Daily Nation where Joe Kadhi was managing editor and would occasionally turn down a "hot" article that might be libelous. Kadhi had helped Tom Mboya to start a newspaper in 1958 and was one of the initial recruits when the Aga Khan decided to start the Nation Newspapers. It was as managing editor that he incurred Mazrui's wrath. After the arrest and detention of fellow intellectual Ngũgĩ wa Thiong'o, Mazrui wrote a scathing article attacking the Kenyatta government but Kadhi refused to publish it on the ground that it could be libelous. Unamused Mazrui confronted Kadhi stating that he did not know that Joe was a coward. But Joe held his ground that it could not be done.[141]

Although for columnists, being turned down because an article is "hot" is normal,[142] the exchange between Mazrui and Kadhi showed a combative side that he rarely displayed and his reaction to Ngũgĩ's incarceration was one of them. The two, Mazrui and Ngũgĩ had a peculiar intellectual relationship. Ngũgĩ had published Mazrui's poem when he was editor of Ghala at Makerere and was systematically making a name as a leading writer in Africa. In turn, Mazrui found opportunities to help and bail Ngũgĩ out of trouble. In 1969 in Dakar when Ngũgĩ fell sick, for instance, he scrawled Mazrui's name and the fellow Kenyan showed up to help. When Ngũgĩ lost his job at Nairobi University, Mazrui came to the rescue by calling on his American friend and leading Africanist of the day Gwendolyn Carter. She arranged for Ngũgĩ a fellowship at Northwestern University where he wrote, Petals of Blood.[143]

Besides Kenya, Mazrui also followed events in Uganda. One of those events was Idi Amin's October 1978 blunder in invading and trying to annex the Kagera Salient in Tanzania. Thereafter President Julius Nyerere sent Tanzanian troops to Uganda to overthrow the Amin regime.[144] By then Mazrui was in Michigan and celebrated "the news of Uganda's liberation from Amin's misrule."[145] The liberation, besides Tanzanian troops, involved many Ugandan factions that were wrangling for power and briefly settled for Yusuf

---

141 Several Discussions with Joe Kadhi at USIU and on telephone. The latest being on October 3, 2015 through a WhatsUp link with Joe reconfirming what had taken place.
142 Macharia Munene, "Column Has been Insightful, Experience," December 30, 2014.
143 Ngũgĩ, "How Ali Mazrui"
144 Justus Mugaju, "The Historical Context," in Justus Mugaju, editor, Uganda's Age of Reforms: A Critical Overview, (Kampala: Fountain Publishers, 1999), p.31.
145 Ali and Molly Mazrui letter to "Friends and Relatives,", Ann Arbor, Michigan, last week of 1979, p.2.

Lule while Obote remained in Dar es Salaam.[146] In June 1979, Mazrui held lengthy ten hour discussions with former President Milton Obote of Uganda, organised by Akena Adako, "Obote's former Chief of Intelligence" in Obote's "residence in Dar es Salaam."[147] In Uganda, the experimental governments of Lule and then Godfrey Binaisa were short-lived which paved the way for the return of Obote in May 1980 as a national hero.[148] Mazrui was then able to return to Uganda for his "first New Year's Day since I scrambled for safety from Idi Amin, seven years previously. I celebrated New Year's Eve last year with President Milton Obote at the presidential suite at the Nile Mansions in Kampala."[149]

Mazrui Redesigned

While Mazrui's Euro-centric views in the 1960s and 1970s were shaped by Euro-scholars at Oxford, he was forced to "redesign" life in the late 1970s and 1980s and he increasingly became such a Euro-critic that he angered former admirers. He actually was part of a three dimensional redesigning phenomenon that stressed reassessment of policies and beliefs. First, the global times were different as the Euros, under the fresh leadership of Margaret Thatcher in England and Ronald Reagan in the United States, displayed a new level of meanness towards the Third World. They reassessed reasons for failures in such places as Vietnam, Iran, Angola, Zimbabwe, and Nicaragua.[150] Second, there was also new leadership in Kenya in which Daniel arap Moi took power in August 1978 and was determined to stamp his authority by redesigning Kenya in his own mental image. In September 1978, for instance, Moi declared that all Kenyans were answerable to him and he was answerable only to God.[151] Third, Mazrui underwent redesigning at the intellectual as well as personal and family levels. He became an anti-imperialist.

Mazrui's latter day conversion into a virtual anti-imperialist was influenced by the times and the events in the United States and Kenya as well as by African scholars who included Walter Rodney, James Karioki, and his

---

146 Mugaju, "The Historical Context," pp.31-33.
147 Ali and Molly Mazrui letter to "Friends and Relatives,", Ann Arbor, Michigan, last week of 1979, p.2.
148 Mugaju, "Historical Context," p.34.
149 Ali A. Mazrui, "Redesigning Life," letter to "Friends and Relatives," Ann Arbor, Michigan, Eve of 1982, p. 2.
150 Macharia Munene, "Cold War Disillusionment and Africa," in G. Macharia Munene, J. Olewe Nyunya, and Korwa Adar (editors) The United States and Africa: From Independence to the End of the Cold War (Nairobi: East African Educational Publishers, 1995), pp. 25-49.
151 Sunday Nation, September 17, 1978, pp.1 and 3.

nephew Alamin. These were among those who held positions that were critical of *neo-colonialism* and were ideologically and diametrically opposed to Mazrui's positions in the 1960s and most of the 1970s. It was Mazrui who gradually moved to their positions as critics of imperialism; and his platform was big. And developments in East Africa, particularly Kenya, helped him move positions.

The initial changes in Eastern Africa in late 1970s seemingly pleased Mazrui. Idi Amin was overthrown in Uganda and Mazrui celebrated by being Obote's guest in Kampala. In Kenya, Moi replaced Kenyatta as president and endeared himself by releasing Ngũgĩ wa Thiong'o and other detainees and giving high appointment in the cotton industry to Jaramogi Oginga Odinga. By 1982, however, an air of intolerance had creeped back into Kenyan body politics characterized by three developments. First, Moi and Odinga fell out and this led to a June 1982 constitutional amendment, declaring Kenya to be a single party state and that KANU was that party. Second, academics thought to be critical of Moi were rounded up in the same month of June 1982 that he amended the constitution to make Kenya a single party state. Third, men of the Kenya Air Force encouraged by the Odinga family attempted a coup in August 1982.

The fall out was Odinga self-inflicted and he annoyed Moi even more by plotting to start another political party to compete with KANU. Since Odinga's logic was that it was not unconstitutional for Kenya to have other political parties and thus challenge the KANU political monopoly, Moi decided to remove that loophole to his rule. KANU top officials met, commended Moi's action of expelling Odinga and then passed a resolution demanding that Parliament declare Kenya to be a single party state. Such a declaration, commented <u>Weekly Review,</u> "preempted the possibility of Odinga, Anyona, or anyone else dissatisfied with KANU policy forming an opposition party."[152] To make it impossible for other parties to exist in Kenya, Njonjo proposed a constitutional amendment that became Section 2A stating that there shall be only one political party in Kenya, namely KANU. Vice-President Mwai Kibaki seconded Njonjo's proposal and parliament passed it.[153] Subsequently only candidates approved by KANU barons were eligible for elected offices. This removed the possibility of any other person challenging Moi.

Of interest to Mazrui in that June of 1982, besides imposing a constitutional amendment to limit political freedom, was the treatment meted out to lecturers. The targeted included those who, sociologist George Katama Mkangi claimed, were "foolish enough to live by the time-honoured tradi-

---

152 <u>Weekly Review,</u> May 28, 1982, p.9.
153 Main Story, <u>Weekly Review,</u> June 4, 1982.

tion of academic and intellectual integrity."[154] Mkangi was one such "foolish" man along with law lecturer Willy Mutunga, historians Maina wa Kinyatti and Mukaru Ng'ang'a, geographer Wachira Kamoji, and literary writer Al Amin. They were locked up in June 1982. Alamin's foolishness was in publishing and staging a play, *Kilio Cha Haki* similar to Ngũgĩ's earlier, *Ngaahika Ndenda,* and so he ended up like Ngũgĩ, in detention.

The academia in the United States, through the African Studies Association (ASA) of which Ali Mazrui was prominent member, then mobilized to have the detainees released on humanitarian grounds as well as academic freedom. Stanford University, where Alamin had obtained his doctorate, blew the alarm. Then geographer Frank Bernard of Ohio University weighed in and challenged the ASA to do something like writing letters to President Moi, attorney general Charles Njonjo, and Law Society of Kenya Chairman Lee Muthoga. Bernard had taught geography at Kenyatta University and knew both Wachira and Mazrui as friends and colleagues. And ASA officialdom responded with Richard Sklar and Crawford Young writing strong letters to remind Moi that he was damaging Kenya's reputation of a free country.[155]

But it was Ali Mazrui's letter to Moi about his nephew that was most personal and heart rending. Reminding Moi that he had also pleaded with the government over the detention of novelist Ngũgĩ wa Thiong'o, Mazrui insisted that the issue was not simply the fact that Alamin was his nephew, it was a matter of ethics, justice, democracy, and refusing to "brutalise individuals in the name of state." He also offered to switch places in custody with his nephew who was then ailing because, despite being older, he was in better health.[156]

The letters that these academics wrote, except for Mazrui's, however, appeared to have been overtaken by events in Kenya in which Moi and attorney general Charles Njonjo fell apart officially due to a failed coup. There was an attempted coup on August 1, 1982 which became the *raison d'etre* for the collapse of the Moi-Njonjo political alliance as Moi accused Njonjo of planning a coup. The failed coup gave Moi reason to purge former 'friends' and to intensify a crackdown on intellectuals and those called dissidents. Of the former friends, the first victim was Njonjo who was accused of

---

154   Munene, The Politics of Transition in Kenya, p. 10.
155   Letters reprinted as part of "Academic Crisis in Kenya," ASA News, Volume XV, No. 4, October-December 1982, pp. 16-19.
156   Ali Mazrui Letter to Daniel arap Moi, June 18, 1982, in ASA Newsletter, Volume XV, No. 4, October-December, 1982, pp 17-18

harbouring treasonous thoughts.[157] The accusation was reinforced by one of the masterminds, political activist Raila Odinga who had supplied logistical and moral support by making his car available to ferry plotters around.[158] The reason he had tried to stage a coup, suspect Odinga claimed, was in order to stop Njonjo from mounting a coup.[159] Bishop Henry John Okullu of Maseno observed that Njonjo was "'crucified' by his own close associates,"[160] and he thereafter was ignominiously hounded out of the political scene.

The irony of the Moi/Njonjo fallout was that in 1980, when he thought he was close to Moi, Njonjo had reminded lecturers that they were "employed to teach but not to mislead students" with Marxist ideas.[161] Moi intensified efforts to contain lecturers as he groomed what he considered "intellectual home guards" to deal with supposed "intellectual terrorist." In his 1986 book, Nyayo Philosophy, Moi had split Kenyan academics into two groups, intellectual terrorists and intellectual home guards. Having found some lecturers to be particularly troublesome, Moi declared them to be intellectuals 'terrorists' and then made universities instruments of recruiting 'intellectual home guards' to suppress critical thinkers who deviated from the authorized line.[162] Moi wrote, "I see no systematic alternative to the intellectual re-education of staff for the purpose of reforming the learning atmosphere" in which students would "evolve into intellectual home guards against intellectual terrorism, political agitation and subversion in the universities." He wanted the "intellectual home guards" to identify "the terrorists", who would then be reeducated.[163]

In that political mind-frame, Mazrui and Ngũgĩ appeared to be part of Moi's "intellectual terrorists" while Bethwell Ogot and his star student William R. Ochieng' seemed to be in the team of Moi's "intellectual homeguards." In the anti-intellectual atmosphere that then prevailed, a new intellectual term, the *Mau Maus,* became a code for referring to government critics. The Ogot team, argues Casper Odegi Awundo, set out to deliver a thorough intellectual beating on the *Mau Maus*. As the intellectual home

---

157 Miller's Report and story in Weekly Review, December 21, 1984, pp. 4-40; see also comments in Weekly Review, October 14, 1988, pp. 6-7.
158 Story on Raila's treason case in Weekly Review, January 14, 1983, pp. 18-19.
159 Story on Raila's treason case in Weekly Review, January 14, 1983, pp. 18-19; see also Raila Odinga with Sarah Elderkin, The Flame of Freedom (Nairobi:), pp. 248-149.
160 Bishop Henry Okullu, Quest for Justice: An Autobiography of Bishop Henry Okullu (Kisumu, Kenya: Shalom Publishers, 1997), p. 114.
161 "Yesterday in Parliament," East African Standard, March 7, 1980, p. 2.
162 Macharia Munene, The Politics of Transition in Kenya, 1995-1998 (Nairobi: Quest and Insight, 2001), pp. 10-11.
163 Daniel arap Moi, Kenya African Nationalism: Nyayo Philosophy and Principles (Nairobi: Macmillan, 1986), pp. 126-133.

guards went about identifying "terrorists", however, their activities occasionally backfired. It happened when Ochieng' and Ogot tried to recruit Odegi to attack and discredit Ngũgĩ in a 1983 history conference. Instead, Odegi caused havoc with his "Rise of the Cheering Crowd" conference paper. At both academic and political levels, Odegi argued, lecturers praised Moi and worked very hard to be in good books so as "to keep a safe distance from Kamiti prison."[164] By then Mazrui and Ngũgĩ were making intellectual waves in the United States.

Mazrui watched all these developments from the vantage point of academic institutions in the United States and he too was being redesigned to discard his previous image. The new "redesigned" Mazrui had a lot on his social and intellectual plate and evolved over time. Domestically, he separated from Molly while he was in Michigan and then he moved to SUNY Binghampton in 1982 as his divorce papers went through. His growing Afro-centricity probably did not quite mesh with Molly's attractions to promoting French matters. He then found his heart throbbing towards Jos in Nigeria where Pauline captured it; they became man and wife. This symbolized completion of Mazrui's triple heritage of Arab, European, and African blood flowing in the veins of his family members.

In some ways, the redesigning of the family Mazrui was also reflected in the intellectual Mazrui. It had started well, with a BBC invitation to deliver the 1979 Reith Lectures, just as his Oxford Teacher Perham had done in 1961. The first woman to give those lectures, she talked of "Colonial Reckoning" and the need to groom African leaders and one of those she mentored, Mazrui became the first African to give the Reith lectures. His topic was "The African Condition." The teacher had aroused interest but the student aroused furious debate by suggesting that Third World countries should have nuclear capacity, if nuclear proliferation was to be limited.[165] The suggestion also indicated a changing Mazrui.

The case for non-aligned nuclear capacity was similar to that of India. It was Jawaharlal Nehru's diplomacy, he argued, that invented the doctrine of non-alignment and influenced Egypt, Ghana, and the Afro-Asian Movement.[166] In developing nuclear capacity, India accused the big powers of exercising "nuclear apartheid", double standards, and hypocrisy. Jaswant Singh, advisor to the Indian prime minister, asserted "that it is impossible to

---

164   Casper Odegi Awuondo, The Cheering Crowd (Nairobi: Basic Books, Kenya, 1997).
165   Ali Mazrui, "Nuclear Proliferation and I," Annual Mazrui Newsletter: Special Chancellor's Edition, Early 2004, pp.4-6; ------ "The Expansion of Western Technology," Annual Mazrui Newsletter No.29, Early 2005, p. 19.
166   Ali Mazrui, Cultural Forces in World Politics (London: James Currey, 1990), pp. 212-214.

have two standards for national security-one based on nuclear deterrence and the other outside of it."¹⁶⁷ It thus became one of the Third World countries that has "a project and strategy" for asserting itself against imperial powers and in the region.¹⁶⁸ Like India, Mazrui was skeptical of big country monopoly of nuclear power and even suggested that the Third World should have its own capacity.

The Reith Lectures, and the suggestion on nuclear proliferation, angered many people of influence who accused Mazrui of being anti-West. Connor Cruise Obrien, editor in chief of <u>The Observer</u>, newspaper in England was furious as he dismissed the entire Mazrui Reith Lecture series as "nonsense" and wondered why BBC allowed Mazrui to air such nonsense. "The notion of one continent 'raping' another is a hollow trope," he wrote, "the reality is one of exploitation of weak people by strong people… The European … got most of the loot. Why not? They were the strongest of the strong"¹⁶⁹ Economist Peter Bauer, sounding like a defender of colonialism and apartheid, complained that Mazrui's lectures were meant to "diminish or undermine the West … another attack on the West by a Western supported Third World intellectual … effectively designed to make the greatest impact on Western feelings of guilt." While Mazrui castigates the Atlantic slave trade, Bauer asserted, he does not refer to the Arab slave trade. What was more treatment of apartheid South Africa is unfair in that those killed at Sharpville and Soweto were probably "part of a mob looting and burning mostly African properties." Bauer's message was that Mazrui should quit blaming the West for the woes in Africa ¹⁷⁰

It took time for people, particularly Africans, to notice the evolving change. As he wrote articles and books, the reputation he had acquired of being an apologist for Euro-exploitation of Africa dogged him even as the

---

167   Jaswant Singh, "Against Nuclear Apartheid," <u>Foreign Affairs,</u> Volume 77, No. 5, September/October 1998, p. 52.
168   Samir Amin, "For a Progressive and Democratic New World Order," in Haroub Athman, editor, <u>Reflections on Leadership in Africa: Forty Years After Independence, Essays in Honour of Mwalimu Julius K. Nyerere, on the Occasion of His 75ᵗʰ Birthday</u> (Dar es Salaam: University of Dar es Salaam, VUB University Press, 2000), p. 51.
169   Conor Cruise O'Brien, "Self-Righteousness: African and European" <u>The Listener Review of Books,</u> Mai 1, 1980 as reprinted in Seifudin Adem, Willy Mutunga, and Alamin M. Mazrui, editors, <u>Black Orientalism and Pan-African Thought: Debating the African Condition, Ali A. Mazrui and His Critics, Volume III</u> (Trenton, NJ: Africa World Press, 2013), pp. 127-130.
170   Peter Bauer, "Ali Mazrui, A Prophet out of Africa: Broadcasting the Liberal Death-Wish," <u>Encounter,</u> August-September 1980 as reprinted in Seifudin Adem, Willy Mutunga, and Alamin M. Mazrui, editors, <u>Black Orientalism and Pan-African Thought: Debating the African Condition, Ali A. Mazrui and His Critics, Volume III</u> (Trenton, NJ: Africa World Press, 2013), pp. 61-81.

scope of his access was wide, money was not an issue, and the lecture circuit for him was attractive. He confronted critics in seminars and conferences and acquired a negative image where African issues were concerned. At one time, at a conference at the Ohio State University in Columbus, Ohio, where fellow Makerere colleague, Mbiti, was in attendance, a young Kenyan "radical", David Wamalwa, promised to deal with him when "revolution" comes. Mazrui smiled. But doubts still remained as to his loyalty until he came up with his ultimate signature in the promotion of African interests and he did it in public glare. He became emotional at Ohio University when his patriotism to Africa was questioned because of the stand he took in the Angolan crisis. He virtually wept and profusely professed his patriotism to the African course.[171]

He also became emotional when attacked by Wole Soyinka and Biodun Jeyifo who belonged to what Mazrui termed "an exclusive club of three racial purists among African intellectuals."[172] With a 1986 Nobel Prize for Literature, Soyinka was an accomplished poet and novelist and in many ways Mazrui's peer even in the command of the English language. Soyinka's global fame hinged on such publications as Kongi's Harvest and The Interpreters. In The Interpreters, Soyinka questioned the tendency of post-colonial elites to imitate their former colonial masters. Soyinka had also quarreled with Chinua Achebe, the other leading Nigerian writer. His public altercations with Soyinka were mainly over two television series on Africa. The first was by Mazrui and the second was by Soyinka's friend at Harvard, Louis Henry Gates.

This was the production of the PBS television series labeled "The Africans: A Triple Heritage." Given his previously "safe" position on matters African, the sponsors of the television series had probably expected Mazrui to live up to his reputation of seemingly exonerating the Euros in Africa; he failed them. There were previews in selected colleges and universities and at the Ohio State University in Columbus, Ohio, this author was one of those who had a preview in 1985.[173] Although the sponsors reportedly chopped off a lot of things they did not like to have aired, they left enough for people to talk about.[174]

---

171 The author, then a graduate student at Ohio University, was present at both instances.
172 Ali Mazrui, "The Politics of Ancestry."
173 The author was then teaching in the Department of Black Studies at the Ohio State University.
174 Betty Jean Craige, "*The Africans* and the Global Village," in Omari H. Kokole, editor, The Global African: A Portrait of Ali. A. Mazrui (Trenton, NJ: Africa World Press, 1996), pp. 207-222.

Mazrui thus disappointed the sponsors in that he did not exonerate the Euros but instead appeared to blame the West. It was not the first time he had done that. His 1979 BBC Reith Lectures on "The African Condition" had also been hard on Euro exploitation of Africa.[175] In this sense, the Triple Heritage was just a visual/television continuation of the radio/audio Reith Lecture series in terms of pro-African tone. They had invited him, so he argued in self-defense, to give an African perspective and he seemingly enjoyed doing it and he could not understand why they were angry. "The thing is, the series was supposed to be all along the view from the *inside*, so I wasn't invited to be professorial," he asserted in defending himself, "I was invited to be an African. And the implication was that I should be speaking as a *participant*-observer. So for them to be astonished that I don't sound American at the end of it seems to be ...absurd you see."[176] Modern Africa, he argued, was a product of "Triple Heritage" comprising indigenous Africans and two migrant communities of Arabs and Europeans and that he was "an example of Africa's triple Heritage."[177]

Part of the anger was because Mazrui had shifted intellectual camp to that of Eric Williams in Capitalism and Slavery and Walter Rodney in How Europe Underdeveloped Africa. Rodney and Mazrui had reconciled ideological differences, before Rodney's 1980 death, and Mazrui increasingly took the anti-imperialist position. To Rodney and the new Mazrui, slave trade and slavery were the foundation of Euro-industrialisation and the net impact of Europe's contacts with Africa was to under develop Africa. Slavery and slave trade, he asserted in one episode, industrialized Europe with the British developing a sweet tooth for sugar grown by slaves in the Caribbean islands. In return for slaves, Mazrui asserted as he stretched his hands holding a gun, Africans received "these". He not only seemed to praise Kaddafy, he even repeated his 1979 nuclear heresy in Reith Lecture Series on the "African Condition" that Third World countries should develop nuclear capacity as a way of curbing nuclear proliferation.[178]

---

175 O'Brien, "Self-Righteousness: African and European", pp. 127-130; Bauer, "Ali Mazrui, A Prophet out of Africa: Broadcasting the Liberal Death-Wish."
176 Judith Michaelson, "'The Africans': An Insider's Non-western View," Los Angeles Times, October 6, 1986.
177 Herbert Mitgang, "Looking at Africa Through an African's Eye," The New York Times, October 1986.
178 Ali A. Mazrui, "Africa's Identity: The Western Aftermath" and "Tools of Exploitation: A Triple Heritage of Technology," The Africans: A Triple Heritage (London: BBC Publication, 1986), pp. 99- 107, 159-177; Mitgang, "Looking at Africa Through an African's Eye"; John Corry, "TV Reviews; "Africans,' A Series on 13," The New York Times, October 9, 1986; Michaelson, "'The Africans': An Insider's Non-western View."

The reception to the series was mixed with most Africans commending the new Mazrui while sponsors and some opinion makers were furious. In Kentucky, an announcer would start each of the series by saying he disagreed with "Professor Mazrui's" views but would air the program as an education program.[179] Chicago Tribune TV/radio critic Clifford Terry considered Mazrui to be was "a man with opinions" that are "at times maddening, at others moving." Among the maddening ones was Mazrui's statement that during the Mau Mau war "'The British Empire was engaged in one of its orgies of militarized righteousness." Despite being "maddening", Terry concluded "'The Africans' deserves to be seen, flaws and all. And whatever one thinks of Mazrui, it is obvious, through it all, that here is a man who deeply cares about what he likes to call 'a remarkable continent.'"[180] The New York Times, what Edward Said termed, "the leading American newspaper," was less generous. It "ran consecutive attacks on the series in articles … by the (then) television correspondent John Corry"[181] In one of the articles, Corry accused Mazrui of being "selective" in a television series whose "scholarship… runs on empty."[182]

More than The New York Times, the big attack on Mazrui came from Lynne Cheney, Director of the sponsoring National Endowment for Humanities. She fumed that *The Africans* "frequently degenerates into anti-Western diatribe" and that the series "moves from distressing moment to distressing moment" and that the "thesis is to blame all the moral, economic, and technological problems of Africa on the West."[183] Complaining that the series "lacked balance and objectivity," she wanted to withdraw the $615,000 her organization had contributed to the project but failing that it removed itself from the line of credit. The sponsors also managed to insert something against Libya's Muamar Kaddafy that was not in Mazrui's original series.[184]

And it was not just American officialdom that was not amused by Mazrui's series. A number of Africans, well known Africans, were displeased by what they considered Mazrui's soft peddling of Arab slave trade and atrocities in Africa while being tough on Euro activities. Two of the African

---

179   The author watched the series from the vantage point of Frankfort, Kentucky.
180   Clifford Terry, "Pbs' Maddening, Moving 'Africans' Deserve to be seen," Chicago Tribune, October 6, 1986.
181   Edward W. Said, Culture and Imperialism, (London: Vintage, 1994), p. 44.
182   Corry, "TV Reviews; "Africans,' A Series on 13."
183   Irvin Molotsky, "U.S. Aide Assaults TV Series on Africa," The New York Times, September 5, 1986.
184   Craige, "*The Africans* and the Global Village," pp. 207-208; Diana Frank, "Producing Ali Mazrui's TV Series *The Africans: A Triple Heritage*," in Omari H. Kokole, editor, The Global African: A Portrait of Ali. A. Mazrui (Trenton, NJ: Africa World Press, 1996), pp.304-305.

critics were West African writer and Nobel Laureate in Literature Wole Soyinka and from East Africa there was Kenya's historian Bethwell Allan Ogot. The probable reasoning for this soft-peddling, Soyinka claimed, was because Mazrui was of Arabic descent. Thereafter, Mazrui wrote in his Annual Newsletter, he and Soyinka "brutalized each other in the pages of the newly revived Transition magazine."[185] The Mazrui series, therefore, became the global talk of the town and transformed Mazrui's image so much that it necessitated production of a new counter series that would exonerate the Euros. And the sponsors sponsored Louis Henry Gates, a Harvard University linguist and head of African American studies to counter Mazrui's presentation. Gates succeeded in producing *Wonders of the African World* that appeared to heap blames on the Africans themselves. In turn, Gates annoyed many people, including Mazrui, because of his seeming attempt to exonerate the Euros.[186]

In Kenya, Mazrui's "Triple Heritage" was not shown for a long time, but he still received criticism. His 1993 suggestion that Kenya's President Moi should relinquish office and the claim that Moi was "guilty of neglect, verging on criminal neglect"[187] was not amusing to those of the Moi establishment. The establishment, noted Ochieng', was not "at ease with him and literary kept him at a distance" with his "anti-establishment statements ... that annoyed the Kenyan leadership." When at a State House luncheon William Ochieng' dared mention Mazrui's name, Moi 'looked at me and asked: So you also admire that strange man?'"[188]

Mazrui's crusade for reparation because of transatlantic slave trade and slavery also sounded strange to some in the Kenyan establishment. A 1993 rejoinder and debate from Ogot, "perhaps Kenya's most distinguished historian", Mazrui wrote, made him "uncomfortable". Ogot, Mazrui commented, initially complained that "Africans were making too much of the issue of slavery" and then seemingly "decided that Africans were not making enough of the Arab slave trade." He concluded that "the verbal exchanges in the

---

185   Ali Mazrui, "Summary of a Year," Mazrui Newsletter(Abridged), Eve of 1992, p.2; ------"The Shadow of Soyinka," Mazrui Annual Newsletter, No. 17, Eve of 1993, pp.11-12.

186   Wole Soyinka, "Ali Mazrui and Skip Gates' Africa Series," and "The Trouble with You, Ali Mazrui! Response to Ali's Millennial 'Conclusion'" as reprinted in Seifudin Adem, Willy Mutunga, and Alamin M. Mazrui, editors, Black Orientalism and Pan-African Thought: Debating the African Condition, Ali A. Mazrui and His Critics, Volume III (Trenton, NJ: Africa World Press, 2013), pp. 183-197

187   Kevin J. Kelley, "Mazrui: 'Prophet' who is least honoured at home," Daily Nation, November 16, 1993.

188   William Ochieng', "Intellectual Achievement: Ali Mazrui is proof that few heroes are respected in life," Daily Nation, September 16, 2009, p. 13.

press were sometimes heated and acrimonious."[189] Although Mazrui was uncomfortable debating Ogot and engaged in "verbal exchanges" that were "sometimes heated and acrimonious," he was annoyed by Ogot's star student, Ochieng' who, along with Wole Soyinka and Bioden Jayefo, Mazrui believed, belonged to "an exclusive club of three racial purists among African intellectuals."[190]

The public climax of the mutual dislike between Mazrui and Ochieng', then Principal of Maseno University College, was displayed through several happenings in July and August 1996 played in the local newspapers. It started with a chance meeting between Mazrui and Ochieng' at the University of Nairobi's Vice Chancellor Francis Gichaga's office as Mazrui prepared to deliver a long expected public lecture comparing American and Kenyan educational systems. He delivered the lecture on July 6, 1996 at Taifa Hall.[191] On the next day Mazrui's article appeared in The Sunday Nation about paradoxes of the Kenyan Coast. In that article, he appeared to romanticize the British colonial experience while accusing post-colonial Kenyan governments of neglecting and marginalizing the Coast. Under British rule, he wrote, "sons of Chief Kadhis could eventually become professors in the United States" and that it was unlikely that in post-colonial Kenya "children brought up in orthodox Muslim homes [would] live to become deans in Kenya's owned university system or distant distinguished scholars in Sweden or the United States."[192]

Ochieng', roughly three weeks later, went on the offensives in a scathing attack that questioned Mazrui's intellectual alertness and patriotism to Africa, seemingly to reply to Mazrui's sentiments. Ochieng', literary critic Chris Wanjala observed, was "boorish" in attacking Mazrui.[193] "He lacked," claimed Ochieng' "the youthful reflexes of age mates like Professors B.A. Ogot and R.T. Odhiambo" as he fiddled "with notes, to which he was most of the time glued.... His lecture was irrelevant and dull." Mazrui, the man of Maseno asserted, "takes pride in being more westernized than Westerners and tries to speak better English than the Queen of England" and yet he had the audacity to call for African cultural rebellion against the West. Ochieng' ended up dismissing "this guy" Mazrui as "simply another harmless coastal chatterbox. He is no better than Mr. Kenneth Matiba and Dr.

---

189   Ali Mazrui, "The Reparation Crusade," Annual Mazrui Newsletter, No. 18, Eve of 1994, p. 4.
190   Ali Mazrui, "The Politics of Ancestry."
191   William R. Ochieng', "The Day the legendary Mazrui lost his stature in my eyes," Sunday Nation, July 21, 1996, p. 7.
192   Ali A. Mazrui, "Paradox of jewel that never shone," Sunday Nation, July 7, 1996, p.7.
193   Chris Wanjala, "Mazrui's fertile pen let best ideas win," The Standard, October 18, 2014, p. 20.

Richard Leakey-with their constant chants of greater freedom and greater human rights." He concluded that Mazrui was not capable of understanding the sacrifices that those who stayed in Kenya endured to build the country "in the face of international and imperialist intrigues!" [194]

This article aroused reaction from Ousseina Alidou of Ohio State University and also irked Mazrui enough to respond four weeks later by lashing back with a challenge that discredited Ochieng'. Alidou accused Ochieng' of being parochial and failing to "understand the difference between objective criticism of someone's intellectual position and obscene attack on the person." She accused Ochieng' of seeking "ways of reducing invaluable achievement to a level of national jingoism."[195] On his part, Mazrui threw the gauntlet at Ochieng' by calling for a public debate on university education in Africa in a public university of Ochieng's choice and "the debate should be entirely without notes."[196] Since Ochieng' did not believe in operating without notes, he declined the challenge,[197] fearing Mazrui's command and use of English as a tool of verbal combat. In such a debate, Ochieng' argued, people would go to listen to Mazrui's English rather than the points. "I cannot agree to such a debate," Ochieng' reportedly told William Mayaka, then a PS in Moi's government, when the two met in Kisumu, "the man would finish me."[198]

Ochieng's purported feud with Mazrui, however, had very little to do with Mazrui as a person. It had a lot to do with his mentor, Ogot, who had little regard for Mazrui. While Ogot dismissed Mazrui as arrogant and Arab slave trade apologist, Ochieng' declared Mazrui to be senile and overrated.[199] Considering Ogot to be the shaper of Kenya's history writing, adoring

---

194   Ochieng', "The Day the legendary Mazrui lost his stature in my eyes," p. 7.
195   Ousseine Alidou, "African Academia and intellectual parochialism: A Reply to Ochieng'," Sunday Nation, August 21, 1996, p. 16.
196   Ali A. Mazrui, "Challenge to a duel of words," Sunday Nation, August 18, 1996, pp. 16-17.
197   Ochieng' Interview in the Daily Nation, "Professor William Robert Ochieng': Ngũgĩ is a tribalist, Tabaan a con and Mazrui overrated," November 30, 2013 as reproduced in Kenya Today www.kenya-today.com/news/professor-william-robert-ochieng-Ngũgĩ-tribalisttaban-con-mazrui-overarated ...
198   Interview with William Mayaka, October 5, 2015 at Villa Rosa Hotel, Nairobi.
199   H.H Waru, "Attack on Mazrui Unfair," Sunday Nation, Nairobi, June 20, 1993 as reproduced in Alamin M. Mazrui and Willy Mutunga, editors, Debating the African Condition: Race, Gender, and Culture Conflict, Mazrui and His Critics (Trenton, NJ: Africa World Press, 2004) p.317; Ochieng' Interview in the Daily Nation, "Professor William Robert Ochieng': Ngũgĩ is a tribalist, Tabaan a con and Mazrui overrated."

student Ochieng'²⁰⁰ was unhappy that Ogot repeatedly appeared to get the short end of the intellectual stick when compared to Mazrui or even novelist Ngũgĩ. He then seemed to go out of his way to attack the two intellectual giants in attempts to belittle them²⁰¹ while trumpeting Ogot. And Ogot returned the favour in praising his star pupil as very brilliant.²⁰²

As Ogot's first doctoral student at the University of Nairobi, Ochieng' thrived in media attacks on Mazrui. When in 2009 Mazrui retired from being chancellor of Jomo Kenyatta University of Science and Technology, Ochieng' wrote an almost obituary. Ochieng' acknowledged that "truly Mazrui is one of the greatest thinkers of our time" and that Mazrui "probably speaks and writes better English than any Englishman alive." Ochieng' then noted that Mazrui "attempted greatly to be accepted by fellow Kenyans.... But while he was widely known and respected in international circles, very few Kenyans knew him personally.... To them, Mazrui was a fairy tale—a story told about magicians and goblins ... people you only meet in novels and not in person." He observed that other chancellors and ministry of education officials failed to turn up for the farewell party with Ogot claiming "that he was not aware that Mazrui was leaving for good."²⁰³ Five years later, in 2014, Ochieng' had changed his mind about Mazrui being "one of the greatest thinkers of our time." He instead dismissed Ngũgĩ as "tribalist" and ridiculed Mazrui for being very good in English and also over-rated in terms of international reputation.²⁰⁴

Deriding the intellectual standing of Mazrui and Ngũgĩ fitted well into Moi's hostility towards intellectuals. Their fortunes in Kenya, however, seemed to improve with the agitation for multi-partyism. The agitation started with the 1988 *Mulolongo* political fiasco which created its own heroes and villains. The July 1990 Saba Saba confrontation led to the formation of FORD as a pressure group because Kenya was constitutionally a single party state. Among the emerging heroes thereafter were Wangari Maathai, Kenneth Matiba, Gitobu Imanyara, Pius Nyamora, Gibson Kamau Kuria, ACK Bishops Henry Okullu and Alexander Muge, and Presbyterian Pastor Timothy Njoya.

---

200   William R. Ochieng', "Introduction" in William R. Ochieng', editor, A Modern History of Kenya, 1985-1980: In Honour of B.A. Ogot (Nairobi: Evans Brothers Limited, 1989), pp. 1-4.
201   Waru, "Attack on Mazrui Unfair," p.317.
202   Ogot, My Footsteps on the Sands of Time, p. 140.
203   Ochieng', "Intellectual Achievement"
204   Ochieng' Interview in the Daily Nation, "Professor William Robert Ochieng': Ngũgĩ is a tribalist, Tabaan a con and Mazrui overrated."

With the intensified agitation for constitutional overhaul, Mazrui jumped into the fray in 1991 by calling on Moi to retire from the presidency. The pressure for constitutional overhaul, best symbolized by the 1995-1997 demonstrations and the IPPG deal, set the stage for review and Mazrui's Oxford college mate, Yash Pal Ghai, became Commission chairman. Ghai remembered Mazrui and invited him to give constitutional advice. The fortunes became even better when Mwai Kibaki was elected in 2002 and then appointed Mazrui to be Chancellor of Jomo Kenyatta University of Agriculture and Technology and Ogot to be chancellor of Moi University. Before Kibaki appointed him chancellor, commented Ochieng', "Mazrui had whined, complained and wailed many, many times about his exclusion. 'I never had a chance to serve as an employee of the government until President Kibaki gave me a chance,' he would later say." [205]

Conclusion

Following his death in October 2014, Mazrui became some kind of commodity to be hoarded as friends and admirers held many symposia and almost turned Mombasa into some sort of Mecca. In one of those Mombasa symposia, Ahmed Idha Salim, Mazrui's childhood playmate, ventured to claim that Mazrui was a reincarnation of his grandfather who was probably being reincarnated in Mazrui's grandson.[206] In reality, however, Mazrui competed with and eventually surpassed his father and grandfather and came close to the 14th Century Berber scholar; Ibn Khaldūn, 600 years earlier. Khaldūn's distinguishing contribution to intellect, in the *Al'Muqadidimah*, Mazrui asserted was the "imaginative concept of *asabiyah*, which is often translated as '*social cohesion."* Mazrui then linked *asabiyah* to modern "nationalism" and "globalization" as "post-modern *asabiyah."*[207]

In between Khaldūn and Mazrui were other giant African intellectuals who towered at different times addressing different issues. Khaldūn had been concerned with the fact that the *Umma* or the Islamic empire was on the decline in part because of internal weaknesses and so he formulated his theory of a cyclical pattern in the rise and fall of empires. His was actually a warning to the *Umma*, a warning that the *Umma* did not heed and because it did not, it was overwhelmed by the Europeans who were busy liberating themselves from the Muslims. In their "triple liberation" strategy of the in-

---

205 Ochieng', "Intellectual Achievement."
206 Ahmed Idha Salim, "Prof Ali A. Mazrui: The Reincarnation of Sh. Ali B. Abdallah Naf'i, Mazrui Mazrui, Reincarnation in Comparative Study," https://www.academia.edu/9857968/Prof_Ali._Mazrui_The_Re-inc... accessed September 7, 2015.
207 Ali A. Mazrui, "Ibn Khaldūn Modernized: Between Nationalism and Globalization," Paper prepared for presentation in Istanbul, Turkey, September 27-28, 2013.

tellect, the territory, and commerce, the Europeans had been systematic.

The success of Europe's triple liberation tended to cover up the fact that the Europeans had long depended on Muslims for knowledge, governance, and commerce. They achieved intellectual liberation by borrowing Moor knowledge from such places as Cordoba in Spain that helped to found great universities like Paris and Padua. Out of Paris emerged such a towing figure as Thomas Acquinas whose <u>Summa Theologica</u> tried to prove the existence of God. Territorial liberation was achieved in 1492 with the capture of Alhambra in Granada. Commercial liberation came in 1498 with Vasco da Gama reaching India by way of the Cape. With the triple liberation, the Europeans then re-invented themselves and they succeeded so well that they ended up dominating the world for the next 500 years. In the process they enslaved, pauperized, and exploited particularly the Africans through slave trade, colonialism, and imperialism.

In the 20th Century, it was the turn of the Africans to seek liberation which explains the rise of what amounted to African intellectual warriors.[208] Some dug up records of the African positive past in which Khaldūn loomed large. Asked by the BBC in 1999 to name the two greatest Africans of the millennium, Mazrui identified Khaldūn as the "man of the *pen*" and Shaka Zulu as "the man of *action*."[209] By then Mazrui had redesigned himself into one of the anti-imperialist intellectual warriors who tended to address the three issues of slavery, colonialism, and imperialism. These intellectual warriors fall into two categories; those who wrote in the colonial period against the slave trade and colonialism and those who wrote in the post-colonial period about slavery, colonialism, and imperialism. These constitute Mazrui's predecessors and contemporaries and some deserve mention.

Six intellectual warriors stand out among those writing in the colonial period. First was W. E. B DuBois questioning the presentation of history as the glorification of everything white and demonization of everything black. He immersed himself deeply into promoting Pan-Africanism. Then there was Eric Williams, in <u>Capitalism and Slavery</u>, showing the linkage between slave trade and industrialization in England and thereby punching holes in the British abolitionist narrative. And the do-gooder narrative came in for intellectual thrashing in Jomo Kenyatta's 1938 <u>Facing Mount Kenya</u> and in Aime Cesaire's <u>Discourse on Colonialism</u> asserting that colonialism was based on a lie. This was followed by post-World War II writers who accused the Euros of being actually very good at disfiguring history through intellec<u>tual thievery that</u> is then merchandised to oppressed people as true record.

---

208   Munene, <u>Historical Reflections on Kenya</u>, p. 60.
209   Ali A. Mazrui, "The Re-inventing of Africa: Edward Said, V.Y. Mudimbe, and Beyond," <u>Research in African Literatures</u>, Volume 36, Number 3 (Fall 2005), p. 73.

Thus Cheikh Anta Diop's African Origins of Civilization and The Stolen Legacy by George James de-clothed the Euros by showing how dependent everyone is to Africans in ancient Egypt.

Several warriors appear to be stuck in between the colonial and post-colonial intellectual battle fields. In many ways, Frantz Fanon and his Wretched of the Earth were stuck in the transitional warrior category. The necessity of anti-colonial violence was a justification for the war in Algeria but the argument could be extended to other places. There is Chinua Achebe, with his Things Fall Apart, as another transitional man agonizing over the passing past in which neither the precolonial nor the colonial centres holds. In addition, Achebe stands out as a promoter of the African literary writers among them being Ngũgĩ wa Thiong'o who writes English as if it was Gikuyu.

Mazrui features in the second group, that of the post-colonial writers and he generated more than his share of controversy. There was Kwame Nkrumah of Ghana whose Neo-Colonialism: The Last Stage of Imperialism popularized the dilemma confronting emerging post-colonial African States as that of *neo-colonialism* or the continuation of colonialism in ways that were not territorial. Nkrumah, the political leader, and Mazrui, the political scientist, had their public differences. The post-colonial warriors also included Rodney, the historian whose How Europe Underdeveloped Africa ended up under-developing admiration for Euro claims. Rodney and Mazrui became friends as Mazrui gravitated to Rodney's position of anti-imperialism. There was John Mbiti, the clergyman, struggling in African Religions and Philosophy to show that Africans did not need European missionaries for them to know God because they are notoriously religious. Mbiti was what Acquinas was to the Catholic Church, a major influence on religious thinking only that Mbiti was a liberator of African religions. And there was Julius Nyerere, *Mwalimu,* experimenting with Ujamaa in Tanzania. More of an idealist than a realist, *Mwalimu* appeared to Mazrui like a kind of philosopher-king. Materially, the Ujamaa experiment flopped but it succeeded as a cementing ideal with which to hold people together. All these were post-colonial intellectual warriors, the group to which Mazrui belonged.

If the importance of Mazrui to the world of intellect was the amount of accolades he received and from whom or the quantity of his output, then his position among the world great would be assured. At least some of his contemporaries recognize that. Hedley Bull, known for his Anarchical Society in the 1970s, considered Mazrui to be the "most illuminating interpreter of the drift of world politics" handling "global" issues.[210] Mazrui was, Bull wrote, "one of the few contemporary writers to have thought deeply" about the question of "justice" in the world.[211] And his intellectual "unflagging adversary", Wole Soyinka, remembers Mazrui as a "perfect host" and reconciler making General Yakubu Gowon and Wole Soyinka sit next to each other during his 70th birthday celebrations. The two Nigerian rivals eased tensions when Gowon "confessed" that he was Soyinka's jailer and Soyinka disagreed by "insisting that I had been merely his fortuitous guest at Kaduna and Kirikiri Prison." Mazrui's passing, concluded Soyinka, "is a great loss to us. I already feel his absence. I miss him."[212]

What will decide his place, however, is the longevity of his ideas which need to be crystalised into singularity. And which of these is likely to be long lasting? It is not his love for verbal combats and binary presentations, defense of Islam, or latter-day anti-imperialism. It is the novelty of the *Triple Heritage*, presented to the public through a television series seen throughout the world that roused the wrath of American establishment or "divided U.S. audiences."[213] He appears as if he is a *post-modern* Khaldūn,[214] and would hardly mind the comparison given his belief that Khaldūn was the greatest African of the pen. Although Mazrui considered "St. Augustine ... one of the most brilliant theologians in the history of Christianity," he believed that Khaldūn was greater than Augustine, as a theorist.[215] The question is whether Mazrui's *Triple Heritage* equals, or comes close, to the *asabiya* or The City of God in terms of time longevity? If it does, the *Mswahili* from East Africa, Mazrui, would come close to the two *Berbers* in North Africa, Khaldūn, and Augustine.

---

210 Quote in Seifudein Adem, "Ali A. Mazrui, Postcolonialim and the study of International al Relations," Journal of International Relations and Development, Volume 14, 2011, p. 506.
211 "Chapter 8: Hedley Bull in his Own Words, Three Essays, 'Order Vs Justice in International Society,'" in Carol Bell and Meredith Thatcher, editors, Remembering Hedly Bull (Canbera: Australian National University, 2008), p. 83.
212 Wole Soyinka, "Remembering Mazrui," Transition, Issue 117, 2015, pp. 192-193.
213 Douglas Martin, "Ali Mazrui, Scholar of Africa who Divided U.S. Audiences, Dies at 81," The New York Times, October 20, 2014.
214 Seifudein Adem Hussein, "Ali A. Mazrui: A Postmodern Ibn Khaldūn," Journal of Muslim Minority Affairs, Volume 23, No. 1, April 2003, pp.127-143; Sheikh Ahmad Kutty, "Ali Mazrui: A Post-Modern Ibn Khaldūn," http://www.onislam.net/english/on-islam-africa/english/478827-ali-maz... Accessed September 29, 2015.
215 Ali A. Mazrui, "The Re-inventing of Africa: Edward Said, V.Y. Mudimbe, and Beyond," Research in African Literatures, Volume 36, Number 3 (Fall 2005), pp. 73-74; also reproduced in Ali A. Mazrui African Thought in Comparative Perspective (New Castle upon Tyne, England: Cambridge Scholars Publishing, 2014), pp. 283-284.

8

Who Killed *Pax Africana*?

Adekeye Adebajo

"The ancestors of Africa are angry. ...what is the proof of the curse of the ancestors? Things are not working in Africa. From Dakar to Dar es Salaam, from Marrakesh to Maputo, institutions are decaying, structures are rusting away. It is as if the ancestors had pronounced the curse of cultural sabotage." "Mwalimu" (Teacher) Ali Mazrui uttered these words in 1986. He died in October 2014 and has himself now become a noble ancestor in the Hereafter he had famously called "AfterAfrica" in his haunting 1971 novel, *The Trial of Christopher Okigbo*. Mazrui was the foremost African public intellectual of the last 50 years, and a dyed-in-the-wool Pan-African who served on two Organisation of African Unity (OAU) eminent panels on reparations and on transforming the continental body into the African Union (AU).

Kenyan scholar, Ali Mazrui, was the intellectual father of the concept of *Pax Africana*. In a seminal study in 1967 published four years after the founding of the OAU (and in the aftermath of the Congo crisis), he called for Africans to create and consolidate peace on their continent through their own exertions. His idea of "continental jurisdiction" was a sort of "Monroe doctrine" that urged outsiders to stay out of the continent and let Africans resolve their own problems themselves. In the related idea of "racial sovereignty," Mazrui argued that inter-African interventions by brotherly outside states was more legitimate than those of outsiders. But, his question posed five and a half decades ago has still not been answered: "Who will keep the peace in Africa now that the colonial powers are departing?" This short essay celebrates Mazrui's life and legacy by seeking to answer another basic question: "Who killed *Pax Africana*?"

In a famous essay published in 2002, Mazrui had posed the question: "Who killed democracy in Africa?" He blamed the demise on five forces: the magician who came in from the North (uncritical importation of Western models of governance); the soldier who came in from the barracks; the spy who came in from the cold (superpower support of African autocrats during the Cold War); the cultural half-caste who came from Western schools and failed to respect African ancestors; and the angry spirit of the ancestors. Mazrui loved murder mysteries and had referred to Agatha Christie's *Murder on the Orient Express* in the 2002 article cited above. As in Mazrui's essay, I also identify five villains in this epic murder mystery. So, who killed *Pax Africana*?

First, *poor governance* has been a scourge that has stalled socio-economic development on the continent. Between 1960 and 1990, only in Sierra Leone did a ruling party lose power in Africa, and just seven leaders (Somalia's Aden Abdullah Daar; Nigeria's Olusegun Obasanjo; Senegal's Léopold Senghor; Cameroon's Ahmadou Ahidjo; Tanzania's Julius Nyerere; Sierra Leone's Siaka Stevens; and Sudan's Abdel Rahman al-Dahab) voluntarily stepped down from power. In Mazrui's most famous article in 1966, he depicted Ghanaian leader, Kwame Nkrumah, as a "Leninist Czar": a royalist revolutionary who ruled in a monarchical fashion and thus lost the organisational effectiveness of a Leninist party structure. Mazrui concluded that Nkrumah would be celebrated more as a great Pan-African than a great Ghanaian. Though he was vilified by many at the time for daring to criticize a Pan-African icon, Mazrui's analysis stood the test of time.

The "men on horseback" – the military – rode onto the national stage 72 times between 1960 and 1990, urging citizens to "stay by their radios" following *coups d'états* that distorted politics. But the soldiers – including those like Uganda's Idi Amin and Liberia's Samuel Doe whom Mazrui memorably termed *lumpenmilitariats* – were no more successful than civilian autocrats at the socio-economic transformation of their countries. Though regular elections now take place in Africa and *alternance* of political parties has occurred in countries like Ghana, Senegal, Zambia, Malawi, and Nigeria while governance has generally improved, polls are still sometimes unfree and unfair, and military brass hats continue to wield influence in Algeria, Madagascar, Ethiopia, and Lesotho. Many military strongmen have, in fact, never left the stage, swapping their military robes for civilian khakis in Chad, Gambia, and Egypt. Elections themselves have sometimes become a way of waging war by other means, with ethnicity and religion mobilised to devastating effect. This has sometimes resulted in violent polls in Nigeria, Kenya, Zimbabwe, and the Democratic Republic of the Congo (DRC).

Who Killed *Pax Africana?*

A major challenge remains the fragility of many African states. The fact that less than 350 rebels could start civil wars that threatened the state in Liberia and Sierra Leone in the early 1990s had already exposed the widespread absence of Leviathans able to monopolise the use of legitimate force over their territories. The roots of many of these conflicts lay in poor governance as well as meddling by external Cold Warriors. These morbid symptoms are still very much present in the three cases of the DRC, Mali, and Central African Republic (CAR). Governments are effectively unable to govern, while their legitimacy remains threadbare.

The second villain in the demise of *Pax Africana* is the *failure of the "responsibility to protect (R2P)"* Africa's one billion citizens: over 3 million people have died in the DRC since 1997; about 800,000 people were killed during Rwanda's 1994 genocide; while over 500,000 fatalities have been recorded in Burundi and Sudan's Darfur region. The proliferation of refugees and internally displaced persons (IDPs) have made Africa the largest generator of conflict nomads in the world, with over 10 million IDPs and 3 million refugees. Mazrui often talked of the African state as a political refugee, desperate and bewildered and in need of external rescue. He also often bemoaned the negative impact of ethnicity in African politics.

The acknowledged father of "the responsibility to protect" – South Sudanese scholar-diplomat, Francis Deng – coined the idea of "sovereignty as responsibility" in 1996, arguing that, in situations of conflict, countries are often so divided that the validity of sovereignty must be judged by the views of local populations rather than by just governments and warlords. Deng thus noted that the best way for governments to protect their sovereignty was to discharge their protection responsibilities properly. Tanzanian diplomat, Salim Ahmed Salim, as OAU Secretary-General between 1989 and 2001 often argued that "Every African is his brother's keeper", and called for the use of African culture and social relations to manage conflicts on the continent. After the Cold War, United Nations (UN) Secretaries-General - Egypt's Boutros Boutros-Ghali and Ghana's Kofi Annan - pushed the world body to support peacekeeping interventions in Africa, while Algeria's Lakhdar Brahimi produced a landmark report on peacekeeping in 2000 which, however, did not focus sufficient attention on the relationship between the UN and Africa's regional bodies.

Mazrui often talked of Africans as having imbibed Western modes of consumption but not Western modes of production. He described the continent as entrapped between the Protestant work ethic and the legacy of the Westphalian state system. The third villain in the death of *Pax Africana* is the *scourge of corruption* which has eaten into the continent's body politic. The

UN panel on illicit financial flows, led by South Africa's former president, Thabo Mbeki, noted that capital flight from the continent between 1970 and 2008 amounted to between $854 billion and $1.8 trillion. CAR's Emperor Jean-Bédel Bokassa squandered a third of his country's national income and all his annual aid budget on staging a grandiloquent coronation in 1977. Zaire's Mobutu Sese Seko stole an estimated $5 billion, which exceeded his country's national debt at the time. General Sani Abacha – immortalised in Nigerian Nobel laureate Wole Soyinka's satirical 2002 play as "King Baabu" – stashed away at least $3 billion in foreign banks. This is all money that should be used to meet the basic needs of Africa's one billion citizens, and build the infrastructure that the continent so desperately needs. There is currently a $35 billion a year gap in funding the continent's infrastructure needs.

The fourth villain in the disappearance of *Pax Africana* has been the *violent extremism* that has wracked Africa, from the Sahel to Somalia, in a perversion of Mazrui's notion of an African "warrior tradition". In Mali, the Tuareg group, the *Mouvement national pour la liberation de l'Azawad* (MNLA); an Islamic splinter group from the MNLA (with its leadership based in Mauritania), Ansar Dine; as well as Algerian-dominated Islamic extremists Al-Qaida in the Islamic Maghreb (AQIM) and the *Mouvement pour l'unicité et le jihad en Afrique de l'Ouest* (MUJAO), launched attacks against government forces that led to their taking over the northern two-thirds of the country in 2012. A subsequent French military intervention into Mali exposed the continuing weaknesses of *Pax Africana*. The ill-conceived North Atlantic Treaty Organisation (NATO) intervention in Libya in 2011 – which has left the country anarchic and acephalous – had facilitated the flow of arms and fighters into Mali, with the government in Bamako and UN peacekeepers still struggling to stabilize the country. The goal of Ansar Dine and AQIM is to impose *Sharia* law across the Sahel. These groups number around 3,000 core fighters and also involve criminal networks. MUJAO and Ansar Dine were reported to be fighting alongside Nigerian militant group, Boko Haram.

Uganda's Lord's Resistance Army (LRA) wreaked death and destruction in an atavistic attempt to implement the biblical ten commandments in the North of the country. Nigeria's nihilistic Salafist militants have killed over 17,000 mostly Muslim civilians since 2009 and represent a brutal embodiment of the grievances of an impoverished Northern Nigeria, where poverty rates are 15 percent higher than in the South. They also have ties with jihadists in Somalia, and seek to implement *Sharia* law throughout Nigeria. In Somalia, al-Shabab continues to wreak havoc on parts of the country (killing shoppers and students), while also launching attacks on Kenya and

Uganda which have troops with the 22,000-strong AU mission in Somalia (AMISOM).

The fifth villain in the demise of *Pax Africana* is the *often pernicious role of powerful external actors in Africa*. *Pax Americana* under the Kenyan-Kansan US president, Barack Obama, between 2009 and 2016, continued to wage a "war on terror", militarising America's Africa policies with 1,500 troops in Djibouti; an African Command in Stuttgart used for the Libya intervention; 100 commandoes in Somalia pursuing "mad mullahs"; and another 100 troops pursuing Joseph Kony. American drones have also been deployed over Somalia, Mali, and Nigeria. In West African countries like Mali, Central African Republic (CAR), and Côte d'Ivoire, *Pax Gallica* has continued the traditional neo-colonial French interventionist policies of a pyromaniac fireman, while *Pax Nigeriana* was weak and incompetent in responding to it during the presidency of Goodluck Jonathan between 2010 and 2015. It is important that Nigeria, South Africa, and Algeria lead efforts at establishing a new *Pax Africana* to ensure that Africa has an effective response to warding off continued external interventionism on the continent.

Mazrui often described the institutions of global governance – the United Nations, the World Bank, and the International Monetary Fund (IMF) – as an international racial caste system of rich Northern *Brahmins* dominating untouchable *dalits* in the global South. The UN – which celebrated its 70th anniversary in 2015 – has five permanent members (P-5) who are mandated to maintain international peace and security. However, these five states account for an incredible 70 percent of arms sales that fuel conflicts around the globe. The "Big Five" have come to resemble several of the characters in *Aesop's Fables*. The US is the lion – the King of the jungle – which lays down the law and hunts other beasts. The Russian bear is a Cold War appellation, and the lion and the bear appropriately fought over a goat in Aesop's fables. China is like the elephant which is sometimes dismissed as "big for nothing". However, the elephant has big ears and listens more than it speaks. It also has a long memory, and appears to be playing a long game to acquire enough power before showing its strength.

France is like the wolf in sheepskin, hunting vulnerable lambs as in its discredited role during the 1994 Rwandan genocide. As in Aesop's tale, the wolf is fooled by its own shadow into believing that it is bigger than it actually is, and suffers from delusions of grandeur. Britain is like the sly fox which is often prepared to betray friends, recalling historical memories of "Perfidious Albion" and Lord Palmerston's dictum that countries have neither permanent friends nor permanent enemies but permanent interests. The games that the UN's "P-5" play often determine peacekeeping outcomes in Africa, since the Security Council is the only body that can start or end peacekeeping missions and whose decisions are binding on all 193 member states. Since 60 percent of the Council's deliberations are on Africa and 82 percent of UN peacekeepers were deployed on the continent in October 2016, prophets of *Pax Africana* must increase their influence on the UN's most powerful body. The undemocratic Council's legitimacy has been greatly eroded, and it must be reformed to bring in new members such as Nigeria, South Africa, Brazil, and India. Financial institutions of global governance – the Bank and the Fund – also launched diabolically devastating twenty-year socio-economic experiments – the Structural Adjustment Programmes (SAPs) – on African guinea-pigs from the 1980s that involved large enforced cuts in health, education, and employment. These were conducted in an utterly unaccountable manner that often undermined democratic governance and fueled social unrest.

Mazrui famously promoted the idea of sub-regional hegemons in Africa spreading security and prosperity as public goods. Africa has sometimes been compared to a gun, with Nigeria as its trigger. On closer inspection of the colonially-inspired map, South Africa would be the muzzle; the DRC, the barrel; Algeria, the grip; and Ethiopia, the bottom of the hammer, of this gigantic gun. If Afro-pessimists often depict the continent as a powder-keg, Afro-realists recognise that the fate of these five countries could largely determine Africa's future. South Africa is the continent's most industrialised state; Nigeria its most populous and largest market; and Ethiopia, Algeria, and the DRC among its geographically and demographically largest countries. These states are collectively rich in oil, gas, gold, copper, and cobalt. It is on these pillars that Africa's future may rest. The national and regional leadership of these countries; their capacity to promote stability or fuel instability, as well as economic integration, in their respective sub-regions; and the "crisis of youth" that afflicts them, will all shape Africa's future.

Finally, I would like to propose three other concrete recommendations for silencing the guns in Africa and reviving *Pax Africana*. First, African governments must observe rules of democratic governance as a condition for obtaining regional and external support. Two five-year presidential term limits must be imposed on leaders across the continent. The capacity of well-governed states to provide social services to their citizens and to extend state authority throughout their territory should then be supported by the international community. Second, Africa's rapid-reaction military capability must be urgently activated in the form of an effective AU-coordinated African Standby Force (ASF) based on five sub-regional brigades; African peacekeepers should be timeously provided with logistical and financial resources; and an effective division of labour must be established with the UN which should lead these missions. Finally, since – by some estimates - in nearly half of the post-Cold War cases, war-torn countries have relapsed back into conflict within five years as a result of inadequate peacebuilding, the international community must urgently provide the resources needed to implement post-conflict activities, particularly restructuring national armies and disarming and demobilizing fighters. This is the only way that soldiers will bid a final farewell to arms and, that - as with the biblical Lazarus – Mazrui's *Pax Africana* can be raised from the dead.

The question Mazrui had famously asked in 1967 was: "Who will keep the peace in Africa now that the colonial powers are departing?" The question our generation of Africans needs to answer is: "Who will keep the peace in Africa now that the Cold War has ended?" We conclude this essay with the paradoxically immortal words of Ali Mazrui: "Death is an exercise in Pan-Africanism". Mazrui described death as the most horizontal form of Pan-Africanism. Until we all meet again in the land of the ancestors in "AfterAfrica", sleep well "Mwalimu". God bless Africa!

9

Kwame Nkrumah and Ali Mazrui:

An Analysis of the 1967 *Transition* Debate[1]*

Michael O. West, Ph.D.

Kwame Nkrumah was the single most consequential figure of African descent in the global movement for decolonization, which swept colonialism from the greater part of Asia and Africa after World War II. Nkrumah began his career as an anticolonial agitator in the British colony of the Gold Coast in 1947. Exactly a decade later, in 1957, the colony attained sovereign nationhood under the leadership of his Convention People's Party, the most storied anticolonial movement in Africa. Ghana, the name the former Gold Coast assumed at independence, was the first territory in Africa south of the Sahara to escape the colonial yoke. Ghana, and Nkrumah personally, became de rigueur, celebrated in music, poetry, sermons and other forms of literary and artistic expressions in Africa and the far-flung African diaspora. A Black Star, a sobriquet accorded Nkrumah, had been born. But then as stars – political and otherwise – often do, Nkrumah precipitously fell. In 1966 he suddenly lost power, overthrown in a military takeover. His ouster spawned an expansive body of work on "the rise and fall of Kwame Nkrumah," as several contributors to this literary genre entitled their accounts of his two-decades-long whirlwind of a political career.[1]

Ali Mazrui contributed one of the first, and most contentious, installments on the narrative on Nkrumah's fall from power. But this was just prelude.

---

* This article, "Kwame Nkrumah and Ali Mazrui: An Analysis of the 1967 Transition Debate" by Michael O. West was originally published in The Journal of Pan African Studies (now titled Africology: The Journal of Pan African Studies), vol.8, no.6, pp.122-140, September 2015 and is printed here with the permission of the original author, and the publisher.

Mazrui's engagement with Nkrumah would have many a sequel, stretching over nearly five decades, which is to say for the rest of Mazrui's life. From a highly critical beginning, Mazrui warmed up to Nkrumah over time, his appraisal of Ghana's first postcolonial leader becoming increasingly more favorable as the years went by. Along the way, Nkrumah's writings came to provide some of the essential building blocks for the trope that is Mazrui's greatest intellectual legacy, for general audiences if not for the cognoscenti – namely, the idea that Africa is a continent with "a triple heritage": African, Islamic and Western. Initially offered as a television documentary on BBC in Britain and PBS in the United States, the triple-heritage idea did double duty, later reappearing in book form.[2]

"Nkrumah: The Leninist Czar."[3] Such was the bold and brash title of the essay Mazrui published in the wake of Nkrumah's fall. In a lifetime as an intellectual gadfly, this was Mazrui's most provocative piece to date. The fiery reaction, mostly negative, was also the first of the many notable debates in which he would become embroiled. The site of the debate also mattered. Mazrui's essay, along with most (although not all) of the responses it engendered, appeared in *Transition*. Based in Kampala, Uganda, *Transition* was a magazine of the arts, culture, and politics. Necessarily, the faculty at nearby Makerere University College (later Makerere University), where Mazrui taught, played an outsize role in magazine. Mazrui himself was an associate editor of *Transition*, which gave his essay unprecedented promotion. The lead article in the issue in which it appeared, the essay was preceded by a lavish and colorful illustration that took up the entire cover of the magazine. (Generally, the cover of *Transition* was in black and white, not color.) The illustration featured an image of Nkrumah's head at one end and that of the Russian revolutionary leader V. I. Lenin at the other, separated by a single shirt with identical collars. The name of the magazine, *Transition*, appeared at both ends of the illustration, except it was transposed at the bottom. When turned upside down, Lenin was on top and Nkrumah at the bottom, which neatly illustrated the point of the essay: that Nkrumah, very consciously so, was an African version of Lenin. Mazrui also received top billing in the section of the journal that listed the contributors: he was the sole author in that issue whose biographical summary was accompanied by a mug shot.

Clearly, a decision had been made to showcase the essay by *Transition*'s associate editor, and to spare no expense in doing so. It assuredly was an investment on which a return was expected – intellectual, political, and commercial. Accordingly, the editors dispatched a copy of the issue with Mazrui's essay to Nkrumah, now in exile in Guinea, with an invitation to respond! If accepted, the resulting Mazrui-Nkrumah exchange would have been a great boon to author and magazine alike. Nkrumah, however, diplomatically refused. No matter. Turning a negative into a positive, *Transition* trumpeted the statement of refusal as a triumph, an acknowledgment that Kwame Nkrumah had read Mazrui's essay, even if he declined to comment on it. For decades to come, Mazrui would regale audiences with the story of Nkrumah's nonresponsive response.[4]

The "Leninist Czar" essay was vintage Mazrui, illustrative as it was of the author's intellectual métier: comparative political studies. Its main argument was that Nkrumah patterned his public life on Lenin, the indispensable leader of the 1917 Bolshevik Revolution. "There is little doubt that, quite consciously, Nkrumah saw himself as an African Lenin," Mazrui wrote.[5] In support of this view, Mazrui pointed to Nkrumah's books, the most recent of which sported the title, *Neo-Colonialism: The Last Stage of Imperialism*,[6] a riff on Lenin's 1917 vade mecum, *Imperialism: The Highest Stage of Capitalism*.[7] Mazrui also attributed Nkrumah's emphasis on organization to Leninist influences, although he took care to note differences in this regard. Lenin's chief concern was to organize an elite revolutionary vanguard, whereas Nkrumah stressed mass organization, which his Convention People's Party was the first in colonial Africa to put explicitly to anticolonial purposes. Mazrui even traced Nkrumah's greatest legacy, his unrelenting advocacy of continental African unity, to Leninist origins.[8] Mazrui failed only to add what he would not have known at time, as it was only later revealed: Namely, that Nkrumah reputedly slept under a portrait of Lenin above his bed, as the African American writer Richard Wright, visiting the Gold Coast in the 1950s to gather material for his book *Black Power*, squealed to United States diplomats.[9]

At one level, Mazrui's essay had said nothing particularly new. From the literary standpoint, at least, Nkrumah's Leninism was no secret. It was certainly evident in his writings and organizational work. Mazrui's novelty was in combining the two, Leninist and Czar. In dubbing Nkrumah "the Leninist Czar," Mazrui, as he was wont to do, upped the rhetorical ante. All good Leninists and students of Lenin knew, or thought they knew, that Leninism had disposed of Czarism, definitively putting paid to Russia's royalist tradition. Now along came the upstart Mazrui, announcing that "while Nkrumah strove to be Africa's Lenin, he also sought to become Ghana's Czar."[10] Lurking in back of Nkrumah's "secular radicalism," Mazrui argued, were deep Czarist impulses inherited from various sources, African and non-African. For Mazrui, the key evidence of Nkrumah's Czarism was his assumption of the title Osagyefo, translated as Redeemer, a title reputedly bestowed on him by Ghanaian royalty. It was not that Mazrui, ever the pragmatist with a high tolerance for inconsistency, objected to the idea of a single individual combining the apparently contradictory ideologies of Leninism and Czarism. He was ready to concede that, "arguably a Leninist Czar was what a country like Ghana needed for a while." Nkrumah's transgression, rather, was what the pragmatic political scientist Mazrui prized above all in human affairs, including in the affairs of state: moderation. "Nkrumah's tragedy," Mazrui offered, "was a tragedy of *excess*, rather than of contradiction. He tried to be too much of a revolutionary monarch."[11]

In the end Mazrui, with usual even-handedness, split the difference. He concluded that Nkrumah ultimately was good for Africa but bad for Ghana. "By leading the country to independence, Nkrumah was a great Gold Coaster," Mazrui offered. "By working hard to keep Pan-Africanism warm as a political ideal, Nkrumah was a great African. But by the tragedy of his domestic excesses *after* independence, Nkrumah fell short of becoming a great Ghanaian."[12] Mazrui's use of the past tense seemed to connote death, physical as well as political.

In fact, Nkrumah would live an additional six years after being removed from power. From his place of exile in Guinea, he had something of a second political coming. He became a theorist of what he called the "armed phase of the African Revolution" and a partisan of the global Black Power movement, which he considered part of the African Revolution.[13]

Mazrui's essay was widely read by the global African literati. The issue of *Transition* in which the piece appeared sold out and went into a second printing.[14] Meanwhile, Nkrumah had turned down the offer to engage Mazrui, conveying his decision to the editor of *Transition* through a secretary. "Osagyefo the President is fairly impressed with the scope of your magazine and would be pleased to see copies of future issues," the secretary wrote of Nkrumah, who continued to insist he was Ghana's rightful leader. "The President has admired the literary effort in Professor Ali Mazrui's article 'Nkrumah: The Leninist Czar'." However, the punch line concluded, "I am afraid it has not quite provoked the President into writing comments on it."[15]

Having failed to provoke Nkrumah into engaging Mazrui, the staff of *Transition* turned to what they apparently considered the best alternative. They turned to K. A. Busia, perhaps the most intellectually able of Ghana's most zealously anti-Nkrumah politicians and a future prime minister of his country. (Busia was trained as an anthropologist, at Oxford, like Mazrui, who of course was a political scientist.) In an interview, the first question the magazine put to Busia was his reaction to Mazrui's essay.[16] Mazrui, Busia retorted, had turned Nkrumah into a better Leninist than he actually was, making "Nkrumahism more orthodox and Marxist than was really practiced."

Socialism, the anti-socialist Busia continued, was "not compatible with the megalomaniac search for eminence of one individual."[17] But Busia was no substitute for Nkrumah, who for *Transition* remained the elusive interlocutor.

Meanwhile, Nkrumah did comment on Mazrui's essay, although not for *Transition*. Nor for public consumption. Several months after the "Leninist Czar" piece appeared, Nkrumah's London-based confidant, publisher and book procurer, June Milne, sent him a copy of Mazrui's new book, *Towards a Pax Africana*.[18] After saying he was glad to receive the book, the critique-averse Nkrumah continued apropos of Mazrui: "I have never met him.[19] I have no idea who he is, black or white. After the coup, he wrote an article in the college paper *Transition*, and called me a 'Leninist Czar', and all sorts of nonsense." But having just denied knowledge of Mazrui's race, Nkrumah then went on to identify him, both racially and politically. "I think he is one of those black neocolonialist intellectuals," wrote the author of *Neo-Colonialism*. "I will read what he has written."[20] It is unclear if Nkrumah actually read *Towards a Pax Africana*. If he did, he apparently did not comment on it, as he sometimes commented on the many works Milne and others sent him, generally disapprovingly. In the event, Nkrumah had not forgotten Mazrui. Nor, it seems, forgiven him. Some eight months later another book by another disfavored African intellectual, *The Gab Boys* by Cameron Duodu,[21] provoked Nkrumah into returning to what he considered the sorry state of the African intelligentsia, with Mazrui as part of the exhibition.

For African intellectuals, Nkrumah offered in gender-specific language that effaced African women intellectuals,[22] "still have the colonial mentality…these chaps are dependent on European publishers, and they write things they think the white man wants to hear." Only a Chinese-style cultural revolution, combined with a socialist revolution, Nkrumah averred, could reeducate and redeem such individuals. "Ali Mazrui is one of them," he added for good measure. "See the trash he writes in *Transition*."[23]

If Nkrumah regarded Mazrui's essay as trash, one wondered what he would have made of another article on the subject of his downfall in the next issue of *Transition*. Appearing under the apparently interrogatory title, "Did Nkrumah favour Pan-Africanism?" the article was written by Russell Warren Howe. A white British journalist with ties to the Central Intelligence Agency, Howe had served as Africa correspondent for various United States publications, including in Nkrumah's Ghana, from which he was deported.[24] Howe began by fastening his sail to Mazrui's wind, lauding the "Leninist Czar" essay as a "penetrating article" that anticipated the main lines of his own argument.²⁵ Mazrui, on Howe's telling, had "stressed the similarity between fascism (or Czarism) and communism." From this premise, Howe concluded, "Ghana under Nkrumah was a fairly typical fascist state."²⁶ Moving seamlessly and promiscuously between fascism and communism, in a manner more reminiscent of Hannah Arendt than of Mazrui's essay,²⁷ Howe announced that Nkrumah "had leanings towards a Communistic society, but seemed to be more at ease with fascism in the end – albeit a fascism allied to Moscow and Peking when it suited him, and seeking to be compared with the successful image of Lenin rather than the disgraced images of Hitler or Peron."²⁸ No sooner had Howe settled on a historical model for Nkrumah, however, than he rejected each one as not quite suitable, and began to cast about for others. After toying with Joseph Stalin, the past master of necropolitics who eventually succeeded Lenin, Howe turned to Benito Mussolini, the negrophobic Italian fascist dictator. As an archetype for Nkrumah, he posited, "the example of Mussolini seems closer to that of the Czars or Lenin."²⁹

Having exposed Nkrumah as a fascist in communist garb, Howe then set out to demolish the most enduring myth about him. Contrary to popular misconception, Howe disclosed, Nkrumah was no Pan-Africanist at all. Far from being a promoter of Pan-Africanism, the former Ghanaian leader was actually a wrecker of African unity. Emphatically no, Howe pronounced, answering the question posed in his article, "Did Nkrumah favour Pan-Africanism?"

By his own lights, Howe had unmasked Nkrumah for the fascist that he was and deconstructed the fallacy of his alleged Pan-Africanism. It only remained for him to explain the makeup and motivation of so bizarre a personality. For this task, Howe turned to psychobiography. Nkrumah, he determined, was literally crazy, mentally unbalanced. He suffered from schizophrenia. Never short of historical precedents, Howe found yet another one to elucidate Nkrumah's condition. This time, though, he did not have to venture out of Africa, having discovered his model in Téwodros II, an Ethiopian emperor from the nineteenth century. Nkrumah, Howe wrote, "showed disquieting similarities with the Emperor Téwodros II [sic] of Ethiopia, who had frankly psychotic periods."³⁰

At this point, Howe took leave of Mazrui, whose analytical lead he claimed to have followed and whose trope had it that Nkrumah, although in the end a bad Ghanaian, was a great African. "I accept the main lines of Mazrui's analysis," Howe noted, "but I think history will see Nkrumah more (like Téwodro) as a colourful scoundrel, a great 'card' (*Transition's* cover was symbolic) and a consummate headline-hunter rather than an activist in history. I do not see him as being a 'great' African."³¹ After charting the tragedy of Nkrumah, Howe ended his article on a note of farce. "Perhaps Nkrumah's great tragedy – and this is not meant facetiously – was the absence, in the present generation, of a lively and prosperous theatre in Africa," Howe allowed. "The stage, rather than politics, would have been the natural vehicle for a man of such eccentric and erratic talents and brilliant pretenses, with a great gift for being, at least temporarily, all or most things to all or most people."[32]

Thus was the leading actor – and this truly is not meant facetiously – on the African political stage for a generation breezily dismissed as a conman and a madman whose only potentially redeeming feature, as a showman, had been aborted by the reputed absence of an arena for the expression of his iniquitous gifts. (Contrary to Howe's assertion, Africa had a theater.) In the flood and fury of ink spilling that followed Nkrumah's fall from power, Howe's article ranked high on the list of the absurd. It truly qualified as trash, the language Nkrumah used to describe Mazrui's essay. Not just by comparison, but also on its own terms, Mazrui's essay was a model of credible (if debatable) analysis and balance, rendering unwarranted Nkrumah's characterization of it. Even Nkrumah's most rabid critics, like the Ghanaian military men who staged the coup against him, refrained from treading where Howe did.[33]

On the face of it, Howe's article was beyond the pale, unworthy of inclusion in a serious journal of African thought, whatever the attitude of the editors toward Nkrumah and the rather inglorious end of his rule – good, bad, or indifferent. The article was so intemperate, tendentious, and unbalanced that even the editorial pages of Howe's newspaper, the *Washington Post*, may have looked askance at it. (By the time of his ouster the US and Western press, whose governments strongly backed the Ghana coup, had turned vigorously anti-Nkrumah.)

Given its literary insipidness and political toxicity, the question of why *Transition*, an apparently serious journal of African thought, chose to publish Howe's article becomes pertinent. It is unknown if Mazrui, who at that point was one of the journal's five associate editors (working alongside a single editor), had a hand in the decision. It seems clear, though, that Howe's article was part of a larger push to generate discussion of Mazrui's essay. That push included headlining the "Letters to the Editor" section of the issue in which Howe's piece appeared with the news of Nkrumah's refusal to engage Mazrui. The letter of refusal was published under the caption, "Literary Effort Admired," which is what Nkrumah's secretary reported him as saying about Mazrui's essay.[34] Further evidence of *Transition's* attempt to keep the debate alive is not wanting.

The issue that followed Howe's piece, itself sparked by Mazrui's essay, carried the interview with K. A. Busia, in which the interviewer's first question was about the Mazrui essay. Unusually, the following issue of the magazine (the one after Howe's article) carried just two letters to the editor. The shorter one castigated Mazrui for asserting that, in the period called Reconstruction after the US Civil War, the freed slaves displayed "flamboyant ostentation."[35]

An accompanying and much longer letter also seemed to be aimed at stoking the fire lit by Mazrui, but with a twist. Its author, Y. Tandon, taught in the Department of Political Science at Makerere, as Mazrui did. Tandon attacked Howe and defended Mazrui, although the defense was mingled with mild criticism. "Ali Mazrui's article, to which Howe apparently responded, was reasoned, well-presented and, after reading Howe's article, also a fair assessment of Nkrumah," Tandon declaimed. "What is most irritating about Howe is that he thinks he can use Mazrui's article to prove his point; that, in fact, he too, like Mazrui, is denouncing Nkrumah – only a little more so," Tandon went on. "The treatment of Nkrumah by Mazrui is brilliant, if incomplete. The treatment by Howe is simply vile. The one is academic, the other a specimen of the worst kind of journalism." Tandon concluded with a warning. "If *Transition* is to retain the respect of its African readership, it has to be careful that it does not become another instrument of the international press," he intoned. "We have already too many international journals which can do the job for Howe and his likes."[36]

Readers of *Transition* perhaps could be forgiven for concluding that Howe, making his maiden appearance in the magazine, wittingly or unwittingly had become a foil, his article being so unreasonable as to demonstrate, by contrast, the reasonableness of Mazrui's. Such a conclusion seemed to be supported by the fact that Tandon had been given ample space in the journal to set up the counterpoint between Mazrui, his colleague and coworker, and Howe, the neocolonialist whom he denounced.

The Ghanaian writer Ama Ata Aidoo was one of many readers of *Transition* who seemed to think the magazine was using Howe's article to put Mazrui's essay in a better light and, just as importantly, to keep the discussion going. Writing from the United States, Aidoo, who was one of the few women to join the debate in the pages of *Transition*, began with Howe before moving on to Mazrui by way of postscript. "'Thank you' to our big white father Howe for an extremely illuminating and rather fresh analysis of Kwame Nkrumah," Aidoo noted, tongue in cheek. "Our ignorance was extreme." In appreciation of Howe's enlightenment, especially in the field of psychiatry, she persisted in the same mocking tone, "we are going to send Kwame

Nkrumah to Bellevue (a hospital for the criminally insane in New York) as soon as possible." In an aside, she then took aim at Mazrui as an enabler of Howe. "Incidentally, we are also grateful to our own Professor Ali Mazrui and all other objective and non-partisan African intellectuals and journalists who make the writing and publication of papers like Mr. Howe's possible."[37]

Munhamu Utete, in another letter that appeared in the same issue as Aidoo's, dispensed with indirection, and sarcasm, and attack Mazrui forthrightly. Utete rounded on the "Leninist Czar" essay, denouncing it, Nkrumah-style, as so much neocolonial sophistry and apologia, "utterly without value." Despite his "spurious objectivity and fake scientism," Utete offered, Mazrui reproduced "all the innuendo, baseless insinuations, and propaganda slanders of world imperialist and reactionary circles that Nkrumah oppressed the people of Ghana." Objectively, Utete determined, Mazrui was allied with the coup makers and their neocolonialist backers who claimed to have "liberated" Ghana.[38]

Utete's critique, including his "excellent shooting down of Howe's sewer-propaganda article on Nkrumah," was lauded by Ken Geering, writing from Britain.[39] Mostly, though, Geering was concerned to directly connect the contents in *Transition* with one of its key sources of funding. "As long as the banner of the Central Intelligence Agency's front organisation, 'the Congress of Cultural Freedom' appears on *Transition's* first page, however inconspicuously, however shyly, just so long will what is in so many ways a fine magazine publish anti-African, American interpretations of African events."[40] Geering had raised a very sore point. The Congress for Cultural Freedom (CCF), the Paris-based, anticommunist outfit and cultural Cold Warrior that funded scores of organizations and publications worldwide, had recently been exposed as a CIA front. While the CCF leaders were well aware of its underwriters, most recipients of its largess were quite ignorant of the ultimate source of their good fortune. It was no secret that *Transition* was one of those recipients, and had been for a number of years. When the news of the CIA connections broke, the editors of *Transition* put out a statement "paying tribute to an important benefactor of this magazine," the CCF, "through its 'no strings' grant." Without directly mentioning the intelligence revelations, the uncharacteristically convoluted statement thanked the CCF for its "truly impartial and disinterested" support "at a time when the 'hidden (or not so hidden) persuasion' fact or in all aid can so easily devalue the integrity of grants [sic]." The statement further noted that, in the wake of the CIA expose, the Ford Foundation had assumed full financial responsibility for the CCF, from which *Transition* continued to receive support.[41]

That the Ford Foundation had picked up where the CIA left off was not good enough for critics like Geering, especially since many former recipients, unimpressed by the changing of fiduciary guards, had severed ties with the CCF. "One would have thought that news of the flight from the Congress of Cultural Freedom would have reached Kampala," where *Transition* was based, Geering acidly reproved. "All over the world organisations are hastening to dissociate themselves from this offshoot of the U.S. spy and murder organisation, the C.I.A. The game is up, the C.C.F. has come to the end of its yard of cloth, and there's no rope left... *Transition* should disassociate too, from this foreign espionage group."[42]

The Kenyan novelist James Ngũgĩ (later Ngũgĩ wa Thiong'o) agreed with Geering. "I remember hearing, quite recently, that this great cultural organization," the CCF, "received funds from CIA pockets," Ngũgĩ offered satirically, in the manner of his fellow imaginary writer, Ama Ata Aidoo. Ngũgĩ noted that *Transition* had recently called attention to a "Project Camelot," which directed CIA funding of cultural organizations, and concluded: "I wonder how many other Project Camelots there are in East Africa to-day!"[43] *Transition*, he implied, was one of them.

Geering and Ngũgĩ had made explicit what was implied in other responses to Mazrui (and Howe). Repeatedly, it was insinuated, or outright asserted, that the attacks on Nkrumah were disingenuous and unprincipled. According to this view, Mazrui was in the service of external forces, indeed anti-African forces, objectively if not subjectively. (There was consensus among the interlocutors, including defenders of Mazrui that Howe consciously served the neocolonialists.) The revelation that *Transition* had been getting CIA money – even if the editors of the magazine, like many if not most recipients of CCF funding, were unaware of that fact – only strengthened the critics in their conviction that the payer of the piper indeed was calling the tune.

The stream of unflattering commentaries on Nkrumah in *Transition*, hard on the heels of Mazrui's essay, seemed to further bolster the view that the magazine had an animus against the ousted Ghanaian president. Some of those commentaries even seemed gratuitous. Consider, for example, a Freudian-inflected article on Shaka, the nineteenth-century founder of the Zulu kingdom in contemporary South Africa. Having been silent on Nkrumah all along, the article suddenly and inexplicably ended by attributing to him a "Shaka complex." (Like Nkrumah and Téwodros, Shaka was labeled as mentally unbalanced by various European writers, some of whom nicknamed him Shaka the Terrible, causing some Africans to respond with an opposing moniker: Shaka the Great.) James Fernandez, the author of the article, thought Nkrumah mirrored Shaka in "his [Nkrumah's] relationship to his mother, his relationship to women, his driving and, in the end, self-defeating ambitions." The title of Nkrumah's self-written life story, *Ghana: The Autobiography of Kwame Nkrumah*,[44] Fernandez informed readers, "is reminiscent of the consuming ambition of Shaka – the nation become [sic] the leader's wish objectified. Politics, for those driven by a Shaka complex, is no longer the process of arbitration and maintenance of balance. It is the creation of a charisma and its imposition upon reality – a charisma let it be said which was first possessed by the child in his mother's eyes."[45] There seemed to be no end to the historical personalities, in and out of Africa, Nkrumah's public life is said to have resembled. Evidence of an anti-Nkrumah design in *Transition,* for those seeking such evidence, apparently was everywhere in the magazine.

Nkrumah's admirers responded by doubling down on their counterattacks. In Mazrui, whose essay they saw as the opening salvo in the campaign against their hero, the Nkrumaists found their chief target. (Nkrumah and his acolytes spelled it "Nkrumaist," without the "h," not "Nkrumahist," as Mazrui joined others in doing.) Mazrui, his pro-Nkrumah critics declared, was a man of talent, but his talent was politically misguided.

He had little sympathy for and even less solidarity with struggling humanity in Africa. Instead, he had put his intellect in the service of the oppressors and traducers of Africa and Africans. By this reasoning he was, in Nkrumah's formulation, a Black neocolonial intellectual.

That was certainly the view of O. F. Onoge and K. A. Gaching'a, respectively from Nigeria and Kenya. Both men were students in North America. In a long coauthored letter to the editor of *Transition*, the pair refused to be drawn into a discussion of the article by Howe, whom they summarily dismissed in language similar to Howe's own invectives against Nkrumah. Howe, they said, was "irretrievably deranged."[46] The coming African revolution, Onoge and Gaching'a declared, would render people like Howe mute and irrelevant. "Unfortunately the Mazrui's will still be with us," they lamented. "It is to him that we must address ourselves." Mazrui's essay, the duo asserted, was "an excellent illustration of the misdirected brilliance of much of current African scholarship." He was a "political science with more politics than science" and, as such, guilty of many wrongs, among them "magical verbal tricks," "intellectual masturbation," and "scurrilous diatribes" against Nkrumah. To Onoge and Gaching'a, Mazrui's essay was "a case of neo-colonial scholarship."[47] Their conclusion, and manner of speech, was too much for the Ghanaian Maxwell Owusu. Confessing that he, like Mazrui, may be a "Eurocentric, neo-colonialist scholar," Owusu scolded Onoge and Gaching'a for using "vehemently abusive" language that was "unbecoming of the budding African social scientists."[48]

But despite the occasional defender like Owusu (and Y. Tandon), the responses in *Transition* ran strongly against Mazrui's essay. The critics included E. R. Ibira and K. Y. Waibike. It may be safely assumed that Ibira and Waibike, writing jointly from Kampala, knew Mazrui personally, although the general tenor of their intervention suggested a less than cordial political and intellectual relationship. Ibira and Waibike found Mazrui's essay "obnoxiously fluent but intellectually hypocritical." On reading the essay, they were "struck by a pervading sense of injustice and cruelty meted out to one of Africa's greatest sons – Nkrumah – by one of Africa's talented professors, but nevertheless whose talent is misdirected – Mazrui. Why does he rejoice at Nkrumah's overthrow by an army clique motivated by greed and financed by external forces?" Accordingly, Ibira and Waibike demanded to know: "On whose side is Mazrui? On Africa's or on the imperialist predators? Mazrui is one of the new Africa's [sic] intellectuals who is a failure. He is a failure because he does not regard himself as being involved in the African struggle, he shapes past history to dovetail into his newly propounded theory divorced from reality and laughs, as a Lucifer would laugh, at efforts made by millions of Africans 'towards colonial freedom'."[49]

Mazrui had the last laugh, though he denied he was any kind of Lucifer.[50] He concluded the debate he began in the pages of *Transition* with a reply to his many critics that was more than half again as long as his original "Leninist Czar" essay.[51] While "irritated" with his detractors, whom he waved off so as many "Nkrumah worshippers," Mazrui insisted that he had tried to be "balanced and fair" in his assessment of Nkrumah.[52]

Claiming to be a dispassionate, objective scholar, Mazrui likened himself to the emerging nation-states of Africa and Asia whose refusal to take sides in the Cold War earned them the scorn of East and West alike. A "spirit of detachment in assessing Nkrumah and a spirit of nonalignment in the cold war have something in common – they share the risk of being despised or blamed by partisans on both sides."[53] His critics, Mazrui suggested, had been unfair to him, in part because they had not taken the time to read him carefully. Perhaps, he added, they could not spare the time. "I realize that it is the business of revolutionaries to be in a hurry," he wisecracked. "And many of my critics in your column sound like revolutionaries. In that capacity perhaps one does not have time to examine too closely what one is about to 'demolish'!"[54]

Whether or not the critics had succeeded in demolishing it, the "Leninist Czar" essay had provoked animated, even angry, discussion and debate on multiple continents, as evidenced by the responses. For better or worse, the profile of the thirty-three-year-old author, a rising star in the East African academy, had been greatly boosted. While belied by Nkrumah's seemingly unruffled, nonresponsive response in *Transition*, mediated by his secretary, Mazrui had even managed to raise the hackles of the former Ghanaian president himself, although that was not public knowledge at the time. (Nkrumah's private correspondence, in which he lashed out at Mazrui, would not be published for another quarter century.) Yet for all the ruckus it caused, in many ways the most provocative thing about Mazrui's nine-page essay was its title. Even so, it launched the first notable debate of a public intellectual who so relished debates, and whose subsequent life in and out of the academy would be studded with such discursive fisticuffs.

For Nkrumah, Mazrui was just one of legions of detractors, albeit one irritating enough to warrant being castigated on at least two occasions in his private correspondence. In this respect, however, Mazrui was not unique. Nkrumah answered many other critics in his personal letters, often in more sustained ways than he dissected Mazrui. In a few instances, Nkrumah seemed to try to convince (or at least engage) his critics by sending them copies of his books and other writings, as he did to Harry Bretton, a white professor in the United States who had written an unfavorable "rise and fall" book on Nkrumah that came out the year after Mazrui's essay.[55] From all accounts, Nkrumah made no similar gesture to Mazrui. If he had, Mazrui surely would have publicized it, just as he publicized Nkrumah's nonresponsive response to his essay. It is known that Nkrumah had a copy of Mazrui's *Towards a Pax Africana*, which came out around the same time as Bretton's book. But, as previously noted, there is no indication that Nkrumah read or commented on Mazrui's book. After his choice words, sotto voce, about the "Leninist Czar" essay, Nkrumah apparently took leave of Mazrui. Mazrui, however, was not finished with Nkrumah.

Some four years after his "Leninist Czar" essay, Mazrui wrote Nkrumah, apparently his first attempt at direct contact with the exiled ex-president. The occasion was the death of Gamal Abdel Nasser, the Egyptian leader. Nasser and Nkrumah had a complex relationship: they were at once overt allies and covert adversaries. Popular lore had it that each man desired to be the preeminent figure on the African political stage and the preeminent African on the global political stage.[56]

Even so, Nasser condemned Nkrumah's overthrow as part a larger "imperialist plan" to undermine African independence; supplied Nkrumah with mangoes during his exile; and materially supported his Egyptian wife and their children, who fled to Egypt after the Ghana coup.[57] Nkrumah and Nasser are reputed to have shared a vision of Pan-Africanism that was, in Mazrui's language, "trans-Saharan."[58] But Nkrumah, at least the exiled Nkrumah, seemed to doubt Nasser's Pan-Africanism (and his revolutionary zeal), believing his real passion was Pan-Arabism. Nasser, Nkrumah observed in private to a correspondent on the death of the Egyptian leader, was "a nationalist but [he] lacked revolutionary socialist foundation. He would have done so much better for Egypt if he had looked towards Africa instead of towards the Middle East."[59]

When Nasser died, Mazrui sought to organize an edited book on his life's work. In view of the connections, and contradictions, between the late president of Egypt and the ex-president of Ghana, Mazrui wrote Nkrumah soliciting a chapter for his proposed collection. Undoubtedly, Nkrumah's contribution would have been the star attraction of such a book. Publishing the subject of his controversial essay would also have been something of a literary and political coup for Mazrui. It would not come to pass. Once again, Nkrumah did not engage. He failed to respond to Mazrui's invitation, his silence substituting for a written refusal this time around. The reason is unclear. Perhaps Nkrumah, who was known to hold a grudge – Mazrui did not – was giving the cold shoulder to someone who, from his standpoint, had kicked him at the very moment he had been knocked to the ground. But Harry Bretton did pretty much the same (even if his book did not generate the kind of discussion Mazrui's essay did), which did not prevent Nkrumah from initiating communication with him. Perhaps also Nkrumah was not then prepared to publicly share his real thoughts on Nasser; among other reasons, he likely would not have wanted to antagonize Nasser's successors, who continued to sustain his family. Again, too, Nkrumah's failure to reply to Mazrui was consistent with a policy he adopted on going into exile, a policy of rejecting virtually all unsolicited requests for essays and interviews. This was the very principle on which he had refused to engage, in the pages of *Transition*, Mazrui's 1966 essay. Furthermore, by the time of Nasser's death Nkrumah's own health had deteriorated, a consequence of his undiagnosed, or misdiagnosed, cancer. In any case, Mazrui's projected volume on Nasser apparently never appeared, whether because of the inability to interest Nkrumah is unknown.

"Kwame Nkrumah is dead."[60] In April 1972 a Russian friend so informed Mazrui, as he was leaving a hotel in Washington, DC. Nkrumah had succumbed to cancer in Bucharest, Romania, where he had gone for treatment months earlier. Mazrui was "deeply moved" by Nkrumah's passing. When Mazrui visited Romania months later, he found himself "enquiring where Nkrumah had spent his last days."[61] These personal reactions prefaced an article, appropriately enough in *Transition*, in which Mazrui lauded Nkrumah's foreign policy, including his attempt to mediate the US war against

Vietnam, as capturing "African aspiration." Nkrumah, who was overthrown while traveling in Asia on his Vietnam peace mission, "lost domestic power partly because he had internationalist concerns," Mazrui noted.[62]

Now, there was no critique of Nkrumah's domestic policies. Nor any mention of the (in)famous "Leninist Czar" essay. Whether because of its quasi-obituary quality or not, Mazrui's treatment of Nkrumah on this occasion was pure celebration, with nary a hint of critique. It was the beginning of a love affair, of sorts.

Mazrui's romance with Nkrumah reached its apogee with what would become his most identifiable intellectual legacy, and the trope for which he is best known, that of an African "triple heritage" consisting of indigenous, Afro-Asian Islamic, and European-Christian civilizations. First presented in 1986 as a BBC/PBS television documentary and then as a book, Mazrui's triple-heritage idea reached a mass audience worldwide. On seeing the television series, Gamal Nkrumah (named after Gamal Abdel Nasser), Nkrumah's son with his Egyptian wife, asked Mazrui how his "concept of Africa's triple heritage was different from his father's consciencism." Gamal Nkrumah had in mind Kwame Nkrumah's book, *Consciencism*, his major philosophical work.[63] Published in 1964, more than two decades before Mazrui's television series aired, this book advanced an argument strikingly similar to Mazrui's, namely that the societies of Africa are a synthesis of African, Islamic and Western cultural traditions.

In response to Gamal Nkrumah's question, Mazrui replied that his triple-heritage trope came from "three great teachers." The first was Edward Wilmot Blyden, perhaps the outstanding black intellectual of the nineteenth-century and author, in 1887, of *Christianity, Islam and the Negro Race*, which indubitably anticipates Mazrui's triple heritage.[64] His "second great teacher," Mazrui told Gamal, was Kwame Nkrumah, the lessons coming largely from *Consciencism*. "My third great teacher was my own life," Mazrui finished off. Growing up in the Indian Ocean port city of Mombasa, Kenya, he "crossed those three civilizations several times every twenty-four hours. I was getting westernized at school, Islamized at home and at the mosque, and Africanized at home and in the streets. I was myself a triple heritage in the making."[65] It remained for Blyden and Nkrumah to lay out, in historical, theological and philosophical terms, the foundations of Mazrui's lived triple heritage.

Mazrui's realization of his triple heritage marked a disjuncture, including as it did a revision of his previous views on Nkrumah. At the center of this evolution in Mazrui's thinking was Nkrumah's book, *Consciencism*. Several critics of Mazrui's "Leninist Czar" essay had called attention to its neglect of *Consciencism*. No serious analysis of Nkrumah, the critics argued, could fail to take account of his major philosophical work.[66] Mazrui, as usual, had a ready response. "I do not think *Consciencism* is an interesting work," he shot back. Quoting from his own inaugural lecture at Makerere, Mazrui went on: "the most intellectual of all Nkrumah's own works is *Consciencism*... Yet *Consciencism* is also the least Africa-oriented of all Nkrumah's books." Intellectually, Mazrui also had a less than exalted opinion of Nkrumah. "On the whole I do not think Nkrumah is a particularly original thinker," he offered. Mazrui rated Nkrumah "significantly below" the Tanzanian leader, Julius Nyerere, "in sheer intellectual freshness."[67]

From this unpromising beginning, Mazrui arrived at a much more hallowed view of Nkrumah's mind a generation later. From the unoriginal thinker of his relative youth, Nkrumah was promoted to the post of preceptor, the "second great teacher" of the mature Mazrui, after the very intellectually imposing Blyden. *Consciencism*, previously dismissed by Mazrui as uninteresting and the least African-centered of Nkrumah's works, became one of two sturdy epistemic legs on which he rested his career-defining triple-heritage trope, the third leg of the triad being experiential, that is, Mazrui's own life. It was a remarkable about-face, but one Mazrui never explained. How then to explain it? Had the mature Mazrui adopted as his mentor an unoriginal thinker, and then taken inspiration in his uninteresting and non-Afrocentric book? That seems unlikely. It is more likely that Mazrui changed his mind about Nkrumah's intellectual worth, and about the Africanist value of *Consciencism*, albeit without advertisement.

The reason for the reversal obviously had nothing to do with Nkrumah, long since dead, and everything to do with Mazrui. In part, the explanation may have to do with location, and the experiences derived therefrom. Responding to critics of his "Leninist Czar" essay, Mazrui had observed that they were all non-Ghanaians.[68] He may also have noted that many of those critics, although hailing directly from Africa, were writing from outside the continent. In fine, they were in the diaspora, temporarily or permanently. As the postcolonial African universities declined in the 1970s and 1980s, along with the journals they sustained, including *Transition*, many African scholars, including Mazrui, also joined the growing new African diaspora in North America and Europe. It was from his perch in the diaspora that Mazrui completed his reexamination of Nkrumah, whose own political consciousness was decisively shaped during his twelve-year-long sojourn outside of Africa, as a student, worker, and organizer in the United States and Britain. Mazrui never became an Nkrumah worshipper, as he had accused critics of his essay of being. He was too good a scholar to be uncritical of anyone, and too good a Muslim to worship any but the almighty. He did, however, in due course come to a greater appreciation of Nkrumah's mind and of his intellectual (if not always his political) labor.

The evolution in thought coincided with an evolution in practice. The diaspora-based Mazrui could hardly be described as detached from struggles outside the academy, as his detractors previously asserted; or as a neocolonial shill, as Nkrumah declaimed. Remade in the diaspora into an insurgent and transgressive organic intellectual, Mazrui proved ever more willing, even eager, to enter the antinomian political arena, the many causes he championed including reparations for slavery and colonialism for black folk and Palestinian national rights against Israeli apartheid and settler colonialism. A pair of critics of his "Leninist Czar" essay, E. R. Ibira and K. Y. Waibike, had rhetorically posed the question: "On whose side is Mazrui? On Africa's or on the imperialist predators?" The question had since become academic. Mazrui transparently was now on the side of Africa and struggling humanity everywhere. This Mazrui, the fighter of the good fight based in the diaspora, was in part a product of engagements with Nkrumah and his life and legacy. Indeed, two Nkrumah-centered projects, the "Leninist Czar" essay and the triple-heritage trope, may be seen as veritable bookends to Mazrui's public life, intellectuall, and political. It was a significant part of a significant life, Ali Mazrui's interlocution with Kwame Nkrumah.

Notes

1 See, for example, C. L. R. James, "The Rise of Fall of Nkrumah," in Anna Grimshaw, ed., *The C.L.R. James Reader* (Oxford, UK: Blackwell, 1993; first pub. 1966), pp. 354-361; William Bedford van Lare, *The Rise and Fall of Kwame Nkrumah and Its Impact on the Rest of Africa* (Accra-Tema: State Publishing Corporation, 1967); Harry L. Bretton, *The Rise and Fall of Kwame Nkrumah: A Study of Personal Rule in Africa* (New York: Praeger, 1967).
2 Ali A. Mazrui, *The Africans: A Triple Heritage* (Boston: Little, Brown, 1986).
3 Ali Mazrui, "Nkrumah: The Leninist Czar," *Transition* 26 (1966), pp. 8-17.
4 See, for example, Ali Mazrui, *Nkrumah's Legacy and African's Triple Heritage: Between Globalization and Counter Terrorism* (Accra: Ghana Universities Press, 2004), p. 12.
5 Mazrui, "Nkrumah," p. 9.
6 Kwame Nkrumah, *Neo-Colonialism: The Last Stage of Imperialism* (London: Nelson, 1965).
7 Vladimir Ilyich Lenin, *Imperialism: The Highest Stage of Capitalism* (Moscow: Foreign Language Pub. House, 1951; first pub. 1917).
8 Mazrui, "Nkrumah."
9 Richard Wright, *Black Power: A Record of Reactions in a Land of Pathos* (New York: Harper, 1954). Although an exile from American apartheid living in France, Wright became an (apparently unpaid) informer for the United States government, betraying

over several years the confidence of Nkrumah and even more so of George Padmore, Nkrumah's London-based close advisor and supposedly also Wright's close friend. See Hazel Rowley, *Richard Wright: The Life and Times* (New York: Henry Holt and Company, 2001), pp. 436-437; Carol Polsgrove, *Ending British Rule in Africa: Writers in a Common Cause* (Manchester: Manchester University Press, 2009), pp. 118-144.
10 Mazrui, "Nkrumah," p. 9.
11 Ibid.
12 Ibid., p. 17.
13 For a sampling of Nkrumah's writings in exile, see Kwame Nkrumah, *Revolutionary Path* (New York: International Publishers, 1973).
14 *Transition*, 30 (1967), p. 27.
15 *Transition*, 27 (1966), p. 5.
16 "Interview with Dr. K.A. Busia," *Transition*, 28 (1967), pp. 20-23.
17 Ibid., p. 20.
8   Ali A. Mazrui, *Towards a Pax Africana: A Study of Ideology and Ambition* (Chicago: University of Chicago Press, 1967). Nkrumah's Ghana is the subject of chapter 4 of this book, pp. 59-73.
19 Mazrui said as a student he encountered Nkrumah at a reception ("sherry party") in New York around 1960 and subsequently in Ghana. See Ali A. Mazrui, "A Reply to Critics," *Transition*, 32 (1967), pp. 48-52; Mazrui, *Nkrumah's Legacy and African's Triple Heritage*, p. 4.
20 June Milne, ed., *Kwame Nkrumah, the Conakry Years: His Life and Letters* (London: PANAF, 1990), p. 116.
21 Cameron Duodu, *The Gab Boys* (London: Deutsch, 1967).
22 On Nkrumah's elision of women in Ghanaian nationalism, see Jean Allman, "The Disappearing of Hannah Kudjoe: Nationalism, Feminism, and the Tyrannies of History," *Journal of Women's History*, 21, 3 (2009), pp. 13-35.
23 Milne, ed., *Kwame Nkrumah*, p. 184.
24 Howe blamed his deportation on Nkrumah advisor George Padmore, "a rather terrifying figure." See Posgrove, *Ending British Rule in Africa*, p. 162.
25 Russell Warren Howe, "Did Nkrumah favour Pan-Africanism?" *Transition*, 27 (1966), pp. 13-15.
26 Ibid., p. 13.
27 Hannah Arendt, *The Origins of Totalitarianism* (New York: Harcourt, Brace, 1951).
28 Howe, "Did Nkrumah favour Pan-Africanism?", p. 13. Juan Peron was the Argentinian leader who modeled himself on European fascists.
29 Ibid., p. 15.
30 Ibid.
31 Ibid.
32 Ibid.
33 See, for example, Colonel A. A. Afrifa, *The Ghana Coup: 24th February 1966* (London: Frank Cass & Co. Ltd, 1967).
34 *Transition*, 27 (1966), p. 5.
35 *Transition*, 28 (1967), p. 5. Others also took Mazrui to task for "patronizing and glaring distortion of Afro-American history." Mazrui, in turn, defended his characterization. See O. F. Onoge and K. A. Gaching'a, "Mazrui's 'Nkrumah': A Case of Neocolonial Scholarship," *Transition*, 30 (1967), pp. 25-27 (quotation on p. 26); Mazrui, "A Reply to Critics," p. 51.

36 *Transition*, 28 (1967), pp. 5-6. Howe responded to Tandon. See *Transition*, 29 (1967), p. 5.
37 *Transition*, 29 (1967), pp. 5-6.
38 Ibid., pp. 6-8.
39 *Transition*, 32 (1967), p. 7.
40 Ibid., p. 8. The organization was actually named Congress *for* Cultural Freedom, not Congress *of* Cultural Freedom, as Geering called it.
41 *Transition*, 29 (1967), p. 3.
42 *Transition*, 32 (1967), p. 8.
43 Ibid.
44 Kwame Nkrumah, *Ghana: The Autobiography of Kwame Nkrumah* (New York: Nelson, 1957).
45 James W. Fernandez, "The Shaka Complex," *Transition*, 29 (1967), pp. 10-14 (quotation on p. 14).
46 Onoge and Gaching'a, "Mazrui's 'Nkrumah'," p. 25.
47 Ibid., pp. 25-27.
48 *Transition*, 31 (1967), pp. 7-8.
49 Ibid., pp. 5-7. The phrase, "towards colonial freedom," is derived from Nkrumah's first book, *Towards Colonial Freedom*, which, together with *Neo-Colonialism* (then Nkrumah's latest book), is used to bookend Mazrui's essay. For additional contributions to the debate, see *Transition*, 30 (1967), p. 5; Kenneth W. Grundy and Michael Weinstein, "The Political Uses of Imagination," Ibid., pp. 20-24; *Transition*, 31 (1967), p. 5.
50 Mazrui may or may not have taken comfort in the fact that Nkrumah was also accused of possessing satanic qualities: a poster in a march organized by the military men who overthrew Nkrumah called him a "devil in a Christian suit." See K. A. Bediako, *The Downfall of Kwame Nkrumah* (Accra: Published by the Author, 1966?), p. 9.
51 Mazrui, "A Reply to Critics."
52 Ibid., p. 48.
53 Ibid.
54 Ibid., p. 49.
55 Bretton, *The Rise and Fall of Kwame Nkrumah*. Howard University Archives, Moorland-Spingarn, Kwame Nkrumah Papers, Box 154-2, folder 48: Bretton to Nkrumah, 12 June 1969.
56 Mazrui himself has discoursed on "Nkrumahism versus Nasserism." See Mazrui, *Nkrumah's Legacy and Africa's Triple Heritage*, pp. 9-11.
57 Milne, ed., *Kwame Nkrumah*, pp. 21, 68, 382-283. Nasser himself reportedly selected Nkrumah's Egyptian Coptic (Christian) wife, Fathia Rizk. The dynastic-like arrangement was made sight unseen, the couple first encountering one another when the bride arrived in Ghana for the nuptials. The marriage, in 1957, the year of Ghana's independence, lasted as long as the Nkrumah regime. Although correspondence passed back and forth, wife and husband never saw each other again after she returned to Egypt. Nor, apparently, did Nkrumah see his children after going in exile.
58 Mazrui, *Towards a Pax Africana*, p. 212.
59 Milne, ed., *Kwame Nkrumah*, p. 382.
60 Ali A. Mazrui, "Nkrumah, Obote and Vietnam," *Transition*, 43 (1973), pp. 36-39 (quotation on p. 36).
61 Ibid., p. 36.
62 Ibid., p. 37.

63. Kwame Nkrumah, *Consciencism: Philosophy and Ideology of De-Colonization* (New York: Monthly Review Press, 1970; first pub. 1964).
64. Edward Wilmot Blyden, *Christianity, Islam and the Negro Race* (Edinburgh: Edinburgh University Press, 1967; first pub. 1887).
65. Mazrui, *Nkrumah's Legacy and Africa's Triple Heritage*, p. 1.
66. See, for example, Onoge and Gaching'a, "Mazrui's 'Nkrumah'"; *Transition*, 31, pp. 5-7.
67. Mazrui, "A Reply to Critics," p. 52.
68. Mazrui was in error; there was at least one Ghanaian critic, Ama Ata Aidoo, in addition to at least one Ghanaian defender of his, Maxwell Owusu.

10

Global Citizen, Dialectical Thinker:
Ali Mazrui and the Analytical Potency of Mazruiana

Wanjala S. Nasong'o, PhD

Introduction

Ali Al 'Amin Mazrui was born on February 24, 1933, in Mombasa, Kenya to an eminent Muslim scholar father who was the Chief Kadhi (Islamic judge) of Kenya. Not a particularly good student, Mazrui was rejected by Makerere University College on account of his poor grades in the Cambridge Certificate Exams. As a junior clerk at the Mombasa Institute of Muslim Education, his speech in 1952 in celebration of Prophet Mohammed's birthday earned him a scholarship. The event was attended by Kenya's colonial governor, Sir Philip Mitchell who was impressed by Mazrui's speech and invited him for a chat. Keen to follow in his father's footsteps and become an Islamic lawyer, Mazrui spoke to the governor about his interest in legal studies. Governor Mitchell discouraged him from pursuing law, but still recommended him for a scholarship, first to Huddersfield College in the UK to finish his secondary education, then to the University of Manchester where he obtained his BA degree in 1960. He got a Rockefeller fellowship to study for his MA degree at Columbia University in New York in 1961 before returning to England for his doctoral studies at Oxford University which he completed in 1966. Mazrui's scholarly prowess was on display one year after his doctoral graduation when he published three books on African politics all in 1967 and went on to publish three others between

1972 and 1973! Mazrui taught political science at Makerere University between 1963 and 1973, where he chaired the Department of Political Science and rose through the ranks to become full professor in 1965 at the age of 32, and was the first African Dean of the Faculty of Social Sciences. In 1973, Idi Amin's excesses forced him into exile in the U.S. where he taught at the University of Michigan, Anna Arbor for 16 years. In 1989, he moved to Binghamton University in New York, where he remained for a quarter century till his passing in 2014.

Prof. Mazrui considered himself a product of three civilizations; Africanity, Islam, and Western. That he was a global citizen is evidenced at multiple levels. First is his education in Kenya, Britain, and the U.S., His education in Britain deepened his westernization and, paradoxically, also reactivated his interest in Arab culture beyond just Islam (see Mazrui 2006: xi). Second are his teaching, lecturing, and simultaneous appointments in multiple institutions across the globe including visiting professorships at Chicago, Harvard, University of California Los Angeles, Oxford, Leeds, Nairobi, Teheran, Denver, London, Baghdad, and Sussex, as well as at-large professorial appointments at the University of Jos, Nigeria and Cornell University, U.S. Third, Mazrui's globalism manifests in his marriage and family. His first wife, Molly Vickerman, was British while his second wife, Pauline Uti was Nigerian. Molly bore Mazrui three sons (born in East Africa) while Pauline bore him two sons (born in the U.S.) and together, they adopted a daughter, Grace. In Mazrui's own words; "... my youngest children, Farid and Harith ... are products of the Eden of achievement, the United States of America. My first three sons – Jamal, Al 'Amin, and Kim – were born in the Eden of human ancestry, East Africa. In my family, the two Edens have once again converged" (Mazrui 2004: x). Interestingly, despite his many decades living and teaching in the U.S., Mazrui never took up American citizenship, choosing to remain Kenyan instead. Overall, Mazrui's role as a scholar is said to have been globalized and Islamized from the 1970s onward with a major milestone in 1979 when the British Broadcasting Corporation invited him to give radio lectures entitled *The African Condition* that were heard by an estimated 80 million people globally. His nine-part television series, *The Africans: A Triple Heritage* marked a climax in Mazrui's globalization as a scholar and Islamization as a political analyst (see Mazrui 2006: xiii).

Throughout his scholarly career, Prof. Ali Mazrui wrote copiously on Africa, publishing more than three dozen books and hundreds of book chapters, journal articles, and newsmagazine commentaries. The breadth and profundity of the corpus of Mazrui's scholarly works has come to be simply referred to as 'Mazruiana.' The most outstanding uniqueness of Mazrui's scholarship is his effective employment of the dialectical method in his analysis of social phenomena. This penchant for the dialectical style put Mazrui in a class of his own among his peers. On account of Mazrui's scholarly proclivity, he has been acknowledged as 'Africa's gift to the world' by former United Nations Secretary General, Kofi Annan. In 2005, the American *Foreign Policy* and the British *Prospect* magazines named Prof. Mazrui one of the top 100 public intellectuals in the world, ranking him 73rd. Morgan State University awarded him the Du Bois-Garvey Award for Pan-African Unity and he was elected an 'Icon of the Twentieth Century' by Lincoln University among many other honors. This chapter focuses on the uniqueness of Prof. Mazrui's analytical style. It begins with a discussion of the essence of the dialectical method whose central feature is the notion of opposites, of contradictions, of paradoxes. It then turns to an exposition of Prof. Mazrui's utilization of the dialectical method in a sample of his works. The main objective of the chapter is to underscore Prof. Mazrui's analytical prowess as a dialectical thinker with a view, to highlighting the analytical potency and explanatory clarity he derives from this approach.

The Dialectical Method and The Essence of Paradoxes

The dialectics as a conversational or debating method of arriving at the truth about social phenomena by exchanging logical arguments is traced to Socrates, and is generally referred to as the Socratic method that was popularized by Plato's 'Socratic dialogues.' However, the method has been appropriated, applied, debated, elaborated, and even subverted by many subsequent scholars and thinkers including Georg Wilhelm Friedrich Hegel, Karl Marx, Friedrich Engels, and Vladimir Ilyich Lenin among others. According to Friedrich Engels (1993), the dialectic method is principally a science of the general laws of motion and development of nature, human society, and thought. Engels argues that in his idealistic philosophy, Hegel assembled three laws of dialectics: (1) the law of the unity and conflict of opposites; (2) the law of the passage of quantitative changes into qualitative changes; and (3) the law of the negation of the negation. The dialectical method is thus said to be the simultaneous application of these three laws for purposes of understanding the real nature of our interdependent world with particular clarity.

The Unity and Conflict of Opposites

Both Lenin (1965) and Engels (1973) note that the law of contradiction (the unity and conflict of opposites) in phenomena is the basic law of materialist dialectics. Engels illustrates this by positing that the world in which we live is essentially a paradoxical terrain characterized by a unity of contradictions, a unity of opposites. We have birth vs. death, wealth vs. poverty, capital vs. labor, sale vs. purchase, rulers vs. ruled, above vs. below, right vs. left, light vs. darkness, boom vs. bust, etc. Engels goes on to demonstrate the universality of these contradictions by providing examples in different intellectual disciplines: in mathematics, there is the integral and the differential (plus and minus); in mechanics, there is action and reaction; in physics, there is positive and negative electricity (by which we can cook food and freeze the same); in chemistry, there is fusion and fission of atoms (combination and dissociation); in social science, there is the haves and have-nots (the basis of class struggle); in war, there is defense and offense, advance and retreat, victory and defeat; indeed, even the human individual is made up of opposites, the spirit (what Engels calls 'the divine spark inside') and the material body, which, even the Bible (English Standard Version) notes in Galatians 5: 17, are always at odds with one another: "For the desires of the flesh [the body] are against the spirit, and the desires of the spirit are against the flesh, for these are opposed to each other, to keep you from doing the things you want to do."

The essence of the dialectics is that everything is composed of contradictions, of paradoxes, of opposite forces and tendencies. Gradual changes in either of the forces create crises within phenomena which crises reach turning points in which one force quantitatively grows in strength and overcomes its opposing force resulting in qualitative change. The existence of the phenomenon with inherent contradictory tendencies is the thesis; the strengthening of one force against the counter-force is the anti-thesis and the resulting qualitative change is the synthesis. It is this logic of the dialectical method that Karl Marx (2002 [1848]) worked into his materialist interpretation of historical development (see Marx 1992 [1867]). According to Karl Marx, at any given historical moment, every society is divided into two classes – the dominant class and the dominated class, the exploiters and the exploited, the owners of the means of production and those who sell their labor in order to subsist. Given their relationship to the material forces, to the modes of production, the relationship between these classes is always antagonistic. As the class of the dominated grows in strength and increasingly becomes aware of its own exploitation by the dominant class, it rises up and eventually overthrows the dominant class and reshapes the mode of production in its own image and thereby restarts the antagonistic process anew. A powerful statement made by Karl Marx in this regard is that every mode of production contains within itself the seeds of (or contradictions that lead to) its own destruction – that is, until society attains communism, a classless society wherein there are no contradictions because of collective ownership of everything, with no haves and have-nots. In this utopian society, the contribution to the production process and distribution of benefits is based on the principle of 'from each according to ability and to each according to need.'

According to the dialectical method, in order for us to fully understand the essence of something, of any social phenomenon, it is necessary for us to seek out its internal contradictions. Under certain circumstances, the universal is the individual, and the individual is the universal. That things turn into their opposites – cause can become effect and effect can become cause – is because they are merely links in the never-ending chain in the development of matter (see Marx 1992, Engels 1973, McTaggart and McTaggart, 2011).

From Quantitative Change to Qualitative Change

The basic argument here is that for us to fully understand the essence of change, both social change and physical change, we have to grasp the law of the transformation of quantitative change to qualitative change. From this perspective, change, development, or evolution is not unidirectional, unilinear, nor does it occur gradually in a straight smooth line. There are long periods of time when nothing seems to be taking place with regard to change, development, or evolution. Then, out of the blue, something seemingly miraculous happens: a major social revolution, a physical catastrophe, a breakthrough in scientific discovery, an innovative discovery. The point here is that at moments when nothing seems to be happening, there are small quantitative changes taking place that eventually add up to a major qualitative change that we then view as a major leap forward.

This law of the transformation of quantitative change into qualitative change, from quantity to quality, is said to have an extremely wide range of applications, from the smallest particles of matter at the subatomic level in chemistry to the largest physical and social phenomena known to humans. Although this law has not received universal recognition according to its proponents, it is evident and manifest in our daily lives at every level. Engels (1973) writes that the transformation of quantity into quality was already known to the Megaran Greeks, who used it to demonstrate certain paradoxes, sometimes in the form of jokes. He provides the example of the 'bald head' and the 'heap of grain.' Does one hair less mean a bald head, or one grain of corn a heap? The answer is no. And if you add one more hair and add another grain of sand? The answer is still no. The question is then repeated until there is a heap of corn and a bald head. We are faced with the contradiction that individually, the small changes are powerless to effect a qualitative change, but at a certain level, they collectively do exactly that: quantity changes into quality.

The notion that under certain conditions, even small things can cause big changes, it is pointed out, finds its expression in all kinds of sayings and proverbs: 'the straw that broke the camel's back,' 'many hands make light work,' and 'constant dripping wears away the stone,' among others. Leon Trotsky (1994) argues that in many ways, this law of the transformation of quantity into quality has penetrated the popular consciousness. He notes that every individual is a dialectician to some extent or other, in most cases, unconsciously. A housewife knows that a certain amount of salt flavors soup agreeably, but that adding more and more salt makes the soup unpalatable. Consequently, Trotsky concludes, an illiterate peasant woman guides herself in cooking soup by the Hegelian law of the transformation of quantity into quality. Despite the seeming triviality of these examples, it is argued that they do reveal a profound truth about the way the world works. They demonstrate that our methods of thought, both formal logic and the dialectic, are not arbitrary constructions of our reason but rather expressions of the actual inter-relationships in nature itself, which is replete with 'unconscious' dialectics (Engels 1973, Hegel 1991, Trotsky 1994, McTaggart and McTaggart 2011).

The Law of the Negation of the Negation

The law of the negation of the negation explains the repetition at a higher level of certain features and properties of the lower level and the apparent return of past features. In the development of social and physical phenomena, there is a constant struggle between form and content and between content and form, resulting in the eventual shattering of the old form and the transformation of the content. According to Engels (1973), this whole process can be best pictured as a spiral, where the movement comes back to the position it started, but at a higher level. In other words, historical progress is achieved through a series of contradictions. Where the previous stage is negated, this does not represent its total elimination. The new stage does not wipe out completely the stage that it supplants.

Engels (1973) explains a whole series of examples in the physical world to illustrate the negation of the negation. One example he provides is of a grain of barley. Millions of such grains of barley are milled, boiled, and brewed and then consumed. However, if such a grain of barley meets with conditions which for it are normal, if it falls on suitable soil, Engels notes, then under the influence of heat and moisture a specific change takes place, it germinates; the grain as such ceases to exist, it is negated, and in its place appears the plant which has arisen from it, the negation of the grain. Given its normal life process, the barley plant grows, flowers, is fertilized and finally once more produces grains of barley, and, as soon as these have ripened, the stalk dies, is in its turn negated. As a result of this negation of the negation we have once again the original grain of barley, but not as a single unit, but ten, twenty or thirty fold. The barley thus lives and evolves by means of returning to its starting point – but at a higher level. One seed has produced many. Additionally, over time, plants evolve qualitatively as well as quantitatively. Successive generations have shown variations, and become more adapted to their environment.

This is the essence of Marx's dialectical materialism and his formulation of the thesis, antithesis, and synthesis to explain revolutionary social change as referenced above. The thesis is the established social order. Contradictory forces – the antithesis – emerge within it leading to a revolutionary crisis. The revolution occurs, leading to a synthesis whereby the old conditions are smashed, though not completely, and a new social order emerges. The process then starts all over again with the synthesis constituting the new thesis. In other words, the original thesis is negated, but the negation is also subject to negation (see Marx 2002). In materialist dialectics, according to Hegel (1991), the law of the negation of the negation is considered a law of the development of nature, society, and thought. If the law of the unity and struggle of opposites discloses the source of development, and the law of the transition of quantitative changes into qualitative changes reveals the mechanism of development, the law of the negation of the negation expresses the direction, form, and result of development. The significance of the law of the negation of the negation is its demonstration of the role of change and continuity and the non-linear character of the process of development.

Mazrui's Penchant for the Dialectical Method

The corpus of Prof. Mazrui's scholarly work is broad and profound. On account of its breadth and profundity, the work has come to be referred to simply as 'Mazruiana.' The appealing nature of Mazrui's work is a function of his commitment to the dialectical method in his analysis, his penchant for the paradoxical, and the contradictory, and his uncanny ability to coin memorable phrases to describe socio-political phenomena. For instance, in his *A Tale of Two Africa's: Nigeria and South Africa as Contrasting Visions* (2006), Mazrui does a comparative study of Nigeria and South Africa, the two most influential countries on the African continent. In his estimation, the two countries represent alternative faces of the continent, mirroring the political and socio-economic contrasts inherent in the African condition. To demonstrate this, Mazrui simply points to the contradictions or paradoxes inherent in the realities that obtain in the two countries. Nigeria is the Africa of human resources; South Africa is a land of mineral resources. Nigeria is repellant to European settlement; South Africa is a magnet for such settlement. Nigeria is a mono-racial society; South Africa is a multiracial society. Nigeria is grappling with the politics of religion; South Africa is pre-occupied with the politics of secularism. Nigeria is Africa's largest exporter of oil; South Africa is the continent's largest consumer of oil. Nigeria is a paradigm of indigenization; South Africa is a paragon of Westernization (Mazrui 2006).

Similarly, in *The African Predicament and the American Experience: A Tale of Two Edens* (2004a), Mazrui puts the dialectical method to work, exploring the historical, cultural, and economic significance of Africa to the development of the Western world, especially the United States. Mazrui contrasts this demonstrated significance of Africa to the development of the West with the combination of neglect and malice directed at the African continent and to peoples of African descent by the West in general and the United States in particular. Throughout this study, Mazrui demonstrates that this is a tale of two Edens: 'Africa as the Eden of Lost Innocence' and 'America as the Eden of Current Power and Future Fulfillment.' People of African ancestry have, he argues, been part of the vanguard for the Edenization of America. But America is also influencing Africa, the first Eden. He observes that the United States is a major force in the liberalization of black people in Africa; but also, black people are a major force in the democratization of all people in the United States.

This penchant for the dialectical runs through Prof. Mazrui's works, from diagnosing the African condition through juxtaposing Islam between globalization and counterterrorism to analyzing the politics of gender and the culture of sexuality (see Mazrui 1986, 2004, 2014). He has analyzed the crisis of habitation in Africa – Africa as the earliest habitat of mankind but the last to become truly habitable. He has focused on the basic paradox of Africa's location – the reality that despite the centrality of its geographical and cultural position, Africa remains the most marginal of all of the world's continents. Mazrui has also lamented the humiliation of African peoples; a humiliation that arises from the triple burden of slavery, colonialism, and racism (see Mazrui 1980, 1986). In an article as early as 1966 on Ghana's Kwame Nkrumah as 'the Leninist Czar,' Mazrui's dialectical prowess was evident. He argued that Nkrumah strove to be Africa's Lenin (a revolutionary theorist) while at the same time he sought to be Ghana's Czar! He contended that Nkrumah's Czarism was not necessarily the worst side of his personality and behavior. On the contrary, his Czarism could – in moderation – have mitigated some of the harshness of his Leninism, and that arguably, a Leninist Czar was what a country like Ghana needed for some time. "Nkrumah's tragedy was a tragedy of excess, rather than of contradiction. He tried to be too much of a revolutionary monarch" (Mazrui 1966: 106).

To fully grasp the analytical potency and explanatory clarity of Prof. Mazrui's dialectical method, the next section focuses on Mazrui's study of the origins of pan-movements. Herein, he analyzes the rise and development of Pan-Africanism and juxtaposes it with Pan-Europeanism that culminated in the formation of the European Union.

On The Origins of Pan-Movements

According to Ali Mazrui (1995: 35-38), pan-movements are born out of a combination of nightmare and dream; anguish and vision. According to him, the nightmare and the dream that released the forces that successfully culminated in the formation of the European Union was war and poetry. Poetry provided the vision and the sensibilities of being European. War provided the practical impetus either through conquest – as European nations expanded and contracted – or through a desire to avoid some future war. This was the combination of nightmare and dream; of anguish and vision that resulted in the consolidation of Pan-Europeanism. Mazrui notes that after World War II, the Schuman Plan and the European Coal and Steel Community illustrated the creation of deliberate Pan-European interdependence designed to avoid the future risk of war – that was the combination of nightmare and dream. The Cold War may have divided Europe – between east and west – but it also united Europe within each camp. Once again nightmare and dream played their paradoxical integrative roles (Mazrui, 1995: 35).

Mazrui notes that the poetry of Pan-Europeanism goes back at least to the European Renaissance as Europeans were stimulated by a new sense of shared civilization. Mazrui (1995: 35) quotes the English romantic poet, William Wordsworth who, in an exuberance celebration of the commencement of the French revolution passionately proclaimed:

> Oh! Pleasant exercise of hope and joy!
> For Mighty were the auxiliars which then stood
> Upon our side, we who were strong in love!
> Bliss was it in that dawn to be alive,
> But to be young was very heaven! – Oh! Times,
> In which the meager, stale, forbidding ways
> Of custom, law and statute, took at once

> The attraction of a country in romance!
> When reason seemed the most to assert her rights,
> When most intent on making herself
> A prime enchantress – to assist the work,
> Which then was going forward in her name!

Mazrui thus argues that even the French revolution was a combination of poetry and war, of dream and nightmare, the two major catalysts of Pan-Europeanism.

Mazrui juxtaposes Pan-Europeanism and Pan-Africanism and contends that for Pan-Africanism, its great impetus lay in the combined power of poetry and imperialism, rather than poetry and war. He delineates two paradoxical forms of Pan-African cultural nationalism that constitute the poetry of Pan-Africanism, what he calls *Romantic Primitivism* and *Romantic Gloriana* both of which were responses to European imperialism. Romantic Primitivism celebrates what is simple about Africa; it salutes the cattle herder, not the castle builder. Mazrui (1995: 35) cites the poet Aimé Césaire to illustrate this:

> Hooray for those who never invented anything
> Hooray for those who never discovered anything
> Hooray for joy! Hooray for love!
> Hooray for the pain of incarnate tears.
> My negritude [blackness] is no tower and no cathedral
> It delves into the deep red flesh of the soil.

For its part, Romantic Gloriana celebrates Africa's legends, heroes, and makers of African history. It celebrates the continent's more complex achievements, including "… the pyramids of Egypt, the towering structure of Aksum, the sunken churches of Lalibela, the brooding majesty of Great Zimbabwe, the castles of Gonder. Romantic Gloriana is a tribute to Africa's empires and kingdoms, Africa's inventors and discoverers, great Shaka Zulu rather than the unknown peasant" (Mazrui 1995: 35).

Both forms of Pan-African cultural nationalism were responses to European imperialism and its cultural arrogance. Mazrui notes that Europeans claimed that Africans were simple and invented nothing (an alleged *fact*); and that those who were simple and invented nothing were, ipso facto, uncivilized (a *value* judgment). It was on the basis of such alleged facts and value judgments that slavery and colonialism were justified on the 'civilizing mission' of taming the barbaric races. Mazrui writes that Romantic Primitivism accepted Europe's alleged facts about Africa – that Africa was simple and invented nothing; but rejected Europe's value judgment – that having invented nothing, Africa was thus uncivilized. To Romantic Primitivism, simplicity was one version of civilization. African simplicity was a function of the fact that the African lived in a paradise, in a Garden of Eden – where food was provided for by the bounty of nature and where the climate was without winter. Mazrui argues that the African simplicity of living in huts, going barefoot, and wearing limited clothing was a function of what he calls the 'winter gap theory.'

Because of winter in the Western world, Mazrui writes, wearing clothes is not just a matter of sexual modesty; it is a matter of physical survival. Wearing shoes is not just a matter of social etiquette; it is a matter of avoiding frostbite. "Where the winds are cold, thicker walls are erected, engineering begins to advance. Where warmth is a matter of life and death, fire is tamed and harnessed. Where the growing season is short, survival depends on planning for winter" (cited in Mazrui and Mutunga 2004: 112). Conversely, the nearer to the Equator an African society was, the less it needed elaborate shelters and complicated tools. The simplicity of the African was thus a function of his ecology. An abundant and friendly ecology explains the lack of technological advancement and engineering prowess in many African societies. This reality, in Mazrui's estimation, was not a bad thing. Its only downside emerged when the colonial imperialists arrived on the scene with their technologically superior weapons. "This time, ecology conspired with colonialism to victimize Africa" (Mazrui and Mutunga 2004).

On the other hand, Romantic Gloriana rejected Europe's alleged facts about Africa – that Africa was simple and invented nothing, but seemingly accepted Europe's values – that civilization is to be measured by complexity and innovation, hence its focus on Africa's great empire builders, on Africa's legendary leaders, great monuments, and extraordinary historical feats. Mazrui notes that the same African country can produce both types of Pan-African nationalists. He gives the example of Senegal wherein Léopold Sédar Senghor, a major thinker and poet in the Negritude School belonged to the Romantic Primitivism School while his compatriot Cheikh Anta Diop belonged to the Romantic Gloriana one. Whereas Senghor accepted Europe's alleged facts and value judgments about Africa, going so far as to posit that 'emotion is black and reason is Greek', Diop spent much of his scholarly life demonstrating Africa's contributions to global civilization and emphasizing that Pharaonic Egypt's civilization was a black civilization. Overall, Mazrui argues that the reality on the African continent was one of fusion of the simple and the complex, the cattle-herder and the castle-builder. It was much more than Romantic Primitivism and Romantic Gloriana. In his view, real Pan-Africanism must go beyond the stimuli of poetry and imperialism if it is to succeed in constructing institutions to overcome its political, social, and economic problems.

Pan-Africanism: Realities and Prospects

Having traced its origins in poetry and colonial imperialism, Mazrui delineates, in his dialectical style, what he calls a fundamental duality in the paradigm of Pan-Africanism – the Pan-Africanism of liberation and the Pan-Africanism of integration. The former is embodied in the solidarity of Africans in Africa and the diaspora who fought against colonialism, who confronted racism and fought against apartheid South Africa. The Africans in Africa found solidarity in Pan-Africanism on the basis of their having been jointly colonized. Africans in the diaspora found unity in Pan-Africanism on the basis of their having been jointly enslaved. The two groups of Africans found solidarity in Pan-Africanism on the basis of their having been jointly exploited by the Western world (see Mazrui and Mazrui, 2002). The Pan-Africanism of integration on the other hand, has sought regional economic integration, "… at least a free trade area, or perhaps a development alliance, or an economic union or economic community. Sometimes the effort is to sustain military cooperation. The ultimate dream has been to try to create whole new federations out of disparate nation-states" (Mazrui, 1995: 35). Examples here include the East African Community, the South African Development Community, and the Economic Community of West African States among a host of others.

According to Mazrui, the Pan-Africanism of liberation has been impressively victorious. But the Pan-Africanism of integration has proved a dismal failure. Accordingly, he concludes that Africans are better at uniting for freedom than at uniting for development. Solidarity in the quest for political freedom has been easier than solidarity in the cause of socio-economic transformation. In his view, Kwame Nkrumah epitomized this paradox: "He led Ghana's independence in 1957, and inspired Pan-Africanists worldwide. But his Ghana-Guinea and Ghana-Guinea-Mali unions were fiascoes in integration" (Mazrui, 1995). Nevertheless, Mazrui does point to the fact that the prospects for regional integration remain positive and, in his view, different regions of the continent are suited to different forms of integration and should take the lead on these aspects accordingly if the Pan-African ideal is to be actualized on the continent.

The first form of integration Mazrui identifies is economic integration. In his view, the best prospects for economic integration in Africa lie with the

Southern Africa Development Community. Writing at a time when South Africa had just been added to the original Southern African Development Coordination Conference, Mazrui argues that the success of the SADC scheme will be partly on account of the fact that South Africa is more equal than the other members. Existence of such a pivotal state helps to assure the success of a regional integration scheme. He gives the example of the European Economic Community which, he asserts, survived after 1958 because some members were definitely more equal than others: "The Franco-German axis was, under Charles De Gaulle, more 'Franco' than German" (Mazrui, 1995: 36), although German economic might has restored the balance in the current European Union. Similarly, Mazrui argues that the pivotal power of South Africa as the indisputable first among equals within the rubric of SADC will be the basis for the scheme's success.

Cultural integration is the second form of Pan-Africanism that Mazrui identifies. In his view, East Africa is well poised to be Africa's leader in the achievement of this form of Pan-Africanism. This is on account of the region having the fortune of an indigenous lingua franca in the name of Kiswahili that binds Kenya, Tanzania, and to some extent, Uganda, Somalia, and potentially, Rwanda, Burundi, and Eastern Zaire. Even northern Mozambique and Malawi are experiencing the influence of Kiswahili which, Mazrui asserts, is spoken by more people than any other indigenous language of Africa: "It will hit its 100 million people early in the 21st century if not sooner. Kiswahili is expanding more rapidly than any other lingua franca in the continent" (Mazrui, 1995).

Third is the Pan-Africanism of political integration which, Mazrui writes, will probably be led by the North African region encompassing the countries of Algeria, Egypt, Libya, Mauritania, Morocco, and Tunisia. Although the region is still a long way away from political integration, Mazrui avers that it is the best placed in Africa for the adventure of political union because of its shared religion in Islam, common Arabic language, a shared Arabo-Berber culture, and a substantial shared history across centuries. Additionally, European integration is viewed by Mazrui as providing stimuli for North Africa's political integration: "The economies of North Africa and Southern Europe are to some extent competitive. The deeper integration of countries like Spain and Portugal and Greece into an Enlarged European Union is ringing economic alarm bells in North Africa. This could help Pan-Africanism in Arab Africa" (Mazrui, 1995).

Fourth and finally is the Pan-Africanism of military integration which, Mazrui writes, is likely to be led by the West African region given the precedent-setting experience of ECOMOG under the auspices of the Economic

Community for West African States. Despite its mixed fortunes and difficulties in its rescue missions in Liberia and Sierra Leone, ECOMOG has been a pioneering enterprise in what Mazrui calls the history of Pax Africana. Mazrui underscores the urgency of the military integration form of Pan-Africanism by arguing that it is precisely the Achilles' heel of Pan-Africanism as a whole. He asks: who will keep the peace in the Africa of the new millennium? If we do not want American troops in Somalia, or French troops in Rwanda, should we just be spectators to carnage in Africa? The answer to Mazrui's questions seem to have been provided by the African Union's establishment of the Peace and Security Council whose protocol came into force in December 2003 following ratification by the requisite number of AU member states. Its functions include promotion of peace, security, and stability in Africa; preventive diplomacy and the maintenance of peace; and the management of catastrophes and humanitarian actions. It is also mandated to deploy peacekeeping and quick intervention missions to assist in cases of genocide, war crimes, and crimes against humanity. It was within the framework of the AU's PSC that AMISOM was deployed to Somalia in 2007. The biggest drag on the operations of the Peace and Security Council is the paucity of logistical resources related to deployment of peacekeeping and quick intervention missions.

In the final analysis, Mazrui argues that while Africans have been successful in uniting to achieve national freedom, they have utterly failed to unite for economic development and political stability. Consequently, war, famine, and state collapse remain the post-colonial legacy for far too many Africans. "As a result, external recolonization under the banner of humanitarianism is entirely possible" (Mazrui, 1995: 36). To avoid this, Mazrui advises, Pan-Africanism needs to devise institutions to help Africa deal with its political and socio-economic malaise. It is only in this way that Pan-Africanism of integration might eventually parallel the record of achievement set by Pan-Africanism of liberation. He warns that unless Pan-Africanism of integration – uniting for development – succeeds, the accomplishments of Pan-Africanism of liberation – uniting for freedom – risk being reversed: "Africa could be colonized in new ways. From nightmare to nightmare, with no poetry in sight" (Mazrui, 1995: 38).

Conclusion

Mazrui's immense contribution to the study of Africa and his unique analytical style put him in a class of his own. On account of this, he has been acknowledged as 'Africa's gift to the world' by former United Nations Secretary General, Kofi Annan. In 2005, the American *Foreign Policy* and the

British *Prospect* magazines named Prof. Mazrui one of the top 100 public intellectuals in the world. Morgan State University awarded him the Du Bois-Garvey Award for Pan-African Unity and he was elected an 'Icon of the Twentieth Century' by Lincoln University. These are just a few of his numerous awards across the globe. Yet Mazrui's scholarship has not been without controversy. His nine-part television series entitled *The Africans: A Triple Heritage*, which propelled him to fame outside of the academic world, generated some heated controversy especially in the United States following its simultaneous airing by the British Broadcasting Corporation in the United Kingdom and the Public Broadcasting Service in the United States.

Conservatives, led by the then National Endowment for the Humanities chairperson Lynne Cheney, wife of former Vice President Dick Cheney, condemned the series for what they saw as its anti-Western bias. Lynne Cheney dismissed it as an anti-western diatribe that was worse than 'unbalanced.' Among their complaints were that Mazrui spoke favorably of Libyan leader Muammar Qaddafi, saying that he inspired Africans to have a sense of destiny and become actors on the world stage. Lynne Cheney's National Endowment for Humanities, which contributed US$ 600,000 toward the US3.5 million budget for the television series, went so far as to demand that its name be removed from the show's credits (Jacobson, 1996).

However, the fact that the series was also criticized by apparently liberal-leaning newspapers like the *New York Times* and *The Washington Post* and, quite paradoxically, banned in Mazrui's native Kenya ostensibly for being 'anti-African' is ample testimony to the objectivity of Prof. Mazrui's television series. *The New York Times* dismissed the series as 'a pretentious fraud.' Reviewing the series for *The New York Times*, John Corry (1986) called its scholarship 'empty' and said that it was a vehicle solely for Mr. Mazrui's feelings; while *The Washington Post* criticized it as 'biased and preachy.' Nevertheless, Clifford Terry (1986), writing in *The Chicago Tribune*, suggested that this personal perspective was in fact a strength. "It is obvious, through it all," he wrote, "that here is a man who deeply cares about what he likes to call a 'remarkable continent.'" Similarly, Tom Shales of the *Washington Post* applauded the program's abrasiveness, arguing that the alternative would be an innocuous, safely 'balanced' documentary on Africa that made no ripples and provoked no discourse (Martin 2014).

Mazrui responded that he was merely restoring balance to the previous colonialist interpretations of Africa and saying what Westerners did not want to hear. Rather than presenting an unbalanced view of African issues, Mazrui insisted that part of the intent of his television series was to restore balance to the overwhelmingly pro-Western coverage of African matters generally seen in America, by presenting a purely African perspective. He noted that there were many parts in the series that were anti-imperialist and observed that Africa was concerned about past domination and afraid of re-domination. Mazrui concluded, in his characteristic dialectical lexicon, that the 'United States is a great communicator, but a poor listener.' Interestingly, while the controversy still raged, Prof. Mazrui was named Andrew D. White Professor-at-Large at Cornell University and, in 1989, the then New York Governor, Mario Cuomo personally lured Prof. Mazrui from Michigan State University to the State University of New York, Binghamton, where he remained for a quarter a century until his death in October 2014.

References

Brockman, Norbert C. *An African Biographical Dictionary*. New York: Grey House Publishing, 2006.

Corry, John. "TV Reviews; 'Africans,' a Series on 13," *The New York Times*, October 9, 1986.

Engels, Friedrich. *Dialectics of Nature*. New York: International Publishers, 1973 [1940].

Engels, Friedrich. "Karl Marx, a Contribution to the Critique of Political Economy," Review of Karl Marx's *Critique of Political Economy*, *Das Volk*, Nos. 14 and 16, August 1859, accessed January 8, 2015 at: https://www.marxists.org/archive/marx/works/1859/critique-pol-economy/appx2.htm.

Gadamer, Hans-Georg and Christopher P. Smith. *Hegel's Dialectic: Five Hermeneutical Studies*. New Haven: Yale University Press, 1982.

Hegel, Georg Wilhem Friedrich. *The Science of Logic*. New York: Random House, 1991.

Jacobson, Robert. "Mazrui, Ali, 1933—" in *Contemporary Black Biography*. 1996. Available at: http://www.encyclopedia.com/doc/1G2-2871400044.html#B, 1996.

Lenin, Vladimir I. [Translated by Clemens Dutt]. *Lenin's Collected Works, Vol. 38*. Moscow: Progress Publishers, 1965.

Martin, Douglas. "Ali Mazrui, Scholar of Africa who Divided US Audiences Dies at 81," *The New York Times*, October 20, 2014.

Marx, Karl. *Capital: A Critique of Political Economy Volume I*. New York: Penguin Classics, 1992 [1867].

Marx, Karl. *The Communist Manifesto*. New York: Penguin Classics, 2002.

Mazrui, Alamin M. and Willy M. Mutunga, eds. *Race, Gender, and Culture Conflict: Debating the African Condition: Mazrui and His Critics Volume I*. Trenton: NJ: Africa World Press, 2004.

Mazrui, Ali. A. [edited by Etin Anwar]. *The Politics of Gender and the Culture of Sexuality: Western, Islamic, and African Perspectives*. Lanham, MD: University Press of America, 2014.

Mazrui, Ali A. [edited by James N. Karioki]. *A Tale of Two Africas: Nigeria and South Africa as Contrasting Visions*. Adonis and Abbey Publishers, 2006.

Mazrui, Ali A. *Islam: Between Globalization and Counterterrorism*. Trento, NJ: Africa World Press, 2006.

Mazrui, Ali A. *The African Predicament and the American Experience: A Tale of Two Edens*. Boulder, CO: Praeger, 2004.

Mazrui, Ali A. "Pan-Africanism: From Poetry to Power," *Issue: A Journal of Opinion* (Vol. 23, No. 1, 1995), pp. 35-38.

Mazrui, Ali A. *The Africans: A Triple Heritage*. New York: Little, Brown, and Co., 1986.

Mazrui, Ali A. *The African Condition: A Political Diagnosis*. London: Heinemann, 1980.

Mazrui, Ali A. "Nkrumah: The Leninist Czar." *Transition*. Vol. 26, Nos. 75/76, 1966.

Mazrui, Ali A. and Alamin M. Mazrui. *Black Reparations in an Era of Globalization*. Binghamton, NY: Institute of Global Cultural Studies, 2002.

McTaggart, John and Ellis McTaggart. *Studies in the Hegelian Dialectic*. Toronto: University of Toronto Libraries, 2011.

Molotsky, Irvin. "U.S. Aide Assails TV Series on Africa," *The New York Times*, September 5, 1986.

Musambi, Evelyne. "The Life of Prof. Ali Mazrui: 13 Things You Should Know," *Daily Nation*, Nairobi, Kenya, October 15, 2014.

Terry, Clifford. "PBS' Maddening, Moving 'Africans' Deserves to be Seen," *Chicago Tribune*, October 9, 1986.

Trotsky, Leon. *In Defense of Marxism: The Social and Political Contradictions of the Soviet Union*. Atlanta, GA: Pathfinder Press, 1994.

11

The African Impact on American Higher Education:
Ali Mazrui's Contribution*1

Alamin M. Mazrui

While the birth of the baby Jesus was heralded by the arrival of the three wise man, the birth of every Swahili child in Mombasa in the 1930s was preceded by the convergence of three civilizations. Ali Mazrui was born in the context of a confluence of three cultures-Africanity, Islam, and the new Western impact.

By a strange coincidence the year of Ali Mazrui's birth was 1933 – the only year in the twentieth century that had more than one three. Ali A. Mazrui therefore had the traid woven into his year of birth. He was what he himself later designated as "a triple heritage baby" – a bundle of three civilizations.

His life was also destined to traverse three continents particularly strongly – Africa, Europe, and North America. In each of those regions he spent many years.

But this chapter is about the American phase of his life, and whether that phase made a difference to American higher education.

In the film *It's a Wonderful Life* with James Stewart, an angel enables a suicidal and despondent man to experience what the world would have

---

1 * This chapter, "The African Impact on American Higher Education: Ali Mazrui's Contribution was originally published in The Scholar Between thought sn Experience: A Biogrpahical Festschrift in Honor of Ali A. Mazrui, ed. Parviz Morewedge (Institute of Global Cultural Studies Global Publications, Binghamton Univeristy, 2001 pp. 3-22, and is printed here with the permission of the original author and the publisher.

been like if he had never been born. In the United States this brilliant film is shown every Christmas season.

If Ali Mazrui were ever to contemplate suicide like the character in *It's a Wonderful Life*, perhaps an angel would show Mazrui how the twentieth century would have been different had he never been born. Mazrui would have re-discovered that an African, relatively illiterate electronically, reached one of the biggest electronic audiences reached by any African in history, and certainly the twentieth century. Mazrui's electronic impact was first by his BBC Reith Lectures *The African Condition* in 1979, second by his PBS/BBC television series *the Africans: A Triple Heritage* (translated into multiple languages) which first aired in 1986, and third by his widely-publicized Internet critique of Henry Louis Gates' television series *Wonders of the African World* in 1999. By his electronic impact alone Ali Mazrui was perhaps a unique African of the twentieth century. His television series has become an essential text in a wide range of African-related courses in the American academy, from literature to history, from political science to anthropology. His radio and television work has reached millions of people worldwide, in multiple languages.

Our focus in this essay remained American-centric. In what other ways has Ali Mazrui essentially helped to redirect American higher education? What have been Ali Mazrui's contributions to higher education in the United States? These have been multifaceted. At least as significant as the content of such contributions have been made.

Those instrumentalities can be translated into the various roles Ali Mazrui has played. These are, first, Ali Mazrui as a classroom teacher on campuses; second, Mazrui as a writer of books and scholarly articles; third, Mazrui as a broadcaster on radio and television; fourth, Mazrui as a public speaker who is in demand nationally from New York to Austin, Texas, and from Boston to Berkeley, California; fifth, Mazrui as a feature writer for newspapers and magazines; sixth, Mazrui as a leader in academic and educational associations; and seventh, Mazrui as a consultant to bodies which range from World Bank to emerging colleges.

However, let us first look more closely at Ali Mazrui's life before the American phase if we are to understand what he brought to America. We must also scrutinize the assets and liabilities that came with him to the United States.

Ancestry and Ascent

Ali Mazrui came from a highly devout Islamic Swahili family headed by his father, who was for a while the Chief Kadhi (or Chief Islamic Justice) of

Kenya. In his childhood in the 1940s, Ali Mazrui accompanied his father on some of his trips across Kenya to hear appeals under Islamic law. Ali Mazrui's first exposure to the Akamba and Gikuyu Muslims in Kenya hinterland, for example, was through the judicial duties of his father as a roving court of appeal.

Ali Mazrui's father died in 1947 when Ali was only fourteen. Had the father lived, Ali would have been trained as an Islamic jurist, culminating at Al-Azhar University in Cairo. In his father's absence, Ali applied for scholarships and finally succeeded in winning a Kenyan Government scholarship (colonial) to enable him to complete his secondary education in Huddersfield, England, and to enable him to do his first degree at the University of Manchester, England.

Ali Mazrui's first exposure to the United States was as a graduate student at Columbia University, New York. He completed his Masters' degree at Columbia in nine months. He used the summer to take courses at the University of Mexico, Mexico City, and at the University of California, Berkeley, and while still under Rockefeller Foundation sponsorship.

Ali Mazrui did his doctoral work at Oxford University, England, funded by Nuffield College, Oxford, where Mazrui was a student. He also did some broadcasting for BBC radio during his Oxford years.

His first regular academic position was as a Lecturer at Makerere University in Uganda where he subsequently became both head of the Department of Political Science and the Dean of the Faculty of Social Services. After General Idi Amin captured power in a military coup in January 1971, Uganda became increasingly unstable. This instability and violence finally forced Ali Mazrui and his family to leave Uganda and move to the United States. The option of going back to Kenya instead of coming to the United States was not an option for him because the University authorities in Kenya would not hire him for political reasons. Mazrui was regarded as a political dissident.

Ali Mazrui was appointed Fellow of the prestigious Center for Advanced Study in Behavioral Sciences in Palo Alto, California (1972-73) and a senior Fellow at the Hoover Institution on War, Revolution and Peace at Stanford in California (1973-4). He then accepted a tenured professorship in the Department of Political Science at the University of Michigan, Ann Arbor, in 1974 where he remained until 1989. From 1978-1981 Mazrui was also the Director for the Center for African-American and African Studies at Michigan. He moved to the State University of New York at Binghamton in 1989 – but more about that later.

Between Assets & Liabilities

Among the special assets Ali Mazrui brought to the United States was a brilliant dialectical mind – dialectical in the sense of a capacity to discern the unity of opposites. His work is full of paradoxes – sometime genuine, sometimes contrived. Each of the six Reith Lectures on the BBC World Service in 1979 was based on a paradox about "the African condition."[1]

There is also a controversial article "Nkrumah: The Leninist Czar" first published as an evaluation of Kwame Nkrumah when he was overthrown in a military coup in 1966.[2]

Ali Mazrui's second major asset was a highly developed command of the English language. His facility with language has been relatively free of jargon but not entirely free of idiosyncrasies and verbal conceits. He is often tempted to play with words. It works in his oratory but it does not always work in his writings.

Mazrui's third major asset was his enjoyment of writing and the ease with which he could produce competent written material at relatively short notice. He is one author who never seems to suffer from writer's block.

The fourth major asset was his oratorical skill. Although he prefers to have written notes before him, and sometimes even a text, he is capable of departing entirely from his text and to deliver a brilliant lecture almost ex tempore (in the American academic market his lectures often earned him thousands of dollars per performance).

Mazrui's fifth asset has been his capacity to let his three civilizations (Africanity, Islam, and westernism) illuminate each other. One powerful illustration is his description of the birth of Islam as "the first Protestant Revolution" within the Christian tradition.[3]

Mazrui's second book chronologically was entitled *On Heroes and Uhuru-Worship* deliberately echoing Thomas Carlyle's classic, *On Heroes, Hero-worship and the Heroic in History*. Mazrui has repeatedly borrowed from the English literature to point an African moral or adorn an Islamic table.[4]

What about the liabilities that Mazrui brought into this American career? One liability has been an unresolved conflict between his role as a political thinker (which may need no documentation or footnoting) and his role as a social scientist (which does require greater attention to formal evidence). Considering how impatient he has been with the minutiae of formal footnoting, it is astonishing that Mazrui has risen as high as he has, and has published in some of the most respected journals in the Western World.

But is Mazrui a man of ideas or a man of science? When the man of ideas in him prevails, the scientist appears to lack rigor. On the other hand, it has been the originality of many of his ideas that have made his reputation internationally, as well as established in the United States.

Another unresolved conflict in Mazrui has been between the political activist and the scholar. As far back as his Uganda days, Ali Mazrui was asked by President Milton Obote, "Are you sure you know the difference between being a political scientist and being a politician?" President Obote was getting fed up with Mazrui's criticisms of Obote's policies, disguised as political science! In the United States his activism, which may have cost Mazrui greater academic honors in Ivy League circles, has been his defense of the rights of Palestinians in some of his public lectures, and even debates within his classes. In his book *Cultural Forces in World Politics* he devotes chapter eight to a comparison of the logic of Zionism (separating Arabs from Jews) with the logic of apartheid (separating Whites from Blacks).

And yet even on the question of the Jews, the dialectical nature of Mazrui's mind has been in evidence again. In the same book Mazrui devoted a separate chapter – seven – in praise of Jewish intellectual achievements and calling upon Black people to learn from Jewish experience. In shore, Ali Mazrui has been an admirer of the Jewish people while remaining a passionate critic of the policies of the Israeli state.[5]

The third unresolved conflict in Ali Mazrui has been whether he is a journalistic popularizer or a solemn and profound scholar. This ambivalence has caused him to be courted by both the media and the academic world. It is possible that no African scholar in history has been heard by more radio listeners (e.g. Mazrui's BBC Reith Lectures), seen by more television viewers (e.g. Mazrui's PBS, BBC, and NBC programs) and read by more readers of magazines and newspapers in his own words (such as Mazrui's syndicated articles for the *Los Angeles Times* and others).

And yet Ali Mazrui has also been published in such highly competitive scholarly journals as *Political Studies* (U.K.), *Journal of Modern African Studies* (Cambridge), and the *American Political Science Review* and the *Harvard Educational Review*.

Ali Mazrui's fourth liability in the United States was a flaw in the American society rather than a fault in Ali Mazrui. "Driving While Black" captures the burden of Black people on American roads and under police surveillance. What about "Professing While Black." Do Black professors confront special obstacles?

Ali Mazrui believes that he both gained and lost as a Black professor. He arrived in the United States in the era of affirmative action. This did help most Black academics. But the wider society was still fundamentally racist. His career suffered in less obvious ways as a result.

The fact that he was an African and not an African American also closed certain doors of advancement for him. For a political scientist the loss was particularly great in terms of comparative access to the Washington power elite. An African American scholar of comparable stature would (if he or she wanted it) have had much easier access to the Congressional elite and the White House.

The fifth unresolved conflict in Ali Mazrui has been between being secular and being religious. Mazrui's life style in the United States has been basically secular. He has been married twice, in each case to a woman from a Christian family. The three sons of his first marriage (all of them in their thirties now) have grown up as liberal, secular Americans. Their father's influence has been more towards liberalism than towards religion – whether the father intended it or not.

And yet to the six of seven million Muslims of the United States, Ali Mazrui is regarded as a major intellectual resource for Islam. Indeed, he and Professor Sulayman Nyang of Howard University are probably the most prominent Black African Muslims in North America. Two major factors propelled Ali Mazrui towards high visibility among American Muslims. One factor was his television series, *The Africans: A Triple Heritage*, which includes extensive treatment of Islam in Africa. The other factor that helped to give Mazrui instant fame among non-Africanist Muslims was his attack on Salman Rushdie's novel *The Satanic Verses*. His attack was made in a public lecture given at Cornell University in 1989 soon after the publication of Rushdies's novel in the United State. Muslims present at the lecture audio-recorded it. To American Muslims the lecture was regarded as sensational. Tapes of it were distributed far and wide. Academic America also sat up and took notice. The lecture was published in two American academic journals and one British. It was also translated into other languages. The lecture was entitled "The Satanic Verses or a Satanic Novel?: Moral Dilemmas of Rushdie Affair."[6]

Ali Mazrui has continued to combine a relatively secular life-style with strong loyalty to Islam. This has remained an unresolved conflict. Has it been a liability in the American context?

The sixth overlapping liability with which Ali Mazrui arrived in the United States was in any case precisely in belonging to a minority religion and often a suspect community – the Muslims of America. In reality African Muslims suffered far less in the United States for their religion than, say, Arab Muslims. African Muslims were seen much more as Africans than as Muslims. They were more likely to suffer for their race than for their religion.

However, there have been occasions when being a Muslim was a liability in mainstream American institutions. Mainstream Zionists or Christian fundamentalists have sometimes treated Muslims with suspicion when it came to appointments, promotion, and publication. Ali Mazrui has been caught up in these issues.

And yet, America being what it is, Ali Mazrui has taught hundreds of Jewish students at Michigan, Binghamton, Cornell, Stanford, Chicago, and elsewhere. American pluralism has repeatedly responded to what Ali Mazrui has had to offer.

Between Africa and the Diaspora

But what is the content of Mazrui's contribution to higher education in the United States? Here two distinctions have to be made between different areas of study. These include new perspectives on, first, Africana studies; second, conflict studies; third, cultural studies; fourth, global studies; and fifth, Islamic studies. These areas are of course overlapping.

For example, his concept of Africa's "triple heritage" is a contribution to both African studies and Islamic studies in America higher education. By "the triple heritage" Mazrui means the convergence of African culture, Islam, and the Western impact upon Africa. Mazrui also coined or re-invented the term "global Africa" to signify the emerging network of relationships among people of African descent scattered worldwide. He gave the concept "global Africa" visibility by making it the title of his program 9 in his television series *The Africans: A Triple Heritage* (PBS and BBS 1986). "Global Africa" was also the title of a course Mazrui taught at Cornell University every year throughout the 1990's. The term "global Africa" has since also crept into the writings of other scholars, and the concept of "global African Studies" is sometimes used in Centers of African-American and African studies.

An even older concept brought to African studies by Mazrui was the concept of "Pax Africana," meaning a system under which Africa becomes its own "policeman" for keeping the peace and maintaining stability. He first launched this concept to the U.S. academic community in a book published by Chicago University Press in 1967 under the title *Towards a Pax Africana: A Study of Ideology and Ambition*. (The British publisher was Wiedenfield and Nicholson, London, 1967). The concept of "Pax Africana" has assumed even greater urgency by the twenty-first century.

Can Africa be one entity if it is part Black and part Arab? Ali Mazrui's most original solution has been to make the Arabian Peninsula part of Africa:

> The most pernicious sea in Africa's history may be the Red Sea. This thin line of water has been deemed to be more relevant for defining where Afri-

ca ends than all the evidence of geology, geography, history, culture [linking the continent to the Arabian Peninsula].[7]

He goes on to argue that while Madagascar is separated from the African continent by the 500-mile-wide Mozambique Channel, Greater Yemen is "separated from Djibouti by only a stone's throw at the strait of Bab-el-Mandeb." He goes on to ask: "Why should Tananarive be an African capital when Aden is not?"[8]

Ali Mazrui coins two compound terms that capture the paradoxical intimacy between Africa and Arabia. He introduced the concept of "Afrabia" in an article published in the University of California journal, UFAHAMU. On the narrower relations between Africa and the Persian (Arabian) Gulf which include the historic impact of the Sultanate of Oman on Zanzibar and the East African coast, Mazrui has coined new terms to summarize complex political or historical phenomena.[9]

Ali Mazrui has also been fascinated by the African Diaspora. He had developed a distinction between the Diaspora of slavery, such as "Survivors of the Middle Passage in the Americas," and the Diaspora of colonialism, the new African migrants to other lands in the wake of the disruptions of colonialism and its aftermath.

He has also developed the concept of *American Africans* (relatively new African settlers in the Americas) to be distinguished from African Americans (in the usual sense of descendants of the survivors of the Middle Passage within the United States, such as Jesse Jackson, Martin Luther King Jr. and Toni Morrison).

A third important distinction Ali Mazrui began developing in the 1990s has been between Africans of the soil (Africans who are part of the African continent but not necessarily part of the Black race) and Africans of the blood (Africans who are part of the Black race but not necessarily part of the African continent). Most Tunisians and Algerians are Africans of the soil but not of the blood. Most African Americans and Black Jamaicans are Africans of the blood but not of the soil. Most sub-Saharan Black people are both African of the blood and African of the soil.

Ali Mazrui has discussed these pairs of concepts on different campuses as a public speaker and in his own classes. Perhaps the most extensive elaboration was in his First Macmillan-Stewart lecture "African Migrations and American Diversity," delivered at Harvard University in March 2000 as part of a series of three lectures sponsored by the W. E. B. Du Bois Institute.[10]

An influential Diasporic course Mazrui has never quite developed into a book is "Comparative Black Political Thought," which he taught at the University of Michigan in the 1970s and 1980s. The course attempted to compare political thought in Africa, Black America, and the Caribbean. Some of Mazrui's former students subsequently developed their own versions of the same comparative course when they became college professors elsewhere. Mazrui has also published comparative philosophical papers in journals ranging from *Ethics* and *Journal of African Philosophy* to *Comparative Studies in Society and History.*

Between Culturology and Global Studies

This interest in the comparison of African cultures links up with Mazrui's work on cultural studies (culturology) and global studies (globalogy), Ali Mazrui tends to use the word "culture" in its sociological sense (the values and institutions of a society) rather than in its aesthetic sense (works of beauty and creativity, like music, paintings and poetry). When he was a professor at the University of Michigan (1974-89), Mazrui organized a special course of his own on what he called "International Political Culture," and taught it at both graduate and undergraduate levels. The course subsequently developed into the more comprehensive course on "Cultural Forces in World Politics" which has been taught at different levels at the State University of New York at Binghamton. The course explores the impact of such forces as religion, language, ideology, and sexual division of labor not only on politics within societies but also on relations between societies. The course has become so successful at Binghamton that when Mazrui is not teaching it, the department of political science asks another professor to take it on.

Ali Mazrui has his own paradigm of culturology. He sees culture as serving seven or eight functions in society. In his paradigm, culture can be our lenses of *perception*, or our source of *motivation*, or our means of *communication*, or the basis of our *stratification*, or our mode of *production*, or the pattern of our *consumption*, or our standard of *evaluation*, or the very foundation of our *identity*. He started developing this paradigm of culture from his BBC Reith Lectures in 1979, and has been promoting and developing it ever since.

He developed even earlier his concept of *counterpenetration* as a separate aspect of his worldview. At a time when most Third World intellectuals were recommending that their countries should attempt to "delink" from the economies of the North from within. Even before the word "globalization" gained currency, he argued that "delinking" went against globalizing trends and was unrealistic. The correct solution would be for the developing countries to use their resources in a manner that empowered them (counterpenetration) rather than allow the North to reduce those countries to further dependency. Delinking would involve under-utilizing their resources.

Ali Mazrui even developed five strategies for making developing countries less dependent upon the North. These strategies were what he called indigenization (emphasizing indigenous resources and skills), domestication (making imported institutions like universities more relevant); diversification (diversifying crops, trading partners, aid donors); horizontal integration or interpretation (greater unity among less developed economies) and vertical counterpenetration (increasing the power of developing countries upon the North – as South Korea has done or the countries of OPEC have tried to do from time to time).

Mazrui's dual strategy has been to reduce the power of the North upon the South (reduced dependency) and enhance the power of South upon the North (counterpentration). But his fascination with Western literary and philosophical classics has sometimes led him to use a Western classic to illuminate an African experience. Quite early he wrote an article entitled "Edmund Burke and Reflections on the Revolution in the Congo." In reality Burke had written about the French Revolution in the eighteenth century. Ali Mazrui used Burkean ideas about the basics of society and governance and applied them to the Congolese situation in the early 1960s. Mazrui's article had quite an impact on conservative circles in the United States.[11]

Mazrui has also written about "Rousseau and Intellectualized Populism in Africa" (co-author G.F. Engholm).[12]

Nor must we forget that Ali Mazrui's inaugural lecture when he was first appointed full professor at Makerere University in Uganda was entitled "Ancient Greece in African Political Thought" (1967). All these are illustrations of Mazrui using Western classics to illuminate the African experience.[13]

When Ali Mazrui Africanizes such Western classics as Burke, Rousseau, Aristotle, and Shakespeare, is he c ontributing to Africa's intellectual dependency? Or is he applying his strategy of domestication, which is part of his process of reducing dependency? In the ultimate analysis, he may be doing *both*!

In 1990, Ali Mazrui published his book *Cultural Forces in World Politics*.[14] It was Mazrui's second most ambitious book on culture on the global scale. His first one was *A World of Federation of Cultures: An African Perspective* (New York: Macmillan Press, 1976).

One meeting point between his African concerns and his global concerns has been his interest in language. In the 1970s he published a book entitled *The Political Sociology of the English Language*, which has been widely quoted. In the 1990s he went into academic partnership with Professor Alamin M. Mazrui, a relative at Ohio State University. Together they have so far published two books – *The Power of Babel: Language and Governance* in the *African Experience* (1998) and before that *The Political Culture of Language: Swahili, Society and the State* (1996).

Between Islam and Conflict-Resolution

With regard to Mazrui's impact on Islamic studies in the United States, some have traced the origins to his television series *The Africans: A Triple Heritage* (1986). By doing research on Islam in Africa, Mazrui reactivated his wider interest in the Islamic religion and in Islamic civilization. Moreover, the television series' Muslim viewers – who had previously thought of Mazrui on as an Africanist – suddenly discovered an Islamic side to Mazrui, both as a person and as a scholar. In the United States this resulted in the growth of a whole new academic constituency for Mazrui as different Muslim organizations turned to him. They invited him initially as a public speaker, but later he was called upon to be a member of Governing Boards of different associations and institutions. By the year 2000 Ali Mazrui was the Chair of the Center for the Study of Islam and Democracy; a member of the Board of the American Council; a member of The Board of the Center of Muslim-Christian Understanding, Georgetown University; and a member of the International Board of Advisors of the Graduate School of Islamic and Social Sciences, Leesburg, Virginia. Outside the United States Ali Mazrui was also a member of the Board of the Oxford Centre for Islamic Studies, Oxford, England.

At the State University of New York at Binghamton and at the Graduate School of Islamic and Social Sciences, Ali Mazrui has taught such courses as "Islamic in World Affairs," "Islam in Global Africa and the Black World," and "Islam and the West." Indeed, for about four years (1996-2000), Ali Mazrui served as Ibn Khaldūn Professor-at-Large at Graduate School of Islamic and Social Sciences, Leesburg, Virginia.

Apart from *The Africans: A Triple Heritage*, Ali Mazrui has not published a book specifically about Islam. However, he has published articles about Islam in such journals as *Foreign Affairs* (New York), *Harvard international Review* (Cambridge, Mass.), *International Affairs* (London), *The American Journal of Islamic Social Sciences, African Arts* (University of California, Los Angeles and Berkeley), and the *Oxford Journal of Islamic Studies* (Oxford, England).

Ali Mazrui's interests in conflict has been combined with a fascination for conflict-resolution. As indicated earlier, his first book published in the United States was entitled *Towards a Pax Africana* (1967) – posing the question of who was to keep the peace in Africa now that Pax Britannica and its European imperial sisters were withdrawing.

Within two years after *Towards a Pax Africana* Ali Mazrui published his collection of essays entitled *Violence and Thought: Essays on Social Tensions in Africa* (1969). The book included the following chapters:

> Chapter 5. Conflict and the Integrative Process
> Chapter 9. Thoughts on Assassinations in Africa
> Chapter 10. The Monarchical Tendency in African Political Culture
> Chapter 14. On Revolution and Nakedness
> Chapter 15. Political Sex
> Chapter 16. Sacred Suicide[15]

Mazrui's fascination with different varieties of violence continued until his controversial Reith Lectures for both the British Broadcasting Corporation in 1979. In his sixth lecture he recommended nuclear proliferation in Africa as a way of shocking the nuclear Big Powers to give up nuclear weapons altogether.[16]

At least as controversial was his recommendation in the 1990s that stronger African states should be prepared to "recolonize" temporarily weaker African countries whose state-institutions had collapsed. He suggested that Tanganyika had recolonized Zanzibar in the wake of the Zanzibar revolution of 1964 and created the United Republic of Tanzania. More defensible was Tanzania's temporary occupation of Uganda in 1979 to get rid of Idi Amin. Should Nigeria have temporarily recolonized Sierra Leone in the 1990s? Was there temporary colonization of Rwanda by Uganda in 1994 through proxies in a bid to end the anti-Tutsi genocide?

One of the important roles that Ali Mazrui has played in American higher education has been to raise uncomfortable questions, and initiate fundamental debates in classrooms as well as in media. Mazrui's "recolonization" thesis was first publicized through a syndicated article for the *Los Angeles Times*, and was then published worldwide and translated in many languages. The widely read English version appeared in the *International Herald Tribune* (Paris, dated August 4th, 1994).

A special kind of conflict and response has been Mazrui's attention to slavery and reparations. In 1992 Ali Mazrui and eleven others were "sworn in" by Africa's presidents to create a new body called Group of Eminent Persons on Africa's Reparations for Enslavement and Exploitation (GEP). The group elected Chief Moshood Abiola as its Chair. In June 1993 Abiola was elected President of Nigeria but never allowed by the military to assume office. Instead he was imprisoned and died in detention in 1998.

Ali A. Mazrui, Professor Jacob Ade-Ajayi of Ibadan University, and Ambassador Dudley Thompson of Jamaica have kept the reparations flame alive by having the issue debated every year at the annual meetings of the Africa Studies Association (ASA) of the United States. In the year 2000 they also involved a major African-American speaker at the ASA, Randall Robinson, whose Trans-Africa Forum (Washington DC) has adopted reparations for African Americans as its last crusade. Randall Robinson had himself just published a book entitled *The Debt* precisely on the issue of reparations.

In classroom situations, Ali Mazrui has provoked debates on what he calls "the triple heritage of African slavery – indigenous, Islamic, and Western." Mazrui was less impressed by Professor Henry Louis Gates Jr. of Harvard University and his television series Wonders of the African World. In a heated Internet debate in the United States, Mazrui accused Gates of blaming the trans-Atlantic slave trade primarily on Africans themselves, thus "letting the white man off the hook." Mazrui's critique of Gates' TV series remains the most highly publicized and most often quoted.

Ali Mazrui coined the phrase "the triple heritage" to describe Africa's three legacies of Africanity, Islam and the West. But he himself has been described as "a walking triple heritage," combining all those three legacies. His impact on higher education in the United States has indeed manifested all those three dimensions.

Notes

1   See *The African Condition: A Political Diagnosis* (London: Heinemann Educational Books and New York: Cambridge University Press, 1980).
2   *Transition* Magazine (Kampala) No.26, 1966. It has since been reproduced in the newly revived *Transition* (Cambridge, Massachusetts), No 75/76 1998.
3   See Ali Mazrui, *Cultural Forces in World Politics* (New Hampshire: Heinemann Educational Books and Oxford: James Currey Publishers, 1990), Chapter 3.
4   See Ali A. Mazrui, *On Heroes and Uhuru-Worship* (London: Longmans, 1967). See also Thomas Carlyle's *On Heroes, Hero-Worship and the Heroic in History* (1841) in which he argued, "The history of the World is but the biography of great men."
5   *Cultural Forces in World Politics* (1990), op. cit. Chapters 7 and 8.
6   A version of the lecture is published as Chapter 4 in Ali Mazrui's book, Cultural Forces in World Politics (Portsmouth, New Hampshire: Heinemann Educational Books and London: James Currey Publishers, 1990) pp. 83-101.
7   Ali A, Mazrui, *The Africans: A Triple Heritage* (Boston: Little, Brown and Company, 1986) p. 29.
8   Ibid, p.28
9   See Mazrui "Afrabia: Africa and the Arabs in the New World Order," UFAHAMU, Vol. XX No. 3 Fall 1992.
10 Ali A. Mazrui, The African Condition and the American Experience: A Tale of two Edens. A series of three Macmillan-Stewart lectures sponsored by the W. E. B. Du Bois

Institute, Harvard University, March 6-8, 2000. The lectures may be published by Oxford University Press in 2001.
11   Ali A. Mazrui, "Edmund Burke and Reflections on the Revolution in France," *Comparative Studies in Society and History*, (Ann Arbor, Michigan) 1963.
12   Ali A. Mazrui and G. F. Engholm, The Review of Politics, Vol. 30, No. 1, January 1968.
13   Versions of the essays on Rousseau and Ancient Greece are published as chapters in Mazrui, *Political Values and the Educated Class in Africa* (Berkley and Los Angeles: University of California Press, 1978).
14   *Cultural Forces in World Politics* (New Hampshire: Heinemann Educational Books and Oxford: James Currey Publishers, 1990).
15   *Violence and Thought*, (New York: Humanities Press, 1969, reprinted 1971).
16   Ali A. Mazrui, *The African Condition: A Political Diagnosis* (New York: Cambridge University Press, 1980).

12

Salient Features in Mazrui's Thought on Education in Africa:
Critical Reflections[1]*

N'Dri T. Assié-Lumumba[2]
&
Tukumbi Lumumba-Kasongo[3]

Introduction: General Issues and Main Objectives

In "Pretender to Universalism: Western Culture in Globalization Age," Ali Mazrui relates his experience at Oxford University where his Yugoslav professor from Montenegro articulated the historical observation of "the importance of power in universalizing the culture of the powerful".[4]

One the most effective instruments for the actualization of the universalizing mission of the powerful has historically been education as a social institution. Western European countries that have shaped the contemporary world have forced their permanent mark on other societies through education. The development of educational systems reflects the journey of societies throughout history with critical junctures and moments.

Many analysts of African predicaments in the 20th and this first decade of the 21st Century, especially when they consider European/industrial societies and their achievements as a reference, tend to use a cross-sectional approach

---

1 * This chapter was originally published in *Public Intellectuals and the Politics of Global Africa: Essays in Honor of Ali A. Mazrui*, ed. Seifuden Adem (London: Adonis and Abbey Publishers Ltd. 2011, pp 173- 186) and is reprinted here with the permission of the original authors, Editor, and the publisher.

that does not capture the long processes, trials and errors, and even attainments among these European countries in their development processes and journey. There is a tendency to overlook some of their critical advantages: they benefited from their internal evolution. Their educational institutions embody this evolution whose path expanded to engulf African societies in the context of colonization.

In Europe, the development of centers of higher learning in the Middle Ages constituted the initial foundation of modern universities that in Mazrui's analysis constitutes the equivalent to command centers of multinational corporations. Many African institutions in the medieval period[5] and the nascent European universities of the Middle Ages emerged out of the leadership of religious institutions: Christianity in Europe and Islam in Africa. Indeed, universities created in specific locations in Medieval Europe shared then a common religious authority; the Catholic Church.

The influence of the Church and the religious content of formal education grew and finally, by the end of the eleventh and twelfth centuries, the goal of education became less one-dimensional and the Church was no longer the sole social system which controlled education for the use of its outcome. At that time, there was a certain "urban renaissance" with a "small local bourgeoisie" that understood the relationship between education and the economic system that they were controlling. In its search for an education that would help produce the needed human resources to meet their growing economic needs, the "small bourgeoisie" contributed significantly to create more schools for the acquisition of the knowledge and skills that they needed and that were not included in domains within the sphere of control of the Church. The domains that needed specialized knowledge included trade, administration, and law. This is the context in which more schools were created, many under the initiative of political authorities such as kings, princes, and authorities in the then newly growing urban centers. The graduates of these schools had employment opportunities offered by the socioeconomic structure of the time. This constituted a key factor that triggered the motivation for wanting an education and the development of the urban middle class.

When the process of the development of the universities started in Western Europe, this sub-region was confronted with problems of underdevelopment and social fragmentation in the war-prone nations in the making. However, the social and religious groups that founded and shaped the universities did not spell out a clear societal mission to cure the social ills in a way that can be compared to the unanimous agreement among leaders and the populations throughout Africa at the time of independence, in creating the university with a development mission. In fact, a perceived or actual initial social disconnect led to the notion of the university as an "ivory tower" wherein reflection becomes an end in itself. In African societies of the era of independence, leaders and common people in urban and rural communities, the overwhelming majority of whom did not receive any type of European formal education under colonial rule, saw in the European university, located in the European metropolis or newly built on African soil, the instrument par excellence for individual upward mobility and societal/national progress. However, unlike in Europe where the universities were mostly the product of European internal evolution despite wars in post-colonial Africa, the European model was very much epistemologically and structurally alien.

Due to the sheer magnitude and long period of external interventions, from the cataclysmic rupture that started with the Trans-Atlantic enslavement and lasted centuries and continued through the informal colonization to decades of formal colonial rule, African institutions generally were forced to halt the genuine pursuit of their historical process development. By the time of independence, African countries had been caught in the tangled web in which Western education, especially the University, was set to play a critical role in the social and economic reproduction. Thus, in spite of, and perhaps because of, the expectation from the Africans to use this externally a double-sided sword. The ensuing issues constitute an important component of Mazrui's analysis of African contemporary education, a selection of which is presented in this essay.

What are our intellectual perspectives in this chapter? We are not interested in singular or personal stories about, and/or on, Ali A. Mazrui, though some of these stories may help depict his intellectual and education trajectory. Our intellectual guidelines are shaped by structural historical paradigms in that Mazrui's thought and works on education are examined and understood as part of a broad system of thought and how this system has been shaped and conditioned by many historical and contemporary national and international factors as they all relate to world system.

Based on the philosophical assumptions of historical structuralism, which project the relationship among social phenomena as parts of the systems, and subsystems, and their historical development, we argue that formal and non-formal education as arenas of learning and a process of acquiring and producing knowledge and skills is not an autonomous sector from the system of power, ritual of changes, or actual process of change and socialization at individual and social levels. To try to do justice to Mazrui's elaborate and complex ideas on education, it is necessary to localize them in historical, sociological, and political contexts through which these thoughts become more relevant and appreciated. Furthermore, the contexts provide several layers of sociology and history that are parts of the world system, namely, regional (African/developing world), international, (transnational institutions and cross national) and Western/industrial countries. Within these contexts, we have examined Mazrui's thoughts on education on broad generalized views and also on African regional perspective. History and culture link these perspectives in a dynamic way.

Influential Factors and General Characteristics of Ali Mazrui's Perspective on Education

Like many other public intellectuals, Ali A. Mazrui, an all-rounded African academic and Renaissance scholar, strongly believes in power of education in transforming the world and its value systems as the instruments of positive change. The big question is what kind of education can contribute to the progressive reconstruction of the African societies, states, and their political economies? While formal education should be, in principle, an ally or instrument for social progress, such an education has also been part of the African problematic. Drawing on selected works of Ali A. Mazrui, we reflected work on these dialectical relationships between negative and positive dimensions of education as projected in the Africa's search for solutions to its problems and Africa's underdevelopments.

Although it is difficult or not even probably fair to reduce Mazrui's works with some simple intellectual characterizations without either offending him or those who agree or disagree with his ways of thinking or perceiving the world, we think that identifying some dominant characteristics in his way of thinking is a legitimate process through which we can follow the thread of his thoughts and compare them over a given historical period.

Based on his spectacular cumulative academic professional experiences and his visibility in the world affairs, we have characterized Mazrui to be essentially a liberal, cultural globalist thinker and critic with strong African nationalist views and perspectives shaped by three cultural heritages-African traditions, Islam, and Western values. For him, culture is about power or power of ideas[6]. Even some of his early writings and talks before he became much more widely known for his 1986 television programs[7] as a commentator within British Broadcasting Corporation (BBC) in London in the 1960 s, while studying at Oxford University, reflect his enthusiasm and commitment to explain African events in Kiswahili culture and language. Since his tenure at the University of Makerere in the 1960s, he has been explaining and promoting an understanding of the complexity of interactions between these three worlds and their respective significance in the contemporary world, especially in Africa. His explanations have been far from being monolithic and intellectually narrow.

As it is well known, anyone or any institution that controls the mind, intellect, and reason of a person or a people, is very likely to control their social destiny as a human being and their way of imagining their world. Mazrui is among very few world personalities in the 20th Century and in the beginning of this 21st Century who have clearly emancipated themselves from the world of ignorance through the highest quality of exceptional capacity to imagine and to interpret the world with intellectual consistency, a sense of historical direction and a deep commitment to explaining the global values in the global humanity. His contributions to innovate and invent elements of the new paradigms about education in the world and in Africa in its broad diversity are well known. He is of the view that, European Education acquired by the Africans, regardless of the initial intention, processes, and inadequacy, can be a tool for emancipation, affirmation, and freedom to imagine a different and better world in which the Africans can and do contribute to not only the design for change in Africa, but also they play significant roles on the world stage. As actors they contribute to frame the paradigms of change. Leaders such as Kwame Nkrumah and Mazrui himself illustrate this view.

Furthermore, the richness of Mazrui's views and thoughts on education reflects a strong continuity and consistency that can be located in the culture of his upbringing as part of nobility in Mombasa and his British colonial experience in Kenya. His education at the University of Manchester, Columbia University, and Oxford University, and also in his professional development as a distinguished professor in many universities, including the University of Chicago, University of Makerere in Uganda, University of Michigan, Cornell University and the University of Binghamton in the United States, University of Jos in Nigeria, to cite only these few, chair, director, and Chancellor (the Jomo Kenyatta University of Agriculture and Technology in Kenya), he learned a great deal from the American and British different curricular organizations. Furthermore, his educational experiences in the Anglo-Saxon and English speaking world and Swahilipone countries, complemented with lectures in many parts of the world, have shaped his perspectives on education as an arena of liberal thinking, freedom of expression and, as indicated above, instruments for influencing world views.

Often controversial, firm in his positions and yet flexible and tolerant about differing views, Mazrui is a gentleman in the most vigorous debates in profound intellectual disagreements. He has offered his views and thoughts to various world consistencies on probably every single aspect of education that one can imagine, since the middle of the 20th Century, from primary, secondary, and tertiary education to technical and political levels, from Antiquity to the New Information and Communication Technologies. Thus, logistically and practically, it is beyond the space of this particular work to expand on most of his historical and political thoughts, with pedagogical perspectives, on education. It is necessary to contextualize our perspective in reiterating our main objectives, which are to critically reflect on some broad themes or topics with the aim of identifying and depicting his theoretical and philosophical perspectives on education and its policy implications. We believe that in so doing, we are able to contextualize his views on education within his general social and political thought and his perspectives on the role of education in progressive change, particularly in Africa.

An Overview of Education

Ali Mazrui's general views on education are clearly articulated in his book entitled: "A World Federation of Cultures: An African Perspective"[8]. He writes to World Council on Science and Culture and states that:[9]

> A world which is governed on the basis of a federated system of cultures has to put a special premium on education and training. The whole quest for cultural convergence and shared pool of values necessitates some convergence among processes of education and socialization. Membership on the World Council would be first, by affiliation to a world language; second by region; third, by cooptation by the council itself for reasons of special expertness on specific aspects education; and fourth, by state.

The notion of defining and locating education in a federated system of power and culture is central to the way Ail Mazrui perceives education at large.

Although depending on the subjects or themes under investigation, Mazrui's approaches in education have been essentially multidisciplinary with some tendencies that have been influenced more by anthropological and ethnographic paradigms than by classical discipline of political science, for instance. The European education system brought to the colonial cultures and people significant aspects of openness based on sciences and universal laws. But such an education has its limitations and strengths in its ethos and its objective: colonization of the world. Colonial ideology and enterprise have on aim: control in pursuit of the interest of the colonial masters. Thus, it is also destined to weaken other types of education.

Education is an arena of learning about innovative ideas, thoughts, and skills. It is also a place in which many different ideas and thoughts meet. However, in the colonial context, it is not a space of meeting of ideas. Rather it is a site of sheer and unchallenged power and intolerance that nurtures social reproduction as defined by the colonial powers. Mazrui has not had any problem comparing Edmond Burke, John Locke, Thomas Jefferson, with Kwame Nkrumah, Nnamdi Azikiwe, etc. However, in his major work on "The African Predicament and American Experience,"[10] he cited extensively Western scholars with more liberal perspectives but did not cite many of the contemporary nationalist radical leftist African scholars such as Samir Amin, Claude Ake, Georges Nzongola-Ntalaja, Bernard Magubane, Albert Memmi, etc. Nevertheless, in many other writings, he cited scholars from Marxist and socialist traditions. On the same logic, in the specific book cited above, he does not advocate revolution as a way for radically transforming the African society at large. Yet in his book on "Heroes and Uhuru-Worship: Essays on Independent Africa,"[11] he extensively cited African radical leftists and discussed at length the major ideologies such as Marxism, Leninism, Socialism, and Capitalism which have been adopted in Africa and their impact on the African ideological and policy choices for development.

The Western education is the motto of "modern civilization" which was organized by the missionaries and the colonial administrations. The role of modern education is a medium for global cultural convergence in the intellectual sphere.[12] This education, which was colonial in context, was transmitted through socialization and acculturation (a transcultural phenomenon). It implies the diffusion of particular values, techniques, and institutions and their modifications under different conditions.[13] It should be noted that only selected Western values and techniques were transmitted to Africa as Ali Mazrui stated:[14]

> Of special importance in the homogenization of the intellectual culture of the world is the role of modern education. The impact of the West on the rest of the world has been particularly critical in this regard. The technological triumph of the Western world gave its system of education almost universal prestige. Cultures, which previously trained and socialized their children in radically different ways saw themselves drawn irresistibly toward the Western approach to education.

Issues on African Education

In his Distinguished Africanist Speech Award at the 38th Annual Meeting of the African Studies Association held on November 3-6, 1995, in Orlando, Florida, USA, Ali Marui re-affirmed his commitment to the studies of Africa as he stated:[15]

> What makes a great Africanist? He or she needs a commitment to Africa, a capacity to interpret it, and a spirit of congeniality toward fellow Africans and Africanists. These are the basics of the Africanist-paradigms.

He has written on most aspects of the African life, states, international relations, cultures, nationalism, political theory, elites, religion, etc. However, a few of the themes through which he has explained Africa, Africans, and the diaspora fully with passion have been on 'The Global Africans'[16] and 'The Triple Heritage'[17] (1986).

As already stated, Ali Mazrui's analysis on the above topics and more has been shaped by a philosophy of education organized through the triple heritage traditions associated with the dominant worldviews of Islam, Europe/Christianity, and Africanity. The civilizations that are based on this heritage are unique, but they also complement one another in a system of acculturation by choice or by coercion that has characterized the contemporary world.

Although Ali Mazrui recognized the technical and instrumental values of European education toward the definitions and the advancement of the global culture and civilization, he has also been critical of such an educational system. First of all, only some Western values and techniques were transmitted in Africa. That is to say, that the introduction was based on some selected objectives contained in the so-called "civilizing mission." Second of all, Western education was the motto of the "modern civilization." This is to say that through formal education, Africans acquire the values of the dominant capitalist/Western culture. And third of all, Mazrui noted the clash between the city of God as interpreted by the colonial powers and the city of man (sic) which represented the secular dimensions of the colonialism. As a result, he pointed out the widespread cultural schizophrenia in Africa. This phenomenon is the reflection of the tense ambivalence which arises out of the interplay between dependency and aggression in the process of acculturation.[18] As he stated:[19]

> The technocultural gap has continued to haunt educational systems in Africa. Secular skills were given a religious infrastructure. And when the infrastructure was rejected, there were no alternative supportive values for the new secular ambitions. Many schools taught the virtues of obedience instead of the ethic of initiative. They taught fear of God instead of love of country; they taught the evils of acquisition instead of the strategy of reconciling personal ambition with social obligation. Religious indoctrination was paramount; political education was anathema yet the schools were also intended to help create viable modern societies.

Although the outcome of such an education is more complex and unpredictable than what the colonial and post-colonial powers (or the African political elites) intended to produce, formal education has been an instrument of both processes of decolonization and colonization.

Salient Features in Mazrui's Thought on Education in Africa

It is worth emphasizing the fact that given the centrality of education, it constitutes a crosscutting theme in Marui's works in general. Thus, his thoughts on education are articulated in works that have education as the specific topic as well as numerous publications and other works that include considerable components on education without education either being mentioned in the title or meant to be the focus. Of particular relevance among his works that focus on education, is his seminal book "Political Values and the Educated Class in Africa."[20] In Part Two, entitled "Expanding Intellectual Horizons," he articulates the conflict embedded in the received Western education in the African society as he wrote:[21]

> Western education in Africa came with new intellectual horizons, as well as the seeds of intellectual dependence. The new intellectual horizons were a form of liberation, a new capacity to transcend ancestral ways. But there was also the risk of imitation and blind deference, a tendency to adore western civilization and all that it was supposed to stand for. However, there was in addition a safety valve of potentially decisive implications. This was Africa's cultural nationalism. Concurrent with expanding horizons and reduced indigenous self-confidence was the confused emergence of African cultural nationalism.

A chapter of this book entitled: "The African University as a Multinational Corporation," was published earlier as an article in the "Harvard Educational Review", with the subtitle 'Problems of Penetration and Dependency.'[22] While Mazrui has been considered at times by some intellectuals as a "conservative scholar," this piece placed him square in the Dependency/World Systems theory.

In the articulation of the arguments framed in the dependency school of thought, African leaders (politicians, policymakers) and chief academic officers of higher education institutions are analyzed as having limited power. They accept decisions made in the centre through the technical advisers from industrial countries and experts from international organizations. Focusing on higher education in the aforementioned work, Mazrui compares African universities to subsidiaries of multinational corporations, as they are conceptualized, designed, set up, and operated like extensions of European universities. The fundamental decision adopted in the West, and at times even details and daily routines of Western institutions, are emulated in African countries and their institutions. As multinational cultural subsidiaries, they "naturally" follow the dictates of parent institutions from the West in general, including former colonial powers in Western Europe and their industrial extensions, primarily in North America.

Mazrui[23] articulates the paradox embedded in the role of formal education, especially universities, as an effective instrument that provides the impetus for political liberation within African countries while at the same time perpetuating cultural dependence. In his view, the higher the Africans climb on the Western educational ladder with the expectation of transferring the qualification to the occupational ladder for upward social mobility, the more culturally dependent on the West they become. He stated that, paradoxically, "the same education which has produced nationalists eager to end colonial rule and to establish African self-government has also perpetuated cultural colonialism."[25].

The process of dependence started when African universities were modeled after institutions of former colonial powers, with some being formally attached to parent universities Belgium, Great Britain, and France and their respective extension in other parts of the world. Critical matters of pedagogy, instruction, evaluation, and policy are decided or approved by the parent institution in Europe. Furthermore, African universities were responsible for producing the appropriate human resources and "redefining the market through acculturation"[26] for multinational corporations, thus serving to consolidate economic dependence rather than independence. In the context of the economic and political crises that triggered in the 1980s the phenomenon of massive migration labeled as "brain drain" this argument had been indisputably validated.

Going beyond a simple analysis to an assessment of the nature of the problems Africa faces at large, in "Towards Diagnosing and Treating Cultural Dependency: The Case of the African University,"[27] makes some proposals towards the possible solutions. He argued that Africa will be successful in building a new society that can promote social progress, only if the objective conditions are critically examined and the hindering factors acknowledged and properly dealt with. He articulated the hindering factors embedded in the cultural dependency syndrome. He identified seven functions of culture whose social function is to provide: (i) "lenses of perception and cognition." Indeed, he argues that people's worldview is not neutral. Rather, it is rooted in and shaped by "cultural paradigms"; (ii) "motives for human behavior"; (iii) "criteria of evaluation"; (iv) "a basis of identification"; (v) a common "mode of communication" with language as the core and the "most elaborate system"; (vi) a "basis of stratification"; and finally (vii) "a system of production and consumption."[28] Mazrui identified a "new international cultural order."[29] Characterized by structural inequality, Africa's location at its margin and its dependence on the former colonial powers which constitute the centers of command. Education and more particularly universities constitute a channel of cultural transfer.

With the consistent concern for the need to search for solutions, in his 1975 article, Mazrui,[30] proposed three strategies for development: domestication, diversification, and counter-penetration.

In the domestication strategy, he argues that the initial task of decolonizing modernity must be to balance the influence on university policy with that of the West through local participation. In order to domesticate African educational systems successfully, he proposes three critical areas that require redefinition:

(i) University admission requirements and their implications for primary and secondary curricula;
(ii) Criteria for faculty recruitment; and
(iii) University organization.

One of his main arguments regarding diversification is the imperative of dissociating the quest for modernization from the continued dependence of Western/former colonial powers as the sole external sources that African countries and institutions can learn from. In his views, the diversification strategy of any cultural content is an important process toward modernization. As he argues.[31] "In terms of culture, reliance on one external reference group is outright dependency; reliance on a diversity of external civilizations may be the beginning of autonomy."

The third and final counter-penetration strategy calls for an integration of African cultural content as a sine qua non for the successful domestication of modernity and the diversification.

In the contemporary world of increasing global stature, the African population that has the responsibility should have an interest in creating the developmental momentum to cross a desirable threshold of social progress. In this process, Africa must also include those who are part of what Mazrui has referred to as "Global Africa." Thus the contribution of the African Diaspora, both the historic and recent branches of the African family tree, merits some attention, precisely because the contemporary component of this group is predominantly the product of higher education. Thus, in "Pan-Africanism and the intellectuals: Rise, decline and revival," Mazrui argues that as the origins of modern black intellectual traditions and those of Pan-Africanism are intertwined, African 'intellectuals and educated minds' have the capacity 'to conceive and construct an alternative social paradigm.'[32]

Regarding the inclusion and actual use of African culture, Mazrui proposes both daring and innovative solutions. For instance, the "The Power of

Babel: Languages and Governance in the African Experience," Mazrui in the chapter entitled 'The Language Planning and Gender Planning', proposes the use of African languages in conjunction with the 'relevant' European language. With the exception of a few southern African countries, as a result of different historical and contemporary factors, the African female population is under-represented in the European-received educational systems, with even more negligible proportions at the higher education level. As formal education has been the official criterion and objective factor for access to political positions and occupations in the "modern sector" of the economy, Mazrui proposes innovative ways to include the educational marginalized segments of the population. Thus, he proposes, for instance, the introduction of African languages in the sphere of political power and deliberations, as means for inclusion of women so that they can have their voices heard and participate in a substantive way to governance.

Conclusion

The late Félix Houphouet-Boigny of Côte d'Ivoire, *whom* many of us criticized for some of his questionable roles from the end of the struggle for independence to the neo-colonial context, remembered the global contradictions, the advantages that the colonial power acquired in the process of their development and the constraints of African countries. Thus, he stated in one of his public speeches, "the impulse of European development in the contemporary period was due to its intrusion into other societies, countries, regions, and its ability to forge means of identification of the totality of the resources these societies and decision to use them to the advantage of Europe." For him, African societies and countries can advance if they find ways to wage their own conquest of other societies.

Mazrui's idea that Africa should influence other cultures in more deliberate and decisive ways is, to a certain extent, close to this idea. Thus, Africans need to domesticate foreign ideas, and create a symbiotic system by selectively and purposefully learning from various external sources while simultaneously influencing others. In his idea of counter-conquest, formal education, and especially higher education, plays a major role as a key social institution that triggers migration, knowledge production and labor circulation globally. Mazrui's life, his mastery of the English language while solidly in command of the Kiswahili, his role of a world public intellectual, all embody and actualize his idea of domestication, diversification, and counter-penetration on the global scale.

Notes

1. Ali A. Mazrui, "Pretender to Universalism: Western Culture in Globalization Age," In *Globalization and Civilizations: Are they Forces in Conflict?* Mazrui, Ali A., Dikirr, Patrick M, and Kafrawi, Shalahudin (eds.), New York: Global Scholarly Publications, 2008 p. 9.
2. Cornell University; *Université de Cocody*; and CEPARRED.
3. Wells College; Cornell University; *Université de Cocody*; Suffolk University; and CEPARRED.
4. The first draft of this paper was presented at the Symposium in Honor of Professor Ali A. Mazrui on the occasion of his 75th birthday: Reflections on Ali A. Mazrui's Legacy: Global Africa's Triple Heritage at New York State African Studies Association (NYASA) 2008 Annual Conference entitled Africa in the 21st Century: Reconstruction or Re-Colonization, Cornell University, Africana Studies and Research Center, Ithaca, New York March 28-29, 2008.
5. For further information about the African universities in the Medieval Period, see Diop, Cheikh Anta, *Pre-Colonial Black Africa*, New York, Lawrence Hill and Company, 1987.
6. Ali A. Mazrui and Alamin Mazrui, *The Power of Babel: Language and Governance in the African Experience* (Oxford, England: J. Currey; Chicago: University of Chicago Press, 1998), p. 25.
7. His television work includes the widely discussed 1986 series, *The Africans: A Triple Heritage*. This book became a best seller in Britain and was recommended by various Book Clubs in the USA.
8. Ali A. Mazrui, *A World Federation of Cultures: An African Perspective* (New York: The Free Press, 1976).
9. Ibid., p. 483.
10. Ali A. Mazrui, *The African Predicament and the American Experience: A Tale of Two Edens* (Westport, Connecticut and London: Praege, 2000).
11. Ali A. Mazrui, *Heroes and Uhuru-worship: Essays on Independent Africa* (London, Longmans, 1967).
12. Mazrui, *A World Federation of Cultures*, p. 356.
13. Ibid., p. 356.
14. Ibid.
15. Ali A. Mazrui, 1995, p. 4.
16. See Omari Kokole (ed.) *The Global African: A Portrait of Ali Mazrui* (New Jersey, Trenton: Africa World Press, Inc, 1998).
17. Ali A. Mazrui, *The Africans: A Triple Heritage* (New York; Little Brown and Co., and London: BBC, 1986).
18. Mazrui, *A World Federation of Cultures*, p. 357.
19. Ibid., p. 358.
20. Ali A. Mazrui, *Political Values and the Educated Class in Africa* (Berkeley, CA, University of California Press, 1978).
21. Ibid., p. 8.
22. Ali A. Mazrui, "The African University as a Multinational Corporation: Problems of Penetration and Dependency," *Harvard Educational Review*, Vol. 45, pp. 191-210, 1975.
23. Ibid.
25. Mazrui, "The African University as a Multinational Corporation", p. 194.

26 Ibid., p. 198.
27 Ali A. Mazrui, "Towards Diagnosing and Treating Cultural Dependency: The Case of the African University," *International Journal of Educational Development*, Vol. 12(2), pp. 95-111.
28 Ibid., p. 96.
29 Op cit.
30 Mazrui, "The African University as a Multinational Corporation", p. 191-210.
31 Ibid., p. 206.
32 Ali A. Marui, "Pan-Africanism and the Intellectuals: Rise, Decline and Revival," In *African Intellectuals: Rethinking Politics, Language, Gender, and Development* Mkandawire T. (ed.), Dakar: CODESRIA, 2005, p. 56.

13

The Trial of Ali Mazrui's Trilogy, Scholarship and the Making of a Public Intellectual in Africa:
Revisiting His Legacy in the World of Knowledge

Maurice N. Amutabi

Introduction

I have borrowed the title of my chapter from Ali A. Mazrui's only work of fiction entitled *The Trial of Christopher Okigbo*, on the involvement of academician, poet and scholar Christopher Ifekandi Okigbo who was killed during Biafra war as he defended Igbo's interests. In the novel, Ali Mazrui puts Okigbo on trial for abdicating his responsibility as a scholar and dying for parochial and narrow Ibo interests which were local and rather peripheral in the larger Nigerian nationalist concerns (Mazrui, 1971). My contention is that Ali Mazrui himself was very much on trial much of his life, right from his time as a child to the time he died. The trial took many angles, from his tribulations as a young man being regarded as a failure for getting Third Division in Overseas Cambridge School certificate examinations and being denied opportunity to continue with his education in Kenya, to being denied opportunity to work in Kenya, where he was regarded as a radical intellectual. It was only former President Mwai Kibaki who debunked that thinking and appointed Mazrui as the Chancellor of Jomo Kenyatta University of Agriculture and Technology (JKUAT). Mazrui did not disappoint and carried JKUAT through an important transition from the time when Presidents appointed Vice Chancellors and deputy Vice Chancellors to competitive interview process.

There is no Kenyan intellectual who generated a lot of controversies in public the way Ali Mazrui did. He wrote in purely academic platforms but also popular press. He appeared on TV and radio speaking about new ideas and offering his recommendations, even if they were controversial. We came to know Ali Mazrui as a controversial figure, who often attracted a lot of attention from fellow intellectuals and the media. There are many greenhorns who made a name for themselves for taking on the great scholar. He was perhaps one of the most influential intellectuals to come from Africa in the last hundred years, mentioned alongside Cheikh Anta Diop, Wole Soyinka, Chinua Achebe, Ngũgĩ wa Thiong'o among other great intellectuals. His public intellectual debates were phrased in the most attractive and academic language that made him always to emerge the winner. Wole Soyinka, Archie Mafeje, William Ochieng' are just few of some of the intellectuals who took on Ali Mazrui and often lost badly.

The Ali Mazrui and Wole Soyinka debate was perhaps one of the fiercest and which defined a lot of things on the Continent. The debate was on USA Africa Dialogue list serve moderated by Toyin Falola. It all started with *Mazrui's* uncomplimentary critique of Henry Louis Gates TV Series "Wonders of the African World" which was being cheered and celebrated despite its racist and condescending overtones. Mazrui was accused by Wole Soyinka for being an interested party because he had also started his own series the "Africans: Triple Heritage" which ran on British Broadcasting Corporation TV. Wole Soyinka said many unkind words about Mazrui in a debate that attracted a lot of attention. Ali Mazrui debated Archie Mafeje and William Ochieng', among others. He coined interesting phrases such as Pax Africana, and Nkrumah, the Leninist Czar. He also made controversial proposals such as the need for Africa to colonize itself. He also discussed issues of identity and was at his most vulnerable when he sought to present Islam as an African religion and his attempts to sanitize Arab past in Africa, especially on slavery and slave trade have always surfaced when Mazrui's legacy is examined in totality. These are the germane issues that this article will address. I read and admired Ali A. Mazrui's intellectual life. As a student at the University of Nairobi, University of Florida, and University of Illinois, I had time and opportunity to meet Mazrui in person and share with him many intellectual platforms. I asked him many questions and he also asked me questions, at least on four occasions. My essay will provide some reflections on my encounters with this great mind and some of the intellectual contributions he made to the world of scholarship in Africa and abroad.

My essay examines the life and times of Ali Mazrui from his days at Makerere University in the 1960s where his intellectual life started, to his life in the United States, at Binghamton University, where he became an intellectual global icon admired far and wide. There is no doubt that Mazrui was a public intellectual. Mazrui gave us one the definitions of an intellectual. He defined an intellectual as someone who is fascinated by ideas (Mazrui, 1969). He lived to this, by the way he coined words and phrases and the way he engaged the strong and mighty of this world, taking them on their commissions and omissions. Therefore, that he was a public intellectual is not debatable. What might be debatable is if his ideas transformed the public sphere the way they have been presented.

In conclusion, I argue that Mazrui contributed a lot to what we know today as multicultural and intellectual discourses on knowledge production. He wrote about political science, history, religious studies, linguistics, literature, film and cinema, gender and other development discourses. Some of his ideas were controversial and may not be justified in modern day world. For example, Mazrui's attempt to sanitize actions of Muslim extremists by painting them as rebels has attracted a lot of attacks on his neutrality. He has also been heavily criticised for proposing internal colonization for Africa, which driven largely by the desire for political stability more than other undercurrents. His calling for Ethiopia to colonize Eastern Africa, and South Africa to colonize Southern Africa and Nigeria to colonize West Africa has been regarded by some as 'Mazrui at his worst' whereas others think that his argument has been taken out of context.

Situating Ali A. Mazrui in Africa's Intellectual Realm

African scholars who rose to prominence in the 1960s and 1970s fought many battles against European and other hegemonies on knowledge production on Africa. They were pioneer scholars in many ways because they replaced White expatriate academics who dotted campuses across the African continent, creating dependency that was not easy to break. They went through racial and academic segregation, and fought hard to get their doctorates and academic space. Inevitably, these African pioneers had to do a lot of rethinking and unlearning what they had been taught in order to create new and unique African inventories of knowledge. Prof. Ali A. Mazrui belonged to this category and was one of the greatest intellectuals to ever emerge from the African continent. For almost five decades, Mazrui competed in the world of ideas with the best and proved that the African continent had original thinkers and philosophers, who could create new knowledge and provide intellectual leadership and deep analyses of phenomena. He studied in Europe, taught in Africa and North America, providing a triple heritage of sorts in his academic dalliance and affiliation to the three continents. In this essay, I seek to provide an intellectual examination of Prof. Ali Alamin Mazrui's contribution to the world as a public intellectual and rebel with a cause. My contention is that many of the ideas were dictated by the exigencies of the moment and influenced largely by the Cold War debates, predicated on capitalist and socialist expositions. Mazrui was seen by some scholars as a moderate, seeking to remain in the centre during the Cold War debates.

Postmodern scholars would regard Prof. Ali A. Mazrui as a postmodernist, who engaged in critical discourses, many of which were deconstructive (Nasong'o and Murunga, 2007). My contention is that Mazrui was a public intellectual because of the broad manner in which he debated and the type of topics he pursued, many of which often ignited massive public debates. For example, in 1992, he proposed that Ethiopia should colonize Eastern Africa, South Africa to colonize Southern Africa, and Nigeria to colonize West Africa in order to bring about political and economic stability and avoid balkanization of the continent into small states. Some scholars and analysts saw this as not only naive, but clear indication of Mazrui's position on the colonization process which he did not see as violent. Many did attack his Arab background due to his interpretation of the colonial project as innocent and normal. Some wondered how any scholar of sane mind would prescribe colonialism, even in extreme circumstances. They had misgivings about such recommendation due to the hegemonic manner in which colonial projects had been pursued before, especially the violent manner in which natives were displaced and exploited. Many natives suffered from colonial trauma many years after the fact.

In this article, I demonstrate how Mazrui ignited debates that attracted friends and enemies alike, in Kenya and abroad. For example, he argued that Islamic slavery was more benign and benevolent compared to Christian European powers, an argument that was vehemently opposed by scholars who accused Mazrui or being an apologist to Muslim slavery. They pointed out that what Mazrui did not do is reveal that slaves taken to Muslim countries were often castrated before being introduced as domestic labour in Muslim homes and harems, different from European slavery where black people were allowed to procreate in captivity hence the present huge populations of black people in the Western and Northern hemisphere. Mazrui's friends and admirers created a huge base full of Mazruiphilia while his enemies accumulated to create a big base of Mazruiphobia. Although I confess to belong to the former category, I understand that in order for me to pursue my objectives in this essay fairly, I should seek to be neutral, not to be seen to belong to any of these two groups, and whose debates I will be using in this essay to assess the life and times of Ali Mazrui as a public intellectual and a rebel. He was fearless and attacked his detractors without fear. But Mazrui had also an easy smile and was an active listener, who would not belittle anyone. He made you feel that your ideas were as important. He made you realize that he was listening to you. I met him more than ten times, and made sure that I took a picture with him each time we met. We were friends, but not close friends. I would say that I am closer to Prof. Alamin Mazrui, his nephew than I was to his fallen uncle, Prof. Ali A Mazrui.

Was Mazrui a rebel with a cause? Partly, yes because he was regarded by some as anti-western in his essays and commentaries, many of which tended to point fingers in their direction; and partly no, because he has sometimes been accused of having pandered to Muslim and Islamic interests. This is an issue that Zeleza brings out strongly in his book *Rethinking Africa's Globalization* (Zeleza, 2003: 339-42). Mazrui was also a rebel in many ways because he did not agree with all the Presidents in Africa, from Jomo Kenyatta and Daniel Moi of Kenya, Milton Obote and Idid Amin of Uganda, to Julius Nyerere of Tanzania and Kenneth Kaunda of Zambia. He honed his skills of being a rebel as a young don at Makerere University from where he attacked the manner in which the political big wigs ruled in their respective countries. He was critical of Kenyatta's pro-Western fraternizing and attacked Daniel Moi's autocratic structures that locked him out of any role in Kenya. Mazrui was unhappy with Obote and Amin for creating ethnic tensions in the country which occasioned breakup and instability of the state before Museveni rescued the state from collapse in 1986.

Encounter with Ali Mazrui and His Ideas

I joined the University of Nairobi as an undergraduate in 1986 and by then Prof. Ali A Mazrui was a household name in Kenya, regarded by many as a moderate, in the middle, at a time when many intellectuals were leftists and hardnosed Marxists. In the 1980s, Prof. Ali Mazrui was famous and already a famous name in Kenya cited and quoted extensively by students and lecturers in their academic discourses on campus. He was mentioned alongside academic luminaries and heavyweights such as Cheikh Anta Diop, Walter Rodney, Frantz Fanon, Samir Amin, Amilcar Cabral, Thandika Mkandawire, Wole Soyinka, Théophilus Obenga, Paul Tiyambe Zeleza, Toyin Falola, Issa Shivji, among others. He was one of the leading lights in the dependency debates of the 1970s (Mazrui, 1977). His name was dropped by every undergraduate or graduate student who wanted to make an impression or demonstrate that he belonged to the big league and was aware of contemporary debates and issues. In my 2007 article entitled "Intellectuals and the Democratization Process in Kenya," Prof. Mazrui was one of the public intellectuals I embellished and analysed, pointing out how he was one of the vitriolic critics of the Kenyatta and Moi regimes (Amutabi, 2007). He faulted former President Jomo Kenyatta and former President Daniel Moi's regimes for various excesses.

My earliest encounter with Ali Mazrui started in the 1970s through newspaper columns and articles when I was still in high school. I liked the way he wrote and particularly his language. He was clear and persuasive and not vitriolic in his responses and did not hit his opponents below the belt. He never got personal in many of his disagreements with his detractors. Ali Mazrui wrote in national newspapers and his essays raised a lot of debates, some of which lasted for weeks. I first met Ali Mazrui in 1986 in rather unusual circumstances. I was an undergraduate student at the University of Nairobi when his planned public lecture was cancelled at the eleventh hour, during those depressing KANU days, when all kinds of freedoms were curtailed. Despite the ban, Mazrui came to the University of Nairobi bookshop to 'buy' some books, and word immediately went round that the Great Scholar was on campus. There was a stampede from the library and a handful of us caught up with him at the parking lot between Gandhi Wing and the Geography building, just next to the Fountain of Knowledge. We appealed to the Vice Chancellor Prof. Philip Mbithi to allow the great scholar to address us at Taifa Hall, an appeal that was flatly declined. Prof. Mbithi told us that we were asking him to choose between his job and us having to listen to Mazrui. He chose his job which was a choice almost everyone who worked for the government at the time made in Moi's Kenya.

We persuaded Mazrui to give us an impromptu address in the University Way Car Park. For almost ten minutes, we listened to one of the greatest intellectuals that Kenya has ever produced, talking about democracy and human rights, using impressive vocabulary in flowery English. He told us how he had applied for teaching positions in Kenyan universities and how he had not even received a reply. He told us that some friends had whispered to him that the Kenyan government had vowed never to employ him because he was a radical and troublemaker. We could not help but admire the great scholar. He told us not to worry about a dictatorship because it has a lifespan and is not immortal. He told us not to agree to be silenced and do everything possible to regain democracy in Kenya. Speaking in parables and political metaphors, he told us how dictators such as Josef Stalin could not live forever. We asked him to return to Kenya and become our Vice Chancellor and he agreed, saying "...there is no problem, I would love to come back home. Just ask President Moi to appoint me and I will gladly come." The problem was passing this information to the appointing authority, but we did fantasize about life with Prof. Mazrui as our Vice Chancellor, perhaps having an address from the VC every Friday in Taifa Hall which was a better idea than watching re-runs of films such as *The Rise and Fall of Idi Amin* or *Cry Freedom*. During our reflections on the short address by Ali Mazrui, we wondered why he had been locked out of teaching in Kenya. Why would any government lockout such as great mind?

The fascinating thing about our encounter with Ali Mazrui in the Car Park was his courage and capacity to package his points and deliver them as punch lines as if he had rehearsed them. He attacked the regime in Kenya without making it so obvious and open. He made us begin to understand problems of institutional and structural failure in Kenya. His remarks drew our attention to the lack of social justice in the country and how the country suffered structural violence, in which we were also victims. We realized how the 'peace' we had in the country was an illusion, negative peace, a smokescreen for the intelligentsia to exploit the hoi polloi. Many years later, after listening to over ten of his speeches, I realized that those were issues that recurred in Mazrui's academic discourses from time to time and were so dear to him. He was concerned about the gap between the rich and the poor, and the political intolerance in the country, where those who differed with the state were detained or haunted into detention. Therefore, although he did not teach at the University of Nairobi, his views were highly respected. To be associated with the ideas of Ali Mazrui was to be seen to be greatly knowledgeable and familiar with the great intellectual debates of the time. Many student leaders quoted him at Kamukunjis (public rallies) and paraphrased his great lines. In my 2002 article entitled "Crisis and Student Protest in Universities in Kenya: Examining the Role of Students in National Leadership and Democratization Process" I paid great attention to his inspiration to many a Kenyan youth, particularly university students (Amutabi, 2002).

Proper articulation and issued based debating was the hallmark of Ali Mazrui's public engagement. As a public intellectual, he always sought to make his arguments with a view of wining some on his side. From the support that people voiced for some of his ideas, it did seem like he sometimes convinced some readers to join his side. Absent in his writing was the bare knuckle attack that we often witnessed as the University of Nairobi and among Kenyan intellectuals. Some of my earliest encounters with Ali A. Mazrui were second hand, through his commentaries in newspapers and magazines, books and some of his critics in popular media. One of the fiercest critics of Ali Mazrui was William Robert Ochieng' whose essays which were written in the 1970s and 1980s were published by the Jomo Kenyatta Foundation on three little sequels (Ochieng', 1984, 85, 88).

Many years later in 1994, I met Ali Mazrui again at the University of Florida, Gainesville, USA where I was at the time, a Ford Foundation governance fellow, where Mazrui was giving a public lecture on "The Wind of Change in Africa" at the invitation of the Center of African Studies. It was a full house. The hall was full to the brim, the type I saw when the late poet Maya Angelou and Cornell West had visited. I felt proud to be a Kenyan. That fall, another Kenyan, wildlife expert Dr. David Western had come to the University of Florida as well and spoke about eco-tourism and wildlife management in Africa but did not even get half of what Mazrui got for an audience. We sang 'Jambo Bwana' for Ali Mazrui but substituted Kenya with Africa. The Great Mwalimu just smiled as we milled round him, struggling to have a handshake with him. He was ours, all the way from Kenya, but Nigerians and other Africans insisted that he was also theirs, African. When he took to the podium, Prof. Mazrui was at his best, in his true elements. He was impressive and spoke so eloquently. He tore into all African dictators but surprised us by saying that some of them were going to survive the tide of the wind of change blowing across the continent due to lack of enough force, pull and push factors, to push them aside. He predicted that some would still be elected under democratic dispensation because of ethnicity. He was right and was vindicated on the account of rulers such as Paul Biya, Yowerri Museveni, and Daniel Moi serving two 'democratic' terms, among others.

Mazrui was balanced in his analysis. If someone was doing the analysis in 1994, the conclusion would have been that everything ought to be done to rid Africa of the dictators and mostly end up with a call for the international community to help. Mazrui realized what was possible at any given time and what was not possible. He based his arguments on facts and sometimes objective analysis. During a time when many analysts were predicting the end of authoritarian regimes on the continent, Mazrui was realistic in envisaging their survival in the near future due to ethnicity. What Mazrui did not anticipate was the role and influence of legacies of founding fathers in African politics, where their influences would still be felt beyond the grave, to the extent that in 2015, Uhuru Kenya, the son of Kenya's first President Jomo Kenyatta would be in power, and in Botswana, Ian Khama, the son of Botswana's first president would be in power as well.

Ali Mazrui has always remained polite and scholarly in his responses to Ochieng', but Ochieng' has not been as courteous. In 1992, at the height of the success of multiparty forces, Ali Mazrui was invited to speak at Taifa Hall at the University of Nairobi. I attended the forum and so did William Ochieng'. What surprised was the report that William Ochieng' produced on Ali Mazrui's talk the following Sunday. He went personal. In 1992, Ochieng' wrote that during his presentation, Mazrui looked frail, a bit tired and sometimes appeared disoriented. There was an outrage by readers of the leading newspapers in Kenya, attacking William Ochieng' for his disrespect for Mzee Ali Mazrui. The lambasted Ochieng' for boxing below the belt and asked him to discuss the ideas of Ali Mazrui and not his age. I was among some of the writers and wrote the editor, complaining about negative debating in the minds of some Kenyan intellectuals.

In September 15, 2009, Ochieng' penned an opinion piece in the *Daily Nation* on Ali Mazrui, who was marking his retirement as the Chancellor of Jomo Kenyatta University of Agriculture and Technology (JKUAT), in which he wrote, "Today the professor [Mazrui] looks exhausted, frail and aged; but he still retains his bold and critical character." This is not a compliment, if it begins with a negative comment. He told readers that before President Mwaqi Kibaki appointed Ali Mazrui as the Chancellor of Jomo Kenyatta University of Agriculture and Technology (JKUAT), he had "whined, complained and wailed many times about his exclusion. He quoted Mazrui as saying, "I never had a chance to serve as an employee of the government until President Kibaki gave me a chance." The fact that Ali Mazrui was never happy that he had never been offered a public job in Kenya was in the public domain and many of us did not see it as whining, complaining and wailing. Mazrui was a Kenyan and just like William Ochieng' and other Kenyans who occupied public posts, he deserved a chance to be employed. In 1986, while addressing us in a parking lot at the University of Nairobi, Prof. Ali A Mazrui had made it clear to us that he would have really loved to hold a job in Kenya but authorities were suspicious of him and his opting to go into exile was forced on him. It was therefore preposterous for someone to suggest that Prof. Ali Mazrui created the conditions for his own victimization and he should not have lamented about his situation. Mazrui made his dissatisfaction on the way he had been treated in a very academic and gentle manner and any reasonable person should have seen the point. After 2010, it was clear that age was catching up with Mazrui, but his intellectual energy and production had not waned.

Generous and Selfless Mwalimu Ali Mazrui

Mwalimu Ali Mazrui was generous in ways that contradicted his material possessions. His huge heart of giving to others may have presented one with the wrong image of Mazrui as a rich person, sufficiently philanthropic to give to others. He denied himself many luxurious in order to assist others. In 1994 at the University of Florida he gave me two copies of his new books for free. I still keep the books with his signature, signed with my parker pen. During his presentation, Mazrui spent time trying to explain why Africa needed democracy more than foreign aid. He said democracy would allow for more equitable distribution of resources, which were enough but were unfortunately concentrated in few hands such as those of Mobutu Sese Seko and Muamar Gaddafi. Mazrui responded to questions with amazing precision and persuasion. He predicted that Nelson Mandela was going to become the first black President of South Africa due to the number of black voters unless they were killed by some malevolent forces such as nuclear bomb or massive pandemic like the plague.

In 2001, when I was serving as Fulbright Scholar-in-residence at the University of Illinois at Urbana-Champaign, Prof. Mazrui paid for an air ticket for me to fly from Chicago in Illinois to New York, Binghamton to attend a conference which he was organizing. He asked Dr. Patrick Dikirr, then his personal assistant to take care of us while in Binghamton. It was four days of great enjoyment, listening to the grand doyen move from one idea to another with the agility of a master. At the time, I was at the University of Illinois at Urbana-Champaign, where I was doing tour of duty at the Centre for African Studies under the care of Prof. Paul Tiyambe Zeleza, the Director. I took massive notes from this Fountain of Knowledge. I have been looking at the notes I took and wonder if Kenya will ever have such a great mind. He talked about wide range of issues such as why Africa may have the first female president before US. He said intermarriage between races and ethnic groups produced beautiful, bright and resilient people (perhaps anticipated the rise of Barrack Obama). He talked about why Ethiopia should colonize Eastern Africa, Nigeria should colonize West Africa and independent South Africa should colonize Southern Africa to bring about stability. He explained how US presence in the Western hemisphere had stabilized Latin America.

In 2002, Prof. Ali Mazrui and I met again at a conference organized by the Association of Third World Studies (ATWS) in Savannah, Georgia, where we drove for almost 15 hours from Illinois to Georgia with Prof. Moses Oketch (of University of London). The conference was organized by Prof. Harold Isaacs. We shared the same hotel with Prof. Moses Oketch and Prof. Shadrack Nasong'o (of Rhodes College, Memphis) and discussed Mazrui's keynote address late into the night. At the conference, Prof. Abdul Bangura loudly confessed to Prof. Ali A Mazrui that "Mwalimu Mazrui, we have admired you, plagiarised you and continue to hold you with great esteem as the greatest scholar from the African soil residing in America today." There was a long line of scholars from all over the world, seeking to greet Prof. Ali Mazrui. We posed for pictures with the Great Mazrui. Mazrui was a true globe trotter. He had just arrived in Savannah, Georgia from Latin America via Miami International Airport and after Savannah; he was headed to France, Europe where he was going to speak at a UNESCO meeting. We heard that ATWS paid him US$10,000 for the three hours he was in Savannah.

Mazrui loved sharing knowledge. Many scholars in Mazrui's league such as Cornell West and Wole Soyinka took over US$50,000 per speaking engagement but Mazrui sometimes took US$10,000. I recall when I was working in the African Studies Programme at Central Washington University; we paid Prof. Wangari Maathai US$50,000 to come to our campus at Ellensburg and speak about environment. I received her from the airport at Seattle and while driving to Ellensburg through the Cascade Mountains, I remember her extolling the virtues of Prof. Ali Mazrui, and how his 'talking fee' was unbelievably low for the great ideas that he produced. Of course some scholars have been wondering not so loudly if the talking engagements may have slightly contributed to the burning out of the Great Professor Mazrui. Although it remains in the realm of speculation, it is obvious that Mazrui's intellectual engagements may have had a contribution to his fast mortality.

In 2003, at Erie State University in Ohio, Mazrui asked me and Dr. Godwin Murunga (currently of the University of Nairobi) to ride with him in an official limousine from the conference venue, to his hotel room in downtown Erie. He entertained us in his hotel room for over one hour on juicy intellectual stories and paid for our dinner. As we made our presentations, we did not know that the good Professor had recorded all that we had said and spared us the embarrassment and humiliation in public. He told Dr. Godwin Murunga that he needed to map the collapse of the Somali to broader factors and create a comparative matrix of similar states elsewhere in Africa and find out why even creation of smaller states from the Greater Somalia was not accepted by the Somali and the rest of the world. He seemed to move Dr. Murunga away from Islam as a factor in the problems of the Somali state. He went back to the colonial history where Somalia was divided into three colonial spheres for the British, Italians and French and how this legacy remained after independence.

For my presentation, Prof. Mazrui asked me to complicate cattle rustling in Northern Kenya into a more intellectual argument, and look at external and internal factors and examine the role of politicians more critically than

Islam. He said that Muslims also lost cattle in northern Kenya and were also killed. He said that before Islam arrived in Northern Kenya, there were cattle raiding activities most of which were cultural and had nothing to do with Islam. He encouraged me to look for pull and push factors such as poverty than radical Islam. He said Muslim countries did not manufacture AK47 or M16 used to kill people in northern Kenya, and it was therefore wrong to blame Muslims for the violence in northern Kenya. This was one among many conferences where Mazrui cleverly deflected any discussion of Islam in negative form.

My Personal and Experiential View of Ali Mazrui

I had a good, cordial, intellectual relationship with Prof. Ali A. Mazrui whom I greatly admired. When he died, I was in shock and watched as his peers mourned him. Among the Abaluhya, young people mourn older people after burial, during "amachienga" (last ambers of funeral fire), after the real fire of mourning is gone. This is Abaluhya culture's way of saving young people from trauma and big shocks. Many people asked me why I had not written about my great friend and mentor. I cited my Luhya culture, because we are very cultural. I penned a tribute in the Daily Nation, one week after his burial, and later paid homage to his burial site near Fort Jesus in the Mazrui family Graveyard that dates back 500 years. Prof. Mazrui was like a father to me, only three years older than my biological father. He attended many of my presentations and said I was a provocative presenter. I have over a dozen personal letters written to me by Prof. Ali Mazrui is his own handwriting and which I now cherish more than before.

I was very excited when I was invited to participate in this book project in honour of the late famous Professor Ali Alamin Mazrui, for three reasons. First Ali Mazrui was a friend and I regarded him as a mentor. He replied to all letters that I wrote to him. He wrote me at least ten personal letters, many of them replies to requests for favours and others I made to him from the 1980s and 1990s when I was looking for an opportunity to study in the United States, and in the 2000s when I was working in the US. The last letter he wrote to me was a congratulatory one, on my appointment as the Deputy Vice Chancellor at Kisii University, and the second last one, was encouraging me to ignore attacks from Prof. William Robert Ochieng' appearing in the Kenyan media. Second, Ali Mazrui was one of the only three mega-professors (besides Wole Soyinka and Ngũgĩ wa Thiong'o) from Africa and could not be ignored, for his opinion really counted. He was articulate and spoke eloquently. He was a wordsmith and engaged in a lot of linguistic engineering in which he coined dozens of new words and phrases. For example, in his 1967 book, he coined the word Pax-Africana from Pax Britannica and Pax Americana (Mazrui, 1967).

Mazrui courted controversy, which made him an original thinker, taking on weak and mighty in equal measure. Third, Mazrui wrote many books which influenced me from my days as undergraduate at the University of Nairobi. Many of his books were found at the Jomo Kenyatta Memorial Library and I hear that he made sure that he sent a copy of all of his books to Kenya's premier university. Mazrui wrote deeply intellectual commentaries and wrote impressively and anyone interested in intellectual debates had to love or hate the old professor. There is no public intellectual in Kenya who has engaged in open discourses on many issues more than Prof. Ali A. Mazrui. A friend of mine, Dr. Bethuel Owuor stumbled on what he regarded as an excellent essay on the life and times of Ali A. Mazrui on the internet. The thought this was a must read for anyone interested in knowing something new about the intellectual life of the great thinker and philosopher, Ali Mazrui. He promptly forwarded the essay to me, saying that since I regarded Mazrui as my mentor, the essay would obviously benefit me. The essay had been widely shared and distributed on many listserves and sites such as Facebook on the internet. A few minutes later, Dr. Owuor sent me another message, apologizing for sending me my own essay. He had read the essay again and noticed that I was the author of the apparently excellent essay and felt embarrassed about it. Ali Mazrui was perhaps one of the most famous public intellectuals in Kenya. For over fifty years, his ideas dominated Kenya's media and shaped a lot of concepts and ideas on the Continent.

Mazrui, the Intellectual Maverick

I regarded Prof. Mazrui as a mentor and did learn a lot from the Great Professor. Ali Mazrui liked me, and I greatly admired him too. I regarded myself like his protégé, always learning from the grand master. He was encouraging and pleasant as a person. He wrote me each time I took on William Ochieng' or other academic heavyweights in the national media. When Ochieng' replied to me through the *Daily Nation* in an article that was headlined "Amutabi talks tough, but show us his books," Mazrui wrote to me telling me not to worry, he told me to be strong because I had arrived as a great scholar in Kenya and Africa and should now just write without fear. He told me that Ochieng' never attacks an idea he does not fear and taking on me meant that he regarded me as a threat and the next big thing, for he was not comfortable to be succeeded. He told that that Ochieng' was not happy with the debates in the media which all focused on my article, especially the emergence of the pro-Amutabi and anti-Amutabi groups which were elevating me to a national figure. Mazrui shared with me the need for mentoring younger scholars and being fair and civil even as one engaged in public discourse and debates. He told me to be prepared to be disappointed sometimes when some scholars hit me below the belt or use vulgar language or get personal. He made me remember how my daughter cried in school after Ochieng' had attacked me in a national newspaper.

I liked Ali Mazrui's intellectual flare but did not agree with him on some of the issues he postulated. He was kind and polite. I liked his capacity to coin new words and phrases and always told him about it whenever I had opportunity to do so. I looked back at many of Mazrui's writings and saw the same trajectory. I noticed that Mazrui was an apologist for Islamic and Muslim excesses in Africa and abroad (Mazrui, et al, 2008). I looked at his famous film series, *Africa: A Triple Heritage* and realized how he worked so hard to privilege Muslims and attributed great African success stories to Islamic presence in Africa. I started having mixed feelings about Ali Mazrui and wondered if he was sincere and honest in his academic pronouncements. I even started to believe some people who had told me over twenty years ago in Florida that Mazrui was a CIA agent. I was surprised when he said that Arabs did not exert a lot of violence on Africans compared to white European slave traders (Mazrui, et al, 2006). I found it strange that the Great professor was covering the fact that many African men who ended up in the Arab and Muslim countries were castrated or killed; while African women had their fallopian tubes surgically removed so as not to create black people in the Muslim world. This was different from white Europeans who allowed African slaves to procreate and have families in captivity.

So as not to be misunderstood, let me state that slaves were treated badly by both Europeans and Arabs, by Christians and Muslims and no amount of justification will ever erase the grotesque and dark memories that this evil practice exerted on the people of Africa and their descendants to this day. But there are now 400 million blacks in the New World, from Brazil where there are 100 million, to the US where there are 50 million, to Jamaica, Cuba, Honduras, El Salvador, Panama, Peru, Chile, Argentina, there are many black people in these places yet they received the same number of slaves as Arab countries. At least India preserved black slaves and even intermarried with them, but in the Muslim counties black people were systematically eliminated and in ways that we see African house-helps treated in many Muslim countries. This is a topic that Ali Mazrui avoided in many of his writings and lectures, something he preferred to sweep under the carpet.

Prof. Mazrui was very vocal on reparations for slavery and slave trade from the West but not from the East (Mazrui and Mazrui, 2002). He was a member of the eminent Africans appointed by the African Union to pursue reparation or compensation for Africans for the trauma of slave and slave trade. He was an apologist of Islamic excesses and did not appreciate the resilience and forgiving hearts of Africans. Unlike Arabs who experienced oppression from 1948 when the state of Israel was created, Africans have suffered over three thousand centuries of oppression and invasion by other cultures and have never engaged in suicide bombing, Africans have never created a Black Al Qaeda to kill Arabs and Europeans despite many years of oppression and enslavement.

Prof. Ali Mazrui has left a lot of academic legacies in the world. His famous TV series *Africa: A Triple Heritage* will be remembered for the many good things it did in preserving Africa's past (Mazrui, 1986). His many books on topical issues will continue to remind us about his great mind. I first learnt the idea of interdisciplinary research and writing from Prof. Ali Mazrui. It was only recently when I was looking at newspaper cutting from the 1980s when I realized that I had more newspaper cutting of Mazrui's articles more than any other scholar alive or dead, and interestingly followed by those of Prof. William Ochieng' whom I also admired a lot. Mazrui wrote about anything and was perhaps the greatest public intellectual that Africa has ever produced. He was certainly a man who was ahead of his peers in many ways. Mazrui loved debates and was at his sharpest wit during questions and answer sessions, when he would widen his eyes and lengthen his neck looking at the audience as if to hold them in his spell, like a hypnotist. He often left audiences asking for more, because of his articulateness and eloquence.

Many scholars in Kenya often looked for a day when Prof. Ali Mazrui would debate William Ochieng'. Now that they are both dead, perhaps their academic sons and daughters will debate one day. I look forward to one day debating an academic son of Ochieng', looking at the influence of triple heritage on former Ruothdoms in Usenge or Uyoma and how Ochieng' and Mazrui would have responded to such. We shall forever be indebted to Ali Mazrui for illuminating our intellectual minds and pointing to new horizons of knowledge, many of which ideas have inspired hundreds of doctoral and master's dissertations world over. I regard myself as one of the followers of Mazrui who was regarded as historian, political scientist, literary scholar and political analyst, among other references. Asante Mzee, Mwalimu, Professor Ali A. Mazrui for giving it all and rest in peace.

Conclusion

Prof. Ali A. Mazrui was celebrated as one of the most influential intellectuals from Africa. He was a thinker, philosopher, and public intellectual per excellence. He was courageous and never feared to pen his ideas, whether popular or not. He allowed us opportunity to see and experience new discursive spaces, shifting paradigms, African agency, and voice in many debates. Through his analytical vigour and rigour, we were able to learn and unlearn new and old ideas, presented in ways that we could easily understand. He spoke just like he wrote, in simple and clear English.

Prof. Mazrui coined new words and concepts, many of which will remain embedded in our intellectual psyche and inventories forever. As a public intellectual, Mazrui has contributed a lot to what we know today as multicultural and intellectual discourses on knowledge production in Africa. Like we have seen, his intellectual breadth was wide and he wrote about political science, history, religious studies, linguistics, literature, film and cinema, gender, and other development discourses. True, some of his ideas were controversial because they went against the grain. There are many scholars who were incensed by his ideas but this did not discourage him. For example, Mazrui's attempt to sanitize actions of Muslim extremists by painting them as rebels with justified actions has attracted a lot of attacks on his neutrality. He has sometimes been cited as having promoted anti-Jewish feelings in some of his writings. Mazrui has also been heavily criticised for proposing internal colonization for Africa, a theoretical understanding which many believe was driven largely by the desire for political stability more than other undercurrents. His calling for Ethiopia to colonize Eastern Africa, South Africa to colonize Southern Africa, and Nigeria to colonize West Africa has been regarded by some as 'Mazrui at his worst' whereas others think that his argument has been taken out of context. Through his writings and speeches, we will continue to enjoy and benefit from his scholarship many years to come.

References

Amutabi, Maurice N. (2007). "Intellectuals and the Democratization Process in Kenya" in S. W Nasong'o and Godwin R. Murunga. (Eds). *Kenya: The Struggle for Democracy.* London: Zed Books, 2007. Pp. 197-226.

Amutabi, Maurice N. (2002). "Crisis and Student Protest in Universities in Kenya: Examining the Role of Students in National Leadership and Democratization Process." *African Studies Review*, Volume 45, Number 2 (September 2002). Pp.157-78.

Amutabi, Maurice N. (2010). **The rivalry between William Ochieng' and Ali Mazrui. May 15, 2010.** https://kenyasocialscienceforum.wordpress.

com/2010/05/15/the-rivalry-between-william-ochieng-and-ali-mazrui/ (Accessed on November 14, 2014).

Amutabi, Maurice N. (2007). Prof. Ali A Mazrui and I. November 4, 2014. https://kenyasocialscienceforum.wordpress.com/2014/11/04/prof-ali-a-mazrui-and-i/ (Accessed on December 9, 2014).

Amutabi, Maurice N. (2013). "Arrogant Ochieng' cannot hold candle to great writers like Ngũgĩ and Mazrui." Daily Nation, November 29, 2013 http://mobile.nation.co.ke/News/Arrogant-Ochieng--cannot-hold-candle-for-Mazrui/-/1950946/2093652/-/format/xhtml/-/2wmw7nz/-/index.html (Accessed November 22, 2014).

Mazrui, Ali A (1967) *Towards a Pax Africana: A Study of Ideology and Ambition*. London: Weidenfeld and Nicholson, and University of Chicago Press.

Mazrui, Ali A (1969) *Violence and Thought: Essays on Social Tensions in Africa* (London and Harlow: Longman).

Mazrui, Ali A. (1971). *The Trial of Christopher Okigbo*. London: Heinemann Educational Books and New York: The Third Press.

Mazrui, Ali A, (1977) *Africa's International Relations: The Diplomacy of Dependency and Change*. London: Heinemann Educational Books and Boulder: Westview Press.

Mazrui, Ali A (1986) *The Africans: A Triple Heritage*. New York: Little Brown and Co., and London: BBC.

Mazrui, Ali A (1990). *Cultural Forces in World Politics*. London and Portsmouth, N.H: James Currey and Heinemann.

Mazrui, Ali A (2008a) *Euro-Jews and Afro-Arabs: The Great Semitic Divergence in History* [editor: Seifudein Adem]. Washington DC: University of America Press.

Mazrui, Ali, Patrick Dikirr, Robert Ostergard Jr., Michael Toler and Paul Macharia (eds). (2008b) *Islam in Africa's Experience*. New Delhi: Sterling Paperbacks.

Mazrui, Ali A, Shalahudin Kafrawi, Alamin M. Mazrui and Ruzima Sebuharara (eds) (2006) *Islam: Between Globalization & Counter-Terrorism*. Trenton, NJ and Asmara, Eritrea: Africa World Press.

Mazrui, Ali A and Alamin Mazrui. (2002). *Black Reparations in the era of Globalization*. Binghamton: The Institute of Global Cultural Studies.

Mazrui, Alamin M and Willy M. Mutunga (eds). (2004). *Race, Gender, and Culture Conflict: Mazrui and His Critics*. Trenton, New Jersey: African World Press.

Mazrui, Alamin M and Willy M. Mutunga (eds). (2003). *Governance and Leadership: Debating the African Condition* (Trenton, New Jersey: African World Press).

Nasong'o, S. W and Godwin R. Murunga. (Eds). *Kenya: The Struggle for Democracy.* London: Zed Books, 2007.

Ochieng', William R. (1975), *The First Word*: *Essays on Kenya History.* Nairobi: East African Literature Bureau.

Ochieng', William R. (1977), *The Second Word*: More *Essays on Kenya History.* Nairobi: East African Literature Bureau.

Ochieng', William R. (1984), *The third word: Essays on Kenyan history and society.* Nairobi: East African Literature Bureau.

Mayaka, Emeka G and Sigei Julius (2013). Professor William Robert Ochieng': Ngũgĩ is a tribalist, Taliban a con and Mazrui overrated. Daily Nation, November 30, 2013 http://mobile.nation.co.ke/lifestyle/Ngũgĩ-is-a-tribalist-Taban-a-con-and-Mazrui-overrated/-/1950774/2084944/-/format/xhtml/-/j48rwfz/-/index.html (Accessed December 8, 2014).

Zeleza, P.T. (2003*). Rethinking Africa's Globalization. Volume 1: The Intellectual Challenges*. Trenton, New Jersey: Africa World Press.

14

Terrorism and Counterterrorism in Ali Mazrui's Political Thought

Oscar Mwangi

Introduction

Political thought is socially constructed based on the social milieu of the thinker. This chapter examines the depiction of terrorism and counterterrorism in Ali Mazrui's political thought. Using social constructivism as a framework of analysis, this article looks at Mazrui's scholarly works and examines the relationship between his social milieu and his construction of terrorism and counterterrorism as a reality in the political world. Mazrui's political thought is heavily influenced by Islamism as a political ideology. This chapter is divided into three sections. The first section looks at the relationship among social constructivism, politics, and terrorism so as to provide a framework of analysis. The second examines Islamism so as to have a sound theoretical background of the issues under discussion. The third section examines the construction of terrorism, counterterrorism, and counterterrorism in Mazrui's political thought at the normative level as influenced by Islamism as a political ideology, and at the empirical level, influenced by his real life experiences as a Muslim.

Social Construction, Politics, and Terrorism

This article adopts the social constructivism approach as used in the analysis of international relations, comparative politics, and terrorism studies to examine the depiction of terrorism and counterterrorism in Ali Mazrui's political thought. Social constructivism pays attention to the role of ideas, norms, knowledge, culture, and argument in politics, emphasising the role of collectively held ideas and understandings of social life. It stresses that human interaction is shaped mainly by ideational factors, not merely material ones, and that most of these ideational factors are commonly shared beliefs that are not reducible to individuals (Wendt, 1999; Finnemore and Sikkink, 2001, pp. 392-393; Price, 2008, pp. 193-194). Constructivist analysis explains how social facts change and influence politics. Most social constructivists in international relations and comparative politics emphasise the 'logic of appropriateness' rather than 'logic of consequences', the latter of which is normally located in the domain of rational choice theories, indicating that behaviour is rule-guided. Actors try to do what is socially acceptable rather than maximising or optimising their given preferences. Socially shared ideas both regulate behaviour and constitute the identity of actors. 'Social facts', such as sovereignty and rights, which have no material reality, exist only because people collectively believe they exist and act accordingly. These norms also define the basic rules of politics in which actors find themselves when interacting (Risse, 2000, pp. 4-6; Sterling-Folker, 2000, p. 99; Finnemore and Sikkink, 2001, p. 393; Mwangi, 2015, pp. 382-383).

Based on ontological assumptions, constructivists argue that actors are shaped by the social milieu in which they live hence agents and structures are mutually constituted in ways that explain the 'reality' of the political world. Understanding the constitution of things is essential in explaining how they behave and what causes political outcomes. The constitution of things is causal since it affects political behaviour. Hence, what counts as 'true', as 'objective', and as 'fact' are determined by the contending accounts of reality. Knowledge is regarded as collectively owned and thus knowledge is never impartial and separate from particular social constructs. In short, social constructivism views politics as socially constructed (Wendt, 1999, p. 1; Finnemore and Sikkink, 2001, p. 394; Grint, 2005, pp. 1470-1472; Mwangi, 2015, pp. 382-383).

Social constructivism can be characterised into three broad variants: conventional, interpretative, and critical/radical. In general, conventional constructivism examines the role of norms and identity in shaping political outcomes by advocating bridge-building among diverse theoretical perspectives. Interpretative constructivists focus on the 'how possible' questions as opposed to the explanatory 'why' kind. They adopt an in-depth inductive research strategy that pays attention to the reconstruction of identities and making use also of methods that involve a variety of discourse-theoretic techniques. Critical variants add an explicitly normative dimension by examining a researcher's own implication in the reconstruction of the identities and world being studied. In this variant, discourse-theoretical methods are also emphasised but with a greater emphasis on the power and domination inherent in language (Checkel, 1998, pp. 230-231; Mwangi and Mwangi, 2014, pp.42-43).

Constructivist perspectives on terrorism are not yet common within the mainstream field of terrorism studies. However, in the post 11 September 2001 period, a discourse-centred terrorism studies has emerged with the rise of Critical Terrorism Studies whereby terrorism is not perceived as a physical fact, but as a social construction. The central notion is that terrorism is constituted through discourse. This does not mean that such a constructivist perspective denies the 'real' existence of terrorism. There are real people who conduct real actions, but what these people and their deeds mean is a matter of interpretation. It is this interpretation in discourse that constitutes a certain group of people as 'terrorists' and their actions as 'terrorism' (Spencer 2012, p. 394). Though methodological criticisms are levelled against social constructivism by scholars of mainstream theories in international relations and comparative politics, it does not reject science or causal explanations. Social constructivism's main criticism of mainstream theories is based ontological, not epistemological issues (Chekel, 1998, pp. 324-349; Risse, 2000, pp. 4-6; Finnemore and Sikkink, 2001, pp. 391-396).

Using social constructivism as a framework of analysis, this chapter looks at Mazrui's scholarly works and examines the relationship between his social milieu and his construction of terrorism and counterterrorism as a reality in the political world. The article attempts to demonstrate that his construction of terrorism and counterterrorism is a function of his social milieu at two levels: the normative and the empirical. At the normative level, his political thought is influenced by Islamism as an ideology, whereas at the empirical level, it is influenced by his real life experiences as a Muslim. It is, therefore, important to first and foremost examine Islamism as a concept and political ideology so as to understand Mazrui's construction of terrorism, counterterrorism, and counterterrorism experiences.

Islamism

The concept Islamism, which is also referred to political Islam emerged during the 1970s to refer to the rise of movements and ideologies articulating a political agenda based on Islamic referents. Islamism refers to the use of Islam by individuals, groups, and organizations as an instrument to pursue political objectives. It provides political responses to contemporary societal challenges by envisioning the establishment of a future Islamic society based on concepts borrowed from Islam (Denouex, 2002, p. 61). Islamists combine strict adherence to the written sources of Islam with 'Islamic activism'. A common goal of all Islamists is to prop up Islamic states in which the *Sharia* law prevails. The strategies for achieving this aim, however, differ immensely (Hoehne, 2009, p. 2).

Islamism or Islamic activism has a number of very different streams. The starting point for understanding these streams is to distinguish between Shiite and Sunni Islamism. Shiism is the minority variant of Islam. Sunnis constitute over 80 percent of Muslims. Shiites, in most cases are minorities in the states in which they are located. Shiite activism is largely centred on defending the communal the interests of the Shiite community in vis-à-vis other non-state and state actors in society. Hence Shiite Islamism has remained unified to a significant degree and has not fragmented into conflicting forms of activism compared to Sunni Islamism. Sunni Islamism is generally seen as uniformly radical and a threat to Western interests. It is, however, not monolithic. On the contrary, it has developed into three main distinctive types: political; missionary; and jihadi. Political Islamists refer to Muslim misgovernment and social injustice and give priority to political reform to be achieved by political action. Missionary Islamists refer to the corruption of Islamic values (*al-qiyam al-islamiyya*) and the weakening of faith (*al-imam*) and give priority to a form of moral and spiritual rearmament that champions individual virtue as the condition of good government as well as of collective salvation. Jihadi Islamists refer to the oppressive weight on non-Muslim political and military power in the Islamic world and give priority to armed resistance (ICG, 2005, pp. i-ii). All these varieties of Sunni activism are attempts to reconcile tradition and modernity. They, however, differ in their perceptions on the problems facing the Muslim world, and their strategies of tackling these problems (ICG, 2005, p. i). Ali Mazrui was a Sunni Muslim.

Islamism is a political ideology and not a theological construct. Its main role is not to offer spiritual solace to its followers but more importantly to provide answers to their contemporary political and social predicaments. Hegghammer (2009) argues that conceptualising and labelling actors and currents within Islamism is problematic, and that since the 1980s the tendency in academic literature on Islamism has been to adopt Arabic descriptors found in the discourse of the Islamic actors themselves. Several terms are widely used in the literature to analyse Islamism. The literature, however, suffers from a lack of clear definitions of these terms, as well as inconsistencies in their application to specific groups and ideologues, leading to considerable ambiguity about the precise political content of such terms. Some of these terms are used as labels while others are self-appellations. According to Hegghammer, defining some of these terms is too complex, hence it is more appropriate to focus on how they relate to political behaviour (Hegghammer, 2002, pp. 245-247). This chapter primarily focuses on terrorism committed by jihadi-salafists and the counterterrorism measures effected to contain them. The term 'Jihadi–Salafi' is popular in the academic literature on radical Islam. It is, however, surprisingly difficult to find a politically substantial and specific definition of it. Most definitions tend to be vague. Despite the ambiguity of the term, many scholars understand Jihadi–Salafi movements as having three politically substantial characteristics. First, Jihadi-Salafi groups are perceived as more extremist and intransigent than other groups. Second, they are said to draw on Salafi or Wahhabi extremist religious tradition and discourse as opposed to pragmatic Islamist ideology and discourse. Finally, they are seen as more internationalist and anti-Western than other groups (Hegghammer, 2009, 252-254).

The Concept of Terrorism, Counterterrorism, and Counterterrorism Experiences in Mazrui's Political Thought

The political thought of a thinker is to a large extent determined by the broader cultural and intellectual milieu in which he or she is formally and informally educated. A political thinker does not write about politics in a vacuum. The thinker holds, deeply, a conviction or set of convictions, 'about the proper ordering of society in a world perceived to have gone awry' (Spellman, 2011, p. 2). Political thought does not only cover the reflection on things political but also ideas about political action. Political thought is inherently concerned with public matters, the inclusive property of a community. Such matters are not only empirical but also normative in the abstract sense of collective purpose and directions, a network of social meaning embedded in a particular time and space (Spellman, 2011, pp. 2-3). It is the context of these arguments that this section examines the way in which terrorism, counterterrorism and counterterrorism experience are depicted in Mazrui's political thought which in essence in influenced by Islamism.

Concept of Terrorism

Mazrui's perceptions on the relationship between Islam, terrorism and counterterrorism are constructed on the basis of his social milieu and real life experiences. Mazrui was born in Mombasa Kenya on 24 February 1933. In an interview conducted in 2003, Mazrui points out the extent to which his social milieu informed his political thought. He emphasized that he lived in a situation which he subsequently described as a 'triple heritage' situation that was a convergence of three legacies in Mombasa. These were 'the Africanicity, the influence of Islam, the impact of the colonial west' (Mazrui, 2003). As he was growing up, these three civilizations, African, Islamic and Western were constantly interacting in his daily life thereby crossing civilizations several times a day. Mazrui specifically noted that his father was Chief *Khadi* of Kenya and was constantly dealing with the issue of the *Shari'a* as well as holding Islamic jurisprudence classes in the mosque. Additionally, as Mazrui points out, the family received many guests, some of whom spoke Arabic and others spoke Swahili. All these factors influenced his early life (Mazrui, 2003). His religious background significantly impacted upon his academic and social writings and subsequently his political thought.

Mazrui's initial conception of terrorism prior to 11 September 2001 was largely constructed on the basis of its political objectives. Writing in 1985, Mazrui pointed out that terrorism is a form of warfare that could be perpetuated either by private individuals or by governments with the objective of creating specialized terror among civilians by violent means to promote political ends (Mazrui, 1985, p. 349). For Mazrui, writing then, the political objectives of terrorism were best understood in the context of ultimate goals and immediate targets. The ultimate goals were to seek attention for political causes that would otherwise not be noticed so as to contribute to the realization of those causes whereas the immediate target was the manipulation of fear as a combat mechanism in the context of wide publicity (Mazrui, 1985, p. 349). Later in 2002, following September 11, Mazrui enhanced this perception by stating that:

> In our present situation, where "terrorism" has become the proclaimed enemy of "civilization," one needs to pay particular attention to the ethical and political implications of the meanings ascribed to it. The use of fear and anxiety for political purposes – as terrorism is often defined – is not only generated by explosions, bombs, and kidnapping or other direct means. Manipulation through fear and anxiety fueled by dominant ideological constructs could be as terrorizing – if not more, due to their "indirect" nature (Mazrui, 2001-2002, p. 1).

In relation to 11 September 2001 Mazrui argues that prior to the attacks, all wars were fought on southern soil. However, after 11 September, the borders of violent conflict shifted and it is no longer limited to the South. Mazrui points out that the concept of terrorism also adopted a new identity by emphasizing that the word is used for violent actions penetrated by groups in the South, and it is not a word commonly attached to violence committed by the North (Mazrui, 2007, p.6; 2011, p.5). Mazrui's construction of the concept of terrorism is, therefore, based on the social facts of ethics, politics, and regioness.

Concept of Counterterrorism

On the concept of counterterrorism, Mazrui argues that the way counterterrorism is constructed out of horrific events may be a more significant terror than terrorist acts themselves. He emphasizes that the 'meaning of terror may wane by comparison to the meaning of terror when it is constructed and circumscribed within a mono-cultural exclusive terrain of interpretation (Mazrui, 2001-2002, p.1). Mazrui underscores the importance of constructivism when he says that the rhetoric, ideology, and belief associated with the dominant discourse of the 'war on terrorism' are enhancing rather than mitigating the same blind hatred that motivated the 11 September attacks but on a global scale. Counterterrorism measures, Mazrui, emphasizes, construct 'a cultural superiority based on a generalization that associates a few thugs with vast populations of particular religions and ethnicities' (Mazrui, 2001-2002, p.6). The war on terrorism he states:

> ...is merely a tool of constructing an enemy that would allow the powers to be to evade addressing issues of social equality and of distributive justice on a global scale while empowering them to impose their will on any population that does not comply with their demands – by labeling them as "terrorists" and constructing them as enemies (Mazrui, 2001-2002, p. 6).

In the context of international relations, Mazrui points out that the 'war on terrorism' is shifting the balance of international order in that it disregards that sovereignty of nations subjected to it. He emphasizes that under the guise of pursuing terrorists undermines a basic tenet of international law built of the respect of the sovereignty of nations and peoples (Mazrui, 2001-2002, p.6). Mazrui constructs counterterrorism on the basis of the social facts of cultural superiority, social equality and distributive justice, religion and ethnicity, and sovereignty.

Counterterrorism Experiences

Islamism as a political ideology which has influenced Mazrui's political thought, is used as an agency to pursue political objectives while at the same time providing responses to contemporary political challenges. As already noted previously, the meaning of terms as used in the discourse or rhetoric of Islamism do not provide meaningful explanatory power in the analysis of the ideology hence it would be more appropriate to focus on how these terms relate to political behaviour. Counterterrorism measures or the war on terrorism is largely a response to the political behaviour of the jihadi-salafists on a global scale. The jihadi-salafists and extremist and intransigent, internationalist and anti-western. The give priority to armed resistance. It is in this context that such counterterrorism measures are repressive.

Mazrui's perceptions on counterterrorism experiences is based on his construction of counterterrorism or the war on terrorism in which he argues that aim of counterterrorism or the war on terrorism is to construct a cultural superiority based on a generalization that associates a few criminals with vast populations of particular religions and ethnicities. The few criminals in this case are the jihadi-salafists while the vast populations of particular religions and ethnicities are Muslims and Arabs respectively. According to Mazrui, counterterrorism or the war on terrorism labels the vast majority of Muslims as jihadi-salafists despite the different streams of Islamism, that is political, missionary, and jihadi. He points out that by doing so, countries that conduct counterterrorism measures or the war on terrorism evade addressing issues of social equality and distributive justice on a global scale while empowering them to impose their own will on any population that does not comply with their demands. In short, counterterrorism labels Muslims as terrorists and constructs them as enemies. As such they are subjected to gross human rights violations. Mazrui's construction of counterterrorism at the empirical level is significantly influenced by his experiences as both a member of the Muslim *ummah* and as an individual. Mazrui has authored several works in which he depicts the relationship among terrorism, counterterrorism and Islam, particularly how a terrorist philosophy has ensnared Islam (Mazrui, 2006, p.13). His normative construction of the concept of counterterrorism and the empirical construction of counterterrorism measures and their adverse effects is depicted in the real life experiences of Arab Muslims. Mazrui was both an Arab and a Muslim. It is in this context that he demonstrates through constructivism that Muslims and Arabs like any other faithful's and ethnicities are equally if not more subjected to the adverse effects of both terrorism and counterterrorism. This informs the basis of counterterrorism experiences worldwide.

Mazrui's examines counterterrorism measures as a response to international terrorism particularly in relation to the policies and politics of the Middle East and Africa. He points out that international terrorism is one more area of intermingling between the policies of the Middle East and the politics of Africa given that the peoples of these regions have suffered on the grounds of religion and ethnicities because of counterterrorism measures. Mazrui emphasises that the Middle East and Africa have been paying the price for anti-American terrorism in the form of counterterrorism operations conducted by the United States (Mazrui, 2002, p.2). In spite of assurances that the war on terrorism is not a war on Islam, Mazrui points out that Muslims are paying a disproportionate price for war or counterterrorism measures worldwide (Mazrui, 2004, p. 815; Mazrui, 2010, p. 10). The adverse effects of counterterrorism measures or the war on terrorism are examined in the context of illegal detentions or renditions, enactment of anti-terrorism legislation, political and religious intolerance, harassment at airports, assassinations and executions in occupied areas.

Illegal Detentions and Renditions

With regard to illegal detentions and renditions, Mazrui points out that on and off there are hundreds of people in detention without trial under American jurisdiction, the majority of whom are Muslims. He emphasizes that the great majority of those in detention are not publicly announced as being in detention and that only a handful of these display any evidence of knowing any particular terrorist suspect or being associated with any movement or charity accused of terrorism. The practice of rendition, where people who are suspected of terrorism are handed over to governments who have less misgivings about torturing them, has also led to Muslims being victimised by the security agencies of these governments. (Mazrui, 2002, p.3; Mazrui, 2004, p. 805). Mazrui emphasizes that out of the millions of illegal immigrants in the United States (US), and those whose visas have expired, those detained without trial or those who are deported instantly are mainly Muslim or who come from the Middle East. Mazrui indicates that the US Immigration and Naturalization Services (INS) has been singling out particular nationalities, mainly Muslim for discriminatory treatment, illegal harassment and unconstitutional imprisonment (Mazrui, 2004, p. 806).

To demonstrate some of the humiliating experiences they undergo, Mazrui indicates that many of these suspects who are detained at Guantanamo Bay, Cuba, the level of justice envisaged for them has led to agonising critiques. For the detainees, some regulations relating to the eavesdropping between lawyers and clients have been relaxed, even before they have made court appearances. He gives the examples of the US Attorney General and former President George W. Bush who repeatedly spoke as if those suspected of terrorism were already convicted terrorists, contradicting the US principle that a person is innocent until proven guilty (Mazrui, 2004, p. 806). Mazrui also emphasizes that there is increasing evidence of torture in facilities used for terrorist suspects and that the US, while conducting counterterrorism measures or the war on terrorism came closer to tolerating torture than at any time in the last century. The US, he argues is more comfortable with imprisoning suspects for years at Guantanamo Bay without access to their own lawyers and often without hope of early release (Mazrui, 2007, p. 6; Mazrui, 2010, p. 10).

Anti-Terrorism Legislation

On anti-terrorism legislation, Mazrui argues that there has been pressure on many countries, from the US, to enact new legislation against terrorism which pose newer threats to civil liberties in in such countries. He points out that the post September 11 period compromised some civil liberties in the US itself to the extent that it became a cliche to say 'September 11 changed everything', particularly in regards to the attitudes of Americans toward Muslims. Mazrui emphasizes that what is perhaps more worrisome is the official attitudes and policies that may encroach on the fundamental rights and freedoms of Muslims not only in the US but worldwide (Mazrui, 2002, p. 3; 2004, p. 805). He indicates that Muslims were harassed and continue to be harassed under new anti-terrorist legislation in countries such as Tanzania, Kenya, and a host of other countries that came under pressure from the George W. Bush administration to do so. Mazrui emphasizes that in 'comparative number of victims, Muslims of the world are more sinned against than sinning' (Mazrui, 2004, pp. 804-805; Mazrui, 2007, p.6). He goes on to provide examples of the experiences of Muslims in the US by indicating that US Attorney General John Ashcroft gave the green light to the Federal Bureau of Investigation (FBI) to spy on churches, mosques, and other sacred places, which were once protected from close police scrutiny, to an extent not envisaged in the country for a long period. (Mazrui, 2004, p. 806). Mazrui also indicates that the US Patriot Act provides the US government with immense powers against its own citizens, including authority for federal agents "to 'sneak and peek' at citizens' private records; enter citizens' homes in secret; and hold citizens indefinitely without access to legal counsel or a hearing before a judge" (Mazrui, 2004, p. 807). It is in the context of the human rights violations of Muslims that Mazrui states:

> If the erosion of civil liberties is justified on the grounds of the war against terrorism, this is a war with no recognisable finality of either a peace treaty with the enemy, or a demand of unconditional surrender. What would constitute the end of this war? Would we be able to have a victory parade, open bottles of halal champagne, or hug each other with joy in the streets? After World War II there were VE Day (Victory in Europe) and V-J Day (Victory in Japan). What would constitute such finality in the war on terrorism? (Mazrui, 2004, p. 807).

In other words, Mazrui is arguing that a war fought on the basis of religion and ethnicity and whereby the rights of such religions and ethnicities are violated; then such a way cannot be morally just or ethical and such a war cannot have victors and losers.

Political and Religious Intolerance

On the question of political and religious tolerance between Islam and other religions in the US and other countries, Mazrui emphasizes that in the post September 11 period the trend of tolerant convergence between American people and Muslim people has either been interrupted or is being reversed. To him, most Americans and Muslims, both in the USA and worldwide, are unfortunately in the process of being pulled apart. Muslims in the West are routine targets of harassment in various ways, while Westerners in the Muslim world have to be concerned about hatred and consequent physical harm (Mazrui, 2004, p. 794; Mazrui, 2007, pp. 5-6). According to Mazrui, Americans, however, also have reason to worry about the lack of friendship from Muslims in many other countries who feel that US aid and support for their enemies is perpetuating violence and hardship for them (Mazrui, 2004, pp. 804-805; Mazrui, 2007, p.6). These divergences provide the opportunities for political and religious intolerance to exacerbate. To demonstrate the political and religious intolerance, Mazrui gives an example where he says that although the George W Bush Administration, especially President Bush, did take pains to assure Muslims that the war against terrorism was not a war against Islam, other administration officials were not so charitable. Lt. Gen. William G Boykin, the Pentagon's Deputy Undersecretary for Intelligence, discussing a 1993 battle with a Muslim militia leader in Somalia, said: 'I knew that my God was bigger than his. I knew that my God was a real God, and his was an idol' (Mazrui, 2004, p. 807). This was a high-ranking US official advocating religious bigotry with the aim of demeaning Islam. Mazrui emphasises political and religious intolerance did not end with the Bush Administration but has continued up to the Barrack Obama Administration. He pointed out that Obama's address to the Muslim world in June 2009, stirred hope to the Muslim *ummah* for a new era in relations between the US and the Muslims of the world. Obama also addressed the peoples of Africa. For Mazrui, 'Those were heady days of Americo-Muslim and Americo-African solidarity. All parties have sobered up since then. We are back to a world of tension and banality' (Mazrui, 2009, p. 7). In other words, the hope did not materialize and it was back to business as usual. To construct and demonstrate the religious intolerance and persecution of Muslims as counterterrorism experiences, Mazrui in one of his writing states that, 'There was a time during the Roman Empire when Christians were thrown to the lions for sport. Modern day religious persecution is rarely so callous. But are there global wargames unfolding at the expense of the Muslim world in this day and age?' (Mazrui, 2007, p. 6). In short, for Mazrui, counterterrorism or the war on terrorism is basically a religious war against Islam and Muslims.

Airport Harassment

According to Mazrui, the number of Muslims harassed at American and international airports began to multiply after September 11 (Mazrui, 2004, p. 805). He points out that visitors to the US from countries in Africa, the Middle East, Asia, and South America are being digitally photographed and finger printed on arrival, but visitors from European countries are being exempted (Mazrui, 2004, p. 805). This according to Mazrui is religious and ethnic discrimination.

The harassment of Muslims at airports is best expressed by his own experience as a Muslim. On August 3, 2003, on arrival from overseas, Mazrui was detained at Miami airport for seven hours under repeated interrogation. For him, detaining a 70-year-old man as a potential terrorist is a case-study of the new paranoia at airports (Mazrui, 2007, p. 7). He was interrogated by firstly immigration; secondly customs; and thirdly Homeland Security and the Joint Terrorism Task Force. They all focused on security. He points out that paradoxically, the last interrogators were the most apologetic and the most courteous though they still questioned him behind closed doors. He admitted he was truthful about all the Muslim organizations he belonged to, including the Muslim American Alliance, the old American Muslim Council and the Center for the Study of Islam and Democracy [CSID] (Mazrui, 2007, p. 7). Though he acknowledged the courteous treatment he received from these officials, he nonetheless felt that he would not have been kept for so long if they had not been interested in interrogating him personally. He was kept waiting until they arrived (Mazrui, 2007, p. 7). The discriminatory experience made him reflect about his religious faith and identify by asking himself questions like, after living in the United States for more than a quarter of a century, did he arouse suspicion on August 3, 2003 because of where he was coming from? Was he coming back from Afghanistan? Had he visited Baghdad? Perhaps he was coming back from Indonesia? The answers were a big no. He was coming back from Trinidad and Tobago in the Caribbean where his primary mission in Trinidad had almost nothing to do with Islam. He had been a keynote speaker to mark Emancipation Day, ironically commemorating the end of slavery in the nineteenth century, and had been received by the Prime Minister (Mazrui, 2007, p. 7). The questions he was asked at Miami on his return included whether he believed in Jihad and what did he understand by jihad? What denomination of Islam did he belong to? Since he was a Sunni, why was he not a Shi'a? Mazrui responded by asking the officials, 'If you were a Catholic, and I asked you why were you not a Protestant, how would you deal with that? (Mazrui, 2007, p. 8). The nature of the questions posed to him confirm Mazrui's reflections on counterterrorism that counterterrorism measures or the war on terror are meant to degrade Islamic culture and to label all Muslims as terrorists hence construct them as enemies. Though his ordeal at Miami airport ended amicably, he was however, not complacent. He was afraid it could happen again, emphasizing that Muslims should not be intimidated (Mazrui, 2007, p. 8).

Assassinations in Occupied Areas

The assassination of Muslims, in areas occupied by Western countries, as a counterterrorism measure is a recurrent theme that appears in Mazrui's discourse of counterterrorism in his political thought. It is interesting to note that in his construction of the word assassination, Mazrui points out that it is one of the ironies of history that the etymology of the English word *assassination* can be traced back to the Arabic language. Mazrui says it originally referred to people who got intoxicated by smoking *hashish* [*hashishin* or assassins] and became murderous as a result. He also points out that *Hassa* also means in Arabic, to slaughter people and that this is an alternative etymology (Mazrui, 2009, p. 6).

Mazrui argues that the most unethical and humiliating contemporary form of assassinating Muslims in the war of terrorism is through the use of drones. He states that:

> The drone has become an intoxicant…a *hashish* of modern technology. The resulting process has been a form of assassination. Every single casualty has been a Muslim, without exception. Many have also been speakers of the Arabic language, which had coined the word *assassin* in the first place (Mazrui, 2009, p. 6).

For Mazrui, the US is the main culprit, which specifically targets Arab Muslims. He argues that for the Obama Administration, the drone become a weapon of ethnic-specific targeted assassinations in the war on terror. He points out that Obama has authorized more specific assassinations than any other Head of State since World War II, with the possible exception of Israel's readiness to assassinate some of the enemies of the Jewish state (Mazrui, 2009, p. 1). Mazrui further points out that Muslim intellectuals are speculating whether Obama found it easy to authorize the killing of Pakistanis and Yemenis because these people were neither of European stock nor of Judeo-Christian ancestry (Mazrui, 2009, p. 1). He goes to the extent of declaring that 'Obama has been jury, judge and executioner, not only of Osama bin Laden but of many others' (Mazrui, 2009, p. 1). Mazrui emphasizes that innocent Muslims who have been killed by U.S. drones are estimated to run into hundreds, if not thousands. To this extent the 'Obama presidency has been the presidence of assassination *par excellence*' (Mazrui, 2009, p. 2). Mazrui also emphasizes that this method of warfare is in effect conducted by the Central Intelligence Agency (CIA) rather than the US Armed Forces directly. He points out that the covert use of drones as some kind of warfare has not been subject to the democratic oversight of any Congressional committee whatsoever and that it is 'a form of an unsupervised system of technological assassinations committed by the Obama administration in a blood-letting form of post-democratic foreign policy' (Mazrui, 2010, p. 25). The Obama Administration, he says, 'is indeed still fundamentally militaristic in foreign policy' (ibid, p. 25). It is in this context that he compares the devastating effects of drone attacks with that of the atomic bomb by stating that:

> When President Harry Truman authorized dropping the atomic bomb on Hiroshima and Nagasaki in August 1945, it was asked whether it was easy politically to drop such horrendous weapons on Asiatic populations rather than on European cities. Was President Truman trying out a new deadly weapon on the so-called "Yellow people." Similarly, a question is now asked whether Obama is the new President Truman trying out drone-attacks on Muslim populations (Mazrui, 2009, p. 2).

In short, Mazrui is arguing that drones, as instruments of assassination, are primarily used against Muslims. To demonstrate the humility of Muslims towards these drone attacks, Mazrui says that whether humanity likes it or not, Muslims across the world are more outraged by attacks against *Islam* (the religion itself) – rather than against *Muslims* [the followers of the faith] (Mazrui, 2009, p. 5).

Conclusion

Political thought is socially constructed in the sense that it is largely determined by the social milieu of the thinker. Mazrui's political thought is influenced by Islam as a religion and Islamism as a political ideology. This is evident in many of his scholarly works that have a dominant theme on issues of Islam and Islamism. His construction of the concepts of terrorism, counterterrorism and counterterrorism experiences are at the normative level influenced by Islamism and at the empirical level by his real life experiences as a Muslim. This is significant as it provides a link between the normative and the empirical.

Mazrui's construction of the concept of terrorism is based on the social facts of ethics, politics, and regioness. He constructs counterterrorism on the basis of the social facts of cultural superiority, social equality and distributive justice, religion and ethnicity, and sovereignty. Hence in his political thought Mazrui constructs the 'fact' or 'reality' that terrorism and counterterrorism do not only adversely affect Christians as is often depicted but likewise adversely affects Muslims. Mazrui argues that Muslims are equally affected by acts of terrorism committed by Islamic extremists but more so by counterterrorism measures effected to contain such extremism. In other words, Mazrui constructs terrorism and counterterrorism in his political thought in such a way that they deconstruct the often held negative perceptions of Islamism. Islamism as a political ideology is, therefore, used to negate Islamic extremism and Western cultural superiority hence promote religious toleration.

References

Checkel, J. 1998. The Constructivist Turn in International Relations Theory. *World Politics,* 50, 324-348.

Denouex, G. 2002. The Forgotten Swamp: Navigating Political Islam. *Middle East Policy* IX, 56-81.

Finnemore, M and Sikkink, K. 2001. Taking Stock: The Constructivist Research Program in International Relations and Comparative Politics. *Annual Review of Political Science, 4*, 391-416.

Grint, K. 2005. Problems, problems, problems: The social construction of 'leadership. *Human Relations,* 58, 1467-1494.

Hegghammer, T. 2009. Jihadi–Salafis or Revolutionaries? On Religion and Politics in the Study of Militant Islamism' in R. Meijer (ed) Global Salafism: Islam's New Religious Movement (New York: Columbia University Press, 2009), pp. 245–247.

Hoehne, M. 2009. Counter-terrorism in Somalia: How external influence helped to produce militant Islamism, Max Plank Institute for Social Anthropology, Halle/Saale, Germany.

International Crisis Group (ICG). 2005. Understanding Islamism, Middle Eat/North Africa Report No. 37, Cairo/Brussels, March 2.

Mazrui, A. 1985. The Third World and International Terrorism: Preliminary Reflections. *Third World Quarterly*, 7, 348-364.

Mazrui, A. 2001-2002. Editorial: The Terror of "the war on terrorism". *Institute of Global Cultural Studies (IGCS) Newsletter*, 3 (1-2), 1, 6 and 10.

Mazrui, A. 2002. Afro-Arab Crossfire: Between the Flames of Terrorism and the force of Pax-American. Development Policy Management Forum (DPMF) Occasional Paper, No. 6.

Mazrui, A. 2004. Islam and the United States; Streams of Convergence, Strands of Divergence. *Third World Quarterly*, 25, 793-820

Mazrui, A. 2006. Who is Afraid of Ali Mazrui? *Annual Mazrui Newsletter*, No. 30, Spring, 12-13.

Mazrui, A. 2007. Islam Between Clash and Concord of Civilizations: Changing Relations Between the Muslim World and the United States, Meeting Record, Chatham House, 16 January 2007, AP2007.

Mazrui, A. 2009. Fighting Evil from Nuremberg to Guantanamo: Double Standards in Global Justice.

Mazrui, A. 2010. Between the Pre-Democratic Ummah and the Post-Democratic United States of America. Draft July 2010. Paper presented on a panel organised by the American Muslim Alliance at the annual meeting of the Islamic Society of North America (ISNA) held in Chicago, Illinois, July 3, 2010.

Mazrui, A. 2011. A Fragment; Africa Between the Baobab Tree and the Owl of Minerva: A Post-Colonial Educational Narrative. Draft May 20111. Paper presented at the annual conference of the Comparative and International Education Society (CIES) on the theme "Education is That Which Liberates: Fifty Years of Education for Development: Taking Stock and Looking Forward", hosted by McGill Faculty of Education, Montreal, Canada April 30 to May 4, 2011.

Mwangi C and Mwangi O. 2014, Environmental Conservation, Peace, Democracy and Development: A Case Study of Wangari Maathai's Speeches, in M. Lockhart and K. Mollick (eds), *Global Women Leaders: Studies in Feminist Political Rhetoric* (Lanham, Maryland: Lexington Books), pp. 41-63.

Mwangi, O. 2012. State Collapse, *Al-Shabaab*, Islamism and Legitimacy in Somalia, *Politics, Religion & Ideology*, Special Issue on Non-State Armed Groups and the Dynamics of Community Support, 13, 513-527.

Mwangi, O. 2015. Don't be vague bash the Hague: Votes and Legitimacy in Kenya's 2013 Elections, *Commonwealth & Comparative Politics*, 53, 381-400.

Price, R. 2008. Moral Limit and Possibility in World Politics. *International Organisation,* 62, 191-220.

Risse, T. 2000. "Let's Argue!": Communicative Action in World Politics. *International Organisation,* 54(1), 1-37.

Spellman, W. 2011. *A Short History of Western Political Thought.* Hampshire: Palgrave Macmillan.

Spencer, A. 2012. The social construction of terrorism: media, metaphors and policy implications. *Journal of International Relations and Development,* 15, 393-419.

Sterling-Folker, J. 2000. Competing Paradigms or Birds of a Feather? Constructivism and Neo-Liberalism Compared. *International Studies Quarterly,* 44, 97-119.

Wendt, A. 1999. *Social Theory of International Politics,* Cambridge: Cambridge University Press.

15

Paradox of Gender in Mazrui's Triple Heritage[1]*

Etin Anwar

Ali Mazrui's work on gender examines the trajectory of gender culture in the historical and contextual encounters of the Western and Muslim worlds. They demonstrate a common pattern and common traits of how rules, roles, and rights are constructed and deconstructed within each locality and how defined gender cultures entail systemic values that are relevant beyond the geographical, cultural, and civilizational contexts. As each gender culture emphasizes its unique superior ideology, Mazrui argues that the gender values of Westerners and Muslims become less compatible when compared to the political relations between the two. Within these multilayered nuances of gender systemic divergence and political compatibility, Mazrui's work on gender examines the trajectory of three civilizational dialogues between Western, Islamic and African values of gender culture and the cultures of sexuality across the boundaries of civilizations, religions, race, ethnicities, and languages.

Central to Mazrui's concept of gender cultures is the confluence of indigenous, Islamic and Western civilizations,[1] which has led to him being labeled everything from an Africanist to a political/social scientist, Islamist, and culturalist. However, he is never labeled as a feminist or a gender theorist. Writing from the perspectives of feminist and gender studies, scholars

---

1 * This chapter, "The Paradox of Gender in Mazrui's Triple Heritage," was originally published in *Public Intellectuals and the Politics of Global Africa: Essays in Honor of Ali A. Mazrui*, ed. Seifuden Adem (London: Adonis and Abbey Publishers Ltd. 2011, pp 45-58) and is printed here with the permission of the original author and the publisher.

like Sudarkasa,[2] Ogundipe-Leslie,[3] and Vakil[4] perceive Mazrui's works on gender as less grounded in the feminist literary tradition, the lived experience of women, and the rhetoric common to feminist consciousness-raising movements. Although I have some reservations about labelling Mazrui as a feminist, I believe that Mazrui's writings on gender unfold what shapes the seamless paradox of gender and its effect on the production of the body politic that is patriarchal and masculine in nature.

In this chapter, I will explore the ways in which Mazrui's paradoxical theory of gender cultures in the triple heritage converge with and diverge from feminism. I will first discuss how Mazrui's theory of the paradox of gender demonstrates the convergent sexual reciprocity among men and women regardless of racial, cultural, religious, and civilizational boundaries. Male and female partnership not only centers on biological reciprocity, but also generates the body politic peculiar to the longevity of such partnership, such as state policy as family planning, sexual division of labor, and the familial institution. I will then examine how the male and female partnership across religions, states, and civilizations produces a convergent world culture and politics.

The Paradox of Gender and Sexual Reciprocity

Mazrui formulates the intricacy of gender relationship in the following propositions: "(i) among humans, the senior partner in the creation of new life is the female of the species (woman as mother); (ii) among humans, the senior partner in the destruction of life is the male of the species (man as warrior); and (iii) it is the power of destruction which has given the male of the species dominion over the female (man as ruler)." These propositions are the product of intellectual, historical and cultural specificity that cannot be removed from its context; yet they also transcend the boundaries of civilizations, religions and geo-political locality. Mazrui's compelling proposition of gender is indeed paradoxical in that, even though men and women need each other, they will never collaborate to control the state because women are interested in balance and equality, whereas men seek to capture the state for themselves and monopolize its legitimacy by means of coercion, physical force and violence.[5]

Mazrui's theory of gender offers in the first place a glimpse at how men and women in sexual reciprocity generate the rules, roles and rights governing their relationship. Although sexual discourse and constructs are a common theme among feminists and gender activist, Mazrui looks at a comparative rule that regulates sexual relationality within each culture and its impact on sexual and civilizational politics. Sexual reciprocity between men and women brings together the racial, religious, cultural, and civilizational factors that shape the genealogical relationality and superiority. Cross-sexual relationality however is often seen as danger to the purity of the lineage, resulting in descending and ascending miscegenation of offspring. Barack Hussain Obama would not have been such a controversial candidate for president, had he not been racially black, biologically linked to a Muslim father, and religiously connected to his pastor Rev. Jeremiah A. Wright Jr.[6]

As a comparative theorist, Mazrui analyzes the gender construct of men and women within the hegemonic masculinity and patriarchy common to African, Islamic and Western civilizations. Like many feminists, Mazrui argues that gender construct is cultural and that its underlying principle is embedded in each local culture. He defines a multilayered function of culture as providing lenses of perception and cognition, motives for human behavior, sources of evaluation, a basis of identity, a mode of communication, a basis for stratification, and the system, of production and conxumption.[7] Within the enmeshed rules that culture produces and the roles for which men and women are prepared, as well as the rights that are conferred on men and women; both sexes undergo some sort of gender appropriation within their own cultures and adjustments to the changing roles of gender coming from global cultures.

The most fundamental gendered construct, one common to Islamic, Christian, and Indigenous African traditions, is the compatibility of men and women in procreation. Male and female partnership within African culture takes into account the Islamic and western influences. Although Islam and Western Christianity support the culture of procreation, both shape Africa quite differently. Islam in Africa is more relevant to the culture of lineage and procreation rather than the culture of combat.[8] Islam spread to Northern Africa by conquest, whereas the majority of the African continent was Islamized through migration, trade, missionary work (da'wa), and revivalist movements. This affinity of indigenous Africans and Muslims lies in the importance they assign to fertility rather than to rivalries among ethnic groups. Islam has been assimilated through intermarriages that subsequently produced the hybridization of Africa and Arab cultures. Christianity had only a marginal impact in the level of fertility since African cultures consider children to be a form of insurance for parents in old age.

Islam endorses marriage and the begetting of children. Marriage, as the Prophet Muhammad is said to have declared, is part of one's religion. The culture of procreation encourages fertility, early arranged marriage, and motherhood. It also engenders a set of mechanisms that nurture the basic norms instituted for men and women. Embedded in the culture of procreation is the institution of marriage as a way if maintaining the lineage if the family and of bestowing honor and dignity upon its members. Although honor and dignity are theoretically the mechanism entrenched in marriage in order to protect the lineage, they are practically useful in maintaining the production of lineage and tribal coalition. The construction of lineage not only starts when the selection of a spouse begins on the basis of either religion, beauty, wealth, piety or other merits, but it is also available as an avenue to improve one's dignity and class. An Arab who is married to a slave would grant the newborn his own paternal lineage. This ascending miscegenation was completely different from the situation in the American slavery system in which the faith of the newborn depended completely on the mother.

The Arabs never completely Islamized Africa before the coming of Western Christianity, which along with capitalism, religious missionaries, modern slavery and colonization, changed the landscape of African lands forever. The existing white settlers in many parts of Africa and the creation of artificial boundaries of the African map escalated the ethnic conflicts and rivalries among Africans. Complicating the intricacy of Africanity of such dominant ethnic groups as the Kikuyu in Kenya and the Ganda in Uganda were the westernized elites that controlled the destiny of Africa through their imperial policies without necessarily centering, liberating and empowering African men and women. Mazrui, however, argues that the Arabization of Africa does not lead to bloodshed in itself; violence and war on African soil, such as that which existed between the Hutu and Tutsi in Rwanda, the Kikuyu and Luo in Kenya, the Ibo, Hausa and Yoruba in Nigeria and others, have been caused by ethnic rivalries, demographic ethnic imbalance, rigged votes, and unequal share of power among divers ethnicities.

Although the Islamic and Western impacts in Africa can clearly be seen in the multifaceted resilience of the local and global forces to the politicization of Africa and its cultural and geographical divides, Mazrui insists that the affinity between men and women in procreation remains the hallmark of human partnership. I argue that male and female partnership in Africa and the Muslim world in general is gendered. Male and female biological partnership assumes the enactment of male dominance that feeds what Mazrui characterizes as the paradox of gender. Whereas both men and women desire copulation, both perceive the propensity for sexual behavior differently.[9] The difference lies in male aggression and female receptivity from which the construction of masculinity and femininity is derived. Even at the most intimate moment, men never fail to insert their dominance, as Oakley states:

> Along with the male's greater aggression in other fields, goes his aggression in the sphere of sexuality: males initiate sexual contact, and take the

symbolically, if not actually, aggressive step of vaginal penetration-a feat which is possible even within a frigid mate. They assume the dominant position in intercourse. Males ask females to go to bed with them, or marry them, or both: not vice versa.[10]

Male dominance and female receptivity in sexual relations should come as no surprise since men define the accepted norms and practices of what is culturally and socially appropriate for men and women.

Female passivity and receptivity to male and sexual advance and leadership are often religiously encouraged. In Islamic heritage, the Qur'anic verses 4:34[11] and 2:228[12] are understood to imply "a biological difference between men and women in intelligence, capacity, and piety;"[13] therefore, men and women are not equal because the former are superior to the latter. They control women, provide maintenance, and have the right to beat disobedient wives (*Qur'an*, 4:34). In contrast to the traditional understanding of the term (*d}arb*, wife-beating), Barlas (2002) interprets *d}arb*, as a restriction and a prevention of violence toward women.[14] This is to say that God does not warrant violence toward women universally, but warrants it only in particular cases and the context in which the *Qur'an* was revealed. In our historical context, *d}arb* may well mean *'taharru* (to leave or move). When any disagreements occur in a marital relationship, both parties need to take time to resolve the problems accordingly. When both parties are tempted to break out in violence, they need to calm things down by giving each other some space.

Although the reproductive function of sexuality unites men and women in partnership, the rules, roles, and rights of men and women in marriage are not equal by far. Mazrui comparatively examines the compatibility of men and women in creation, yet the different roles and rights of men and women imposed by the religious, social and political imperatives that often marginalize and oppress women cannot transcend the boundary of the utilitarian union between a husband and a wife. He demonstrates the commonality of the cultural foundation that underlies this in the confluence of Islamic, Western and African traditions. He sees the gender gap between and men and women in private and public spheres globally. This gap is even wider in the Muslim world in particular and the third world in general since women are often subjected to the rules, roles, and rights imposed by the state, religion, and society. As a series of states' policies on women emphasized the control of female sexuality through family planning with fewer rights to safe abortion and reproduction, the appropriation of the role of motherhood as the backbone of the culture is parallel to the way the sexual division of labor is instituted. Women are invariably expected to meet fully the expectations of both the religion and the state in the private and public domains.

The return of religious fervor to many parts of the Islamic world [*] especially among fundamentalists who strive to win the hearts and the minds of Muslims through the control of women [*] brings Islam closer to the center of the family and the state. In the process, women, seen as the carriers of the tradition, are subjected to pressure and sometimes even religious violence (such as by being forced to act as suicide bombers). This institutionalization of traditionalism emphasizes the unchanging roles and rights of women, generating a gap between their modern and traditional portrayals. Mazrui calls for the closure of the gender gap by way of cultural readjustment of the rules, roles, and rights of women at the personal, political and social levels.

Gender Politics and the Politics of Masculinity and Its Vindication

The second aspect of Mazrui's paradox of gender reflects the politics of gender difference and its effect on men and women in Islamic, Western and African traditions. He postulates that the destruction of life and war is characteristic of partnership between men, rather than among females and/or in the male-female partnership. In the Marzuian framework, the exclusion of women from warring and killing is a form of benevolent sexism, a kindness to women extended for their own dignity and protection. Feminists would certainly object to the exclusion of women from public responsibility, even in the area of war and patriotism, on the basis of the biological difference between men and women. Women in many developed and developing countries have been part of the warrior tradition. Parallel to benevolent sexism is benign sexism that neither harms nor bestows advantage, while yet advancing women's interests and needs. Only malignant sexism does actual harm to women, since it subjects women to "economic manipulation, sexual exploitation, and political marginalization."[15]

I will argue that the senior partnership between men in the politics of war and peace is a culturally constructed system directly resulting from both convergent and divergent power relations. Within this enmeshed social, political, and cultural power relation lies women's subjectivity, which is ineluctable from the masculine and patriarchal world that produces rules, roles, and rights for both men and women. Men cross-culturally create the rules and the language of how to live by the rules, define the roles that are appropriated on the basis of sexual and gender difference, and confer the rights that are constructed on the basis of economic and sexual merit. In other words, men not only define what rules, roles, and rights are available to women, but also produce the measures and discipline for cases where ruling ideologies do not function. This gender thinking operates at the epistemological level and finds its application at the personal, familial, social, and political apparatus. Within this trajectory of gender cultures, Mazrui concedes that the categories of sexism, i.e., benevolent, benign and malevolent, are intrinsic to the gender relationship and male alliances in power and war.

This is where Mazrui and feminists diverge sharply. For Mazrui, not every preferential concept or attitude in the treatment of women is fully sexist; since it is the meta-language of sexism that entails its true meaning, as is the case with malignant sexism. For feminists on the other hand, any and all rules, roles, and rights that are bestowed on women on the basis of sexual difference and that are constructed to enhance masculine interests are legitimate targets of the feminist critique of patriarchy and masculinity. Is Mazrui to be blamed for centering the discourse of gender on "a feminist frame of reference"[16] but without feminist nuances and epistemology? Mazrui places his theory of gender culture within an African context that explores themes of the role of men and women at the personal, familial and social levels, looking at gender relationships, their oppression, and empowerment. He combines factual and theoretical construct of how the human condition in its geopolitical locality produces, reproduces and nurtures power and knowledge. The masculine codification of power and knowledge generates out of an accumulated male prowess of domination produces not only the body politic, but also the politics of masculinity that maintains the ruler and the ruled, the self and the other and the dominant and the weak. This dual assumption governs not only the gender relationship, but also human relationality within its own culture and the human encounter with the other.

For many feminists who accentuate the personal as the political, Mazrui's approach fails as an "essentialist," "reductive," and "simplistic" paradigm.[17] Mazrui however painstakingly claims that the fundamental issue in gender discourse is not about men speaking about women or vice versa, but about the survival of the human species that depends on the symbiotic relationship between men and women and the empowerment of women at all levels.[18] Like the feminists, Mazrui focuses on their critique of masculinity and patriarchy that goes beyond the products of "male-centered discourses" and what Wittig calls the "straight mind."[19] De Lauretis argues that

> [if] the goal of feminist theory is to define sexual difference for women, to understand how one becomes a woman, what gives femaleness (rather than femininity) its meaning as the experience of a female subject, then the

starting point can be neither "man" nor "woman": neither the Man with the capital M of humanism, or the lower case M of modernism; nor, on the other hand, women as the opposite or the complement of man: Woman as Nature, Mother, Body, and Matter, or woman as style, figure, or metaphor of man's femininity.[20]

Because the "all-purpose feminist frame of reference" is an emerging field, it has to be inclusive of multiple identities, heterogeneities within women, and a multilayered trajectory of race, gender, sexuality, and ethnicity.[21] In the process of addressing feminist subjects, both male and female voices enhance the feminist epistemology and politics. After all, feminist studies continue to engage rigorously with divergent voices, paradigms, and categories and to engage in interdisciplinary dialogues.

Mazrui's theory of gender complements the feminist rhetoric of how the politics of masculinity, which centers on the exercise of power, affects women.[22] Feminist theories focus on men's "sexual exploitation and violence," "unrelieved villainy," and their role as "agents of patriarchy" as a means to enhance and maintain the patriarchal and masculine domination.[23] Mazrui engages the feminist issue by looking at the causes of women's oppression, empowerment and policy recommendations across civilizations, since many feminists concede that:

> Liberal feminists...believe that women are oppressed insofar as they suffer unjust discrimination; traditional Marxists believe that women are oppressed in their exclusion from public production; radical feminists see women's oppression as consisting primarily in the universal male control of women's sexual and procreative capacities; while socialist feminists characterize women's oppression in terms of revised versions of the Marxist theory of alienation.[24]

As the eradication of oppression from women's everyday life is a daunting task, it takes the united efforts of individuals, the state, women's organizations, and legal practitioners to implement the necessary ideas and programs. Given women's lack of education, property, economy, technology, finance and opportunity, women's rules, roles and rights will continue to be marginal. In the indigenous African traditions, women as the custodians of the earth, water, and fire hardly move beyond this predicament, since in the wake of technological advancement, farming, irrigation, and electricity are often managed and controlled by men.[25] Even if women were to enter the economy and politics, the majority of women would not have the needed skills to plug into the male-dominated markets and political system.

Why then are women continuously marginalized? Is hegemonic masculinity too powerful to be defeated? I think that the resilience of the hegemonization and homogenization of masculinity that has existed since the origin of human existence is a dynamic process. Hegemonic masculinity is not a condition, but "a question of how particular groups of men inhabit positons of power and wealth, and how they legitimate and reproduce the social relationships that generate their dominance."[26] The answer to this question lies in women's subordination, which benefits men, their connection to the institution of male dominance over women, heterosexual regimes,[27] and the patriarchal system that upholds the underpinning of societal institutions produced and protected by men. Hegemony refers not only to "a historical situation, a set of circumstances in which power is won and held," but also a constant contestation of power and the reproduction of power operating at a new level. Although the feminist contestation of masculine hegemony has shifted the dynamic of gender relations, on a larger scale, it has not yet loosened the grip of male domination and power in the private and public spheres, especially in the third world countries.

Mazrui points to examples of women who achieved leadership roles in Muslim-dominated countries, such as Benazir Bhutto (1988-1990 and 1993-1996), the daughter of Zulfikar Ali and Megawati Sukarno Putri (2001-2004), and Khaleda Zia (1991-1996) and Sheikh Hasina (1996-2001) in Bangladesh, all of whom were elected to office due to the kinship relationship to the male leaders. They did earn their jobs by virtue of blood relatives and male connections; hence, their leadership is male-derived. Admittedly, female leadership in the Muslim world is, despite the claim of democracy, granted by men to women. All these female leaders, although they resumed the leadership inherited from the male relatives, did not survive the masculine politics of a husband's, relative's or associates' corruption or the enemy coalitions during their terms of office.

Bhutto's tragic assassination is an example of how a woman's interruption into masculine politics and authority can cost a woman her life, not to mention the dream of democracy. She stood not only against authoritarian and dictatorial leadership, but also against chauvinist radical religious leaders who perceived anyone standing in their way as an enemy. Was Bhutto considered an enemy because she was female? She was not an ordinary female. She was a Western educated female and twice prime minister. Her mistake was to step into the male world as prime minister twice. This time, however, she came with the masculine, 'foreign' rhetoric of the war on terror to crack down on Muslim radicals at the heart of Pakistan. Violence of any background – religious, racial or civilizational – is genderless and merciless to men, women, children, and civilians. In war and conflict zones, women are often targeted with violence as a means to defeat the enemy by way of rape, trafficking, intimidation, and slavery.

The exclusion of women from warfare, while benevolent, is about the inequality of power in the public domain. War is about policy towards the enemy. This political decision has been historically made by men to conquer the other's lands and has always been led my men. A historical, diachronic look into masculine politics has been largely authoritarian, chauvinist, and dictatorial in nature. In this sense, Mazrui's point of senior partnership in the destruction of life and violence is right, in that warfare is initiated and occurs between men. He seems to be saying that women's involvement in warfare is incompatible not only with the reproductive relationship between men and women, but also with benevolent, benign, and even malevolent sexism. Is Mazrui's view of women's rules, rights, and roles underlying the partnership between men and women a gendered one? Does he voice men's view of gender appropriation? It would be misleading to perceive Mazrui's work on gender as an apologetic masculine view, since Mazrui is attentive to women's issues, interests, and needs.

Mazrui regards the virtue of masculinity in politics as common to all civilizations. The term masculinity entails strength, virility, and nobility. Although the virtue of masculinity is exercised on the battlefield, it infiltrates all aspect of life. Islamic, Western, and African cultures all interact in asserting masculine dominance. The Negro symbolizes masculinity; Africa confers the notion of femininity. Africa is discussed in feminine term because it is feminized by the intrusion of other masculine cultures, like Islam and Western Christianity. The use of the beard symbolizes manliness and dignity in times of peace and war. However, as the beard post-September 11th is perceived as the emblem of terrorists and terrorism, it has now become repellent to have it. Although the imposition of beardlessness is political, it also feminizes Muslim men by stripping them of their right to wear a beard. Similarly, polygamous marriage is common to indigenous African and Islamic cultures, but this practice becomes perceived as repugnant as the homogenization of monogamous marriage becomes the accepted ruling ideology. The colorful African and Islamic dress is similarly homogenized by masculine Western suits. If men exercise masculine virtues over women by way of the imposition of masculine rules on the feminine roles and rights, the masculine civilization imposes the feminization of the less powerful civilizations.

Even though the supposed overbearing masculine civilization endorses the masculine premises of power and dominance over less powerful civilizations, the political alliances between the masculine and the emasculative regimes tend to converge. The incontestable Western support for authoritarian and despotic countries in the Muslim world led by men is a living proof of what Mazrui insightfully presents as the collaboration in destructive power. Although the Western-backed regimes envisage the coming of democracy, they utilize various powerful tools to silence indigenous democratic voices and justice along with an unchanging perception of the foundational and institutional structure. In this sense, the political convergence between world civilizations is masculine oriented rhetoric, since they serve each other's purpose of the multilayered hegemony that allows the injustice to gender equality and humanity to exist.

Concluding Remarks

Mazrui's assessment of the divergent gender cultures in the world civilizations correlates with the feminist epistemology in examining the cross-cultural roles of women. Certainly, his theory of gender culture is less founded in what Narayan calls the feminist epistemology,[28] which is rooted in the premise of how women's individual and social position in the world affects ways of thinking and the production of knowledge. Does sexual and biological ownership matter in defining what feminism is and what is not? What defines feminism is not biological commonalities, but the commitment to eradicate "sexism, sexist exploitation, and oppression."[29] In the case of Mazrui, his works should be seen within "broad, generalizing categories for ordering, analyzing, or explaining human behavior, particularly recurrent behavior, characteristic of societies and cultures around the world."[30]

The civilizational encounters on gender issues remain oppressive and burdensome. Women are seen as sexed bodies that are subjected to a series of gendered cultures and as sexual objects whose sexuality is only of interest for reproduction, sexual trafficking, mail bride, and prostitution. The global victimization of women prevails in third world countries; Western feminists are mostly interested in the empowerment of women when the perceived oppression is presumably linked to radical Islam. The liberation of Afghani women, so important to feminists, was imbued with the masculine dialectics of preemptive war on terror. Yet, women in conflict zones continue to find it hard to achieve the basic rights and security needed for everyday life. These women are the victims of double masculine politics. The intricacy of Western masculine politics and its appropriation of the masculine gendered system in the Muslim world strengthen male political alliances and the production of rules for an operative gender system, yet preserves the discontinuity between women's rights and roles.

Notes

1. Alamin Mazrui, "Ali Mazrui and His Critics," in *Race, Gender, and Culture Conflict: Debating the African Condition: Mazrui and His Critics*, Volume 1, eds. Alamin Mazrui and Willy Mutunga (Trenton, NJ: African World Press, Inc., 2004), 1.
2. Niara Sudarkasa, "Mazrui and Gender: A Contextual Essay," in *Race, Gender, and Culture Conflict: Debating the African Condition: Mazrui and His Critics*, Volume 1, eds. Alamin Mazrui and Willy Mutunga (Trenton, NJ: African World Press, Inc., 2004), 199-219.
3. Molara Ogundipe-Leslie, "Beyond Hearsay and Academic Journalism: The Black Women and Ali Mazrui," in *Race, Gender, and Culture Conflict: Debating the African Condition: Mazrui and His Critics*, Volume 1, eds. Alamin Mazrui and Willy Mutunga (Trenton, NJ: African World Press, Inc., 2004), 236-245.
4. Ann C. Vakil, "Addressing Gender Inequality in Africa," in *Race Gender, and Culture Conflict: Debating the African Condition: Mazrui and His Critics*, Volume 1, eds. Alamin Mazrui and Willy Mutunga (Trenton, NJ: African World Press, Inc., 2004), 259-262.
5. Ali A. Mazrui, *Cultural Forces in World Politics* (Oxford: James Currey, 1990), 58-9.
6. Editorial, "Mr. Obama's Profile in Courage," *New York Times*, March 19, 2008.
7. Mazrui, *Cultural Forces in World Politics*, pp. 7-8.
8. Ali. A. Mazrui, "Africa's Islamic Experience: Expansion, Revival and Radicalization," a paper was delivered at the World Affairs Council, San Francisco, California (April 10, 2002).
9. Ann Oakley, "Sexuality," in *Feminism and Sexuality: A Reader*, eds. Stevi Jackson and Sue Scott (New York: Columbia University Press, 1996), 36.
10. Oakley, "Sexuality," in *Feminism and Sexuality: A Reader*, 36.
11. Men are the protectors and maintainers of women, because Allah has given the one more (strength) than the other, and because they support them from their means. Therefore, the righteous women are devoutly obedient, and guard in (the husband's) absence what Allah would have them guard. As to those women on whose part ye fear disloyalty and ill-conduct, admonish them (first), (Next), refuse to share their beds, (And last) beat them (lightly); but if they return to obedience, seek not against them Means (of annoyance): For Allah is Most High, great (above you all)." See Yusuf Ali's translation of 4: 34 in his work, *The Qur'an* (New York: Tahrike Tarsile, 1987), p. 190.
12. "Divorced women shall wait concerning themselves for three monthly periods. Nor is it lawful for them to hide what Allah Hath created in their wombs, if they have faith in Allah and the Last Day. And their husbands have the better right to take them back in the period, if they wish for reconciliation. And women shall have rights similar to the rights against them, according to what is equitable; but men have a degree (of advantage) over them. And Allah is Exalted in Power, Wise." See Ali's translation of 2: 228 in his work, *The Qur'an*, p. 90.
13. Marsam J. Al-Faruqi, "Women's Self Identity in the *Qur'an* and Islamic Law," in *Windows of Faith: Muslim Women Scholars-Activists in North America*, ed. Gisela Webb (Syracuse: Syracuse University Press, 2000), 82.
14. Asma Barlas, *"Believing Women" in Islam: Unreading Patriarchal Interpretations of the Qur'an* (Texas: University of Texas Press, 2002), pp. 184-188.
15. A. A. Mazrui, "The Black woman and the Problem of Gender," in *Race, Gender, and Culture Conflict: Debating the African Condition: Mazrui and His Critics*, Volume 1, eds. Almin Mazrui and Willy Mutunga (Trenton, NJ: African World Press, Inc., 2004), 218.

16 Theresa de Lauretis, "Feminist Studies/Critical Studies: Issues, Terms, and Contexts," In *Feminist Studies/Critical Studies* (Wisconsin: The Regent of the University of Wisconsin System, 1986), p 13.
17 Ogundipe-Leslie, "Beyond Hearsay and Academic Journalism: The Black Women and Ali Mazrui," p. 239 and p. 244.
18 Ali A. Mazrui, "Women as Victim, Woman as Victor: A Feminist Dilemma," in 249-246 in *Race, Gender, and Culture Conflict: Debating the African Condition: Mazrui and His Critics,* Volume 1, eds. Alamin Mazrui and Willy Mutunga (Trenton, NJ: African World Press, Inc., 2004), p. 249-250.
19 de Lauretis, "Feminist Studies/Critical Studies: Issues, Terms, and Contexts," p. 13.
20 Ibid.
21 Ibid., p. 14.
22 Tim Carrigan, Bob Connel, and John Lee, "Toward a New Sociology of Masculinity," in *The Making of new Masculinities: The New Men's Studies,* ed. Harry Brod (Boston: Allen and Unwin, 1978), 64.
23 *Ibid.*
24 Alison M. Jaggar, *Feminist Politics and Human Nature* (New Jersey: Rowman and Allanheld, 1983), 354.
25 Ali A. Mazrui, "The Economic Women in Africa: An African Commentary from a Sociological Perspective," *Race, Gender, and Culture Conflict: Debating the African Condition: Mazrui and His Critics,* Volume 1, eds. Alamin Mazrui and Willy Mutunga (Trenton, NJ: African World Press, Inc., 2004), 253.
26 Carrigan et al., "Toward a New Sociology of Masculinity," p. 92.
27 Ibid., pp. 93-94.
28 Uma Narayan, "The Project of feminist epistemology: Perspectives from a Nonwestern Feminist," Gender," eds. Alison M. Jaggar and Susan R. Bordo, */Body/Knowledge/ Feminist Reconstructions of Being and Knowing* (New Brunswick and London: Rutgers, 1989), p. 256.
29 Bell Hooks, *Feminism is for Everybody* (Cambridge: South End Press, 2000), 1.
30 Sudarkasa, "Mazrui and Gender: A Contextual Essay," 202.

16

Pan-Blackist Conceptualizations of the Black Power Paradigm:
From Cheikh Anta Diop to Ali Al'amin Mazrui

Abdul Karim Bangura

Introduction

After 17 months of intermittent residency in Trainidad, Ivar Oxaal, an American sociologist of Norwegian descent published a book titled *Black Intellectuals Come to Power: The Rise of Creole nationalism in Trinidad and Tobago* in 1968. This book opened doors to Oxaal for research fellowships, other books, tenure and promotion. Writing from a Eurocentric perspective, Oxaal described very well the power dynamics among the various ethnic groups in the country. What is missing in this work on Black Power, however, is the Pan-Blackism or Pan-African dynamics that undergirded the power struggle in Trinidad and Tobago. Had Oxaal been schooled in Pan-Afrcan or Pan-Blackist theories and research methodologies, he would have realized that Creole Nationalism in Trinidad was part and parcel of a larger global Pan-Black and Pan-African struggle that included Creoles in Louisiana, Spanish overseas colonies, Belize, Sierra Leone, Indonesia, Mauritania, and the Americas working with their brothers and sisters in Africa and the Diaspora to advance Black Nationalism. Oxaal would have also realized that Mighty Sparrow, whose words of wisdom he quoted extensively throughout the book, had strong affinity with Sierra Leone, a country he visited several times and wrote songs in its honor.

This essay presents and analyzes the essentiality of Pan-Blackism in the discourse on the Black Power paradigm. This is important because most of the concepts used in works dealing with Africa and/or African issues employ Eurocentric concepts that often do not capture the essence of the phenomena being discussed.

To demonstrate why and how Pan-Blackism promotes greater comprehension of the Black Power paradigm, the rest of this essay is divided into three major interrelated parts. First, I deal with the general import of concepts. Second, I discuss the essence of concepts in communication. Finally, I discuss the postulates of a sample of major Black thinkers around the world on the paradigm.

The General Import of Concepts

> Thinking involves the use of language. Language itself is a system of communication composed of symbols and a set of rules permitting various combinations of these symbols. One of the most significant symbols in a language…is the *concept* (1996:26).

With the preceding excerpt as backdrop, social scientists Chava Frankfort-Nachmias and David Nachmias defined a *concept* as "an abstraction—a symbol—a representation of an object or one of its properties, or of a behavioral phenomenon" (1996:26).

Concepts are generally defined as abstract ideas or mental symbols that are typically associated with corresponding representations in languages or symbologies which denote all of the objects in given categories or classes of entities, events, phenomena, or relationships between them. Concepts are said to be abstract because they omit the differences of the things in their extensions, treating them as if they are identical; they are said to be universal because they apply to every thing in their extensions. Concepts are also characterized as the basic elements of propositions, much the same way words are the basic semantic elements of sentences.

As opposed to being agents of meaning, concepts are bearers of meaning. Consequently, concepts are arbitrary. For example, the concept of TREE can be expressed as *tree* in English, *shajar* in Arabic, *mti* in Kiswahili, *kənt* in Temne, *àrbol* in Spanish, *albero* in Italian, *arbre* in French, *árvore* in Portuguese, *депево* in Russian, and *baum* in German. The fact that concepts are arbitrary, i.e. they are independent of language, makes translation possible— words in various languages have identical meaning, because they express one and the same concept.

For scientific purposes, as social scientists Kenneth Hoover and Todd Donovan have posited, concepts are "(1) tentative, (2) based on agreement, and (3) useful only to the degree that they capture or isolate some significant and definable item in reality." Thus, for these scholars, concepts are important because (a) thought and theory develop through the linking of concepts, and (b) science is a way of checking on the formulation of concepts and testing the possible linkages between them through references of observable phenomena (2004:18-19).

The scientific functions of concepts, according to Frankfort-Nachmias and Nachmias, are fourfold. First, concepts are the foundation of communication. Without a set of agreed-upon concepts, scientists could not communicate their findings or replicate one another's studies. Second, concepts introduce a *perspective*—i.e. a way of looking at empirical phenomena. Concepts enable scientists to relate to some aspect of reality and identify it as a quality common to different examples of the phenomena in the real world. Third, concepts allow scientists to classify and generalize. Stated differently, scientists employ concepts to structure, characterize, order, and generalize their experiences and observations. Finally, scientists use concepts to serve as components of theories and, therefore, of explanations and predictions. Consequently, concepts are the most critical elements in any theory because they define its content and attributes (1996:26-27).

The Essence of Concepts in Communication

The correct or objective use of concepts is essential for successful communication because the latter involves two or more participants in an interaction who must share similar meanings of the former (Crystal, 1992:256). In order to fully grasp this essence, we must turn to the works of linguists.

For linguists, the essence of concepts in communication rests on the notion of *conceptual dependency*, defined by Gillian Brown and George Yule as the relationship between attitudes and behavior; but, when applied to understanding discourse, it incorporates a particular analysis of language (1983:241). Roger Schank set out to represent the meanings of sentences in conceptual terms by providing a conceptual dependency network he terms a *C-diagram*. He defined a *C-diagram* as a network that contains concepts, which enter into relations he described as dependencies.

Riesbeck and Schank pointed out that our expectations are conceptual rather than lexical and that different lexical realizations in the x-position (e.g., *hospital, doctor, medical center*, etc.) will all fit our expectations. Brown and Yule added that evidence that people are 'expectation-based parsers' of texts hinges on the fact that we can make mistakes in our predictions of what will come next (1983:242).

John Lyons introduced the notion of conceptual field by relying on Jost

Trier's general definition of "fields." According to Trier, "Fields are living realities that intermediate between individual words and the totality of the vocabulary; as parts of a whole they share with words the property of being integrated in a larger structure (*sich ergleiden*) and with the vocabulary the property of being structured in terms of smaller units (*sich ausgliedern*)" (Lyons, 1977:253).

Lyons illustrated the notion of conceptual field by employing the continuum of color, prior to its determination by particular languages. According to him, color terminology provides a particularly good illustration of differences in the lexical structure of different language systems. He noted that, actually, there are problems attaching to the recognition of a conceptual area, and in this case psycho-physical definable, field of color, neutral with respect to different systems of categorization. He noted that if we are to accept for the moment that it is reasonable to think of the continuum, or substance, of color in this manner, then different languages and different synchronic states of what may be regarded, diachronically, as the same language evolving through time, can be compared in respect of the way in which they give structure to, or articulate (*gliedern*), the continuum by lexicalizing certain conceptual (or psycho-physical) distinctions and thereby giving lexical recognition to greater or less areas within it.

Pan-Blackist Conceptualizations of Black Power

Ali Ala'min Mazrui (1977:27) provided a general definition of Pan-Blackism as a Trans-Atlantic Pan-African phenomenon constituting links between Africa south of the Sahara and the Black Diaspora—the solidarity of shared blackness is extended to Black/African Americans, West Indians, Black/African Brazilians, and other African/Black people in the Western Hemisphere. Mazrui distinguishes Pan-Blackism with three other Pan-African phenomena. The first is Sub-Saharan Pan-Africanism, an assertion of solidarity among Black Africans south of the Sahara. The second is Trans-Saharan Pan-Africanism, emphasizing the links between Africa south and north of the Sahara; the Organization of African Unity (OAU) was and its predecessor, the African Union (AU), is based on this principle. The third is Trans-Atlantic Pan-Africanism, bringing together the Black Diaspora in the Western Hemisphere with all Africans in the continent, both Black and Arab.

The growth of Pan-Blackism and the other Pan-African phenomena, according to Mazrui (1977:26-27), was the result of race consciousness. Gradually, with improved communications, Africans in East Africa found out about Blacks in West Africa and what was happening to them. Africans in Central and Southern Africa in turn discovered the shared experiences of Africans in Eastern and later in Northern Africa. The bond that brought together Black Africans was that of being all Black; but the bond that linked Black Africans with Arab Africans was in part due to the solidarity of being *non-White*. The link in Sub-Saharan Pan-Africanism was that of shared blackness; but in the continent as a whole, the ultimate unifying principle was that of shared humiliation and colonization by the White races.

As Mazrui (1977:197) also pointed out, it is critical to make a distinction between Pan-Blackism and Pan-Aricanism, as Pan-Blackism is the movement, ideology, or collection of attitudes primarily concerned with the dignity of Black people wherever they might be. The banner of Pan-Blackism, he added, brought Sub-Saharan Africans and African Americans together. Pan-Africanism, on the other hand, gradually became essentially a continental movement within Africa itself, in which the Arabs of North Africa were perceived to play a more important role than African Americans. Mazrui cited Tom Mboya as having argued that the proof that Pan-Africanism was not a *racial* movement lay in the fact that the OAU included both Arab and Black states. But as Mazrui also correctly pointed out, historically, Pan-Africanism was birthed by Pan-Blackism. He insisted that it cannot be repeated too often that it was African Americans such as W. E. B. Du Bois and West Indians such as George Padmore that helped to make Pan-Africanism globally conspicuous. Furthermore, while the foundation of Pan-Blackism remained an affinity of color, the basis of Pan-Africanism became an attachment to a continent.

Despite its history and significance, there are Pan-Africanists who have rejected Pan-Blackism. Tajudeen Abdul-Raheem, for example, rejected Pan-Blackism arguing that it is a reactionary attempt to balkanize Africa behind the so-called Sub-Saharan division. He argued that we must accept as African any citizen, by whatever means acquired, of any of the countries of Africa, from Cape Town to Cairo and all other Islands (Madagascar, Mauritious, Cape Verde, etc.) and also recognize anybody of African descent in the Diaspora. He added that while a majority of Africanns are of Negroid origins, it is not true historically, factually, or even politically, that blackness is the only criterion for Africaness (Campbell, 2009).

Nonetheless, there are other Pan-Africanists who have countered the position proffered by Pan-Africanists such as Abdul-Raheem. Tunde Adeleke (2005), for instance, argued that the color line is rooted in history, and that the experiences of Africans and Blacks in the Diaspora have tragically been informed by a Eurocentric hegemonic *weltanschauung* that has provoked a countervailing racial essentialist ethos contrived to combat the debilitating impact of Eurocentrism. In order words, according to Adeleke, racial essentialism has historically served as pedestal for constructing and sustaining binaries of hegemony and counter-hegemony.

For centuries, pointed out Adeleka (2005), race has served as a defining and unifying construct in African and Black Diaspora historical relations. According to him, Blackness, identified as the basis of negative historical experiences (slavery, colonial exploitation, and discrimination), also became the underpinning of identity and the framework for unity against an equally racially defined and monolithic Euro-American establishment and world order. Race, he added, became the basis of confraternity and the foundation for a Pan-African platform and struggle. Therefore, Adeleke asserted, the color line suggests a Manichean conception of society and reality as theaters of perpetual conflict between two racially constructed and irreconcilable forces: i.e. Black and White. Race became, he added, the medium not only of understanding the nature of the challenges and struggles of Blacks, but also of adequately constructing an effective counter-offensive.

Black Power is generally defined as a political concept used among people of Black African descent throughout the world to emphasize racial pride and the creation of Black political and cultural institutions to nurture and promote Black collective interests, advance Black values, and secure Black autonomy (Scott, 1976; Ogbar, 2005). Black Power expresses a range of political goals, from defense against racial oppression to the establishment of separate social institutions and self-sufficient economy. The Black Power Movement helped to usher in Black radical thought and action against an elusive, yet visible, White supremacy. The earliest known usage of the term is found in a Richard Wright's 1954 book titled *Black Power*. The first use of the term in a political sense is attributed to Robert F. Williams, a National Association for the Advancement of Colored People (NAACP) chapter president, writer, and publisher of the 1950s and 1960s. New York politician Adam Clayton Powell, Jr. is noted to have used the term on May 29, 1966 during a baccalaureate address at Howard University when he said "To demand these God-given rights is to seek Black Power" (Shapiro, 2006).

Noteworthy is the fact that the Black Power symbol and salute that have been employed and continue to be employed in Africa and its Diaspora is traced back to the Ethiopic ideographic character ρ (yä) YÄMAN, literally a term for a fisted right hand. Ethiopic is not only a cultural agency but also a foundation to a great literary tradition in Ethiopia which, for instance, has made a critical contribution to the history of Christianity by originally preserving *The Book of Henok*, which is widely believed to be a precursor of Christianity. The Ethiopic writing system is much older than it has been previously thought, with its origins going as far back as 2000 BCE. The dynamic linkages between the Ethiopic and Egyptian writing systems suggest a possible relationship between all African writing systems of the Nile Valley (Bekerie, 1997).

Some may wonder why these Ancient Egyptian renditions of these concepts are important. The answer can be found in a major challenge Cheikh Anta Diop posed to African intellectuals: i.e. until Africa is able to reclaim the historical and promethean consciousness that is embodied in the achievements of Ancient Egypt, the history of Black Africans and that of humanity in general will "remain suspended in air" (1974a:xiv-vi). According to Diop, such a history can never be written correctly "until African historians dare to connect it with the history of Egypt." In his view, even the study of languages, institutions, etc. cannot be treated properly until this is done: "in a word, it will be impossible to build an African Humanities, a body of African human sciences, so long as the relationship does not appear legitimate" (1974a:xiv).

For us to respond to this historic challenge and be part of the correction of the historical distortion and theft of our African heritages, we must provide deeply thought out and well-conceived vision and mission, with a well-articulated strategy to achieve our objectives. To succeed, our effort must be part of the creation of a counter-hegemonic discourse which can enable, as Odora Hoppers and colleagues characterized it, the "triple agenda of deconstruction, reconstruction and regeneration to be undertaken at the same time" (2002:238). To achieve this counter-discourse, we must engage in work that can help and contribute to reshaping the direction of education on the continent and in the Diaspora towards a more culture-specific and culturally relevant curriculum of liberation. We must carry out theoretical formulations and reflections in a multiplex, interdisciplinary, pluridisciplinary and comparative manner (for more on this approach, see Bangura and McCandless, 2007 and my forthcoming book in press). We must provide conditions for the acquisition of knowledge not only for "its own sake" but for the sake of humanity and African recovery and rebirth. We must develop new methodologies and techniques for accessing, utilizing, and storing all knowledge based on an African epistemology and cosmology. This would imply, according to Dani Nabudere (2002), the development of an all-inclusive approach, which recognizes all sources of human knowledge as valid within their own contexts.

The åtenu/Mapinduzi/Revolutionary Perspective

It is important to note here that while the *åtenu/Mapinduzi*/Revolutionary paradigm of Black Power was, and continues to be propounded by those who are still alive, by the Black thinkers listed within this group in Table 1, Pan-Blackist Revolutionary consciousness is deeply rooted in American history and can be traced back to the early 19th Century efforts by Black leaders to use both slavery and racism as unifying constructs. As Adeleke (2005) correctly pointed out, the tradition became much more pronounced in the mid-19th Century Black nationalist, back-to-Africa push of Martin R. Delany, Henry H. Garnet and others. They had given up on integration, and believed that racism was deeply entrenched, invincible and unconquerable. In his 1854 Presidential Address before the National Negro Emigration Convention in Cleveland, Ohio, Martin Delany proclaimed, in unambiguous terms, the racial essentialist creed that, for generations to come, African American nationalists invoked to justify a Manichean worldview. Underscoring the imperative of emigration, Delany declared that "It would be duplicity longer to disguise the fact that the great issue, sooner or later, upon which must be disputed the world's destiny, will be a question of black and white, and every individual will be called upon for his identity with one or the other." Almost half a century later, William Edward Burghardt (more commonly, W. E. B.) Du Bois echoed Delany's sentiments in what many perceive as a perceptive and prophetic articulation of the racial underpinning of 20th Century history. "The problem of the twentieth century," according to Du Bois, "is the problem of the color line." Both Delany and Du Bois underscored the primacy of the color line as essential dynamics of American history. Yet, both had radically different considerations in mind. The consideration for Delany was separatism—that is, the creation of an independent Black nationality in Africa. Du Bois' consideration was a little ambivalent, albeit he too emphasized race and racial consciousness, but realizing the complexity and duality of the Negro as an equally compelling consideration. While race mattered to Du Bois, and he eventually became active in Pan-Africanism, his analysis took into account the American dimension of the Negro identity and the inherent validity of that identity. Both Delany and Du Bois would go on to use their racial convictions to support paradigms that advanced Pan-African consciousness and movement designed to unify all Blacks around the world behind a platform of economic, social and political struggle and regeneration. This racial essentialism also became a fundamental character of Marcus Garvey's Pan-Africanism of the first quarter of the 20th Century. The tradition continued right through the civil rights epoch to the present.

Mumia Abu-Jamal lost his father when he was nine years old (Smith, 2007). He was named Mumia in 1968 by his Kenyan high school teacher instructing a class on African cultures in which students took African names in the classroom (Burroughs, 2004). The name Mumia means "Prince" and was the name of anti-colonial African Nationalists engaged in warfare against the British in Kenya at the time of its independence movement (Abu-Jamal, 2003). He adopted the surname Abu Jamal, meaning "Father of Jamal" in Arabic, after the birth of his son Jamal on July 18, 1971 (Burroughs, 2004).

Abu-Jamal wrote that during his adolescence, he was "kicked...into the Black Panther Party" after suffering a beating from "whire racists" and a policeman for his efforts to disrupt a George Wallace for President Rally in 1968 (Abu-Jamal, 1996). The following year, at the age of 15, Abu-Jamal helped to form the Philadelphia branch of the Black Panther Party, serving as the chapter's Lieutenant of Information and exercising a responsibility for authorizing information and news communications of the branch. In one interview he gave at the time, he quoted Mao Zedong saying that "political power grows out of the barrel of a gun (Burroughs, 2004). He left the Panthers and returned to his old high school, but he was suspended for distributing literature calling for "Black revolutionary student power." He also led protests to change the school's name to Malcolm X High, albeit he was unsuccessful (Shaw et al., 2007). After attaining his General Education Diploma (GED), he studied briefly at Goddard College in rural Vermont (Burroughs, 2004).

Abu-Jamal worked at WUHY public radio station from 1979 until 1981 when he was asked to submit his resignation after a dispute about the requirements of objective focus in his presentation of news. As a radio journalist, he was called "the voice of the voiceless" and was well known for identifying with and giving exposure to the MOVE commune in Philadelphia's Powelton Village neighborhood, including reportage of the 1979-1980 trial of certain of its members (the MOVE Nine) charged with the murder of police officer James Ramp (*The Philadelphia Inquirer*, 1981). During his broadcasting career, Abu-Jamal interviewed such high profile Blacks like Bob Marley, Alex Haley, and Julius Erving. Abu-Jamal also served as president of the Philadelphia Association of Black Journalists, NABJ (NABJ, 2005).

Jamil Andullah Al-Amin, also known as H. Rap Brown, was born as Hubert Gerold Brown. He came to prominence in the 1960s as chairman of the Student Nonviolent Coordinating Committee SNCC) and later the Justice Minister of the Black Panther Party. He is perhaps most famous for his proclamation during the 1960s that "violence is as American as cherry pie" and that "if America don't come around, we're gonna burn it down." Al-Amin's activism in the civil rights movement led to his arrest in Cambridge, Maryland, and charged with inciting to riot as a result of a speech he gave there. He later opened a store in Atlanta, Georgia and became a Muslim spiritual leader and community activist preaching against drugs and gambling in Atlanta's West End neighborhood. He became affiliated with Dar ul-Islam and became the leader of Ummah, a group of mostly African American converts to Islam which seeks to establish a separate Sharia-law-governed state within the United States according to Federal Bureau of Investigation (FBI) files (Center for Islamic Pluralism, 2008). Nonetheless, the Muslim Alliance in North America (MANA) issued a statement rebuking the FBI characterization and allegations against Al-Amin as "shocking and inconsistent" to those who had worked with him (MANA, 2009).

As C. L. R. James observed in 1967, Al-Amin is prepared to challenge American and racial prejudice to the utmost limit of his strength and the strength of African Americans who will follow him. James further pointed out:

> A word more about Rap Brown. Whether he is what "they" call a racist, or he is not one, does not interest me at all. I am interested in Rap Brown as a political leader. And I know what Rap Brown is doing. He is not a Garvey-ite: Garvey's doctrine was suitable for his time. What Brown is doing is this: he is taking care that the total rejection of second-class citizenship, the single-mindedness, the determination to fight to the death if need be, which now permeates the Negro movement, will not be corrupted, modified, or in any way twisted from its all-embracing purpose by white do-gooders and well-wishers of whom the United States is full. Even when whites go down to the South to face blows and bullets from the Southern police and gangsters, the Negro movement finds that they cause difficulties which impede the struggle (James, 1967:9).

It is not farfetched to assert that no other African-centered scholar has advocated and defended the *àtenu/Mapinduzi*/Revolutionary paradigm, while thoroughly condemning the global hegemonic character of Eurocentrism as Marimba Ani, also known as Dona Marimba Richards. Two of her seminal works titled *Yurugu: An African-Centered Critique of European Cultural Thought and Behavior* (1989) and *Let the Circle be Unbroken: The Implications of African Spirituality in the Diaspora* (1989), for example, are scathing criticisms and deconstructions of the hegemonic character of Eurocentric history and culture. She is also one of the most fervent defenders of the absolutist construction of African identity for Blacks all over the world. Her work on identity deemphasizes the transformatory consequences of the cultural transplantation. As far as she is concerned, Blacks retain their African essence and identity, despite the centuries-old transplantation in the New World. Ani has reaffirmed a cardinal Africancentric conviction—that is, the inherent and absolute hegemonic character of Eurocentric culture—and called for "de-Europeanizing culture" in order to sustain a culture that is relevant and responsive only to the political needs of Blacks. She added to the call for racial and cultural vigilance in a global context in which she believes Blacks continue to be threatened by Eurocentric values and cultural contacts.

Without a doubt, Molefi Kete Asante is one of the leading modern philosophical advocates of the *åtenu/Mapinduzi*/Revolutionary paradigm. In his pioneering work, Asante constructed an intellectual paradigm, Afrocentricity, which encompasses the separatist visions of Pan-Blackism. The Afrocentric framework within which he envisioned the Black struggle is decidedly and essentially culturally constructed upon African historical and cosmological foundations. He called for cultural vigilance and unity against an ever-growing Eurocentric force. Asante insisted that Black survival and eventual triumph in a world order still dominated by Europeans hinge upon Black racial/cultural unity (see, for example, Asante, 1987:190).

As I stated in my forthcoming book titled *African-centered Research Methodologies: From Ancient Times to the Present* (Bangura, in press), Afrocentricity presupposes knowledge of a commonality of cultural traits among the diverse people of Africa which characterize and constitute a worldly view that is some how distinct from that of the foreign world views that have influenced African people. Afrocentricity simply means that the universe is a collection of relationships, and an individual or a group being in that universe is defined by and dependent upon these relationships. Africans, prior to European and Asian dominance, and still to some degree now, considered the Cause or God as being a part of His creation while Europeans on the other hand considered God separate from His creation. Afrocentricity will continue to evolve as more information on African people's past comes to light and as greater and differing demands are placed on African people. It can be defined by its history, the organizations and people who contributed to its development, and the body of ideas that make it up. Applied within its scientific framework, Afrocentricity has greater value and respect. The value of Afrocentricity in regards to the well being and overall development of African peoples is invaluable. It can ultimately give them a greater degree of understanding of themselves. Probably, the most beneficial aspect of Afrocentricity is its potential in uniting people of African descent for their collective well being.

Imamu Amiri Baraka, born Everett LeRoy Jones, founded in Harlem, New York the Black Arts Movement (BAM), an artistic branch of the Black Power movement, in the 1960s. BAM inspired Blacks to establish ownership of publishing houses, magazines, journals and art institutions. Other well known writers who were involved with BAM included Nikki Giovanni, Don L. Lee (later known as Haki Madhubutti), Sonia Sanchez, Maya Angelou,

Dudley Randall, Sterling Plumpp, Larry Neal, Ted Jones, Ahmos Zu-Bolton, and Etheridge Knight. Some of the Black-owned publishing houses and publications that came from the BAM movement included Madhubutti's *Third World Press* and *Broadside Press*, Zu-Bolton's *Energy Black South Press*, and the periodicals *Callalloo* and *Yardbird Reader*. Other literary giants that have shared some of BAM's artistic and thematic concerns include notable African American novelists Ishmael Reed and Toni Morrison and poer Gwendolyn Brooks (Joseph, 2006).

As it sought to link art and politics in a highly conscious manner in order to assist in the liberation of Blacks, BAM helped to increase the number and visibility of African American artistic productions. The movement made it very clear that the literature, drama, and music of Blacks served as an oppositional and defensive mechanism through which creative artists could confirm their identity and express their own unique impressions of social reality. Furthermore, to act as highly visible and unifying representations of blackness, the artistic products of the Black Power movement also utilized themes of Black empowerment and liberation. Black recording artists not only transmitted messages of racial unity through their music, they also became significant role models for a younger generation of African Americans. Updated protest songs not only bemoaned oppression and societal wrongs, they also utilized adversity as a reference point and tool to lead others to activism. Many BAM artists conducted brief mini-courses in the techniques of empowerment. In the tradition of cultural nationalists, these artists instilled the belief that in order to alter social conditions, Blacks first had to change the way they viewed themselves; they had to break free of European norms and strive to be more natural, a common theme of African American art and music. Musicians such as the Temptations sang lyrics like "I have one single desire, just like you / So move over, son, 'cause I'm comin' through" in their song "Message From a Black Man," expressing the revolutionary sentiments of the Black Power movement (Van DeBurg, 1992).

Yosef Alfredo Antonio ben-Jochannan, more widely known as Dr. Ben, is an only child to a Black Puerto Rican Jewish mother named Julia Matta and a Black Ethiopian Jewish father named Kriston ben-Jochannan, a Falasha. He was born in Gonder, Ethiopia. Shortly after his birth, the Ben-Jochannan family moved to St. Croix, Virgin Islands. The young Ben enjoyed playing cricket and working on the sugar plantation of his uncle. In 1938, ben-Jochannan earned a BS degree in Civil Engineering at the University of Puerto Rico and in 1939 a Master's degree in Architectural Engineering from the University of Havana, Cuba. He received doctoral degrees in Cultural Anthropology and Moorish History from the University of Havana and the University of Barcelona, Spain, respectively. He is a well-respected American historian and Egyptologist. He is most notable for his writings and teachings about ancient Egypt and how European culture appropriated its legacy (*HistoryMakers*, 2006).

In one of his famous books, *African Origins of the Major "Western Religions": The Black Man's Religion* (1970), ben-Jochannan pointed out that many African Americans have moved from their "I know a good Negro family in my church..., etc.," window dressing role to positions of minor non-policy making participation in White America's religious institutions. He stated that the "GOOD NEGROES," nevertheless, have decided to act upon, rather than remain quietly within, the White Christian religion (ben-Jochannan, 1970:297). He added that Blacks in the United States, be they Jews, Muslims, Christians, or the traditionally noted indigenous African religious denominations, are also asking whether religion's role and sole purpose is for the existence and perpetuation of the powers that allow it to become wealthy. He then asked the question of how long Black America is expected to worship a God on its knees and stare into the clouds awaiting the coming or return of the promised "MESSIAH" to free them from their earthly bondage (1970:298-299).

Dr. Ben calls upon Blacks to fight for their human rights and reclaim their religions from Europeans. As he puts it,

> It is African-American (Black) and their "*Human Rights,*" guaranteed them by the mere virtue of their birth; and by the world community of nations in its "*Declaration of Human Rights*," "*Rights*" which found much of their fundamental origins in the religious philosophies of the so-called "AFRICANS SOUTH OF THE SAHARA"—"BLACK AFRICA." There can be no doubt that "WESTERN RELIGIONS" is a misnomer of the "*nth*" degree. It is as *racist* as it sounds, "WESTERN RELIGIONS." Like "GREEK PHILOSOPHY," it cannot escape its indigenous African origin, and the inheritors of their African origin—presently indigenous Africans and their descendants in the Caribbean, the Americas, and elsewhere (1970:304).

Amílcar Lopes Cabral, a Guinea-Bissaunian agronomic engineer, writer, Marxist and nationalist guerrilla and politician, and also known by his *nom de guerre* Abel Djassi, led African nationalist movements in Guinea-Bissau and the Cape Verde Islands and led Guinea-Bissau's independence movement. He was assassinated in 1973 by Guinea-native agents of the Portuguese colonial authorities just months before Guinea-Bissau declared unilateral independence (Chabal, 1983). An ardent proponent of the *ãtenu/Mapinduzi/* Revolutionary paradigm, Cabral urged Blacks to "return to the source" and struggle for their identity and dignity in the context of the national liberation movement. He argued that the fact that independence movements are generally marked, even in their early stages, by an upsurge of cultural activity has led to the view that such movements are preceded by a "cultural renaissance" of the subject people. He added that culture is one means of collecting together a group, even a *weapon* in the struggle for independence (Hord and Lee, 1995:74-75).

But the return to the source, according to Cabral, is not and cannot in itself be only an *act of struggle* against foreign domination (colonialist and racist), and it no longer necessarily means a return to traditions. It is the denial by the petite bourgeoisie of the pretended supremacy of the culture of the dominant power over that of the dominated people with which it must identify itself. He added that the return to the source is therefore not a voluntary step, but the only possible reply to the demand of the concrete need, historically determined and enforced by the inescapable contradiction between the colonized society and the colonial power, the mass of the people exploited and the foreign exploitive class, a contradiction in the light of which each social stratum or indigenous class must define its position (Hord and Lee, 1995:77-78).

Cabral further stated that the identity of an individual or a particular group of people is a bio-sociological factor outside the will of that individual or group, but which is meaningful only when it is expressed in relation to other individuals or other groups. This dialectical character of identity, he added, lies in the fact that an individual or a group is only similar to certain individuals or groups if it is also different to other individuals or groups. Thus, for Cabral, the Black struggle, in the face of all kinds of obstacles and in a variety of forms, must reflect the awareness or grasp of a complete identity, generalizes and consolidates the sense of dignity strengthened by the development of political awareness, and derives from the culture of cultures of the masses in revolt as one of its principal strengths (Hord and Lee, 1995:79, 83).

Aimé Césaire, Martinican poet, playwright, and politician, one of the most influential authors from the French-speaking Caribbean, formulated with Léopold Senghor and Léon Gontian Damas the concept and movement of *négritude*, defined as "affirmation that one is Black and proud of it." Césaire's thoughts about restoring the cultural identity of Black Africans were first fully expressed in *Cahier d'un retour au pays natal* (*Return to My Native Land*), a mixture of poetry and poetic prose. The work celebrated the ancestral homelands of Africa and the Caribbean. It was completed in 1939 but not published in full form until 1947 (Tekijä, 2008).

Césaire characterized Western civilization as a decadent civilization that proves incapable of solving the problems it creates, stricken a civilization that chooses to close its eyes to its most crucial problems, and a dying civilization that uses its principles for trickery and deceit. Thus, for him, the so-called European civilization, cum "Western" civilization, as it has been shaped by centuries of bourgeoisie rule, is incapable of solving the two major problems to which its existence has given rise. The first problem is that Europe is unable to justify itself either before the bar of "reason" or before the bar of "conscience." The second problem is that, increasingly, Europe takes refuge in a hypocrisy which is all the more odious because it is less likely to deceive (Hord and Lee, 1995:162).

Stating the equation that colonization equals "thingification," Césaire noted a storm that talked to him about progress, about "achievements," diseases cured, and improved standards of living. He stated that he was more concerned about societies drained of their essence, cultures trampled underfoot, institutions undermined, lands confiscated, religions smashed, magnificent artistic creations destroyed, and extraordinary *possibilities* wiped away (Hord and Lee, 1995:168). Césaire therefore called for revolutionary change because the proof is abundant from the indigenous people of Africa who were demanding schools and colonialist Europe refusing them, the Africans who were asking for ports and roads and colonialist Europe was niggardly on this score, and the colonized people who wanted to move forward and the colonizers holding them back (Hord and Lee, 1995:170).

Cheikh Anta Diop, historian, anthropologist, physicist, and politician, studied the human race's origins and pre-colonial African culture. He is regarded as an important figure in the development of the Afrocentric viewpoint, in particular for his seminal theory that the Ancient Egyptians were Black Africans. For Diop, Black Power hinged upon the origins and history of the Black world. He asserted that in all likelihood, present-day African people are in no way invaders from another continent; they are the aborigines. He noted that recent scientific discoveries that show Africa to be the cradle of humanity increasingly negate the hypothesis of Africa being peopled by outlanders. He pointed out that from the appearance of *homo sapiens*—from earliest prehistory until our time—we are able to trace our origins as a people without significant breaks in continuity. In early prehistory, a great South-North movement brought the African peoples of the Great Lakes region into the Nile Basin. They lived there in clusters for millennia. He noted that in prehistoric times, it was Africans who created the Nilotic Sudanese civilization and what we now know as Egypt (Diop, 1974b:3).

Diop therefore called for a Pan-African Union on the basis of historical, psychological, economic and geographical unity. He urged that we complete such a unity and set it on a modern autochthonous cultural base to recreate our linguistic unity through the choice of an appropriate African tongue promoted to the influence of a modern cultural language. He concluded that linguistics dominates all national life. Without it, national cultural unity is but fragile and illusory, as the wrangling within a bilingual country, such as Belgium, illustrates the point (Diop, 1974b:7-8).

William Edward Burghardt (more commonly, W. E. B.) Du Bois, African American civil rights activist, Pan-Africanist, sociologist, historian, author, and editor, attempted virtually every possible solution, ranging from the realm of scholarship to propaganda, integration, national self-determination, human rights, cultural and economic separatism, politics, international communism, expatriation, and Third World solidarity, to the problem of the 20th Century: that is, racism. Du Bois identified four classes of reasons usually given in defense of race antagonism. The first class of reasons is that racial antagonism is an instinctive repulsion from something harmful and is, therefore, a subtle condition of ultimate survival. The second class of reasons is that racial antagonism, whether instinctive or not, is a reasonable measure of self-defense against undesirable racial traits. The third class of reasons is that racial antipathy is a method of race development. And the final class of reasons is that race antipathy is a method of group socialization (Hord and Lee, 1995:247-248).

According to Du Bois, most persons use all four classes of reasons at once and skillfully skim from one to the other. He noted that each argument has in other days been applied to individuals and social classes, but that we have outgrown that. He added that we now apply it to races because race is a vague, unknown term which may be made to cover a multitude of sins. He asked the questions: What is race? How many races are there? He asserted that what we have on earth are men. He then proceeded to ask more questions: Shall we help them or hinder them? Shall we hate and kill them of love and preserve and uplift them? Which method will do us the most good? These, for Du Bois, are the real questions of race antipathy (Hord and Lee, 1995:249).

It is this race concept, Du Bois pointed out, that dominated his life, and the history of which he had attempted to make the leading theme in his work. He noted that it propelled him to show all sorts of illogical trends and irreconcilable tendencies. He concluded that finally, consideration of his connection, physical and spiritual, with Africa and the African American race in its homeland led him to an attempt to rationalize the racial concept and its place in the modern world (Hord and Lee, 1995:260).

The work of Frantz Omar Fanon—psychiatrist, philosopher, revolutionary, freedom fighter in the war to liberate Algeria from France, and author from Martinique— remains influential in the fields of post-colonial studies and critical theory. Fanon is known as a Marxist thinker on the issue of decolonization and the psychopathology of colonization. His works have incited and inspired anti-colonial liberation movements for more than four decades.

According to Fanon, to study the relations of racism and culture is to raise the question of their reciprocal action. For him, culture is the combination of motor and mental behavior patterns arising from the encounters of man with nature and with his fellow man. He argued that racism can be said to be a cultural element; therefore, there are cultures with racism and cultures without racism (Hord and Lee, 1995:172).

Fanon noted that intellectual and emotional primitivism appeared as a banal consequence, which is the recognition of existence. Such affirmations, crude and massive, he pointed out, give way to a more refined argument. Thus, here and there, however, he believed an occasional relapse is to be noted; therefore, the "emotional instability of the Negro," the "subcritical integration of the Arab," and the "quasi-generic culpability of the Jew" comprise data that one comes upon among a few contemporary writers. These old-fashioned positions, Fanon argued, tend in any case to disappear; thus, this racism that aspires to be rational, individual, genotypically and phenotypically determined, becomes transformed into cultural racism. Thus, according to Fanon, the object of racism is no longer the individual man but a certain form of existence. At the extreme, he contended, such terms as "message" and "cultural type" are employed. "Occidental values" are then oddly blended with the already famous appeal to the fight of the "cross against the crescent." Fanon therefore insisted that we look for the consequences of this racism on the cultural level. Racism, as we have seen, he added, is only one element of a vaster whole: that of the systematized oppression of a people (Hord and Lee, 1995:173).

For Fanon, the logical end of this struggle is the total liberation of the national territory. In order to achieve this liberation, he called upon the inferiorized to bring all of their resources into play, all their acquisitions, the old and the new, their own and those of the oppressor. The struggle has to be total and absolute. He concluded that universality resides in this decision to recognize and accept the reciprocal relativism of different cultures (Hord and Lee, 1995:181).

Louis Farrakhan (born Louis Eugene Walcott) is the National Representative of the Nation of Islam. He is an avid advocate for Black interests, and a critic of American society. Farrakhan has been both widely praised and criticized for his often controversial political views and rhetorical style. In 1996, he was awarded the Al-Gaddafi International Prize for Human Rights founded by Libya's leader Muammar al-Gaddafi.

According to Farrakhan, unity in the global Black community is paramount. As he put it, he is tired of the divisions that we create for ourselves whether they be religious, political, educational, social, financial or other artificial barriers we set up to block dealing with another brother or sister in our community. He stated that Black love is Black Power and it is what we need more (Mustafaa, 2010).

As Farrakhan has stated repeatedly, members of the Nation of Islam want freedom, justice and equal opportunity for people of color. Blacks want reparations, preferably a large tract of land set apart from the United States and given to Black people, plus "our former slave masters are obligated to maintain and supply our needs in this separate territory for the next 20 to 25 years." They want the release of all Blacks convicted of any federal crimes and the release of all Black people convicted of any capital crime requiring the death sentence. Farrakhan has made it very clear that he is opposed to racial integration and against interracial marriage or race mixing (Pement, 1999).

Cyril Lionel Robert (more popularly, C. L. R.) James, who also adopted the pen-name of J. R. Johnson, was an African Trinidadian historian, journalist, socialist theorist and essayist. He was influential in the United Kingdom and the United States in socialist parties and Marxist thought, as well as leading ideas about the end of colonialism. He is also well remembered as a writer on cricket (Rosengarten, 2007:134).

In his essay on the West Indian middle class, James made it very clear that the effects of slavery and colonialism are like the miasma all around choking Black people. He insisted that the ordinary Blacks who have borne the burden for centuries are very tired of it. They do not want to substitute new masters for old; they want no masters at all. Unfortunately, he asserted, middle class Blacks do not know much. Under imperialism, they had little opportunity to learn anything. Thus, according to James, history will take its course, only too often a bloody one (Hord and Lee, 1995:161).

During his 1967 speech titled Black Power given in London, James expressed his belief that the concept of Black Power is one of the great political slogans of the time, albeit only time itself could tell that. Nonetheless, he stated, when we see how powerful an impact this slogan had made, it was obvious that it touched very sensitive nerves in the political consciousness of the world. He then called upon all Blacks in the world to support the fighters for African American rights and for Black Power in the United States.

As he emphasized, this means Blacks *do not* apologize or seek to explain, particularly to British people (and in particular to British Marxixts), or give any justification or apologize for whatever forms the struggle in the United States may take (James, 1967:9).

Maulana Karenga, born Ronald McKinley Everett and also known as Ron Karenga and as M. Ron Karenga, is an African American author, political activist, and college professor best known as the creator of Kwanzaa. Karenga was active in the Black Power movement in the 1960s and 1970s and founded the Black Nationalist group called The Organization Us which remains active to this day promoting the philosophy of Kawaida: a philosophy based on Black social and cultural change (The Organization Us, 1997).

As Molefi Keta Asante (2009) stated in his recent book on Karenga, Kwanzaa rose out of the Black liberation movement, especially its Black Power phase, "defined by its thrust to 'return to the source,' to go 'Back to Black.'" It is this period, according to Asante, which "stressed the rescue and reconstruction of African history and culture, redefinition of ourselves and our culture and the restructuring of the goals and purpose of our struggle for liberation at a higher level of human life based on the Afrocentric model." And Karenga and The Organization Us, Asante added, has served as a vanguard in the emphasis on turning toward Africa for cultural revitalization and the linking of culture and struggle, as Malcolm X, Frantz Fanon, Amilcar Cabral and Sékou Touré had propounded (Asante, 2009:166).

According to Asante, what Karenga discovered in his own research into the nature of knowledge and symbols was the need for ways to implement the lessons learned in the areanas of action and reflection. Kwanzaa, Asante argued, is the most representative creation of the Kawaida tradition in terms of African conception, cultural objectives, and ethical purpose. Initiated by Karenga in 1966, recounted Asante, Kwanzaa is a unique intellectual and cultural creation which is now celebrated by over 30 million Africans throughout the globe. Asante quoted Karenga as stating that he founded Kwanzaa for a number of basic reasons: (a) "to reaffirm and restore our rootedness in African culture;" (b) "to reaffirm and reinforce the bonds between us as a people in both the national and Pan-African sense;" (c) "to introduce and reinforce the *Nguza Saba* (The Seven Principles) and place at the same time emphasis on the importance of African communitarian values in general;" and (d) "as an act of self-determination,…it is important that we as African people speak our special cultural truth (in the world)." What then separates Kwanzaa from other celebrations in the African world, Asante asserted, is its self-conscious nature as an African-inspired form (Asante, 2009:164).

Ali Al'amin Mazrui (born in Mombasa, Kenya) is an academic and political writer on African and Islamic studies and North-South relations. He is an Albert Schweitzer Professor in the Humanities and the Director of the Institute of Global Cultural Studies at the State University of New York at Binghamton, among many other distinctions.

As Mazrui argued, it would be totally inaccurate to even say that the principle of collective self-determination as a nationalist assertion was unknown in Africa before the European intrusion. On the contrary, he asserted, the history of Africa is full of instances of resistance and rebellion against the European colonizer, as many Africans were inspired by a desire to maintain their autonomy and were unwilling to capitulate without a struggle to the new European presence in Africa. According to Mazrui, the range of African resistance is from Sultan Attahiru Ahmadu of the Sokoto Caliphate in 19th-Century Nigeria to the Maji Maji rebellion in Tanzania, from the so-called mad mullah of Somalia to the Shona-Ndebele risings in Zimbabwe in the late 19th Century. These activities were, as Mazrui stated, primary resistance movements against colonialism, to be distinguished from secondary resistance movements which came with modern political parties in Africa. Both forms of resistance, for Mazrui, can be seen as instances of self-determination in the form of nationalist assertion (Mazrui, 1977:27).

In reading the three-volume edited work titled *Africanity Redefined: Collected Essays of Ali A. Mazrui* (1992), which represents compilations of Mazrui's most important essays, it becomes quite evident that with a broad spectrum of Mazrui's writings during his many decades as a scholar and public intellectual, he has redefined the meaning of Africanity across geographical spaces, time, and cultures. The resulting definition is dynamic. It forces us to reject neo-imperialist paradigms and ontologies of what it means to be African. By encouraging us to think about Africanity as an idea rather than as point of origin, the ideas contained in these essays force us to reposition ourselves in the debate of our place in global cultures and civilizations, and they prepare us to take a more active role in social and political affairs.

Kwame Nkrumah (hailed Osagyefo, meaning "the Redeemer" in the Twi language), author, radical thinker, and revolutionary leader, was an influential 20th Century advocate of Pan-Africanism. He was the first President of Ghana, the first Prime Minister of Ghana and a founding member of the Organization of African Unity (OAU), the precursor of the present-day African Union (AU). Kwame Nkrumah was the leader of Ghana and its predecessor state, the Gold Coast, from 1952 to 1966, when he was overthrown with the complicity of the United States.

In his effulgent essay titled "Consciencism," Nktumah stated that practice without thought is blind and thought without practice is empty. Thus, according to him, the three segments of African society—(1) the traditional, (2) the Western, and (3) the Islamic—coexist uneasily. Consequently, he pointed out, the two foreign segments, in order to be rightly seen, must be accommodated only as experiences of the traditional African society. Nkrumah therefore suggested a number of tenets that must undergird the attitudes of Blacks toward the Western and Islamic experience if that experience is to be purposeful and guided by thought. First, any unification must take account, at all times, of the elevated ideals underlying the traditional African society. Second, social revolution must have, standing firmly behind it, an intellectual revolution, one in which our thinking and philosophy are directed toward the redemption of our society. Third, our philosophy must find its weapons in the environment and living conditions of the African people, as it is from these conditions that the intellectual content of our philosophy must be created. Fourth, the emancipation of the African continent is the emancipation of man, which requires two aims: (1) the restitution of the egalitarianism of human society and (2) the logistic mobilization of all our resources towards the attainment of that restitution (Hord and Lee, 1995:55).

The philosophy that must stand behind this social revolution, Nkrumah insisted, is consciencism: i.e. an intellectual map in terms of the disposition of forces which will enable African society to re-Africanize and then digest the Western, the Islamic and the Euro-Christian elements, and develop them in such a way that they fit into the African personality. According to Nkrumah, the African personality is itself defined by the cluster of humanist principles which underlie the traditional African society. He defined philosophical consciencism as that philosophical standpoint which, taking its start from the present content of the African conscience, indicates the way in which progress is forged out of the conflict in that conscience. Its basis, he added, is in materialism, and the minimum assertion of materialism is the absolute and independent existence of matter, a plenum of forces which are in antithesis to one another. The philosophical point of saying this, for Nkrumah, is that matter is endowed with powers of self-motion (Hord and Lee, 1995:55-56).

Jean Price-Mars, Haitian writer born in Grande Rivière du Nord, obtained a degree in medicine and worked as a diplomat. His writings championed the Negritude movement in Haiti, which "discovered" and embraced the African roots of Haitian society. Price-Mars was the first prominent defender of <u>vodou</u> as an actual religion complete with "deities, a priesthood, a theology, and morality." He argued against the prevailing prejudice and ideology, which rejected all non-White, non-Western elements of the cultures of the Americas (Antoine, 1981).

Price-Mars' Haitian Nationalism contrasted its embracement of Haitian cultural identity as African through slavery, while the neighboring Dominican Republic prided itself for being Spanish. Price-Mars' attitude was born when he witnessed the active resistance to the 1915-1934 United States' occupation of Haiti by the *campesinos*. He deplored the elite's abandonment of the tradition that focused on the country's liberation from French colonialism, but he took pride in the conduct of the poor. He attacked the elite for their "inability to promote the welfare of the Haitian masses." He coined the term "collective Bovarism" to describe the elite in identifying themselves with elements of European ancestry while denouncing any ties to their African legacy. He noticed that the elite were composed almost exclusively by people of mixed blood, who embraced their "whiteness," while the rest of the majority shared much of the same features, but his disdain for the elite spread beyond the racial purity of "Bovarism." It also spread to their economic and political influence implied by their status. He understood that their power base in the state system relied heavily on the taxation of crops, especially of coffee, the chief export, grown by the *campesinos* that had come to the country's defense when the elite had abandoned it to protect their own interests (Antoine, 1981).

For more contemporary evidence on the African presence in Asia and working with Blacks in the continent to engage in their liberation struggle, it is no exaggeration to state that no other scholar or activist has done as much work on those aspects as Runoko Rashidi. In his recent work titled "The African Presence in Asia: Introduction and Overview" (2010), Rashidi reminded us that the story of the African presence in Asia is as fascinating as it is obscure, and it began, it would strongly appear, more than 100,000 years ago. In truth, he said, we now know, based on recent scientific studies of DNA, that modern humanity originated in Africa, that African people are the world's original people, and that all modern humans can ultimately trace their ancestral roots back to Africa. Were it not for the primordial migrations of early African people, humanity would have remained physically Africoid, and the rest of the world outside of the African continent absent of human life. Since the first modern humans in Asia were of African birth, the African presence in Asia can therefore be demonstrated through the history of the Black populations that have inhabited the Asian landmass within the span of modern humanity.

Rashidi cited two recent DNA studies that strongly substantiate this claim. According to the first study, titled "Chinese Roots Lie in Africa," most of the population of modern China—one fifth of all the people living today—owes its genetic origins to Africa. An international scientific team has presented research findings that undercut any theory that modern humans may have originated independently in China. Populations from East Asia derived from a single lineage, indicating the single origins of those populations. It is now probably safe to conclude that modern humans originating in Africa constitute the majority of the current gene pool in East Asia.

Paul LeRoy Bustill Robeson, internationally renowned American bass-baritone concert singer, actor of film and stage, All-American and professional athlete, writer, multi-lingual orator, scholar and lawyer who was also noted for his wide-ranging social justice activism, was a forerunner of the civil rights movement. He was a trade unionist, peace activist, Phi Beta Kappa Society laureate, and a recipient of the Spingarn Medal and Stalin Peace Prize, among many others. He achieved worldwide fame during his life for his artistic accomplishments and his outspoken, radical beliefs, which largely clashed with the Jim Crow climate of the pre-civil rights United States. He became a prime target of the right during the McCarthyist era. Despite his being one of the most internationally famous cultural figures of the 20th Century, persecution by the United States government and media virtually erased Robeson from mainstream Ameican culture and subsequent interpretations of American history, including civil rights and Black history. Robeson was the first major concert star to popularize the performance of African American spirituals and was the first Black actor of the 20th Century to portray Shakespeare's *Othello* on Broadway. As of this writing, Robeson's run in the 1943-45 *Othello* production still holds the record for the longest running Shakespeare play on Broadway. In line with Robeson's dissatisfaction with movie stereotypes, his roles in both the American and British film industries were some of the first parts ever created that displayed dignity and respect for Black film actors, paving the way for other Black artists like Sidney Poitier and Harry Belafonte (Duberman, 1995).

At the height of his fame, Paul Robeson chose to become a primarily political artist, speaking out against fascism and racism in the United States and abroad as the United States government and many Western European powers failed after World War II to end racial segregation and guarantee civil rights for people of color. He therefore became a prime target of the Red Scare that lasted from the late 1940s through to the mid-1960s. His passport was revoked from 1950 to 1958 under the McCarran Act and he was under surveillance by the Federal Bureau of Investigation and Central Intelligence Agency and by the British MI5 for well over three decades until his death in 1976. The reasoning behind his persecution centered not only on his beliefs in socialism and friendship with the Soviet people but also his tireless work towards the liberation of the colonized peoples of Africa, the Caribbean, Asia and the Australian aborigines, his support of the International Brigades, his efforts to push for anti-lynching legislation and the racial integration of major league baseball among many other causes that challenged White supremacy on six continents. Condemnation of Robeson and his beliefs came swiftly from both the United States Congress and many mainstream Black organizations, including the National Association for the Advancement of Colored People (NAACP). To this day, Paul Robeson's FBI file is one of the largest of any entertainer ever investigated by the United States Intelligence Community, requiring its own internal index and unique status of health file. Despite persecution and limited activity resulting from ailing health in his later years, Paul Robeson remained, throughout his life, committed to socialism and anti-colonialism as a means to world peace and was unapologetic about his political views. Afrocentrist activists and historians of Paul Robeson's legacy have worked successfully to restore his name to many history books and sports records, while honoring his memory globally with posthumous awards and recognitions (Duberman, 1995).

As Bangura (2006) demonstrated in his essay on Paul's Robeson's linguistics breakthrough, he discovered common links in music through the pentatonic scale—a five-tone scale characteristic of both Chinese and African traditional music. He used this to also demonstrate that the Aorist form of Chinese and African languages has five different tonal patterns, each used regularly under certain conditions. [*Tone* refers to the linguistic function of pitch at word level. Tones are usually classified in terms of pitch range and direction into high vs. low, and rising vs. falling level, with more complex sequences (such as rising-falling and falling-rising). In a tone language, tone is one of the features, which determine the lexical meaning of a word.]

Also, Robeson discovered a common link between Chinese and African languages based on changes of tone and inflection, which give new meanings to words and grammatical constructions. Furthermore, he found that all ancient music from around the world is part of a common body of music based on a common means of expression—the pentatonic scale. These discoveries, arrived at through his own research, provided the historical and cultural foundation for his dedication to world peace (Bangura, 2006).

Robeson's linguistic insight allowed him to sing and analyze spirituals with deep structural linguistic meanings, since the messages of these songs contained a secret language of communication, which arranged escape from slavery. In essence, Robeson was deft in the syntactic (sign vs. sign), semantic (sing vs. concept or universe) and pragmatic (sign vs. context) meanings of the spirituals. This linguistic insight propelled Robeson to stand up at every opportunity and speak out against injustices and degradation that Africans experienced in America and other parts of the world. It also pushed him to embrace the cause of the poor and oppressed people wherever they were, no matter what the price or personal sacrifice (Bangura, 2006).

Walter Rodney, prominent Guyanese historian and political activist, was assassinated in Guyana in 1980. Rodney became a prominent Pan-Africanist and was important in the Black Power Movement in the Caribbean and North America. While living in Dar es Salaam, he was influential in developing a new center of African learning and discussion. Rodney's most influential book is *How Europe Underdeveloped Africa*, published in 1972. In it, he described an Africa that had been consciously exploited by European imperialists, leading directly to the modern underdevelopment of most of the continent. The book became enormously influential as well as controversial. In 1974, Rodney returned to Guyana from Tanzania. He was supposed to take a position as a professor at the University of Guyana but the government prevented his appointment. He became increasingly active in politics, forming the Working People's Alliance against the Guyanese government. In 1979, he was arrested and charged with arson after two government offices were burned. In 1980, Rodney was killed by a bomb in his car while running for office in Guyanese elections. Walter's brother, Donald, who was injured in the explosion, said that a sergeant in the Guyana Defense Force named Gregory Smith had given Rodney the bomb that killed him. Smith fled to French Guiana after the killing, where he died in 2002. Rodney's death was commemorated in a poem by Martin Carter entitled "For Walter Rodney" and by the dub poet Kwesi Johnson in "Reggae fi Randi" (GuyanaCaribbeanPolitics.com, 2010).

In his 1969 essay titled "Black Power: A Basic Understanding," Rodney defined Black Power as a doctrine about Black people, for Black people, preached by Black people. He put it on all of us Blacks that the color of our skin is the most fundamental thing about us and the most biding factor in our world. He stated that in doing so, he was not saying that it is the way things ought to be but simply recognizing the real world—that is the way things are. He argued that under different circumstances, it would have been nice to be color blind, to choose our friends solely because their social interests coincided with ours—but no conscious Black person can allow himself/herself such luxuries in the contemporary world (Hord and Lee, 1995:182).

Rodney made it very clear that Black people comprise non-Whites—the hundreds of millions of people whose homelands are in Asia and Africa, with another few millions in the Americas. He noted a further subdivision with reference to all people of African descent whose position is clearly more acute than that of most non-White groups. He noted that once a person is said to be Black by the White world, then that is usually the most important thing about him/her; fat or thin, intelligent or stupid, criminal or sportsman—these things pale into insignificance. He pointed out that a lot of Whites literally cannot tell one Black from another, partly because a lot of Whites do not personally know many Black people, a reflection of a psychological tendency to deny the individuality of Blacks by refusing to consider us as individual human beings (Hord and Lee, 1995:183).

Rodney warned that apart from local violent protest (riots), the United States faced the possibility of large scale racial war. He cited the book titled *Black Power* (1967) written by Stokely Carmichael (later Kwame Ture) and Charles Hamilton (banned by the 'White Power" Jamaican government) which stressed that its aim was to present an opportunity to work out the racial question, but if that opportunity was missed the society was moving towards destructive racial war. In such a war, Rodney argued, Black people would undoubtedly suffer because of their minority position, but as an organized group they could wreck untold damage on the Whites. He argued that the White racists and warmongers cannot drop their bombs on Black people within the United States, and whatever damage is done to property means damage to White property. Rodney asserted that we Blacks have nothing to lose for Whites are the capitalists. He made it abundantly clear that 22 million Blacks could not be treated as if they did not exists; thus their interests must be taken into account *out of respect for their power*—power that can be used destructively if it is not allowed to express itself constructively (Hord and Lee, 1995:188).

Assata Olugbala Shakur, born as JoAnne Deborah Byron, married name JoAnne Chesimard, is an African American revolutionary, author, activist and ex-political prisoner living in exile in Cuba since 1984. She was a member of the Black Panther Party, the Black Liberation Army—a politico-military organization whose primary aim was to fight for the independence and self-determination of African people in the United States, and the Republic of New Afrika—an organization formed to create an independent Black majority nation composed of South Carolina, Alabama, Mississippi and Louisiana. Between 1971 and 1973, Shakur was accused of several crimes, of which she would never be charged, and made the subject of a multi-state manhunt (Marable and Mullings, 2003:529-530).

Akinwande Oluwole "Wole" Soyinka, Nigerian political activist, writer, poet and playwright, won the Nobel Prize in Literature in 1986, the first African to be so honored. In 1994, he was designated United Nations Educational, Scientific and Cultural Organization (UNESCO) Goodwill Ambassador for the promotion of African culture, human rights, freedom of expression, media and communication. Soyinka has played an active role in Nigeria's political history. In 1965, he made a broadcast demanding the cancellation of the rigged Western Nigeria Regional Elections following his seizure of the Western Nigeria Broadcasting Service studio. He was arrested, arraigned but freed on a technicality by Justice Esho. In 1967, during the Nigerian Civil War, he was arrested by the federal government of General Yakubu Gowon and put in solitary confinement for his attempts at brokering a peace between the warring Nigerian and Biafran parties (NobelPrize.org, 1986).

In his book, *Myth, Literature, and the African World* (1976), Soyinka, posited that the vision of Negritude should never be underestimated or belittled. He argued that what went wrong with the idea is contained in the contrivance of a creative ideology and its falsified basis of identification with the social vision. This vision, he contended, was that of restitution and re-engineering of a racial psyche, the establishment of a distinct human entity, and the glorification of its long-suppressed attributes—on an even longer-term basis, as universal alliance with the world's dispossessed. In attempting to achieve this laudable goal, however, Soyinka asserted, Negritude proceeded along the route of oversimplification. Its re-entrenchment of Black values, he posited, was not preceded by any profound effort to enter into this African system of values. This, he stated, extolled the apparent; its reference points took far too much coloring from European ideas, even while its messiahs pronounced themselves fanatically African. In attempting to refute the evaluation to which Black reality had been subjected, according to Soyinka, Negritude adopted the Manichean tradition of European thought and inflicted it on an African culture which is most radically anti-Manichean. Thus, for him, Negritude not only accepted the dialectical structure of European ideological confrontations, it also borrowed from the very components of its racist syllogisms (Hord and Lee, 1995:84).

To respond to this problematic, Soyinka asked us Blacks to imagine how a mythical Black brother innocent would respond in his virginal village, pursuing his innocent sports, suddenly confronted by the figure of Descartes in his pith helmet, engaged in the mission of piercing the jungle of the Black pre-logical mentality with its intellectual canoe as follows:

> As our Cartesian ghost introduces himself by scribbling on our Black brother's—naturally—tabula rasa the famous proposition, "I think, therefore I am," we should not respond, as the negritudinists did, with "I feel, therefore I am," for that is to accept the arrogance of a philosophical certitude that has no foundation in the provable, one which reduces the cosmic logic of being to a functional particularism of being. I cannot imagine that our "authentic black innocent" would ever have permitted himself to be manipulated into the false position of countering one pernicious Manicheism with another. He would sooner, I suspect, reduce our white explorer

to syntactical proportions by responding: "'"You think, therefore you are a thinker. You are one-who-thinks, white-creature-in-pith-helmet-in-African-jungle-who-thinks and finally, white-man-who-has-problems-believing-in-his-own-existence." And I cannot believe that he would arrive at the observation solely by intuition (Hord and Lee, 1995:92).

Asked about how the major world's news media have reported the large-scale fighting that was going on in the Southeast Asia-Pacific region between the Republic of Indonesia on the one hand, and on the other, the guerilla forces of the Democratic Government of West Papua New Guinea, Tanggahma's answer was that the press fails to inform people about the fact that these are struggles in which poor, disinherited Black populations—both in East Timor and West Papua New Guinea—are fighting against a yellow supremacist, racist, expansionist, colonialist and fascist empire: i.e. the Republic of Indonesia.

About the ignorance of Blacks in other parts of the world, especially in the United States, where people are supposedly in possession of the greatest amount of information about what is going on in the world, there is great ignorance about his people's struggles, Tanggahma's response was that it is true. He added that Black people have been inhabiting all regions of Asia for many thousands of years. In fact, the aboriginal populations of Southern China and the entire Southeast Asia (the Philippines, Kampuchea, Laos, Vietnam, Malaysia, Burma, Thailand, and Indonesia) were Black. They are still in the jungle areas of those nations even today, although living as marginal people and facing many hardships in most cases.

Concerning the Black peoples of the islands of New Guinea and Timor, who also were fighting the Indonesians, and whether they were therefore part of that great belt of aboriginal Black populations that settled in Asia, Tanggahma responded that they are on the island of New Guinea and on the island of Timor which belong to what is known as Melanesia, or Black Islands, if we translate it literally.

Asked about his and his people's relationship with Africa and Africans, Tanggahma made it very clear that Africa is their motherland. He added that all of the Black populations which settled in Asia over the hundreds of thousands of years came undoubtedly from the African continent. In fact, the entire world was populated from Africa. Hence, they, the Blacks in Asia and the Pacific today, descend from proto-African peoples. They were linked to Africa in the Past. They are linked to Africa in the future. They are what one might call the Black Asian Diaspora.

Thirumavalavan is the second child of Tholkappian (Ramasamy) and Periyammal, and was born in the village of Anganur in Ariyalur District in Tamil Nadu, India. His father had studied up to the eighth grade, while his mother remained uneducated. He has a sister and three brothers, but he was the only member of his family who went on to higher education after completion of his schooling. He initially studied Chemistry, and went on to do a master's degree in Criminology, before studying Law at Madras Law College. He then began working in the government's Forensic Department as an assistant scientist (Wikipedia, 2010).

He began growing interested in politics in 1982, when he was still a student, in reaction to reports from refugees of Sri Lankan military atrocities against Tamils in Sri Lanka. He began holding rallies and organized boycotts and conferences to support the Sri Lankan cause. He ran around Madras Law College, but failed. This, he alleged, was due to his being a Dalit. The incident led to his meeting and becoming acquainted with politicians from the <u>Dravida Munnetra Kazhagam</u> (DMK), a major political party in Tamil Nadu (Wikipedia, 2010).

The DPI boycotted elections until the 1999 general elections. Thirumavalavan allied with G. K. Moopanar's Tamil Maanila Congress and represented the Third Front. The party contested in the parliamentary constituencies of Chidambaram and <u>Perambalur</u>. Thirumavalavan contested in Chidambaram, and managed to poll 2.25 lakh votes in his debut election (Wikipedia, 2010).

Ahmed Sékou Touré, revolutionary thinker, prolific author, great orator, political leader and President of Guinea from 1958 to his death in 1984, was one of the primary Guinean nationalists involved in the liberation of the country from France. Touré's early life was characterized by challenges of authority, including during his education. Touré was obliged to work to take care of himself. He began working for the Postal Services (PTT), and quickly became involved in Labor Union activity. During his youth and after becoming president, Touré studied the works of communist philosophers, especially those of Karl Marx and Vladimir Lenin. Touré is remembered as a charismatic figure and while his legacy as president is often disdained by some in his home country, he remains an icon of liberation in the wider African community. Touré served for some time as a representative of African groups in France, where he worked to negotiate for the independence of France's African colonies. In 1958, Touré's Rassemblement Démocratique Africain, or RDA (African Democratic Rally), section in Guinea pushed for a "No" in the French Union referendum sponsored by the French government, and was the only one of France's African colonies to vote for immediate independence rather than continued association with France. Guinea became the only French colony to leave the French Community. In the event, the rest of Francophone Africa gained its independence only two years later in

1960; but the French were extremely vindictive against Guinea, withdrawing abruptly, taking files, destroying infrastructure, and breaking political and economic ties (*Encyclopedia Britanica*, 2010).

During his presidency, Touré led a strong policy based on Marxism, with the nationalization of foreign companies and strong planned economics. He won the Lenin Peace Prize as a result in 1961. His early actions to reject the French and then to appropriate wealth and farmland from traditional landlords angered many powerful forces, but revered in much of Africa and in the Pan-African movement. From 1965 to 1975, he ended all his relations with France, the former colonial power. Touré argued that Africa had lost much during colonization, and that Africa ought to retaliate by cutting off ties to former colonial nations. Only in 1978, as Guinea's ties with the Soviet Union soured, did French President Valéry Giscard d'Estaing first visit Guinea as a sign of reconciliation. Throughout his dispute with France, Guinea maintained good relations with several socialist countries. Nonetheless, Touré's attitude toward France was not generally well received, and even some African countries ended diplomatic relations with Guinea over the incident. Despite this, Touré's move won the support of many anti-colonialist and Pan-Blackist groups and leaders. Touré's primary allies in the region were Presidents Kwame Nkrumah of Ghana and Modibo Keita of Mali. After Nkrumah was overthrown in a 1966 coup, Touré offered him a refuge in Guinea and made him co-president. As a leader of the Pan-Africanist movement, he consistently spoke out against colonial powers, and befriended leaders from the African Diaspora such as Malcolm X and Stokely Carmichael, to whom he offered asylum, and who took the two leaders names, as <u>Kwame Ture</u>. He, with Nkrumah, helped in the formation of the All-African Peoples Revolutionary Party, and aided forces fighting Portuguese colonialism in neighboring Guinea-Bissau, for which the Portuguese launched an attack upon Conakry in 1970 (*Encyclopedia Britanica*, 2010), but the forces of the neo-colonial imperialists were thoroughly humiliated.

In his essay appropriately titled "A Dialectical Approach to Culture" (1989), Touré argued that the path of tribulations the concept of culture has undergone has been long, as the opinions of "committees of intellectuals" cancel one another out in a sterile dialectic. These groups, he noted, bring incomprehension and a hollow humanism as they timidly deal with the historical truth of the greatest calamity known to history: i.e. imperialism.

According to Touré, the intellectuals in countries where a capitalist regime isolates the general populace from scientific and technical attainments must constantly fight to retain their false "freedom" and constantly question themselves in vain about the future of a decadent economic and social structure.

The intellectuals being helpless somehow construct a cultural policy in order to strengthen a society whose upheavals are the undeniable symptoms of degeneration, and as they use the faded light of their poor autocratic reason to seek a new cultural conscience, they sink into skepticism or, rather, into the terror of a future overshadowed by capitalism (Touré, 1989:3).

Touré pointed out that the European trends have dominated the inquiry of cultural problems in Africa. For a long time, he noted, contemporary Anglo-Saxon anthropology, obsessed with justifying the reactionary ideas of colonialism, cited Africa as the home of backward peoples who should be forced to accept colonialist humanitarian civilization. He argued that history has shown that revolutionary maturity cannot be the object of an edict which imperialism would never permit. The Anglo-Saxon school of thought, he noted, gave birth to pseudo-realism in line with David Hume's successors—Alfred Vierkandt's disciples, "culturalists" such as Anton Grabner and Bernhard Ankerman, and functionalists like Bronislaw Malinowski, assumed that they had discovered the basis of African culture. Due to their hatred of historical materialism, these scholars produced a flood of disjointed monographs in which they denied the class war and the imperialists' exploitation of Africans, reducing the phenomena instead to an anti-scientific cultural pluralism (Touré, 1989:3-4).

Archaeologists' pickaxes, Touré suggested, had evidently not reached the African culture that lay too deeply buried under the irremovable heap of dirt left behind by the colonialists, which Africans have now succeeded in uncovering. He noted that the anxiety to extricate an authenticity which was for obvious reasons unrecoverable led Lucien Lévy-Brühl, who was already blind, to present a fairly accurate "prelogism" of African culture. As Touré puts it, "In any case there is no difference of concept between the black man unaware of the logical categories of the classical world on the one hand, and the idea of the essentially sensitive black man as a sort of passive, wax creature, only fit to remain at a primary intuitive level in his perception of the outside world, on the other" (Touré, 1989:4).

Thus, for Touré, it is no accident that African states had to dedicate a symposium to a topic such as that which unites them: "African culture and its realities." He recalled that as late as the 1960s, many pages were devoted to another topic that seemed quite provocative at the time: i.e. "A black man is a human being." He therefore argued that it is incumbent upon Africans to reestablish themselves in a field such as culture, because they are emerging from a long period of eclipse during which the most elementary attributes of man, notably those of his creativity, were contested and denied to Africans (Touré, 1989:4).

According to Touré, a well-nurtured Eurocentric prejudice is that Africans played no role in the general task of shaping civilization. Africans were accused of being without history and without culture because it was necessary that it be so. He pointed out that Europeans slaughtered Native Americans while at the same time admiring their temples and palaces, and admitting that they murdered the men and took over their lands. He mentioned the fact that with their quest to conquer and dominate others, Europeans destroyed millennial civilizations in Asia, but they never denied the existence of these civilizations as such and never contested the quality of their craftsmanship and their human attributes. He further stated that when it came to Africa, Europeans' first notion was not to exterminate the men with the sole idea of seizing their treasures, but to treat them as beasts to be sold into slavery and as they pleased sold on the spot or exported to America, or even killed when their capabilities and selling prices no longer assured adequate profits. To guarantee the success of such a venture, he added, a preliminary step was taken by Europeans to ease their conscience to believe that slavery with its attendant savagery was a question of dealing with beasts and not human beings. He further stated that by Europeans alleging the barbarity of Africans and denying that they have a culture and civilization made it justifiable to Europeans to estrange Africans from the human race (Touré, 1989:4-5).

Despite all this dehumanization of Africans by Europeans, according to Touré, time did not stop, and progress continued to strengthen in the face of opposition and exploitation. Africans began to pay more attention to their legends, the epic poems and the tales passed by word of mouth from generation to generation of the Griots. He added that archaeology finally penetrated the various continents, thrusting deep into the depths of history and the soil to reveal and revive the remains of entombed cultures.

Thus, according to Touré, the whole African cultural evolution, this progressive qualification, is subordinated to reason, to the law of gnoseology, to the transition from ignorance to an increasingly deeper and more exact degree of knowledge. Consequently, for him, any anthology of African culture that situates it outside the realm of reason, of rational thought, of the law and of gnoseology, downgrades it and deviates it from its true end, which is to qualify mankind, and sacrifices it to the myth of singularity and specificity (Touré, 1989:7).

Oba T'Shaka (birth name Bill Bradley), author, political activist, **pro**fessor in the Black Studies Department at San Francisco State University, served as Chair of the Black Studies Department at San Francisco State University for 12 years. T'Shaka is one of the principal architects of the African

Centered Educational Movement (ACEM), which led to the development of an African-centered discipline that incorporates physics, chemistry, biology, and mathematics into the core discipline of Black Studies. He also led the move to define ancient African philosophy as the foundation of the Black Studies discipline. T'Shaka is the national vice chairperson of the National Black United Front (NBUF) and has been active in Black freedom movements since 1960. From 1963 to 1965, he was chair of San Francisco's Congress of Racial Equality (CORE), which spearheaded a campaign for jobs for Blacks and other peoples of color in San Francisco and throughout California. He led an international work project to Tanzania made up of members of the Pan African People's Organization (PAPO) in 1963, and in 1974 played a major leadership role in the Sixth Pan African Congress in Tanzania, chairing the North American Political Committee (First World Conference, 2006).

In his book titled *Return to the African Mother: Principles of Male and Female Equality* (1995), T'Shaka summarized his life's work of struggle to achieve justice for African people. The book is a product of activism and study through engaging the forces of White supremacy on the battlefields of Civil Right, Black Power, Pan-Africanism and Afrocentrism, which makes it clear that Black liberation depends upon knowledge of the enemy and knowledge of ourselves. T'Shaka unveiled the framework and platform for constructing (in our case reconstructing) the "just society." He took us on a journey through varied terrain exploring and contrasting the African world with that of the Aryan, revealing the Aryan incapacity to produce a just society; while the African has several models, Kemet and Dogon being two of them, the latter providing a contemporary example. His was an application for the rebuilding process of the just African society based upon the principles of right and truth (*Maat*), and upon true government of (Ausar and Auset). T'Shaka reconnected the umbilical cord between us Blacks and our antecedents.

Chancellor James Williams, writer, university professor, and historian, had an innate curiosity concerning the realities of racial inequality and cultural struggles, particularly those which involved African Americans, which began as early as his fifth-grade year. Years later, he was quoted in an early interview as saying: "I was very sensitive about the position of Black people in the town... I wanted to know how you explain this great difference. How is it that we were in such low circumstances as compared to the whites? And when they answered 'slavery' as the explanation, then I wanted to know where we came from" (Rashidi, 1998 & 2002).

In 1971, Williams sent his magnum opus, *The Destruction of Black Civ-*

ilization, to Kendall Hunt, a White-owned publishing company, for publication and distribution. The following year, the book received an award from the Black Academy of Letters and Arts. Encouraged by the award, Williams worked for years to expand and revise the book before publishing a second edition. Feeling more comfortable with a Black-owned firm as his publisher, he sent the second version to Chicago's noted Third World Press. When published in 1987, the second edition of the book received a wide wave of critical acclaim, including from such people as New Jersey poet laureate Amiri Baraka and noted professor John Henrik Clarke. Years of cultural change enabled people to see the value of Williams' work. The 21st Century Foundation honored Chancellor Williams, making him the first person to receive its Clarence L. Holte International Biennial Prize. Preparing to release his most famous book, Williams did not wait for grants or fellowships to publish it. On his apparent hastiness, he commented: "I was out of step with tradition." He also said, "I rebelled against overspecialization. Even when I had the required courses for my majors, I would take other subjects in which I was equally interested. I was interested in pure science, for example, even though I was majoring in history. I was also interested in psychology. My transcripts from Howard, where I did most of my formal study, won't give you any idea of what my major really was" (Rashidi, 1998 & 2002).

As Adeleke (2005) succinctly pointed out, in his critically acclaimed study of how the West "destroyed Black Civilization," Williams urged the creation of a "race organization," which he described as "a nation-wide organization of Blacks only." Adeleke also noted that Williams called upon Blacks to begin "building step by step, a race organization so great that it will not only be the voice of a united people but will carry on effectively an economic program to assist them advance on all fronts."

Richard Nathaniel Wright, African American author of powerful, sometimes controversial, novels, short stories and non-fiction, wrote mostly about racism. His work helped redefine discussions of race relations in America in the mid-20th Century. At the age of 15, Wright wrote his first story titled "The Voodoo of Hell's Half-Acre." It was published in *Southern Register*, a local Black newspaper. In 1923, Wright was made class valedictorian. Determined not to be called an Uncle Tom, he refused to deliver the assistant principal's carefully prepared valedictory address that would not offend the White school officials and finally convinced the Black administrators to let him read a compromise version of what he had written. In September of the same year, Wright registered for mathematics, English, and history courses at the new Lanier High School in Jackson, but had to stop attending classes after a few weeks of irregular attendance because he needed to earn money for family expenses. His childhood in Memphis and Mississippi shaped his lasting impressions of American racism (Liukkonen, 2008).

In 1932, Wright began attending meetings of the John Reed Club. As the club was dominated by the Communist Party, Wright established a relationship with a number of party members. Especially interested in the literary contacts made at the meetings, Wright formally joined the Communist Party in late 1933 and as a revolutionary poet wrote numerous proletarian poems: for example, "I Have Seen Black Hands," "We of the Streets," and "Red Leaves of Red Books" for *The New Masses* and other left-wing periodicals. A power struggle within the Chicago chapter of the John Reed Club forced the dissolution of the club's leadership. Wright was told he had the support of the club's party members if he was willing to join the party. By 1935, he had completed his first novel, *Cesspool*, published as *Lawd Today* (1963), and in January 1936 his story titled "Big Boy Leaves Home" was accepted for publication in *New Caravan*. In February, he began working with the National Negro Congress (NNC), and in April he chaired the South Side Writers' Group (SWG), whose membership included Arna Bontemps and Margaret Walker. Wright submitted some of his critical essays and poetry to the group for criticism and read aloud some of his short stories. In 1936, he was also revising "Cesspool." Through the club, Wright edited *Left Front*, a magazine that the Communist Party shut down in 1937, despite his repeated protests. Throughout this period, he also wrote for the *New Masses* magazine (Liukkonen, 2008).

While Wright was at first pleased by positive relations with White Communists in Chicago, he was later humiliated in New York City by some who rescinded an offer to find housing for him because of his race. To make matters worse, some Black Communists denounced the articulate, polished Wright as a bourgeois intellectual, assuming he was well educated and overly assimilated into White society. However, he was largely autodidactic, having been forced to end his public education after the completion of grammar school. His insistence that young Communist writers be given space to cultivate their talents and his working relationship with a Black Nationalist Communist led to a public falling out with the party and the leading African American communist Buddy Nealson. Wright was threatened at knife point by fellow-traveler coworkers, denounced as a Trotskyite in the street by strikers and physically assaulted by former comrades when he tried to join them during the 1936 May Day march (Liukkonen, 2008).

In spite of his financial difficulties, Wright refused to compromise his principles. He declined to participate in a series of programs for Canadian radio because he suspected American control over the programs. For the same reason, Wright rejected an invitation from the Congress for Cultural Freedom (CCF) to go to India to speak at a conference in memory of Leo Tolstoy. Still interested in literature, Wright helped Kyle Onstott get *Mandingo* (1957) published in France. His last display of explosive energy occurred on November 8, 1960 in his polemical lecture titled "The Situation of the Black Artist and Intellectual in the United States," which was delivered to students and members of the American Church in Paris. He argued that American society reduced the most militant members of the Black community to slaves whenever they wanted to question the racial status quo. He offered as proof the subversive attacks of the Communists against *Native Son* and the quarrels which James Baldwin and other authors sought with him (Liukkonen, 2008).

Malcolm X, born Malcolm Little and also known as El-Hajj Malik El-Shabazz, was an African American Muslim minister, public speaker, and human rights activist. While his detractors accused him of preaching racism, Black supremacy, anti-Semitism, and violence, to those of us who admire him, he was a courageous advocate for the rights of Africans everywhere, a man who indicted White America in the harshest terms for its crimes against African Americans and other Africans around the world. He is one of the greatest, and most influential, Africans in history.

Malcolm X's sense of Africa's history of grandeur was impeccable. He talked about the African civilization called Carthage. One of the most famous persons in Carthage was Hannibal The Great. Malcolm X and other Africans had been taught that Hannibal was a White man. This is how they steal African history just as Hollywood produces a movie showing a Black man as a White man, he pointed out. He recalled one day when he told a Black college student that Hannibal was a Black man, and the student had a fit and wanted to fight Malcolm X on that. Hannibal, Malcolm X noted was famous for crossing the Alps Mountains with elephants. Europeans could not go across the Alps on foot by themselves. Hannibal had with him 90,000 African troops, defeated Rome, and occupied Italy for between 15 and 20 years. Malcolm X added that it is because of some of that Hannibal blood that many Italians are dark. Even the Irish got some of the Black blood when the Spanish Armada was defeated off the coast of Ireland. The Spanish in those days were dark; they were the remnants of the Moors, and they went ashore and settled down in Ireland and right to this very day their descendants are called Black Irish (Malcolm X, 1967:32-33).

Indeed, Malcolm X's internationalism and optimism in the future and confidence in the capacities of the oppressed were well founded. The pattern he described continued with the crushing defeat of the United States in

Vietnam in 1975; the defeat of the South African army at Cuito Cuanavale, Angola, in early 1988 by Cuban, Angolan, and Namibian forces; and the democratic revolution against the racist White Rhodesian system in Zimbabwe and the racist Apartheid system in South Africa in the 1980s and 1990 (Malcolm X, 1967:33).

Furthermore, as William W. Sales, Jr. pointed out, the last period in the evolution of Malcolm X's political thought began on April 22, 1964, when he embarked upon the first of two trips to the Middle East and Africa. These trips, according to Sales, pushed forward Malcolm X's development in his thinking. After his return from the first trip in late May of 1964, Malcolm X was no longer satisfied with the formulation of Black Nationalism he had articulated earlier. He no longer felt that the Muslim Mosque, Inc. could be the proper organizational form for moving toward a politics of African American liberation. Upon his return from Africa, Malcolm X was committed to Pan-African internationalism, leading him to form the Organization of Afro-American Unity (OAAU) on June 28, 1964 (Sales, Jr., 1994:84).

During this period of Pan-African internationalism, according to Sales, Malcolm X's formulations were not finished theoretical postulates but a rapidly developing perspective which he was never allowed to complete. Consequently, many of the questions which he addressed were incompletely answered or not answered at all. It was clear, however, that Malcolm X was quite certain that the Eurocentric international system had to be transformed into one which could extend justice and equality to all of the world's people. It was equally evident that Malcolm X believed this had to be done in such a way as to preserve the plurality of cultures and nationalities and not through the forced homogenization of "integration." Malcolm X had only begun to formulate the actual contours and mechanisms which would empower such new social forces, and most often with specific reference not to the entire Third World but to the African American community and Africa (Sales, Jr., 1994:84-85).

According to Sales, historically, Black Nationalism emerged as a response to racism. It was necessary for it to be concerned with the status and treatment of the race no matter the national boundaries. Black Nationalism was therefore at one and the same time a legitimate nationalism but also a "pan" movement, an international movement for the redemption of the race; in fact, scholars often refer to 19th-Century Black Nationalism as "Pan-Negro Nationalism." This, for Sales, might have been obscured in Malcolm X's case because his most explicit formal definition of Black Nationalism did not mention an international dimension. Sales added, however, that whatever ambiguity existed on this point was clarified by Malcolm X in this last period of his development, as late in 1964 at Harvard University, Malcolm X argued that African Americans "are just as much African today as we were in Africa for hundred years ago, only we are a modern counterpart of it" (Sales, Jr., 1994:85).

As a result of his two trips to Africa in 1964, Sales observed, Malcolm X came to recognize the inconsistency of Black control of Black communities in a monopoly capitalistic economy rooted in Western imperialism. He realized that coexistence was impossible in such a system and frequently described capitalism as a "blood sucker." He now felt that capitalism could not be relied upon to eradicate racism and poverty. Malcolm X looked closely and favorably on African nationalists' attempts to create an African socialism. He noticed on his travels that most of the newly independent nations had turned away from capitalism to the direction of socialism. His interaction with heads of state and nationalists of African socialism exposed him to the various theories of African socialism that they espoused. Leaders like Julius Nyerere of Tanzania, Gamal Abdel Naser of Egypt, Sekou Touré of Guinea, and Kwame Nkrumah of Ghana all had some formation of a mixed economy that they labeled socialist. At his death, however, Malcolm X had not established clearly what kind of socialism should supersede capitalism. No information exist that shows Malcolm X's commitment to scientific socialism or communism (Sales, Jr., 1994:86).

Furthermore, as Jan Carew recounted, Malcolm X seemed to be racing against time during the final year of his life. Between December of 1974 and February of 1965, he visited Britain twice. In the course of those visits, Malcolm X made what Carew believed were the most sophisticated, brilliant and conciliatory speeches of his career. In early December, immediately after his second pilgrimage to Mecca, Malcolm X took part in a debate at the Oxford Union, one of the most famous debating societies in the English-speaking world. Less than three months later, on February 11, Malcolm X was invited back to London by the African Society to address a large audience in the Old Theatre at the London School of Economics. In both addresses, Malcolm X moved the political discourse from civil rights to human rights and stated clearly and unequivocally that the Black liberation struggle had to be internationalized rather than "ghetoized." He was welcomed by a Third World immigrant population drawn mostly from the West Indies, Africa, and the Indian subcontinent. As a descendant from a Grenadian mother, as a Pan-Africanist and a Garveyite, and as a Muslim, Malcolm X in 1965 was able to reach people from a broad range of backgrounds. Weaving through that brilliant speech was a pristine belief in the African Revolution. It was a declaration of faith by someone who would not live long enough to see the twists and turns that revolution would take or the brutal and savage low-intensity warfare unleashed against whole societies that were trying to free themselves from the yoke of imperialism (Carew, 1994:viii-ix, 104).

The åtenu m'ţen/Mapinduzi ya Malazi/Revolutionary-Accommodationist Perspective

In her book, *A Voice from the South* (1892), Cooper stated that the two sources from which modern civilization has derived its noble and ennobling ideal of woman are Christianity and the feudal system. Here, she argued, was the confluence of the two streams which stretch before us as a broad majestic river, the resultant of which is destined to be a potent force in the betterment of the world. She posited that after our appeal to history comparing nations destitute of this force and so destitute also of the principle of progress with other nations among which the influence of woman is prominent coupled with a brisk, progressive, satisfying civilization—if in addition we find this strong presumptive evidence corroborated by reason and experience, then we may conclude that these two equally varying concomitants are linked as cause and effect: put differently, the position of women in society determines the vital elements of that society's regeneration and progress. She added that this postulate is so in a priori grounds, not because woman is better or stronger or wiser than man, but from the nature of the case, because it is she who must first form the man by directing the earlier impulses of his character (Hord and Lee, 1995:231).

Thus, Cooper insisted that us Blacks must either break away from dear old landmarks and plunge out in any line and every line that enables us to meet the pressing need of our people, or we must ask the Church to allow and help us, untrammeled by the prejudices and theories of individuals, to work progressively under its direction as we alone can, with God's help, for the salvation of our people. She declared that the time is right for action and that self-seeking and ambition must be laid on the altar. The battle, she believed is one of sacrifice and hardship, but our duty is plain because we have been recipients of missionary bounty in some sort for 21 years. She argued that not even the senseless vegetable is content to be a mere reservoir, for giving without receiving is an anomaly in nature. She then concluded with these words from Ralph Waldo Emerson:

> In ordinary, we have a snappish criticism which watches and contradicts the opposite party. We want the will which advances and dictates [acts]. Nature has made up her mind that what cannot defend itself, shall not be defended. Complaining never so loud and with never so much reason is of no use. What cannot stand must fall; *and the measure of our sincerity and*

therefore of the respect of men is the amount of health and wealth we will hazard I the defense of our right (Hord and Lee, 1995:242).

Angela Davis, African American socialist, philosopher, political activist, gay rights advocate, and retired professor with the History of Consciousness Department at the University of California, Santa Cruz, was the director of the university's Feminist Studies department. Davis was largely active during the Civil Rights Movement and was associated with the Black Panthers and even invited to the launching of the Israeli Black Panthers when she visited the country in 1971. Her research interests are in feminism, African American Studies, critical theory, Marxism, popular music and social consciousness, and the philosophy and history of punishment and prisons. She wrote about the FBI's targeting of the Black Panther Party as part of its Counter Intelligence Program (COINTELPRO). Also, she was tried and acquitted of suspected involvement in the Soledad brothers' August 1970 abduction and murder of Judge Harold Haley in Marin County, California, even though she had purchased the weapons involved, had written letters to one of the prisoners who had escaped, and became a fugitive of the law after the murders. She was twice a candidate for Vice President on the Communist Party USA ticket during the Reagan era. Since moving in the early 1990s from party communism to other forms of political commitment, she has identified herself as a democratic socialist. Davis is the founder of Critical Resistance, an organization working to abolish the prison-industrial complex (Davis, 1989).

Davis called upon African American women to learn from their sisters in South Africa and Nicaragua and all progressive women of other racial backgrounds to join hands to forge a new socialist order—one that will reestablish socioeconomic priorities so that the quest for monetary profit will never be permitted to take precedence over the real interests of human beings. She, nonetheless, was realistic in noting that this strategy does not mean that the problems of Blacks will magically dissipate with the advent of socialism, rather that such a social order should provide us with the real opportunity to extend further our struggles, with the assurance that one day we will be able to redefine the basic elements of our oppression as useless refuse of the past (Hord and Lee, 1995:302-303).

Jomo Kenyata, first Prime Minister (1963–1964) and President (1964–1978) of Kenya, is considered the founding father of the Kenyan nation. In 1928, he launched a monthly Kikuyu-language newspaper called *Mwĩgwithania* (*Reconciler*) which aimed to unite all sections of the Kikuyu. The paper, supported by an Asian-owned printing press, had a mild and unassuming tone, and was tolerated by the colonial government. He also made a presentation on Kikuyu land problems before the Hilton Young Commission in

Nairobi in the same year. In 1929, the KCA sent Kenyatta to London to lobby on its behalf with regards to Kikuyu tribal land affairs. He wrote articles to British newspapers about the matter. He returned to Kenya on September 24, 1930 and was welcomed at Mombasa by his wife Wahu and James Beauttah. He then took part, on the side of traditionalists, in the debate on the issue of circumcision of girls. He later worked for Kikuyu Independent Schools in Githunguri. He returned to London in 1931 and enrolled in Woodbrooke Quaker College in Birmingham. From 1932 to 1933, he briefly studied economics in Moscow at the Comintern School, University of the Toilers of the East (KUTVU), before his sponsor, the Trinidadian communist George Padmore, fell out with his Soviet hosts, forcing Kenyatta to move back to London. In 1934, Kenyatta enrolled at University College London and from 1935 studied social anthropology under Bronisław Malinowski at the London School of Economics (LSE). He published his revised LSE thesis as *Facing Mount Kenya* in 1938 under his new name, Jomo Kenyatta (his old name was Kamau wa Muigai). The name "Jomo" means in English "Burning Spear," while the name "Kenyatta" was said to be a reference to the beaded Masai belt he wore, and later to "the Light of Kenya." During this period, he was also an active member of a group of African, Caribbean and American intellectuals who included C. L. R. James, Eric Williams, W. A. Wallace Johnson, Paul Robeson, and Ralph Bunche. During his presidency, a number of streets in Nairobi were named after those early black-emancipation intellectuals. Kenyatta acted as an extra in the film *Sanders of the River* (1934), directed by Alexander Korda and starring Paul Robeson. During World War II, he worked as a laborer at an English farm in Sussex and also lectured on Africa for the Workers' Educational Association (WEA). In 1942, he married an Englishwoman, Edna Clarke. He also published *My People of Kikuyu* and *The Life of Chief Wang'ombe, a History Shading into Legend*. Edna gave birth to their son, Peter Magana, in 1943. In 1945, with other prominent African Nationalists, such as Kwame Nkrumah of Ghana, Kenyatta helped organize the fifth Pan-African Congress held in Britain. He left Edna Clarke behind in Britain when he returned to Kenya in 1946 (Boddy-Evans, 2010).

Kenyatta returned to Kenya in 1946, after almost 15 years abroad. He married for the third time, to Grace Wanjiku, Senior Chief Koinange's daughter, and sister to Mbiyu Koinange, who later became a lifelong confidant and was one of the most powerful politicians during Kenyatta's presidency. Kenyatta then went into teaching, becoming principal of Kenya Teachers College Githunguri. In 1947, he was elected president of the Kenya African Union (KAU). He began to receive death threats from White settlers after his election. From 1948 to 1951, he toured and lectured around the country condemning idleness, robbery, urging hard work while campaigning for the return of land given to White settlers and for independence within three years. His wife, Grace Wanjiku, died in childbirth in 1950 as she gave birth to daughter Jane Wambui, who survived. In 1951, Kenyatta married Ngina Muhoho, daughter of Chief Muhoho. She was popularly referred to as Mama Ngina and was independent Kenya's First Lady, when Kenyatta was elected President. The Mau Mau Rebellion began in 1951 and KAU was banned, and a state of emergency was declared on October 20, 1952 (Boddy-Evans, 2010). The Mau Mau Uprising was a military conflict that took place in Kenya (then called British East Africa), from 1952 to 1960, between a Kikuyu-dominated anti-colonial-group called Mau Mau and the British Army-cum-adjuncts. The conflict set the stage for Kenyan independence and motivated Africans in other colonies to fight against colonialism. It created a rift between the European colonial community in Kenya and the Home Office in London.

Kenyatta was arrested in October of 1952 and indicted with five others on the charges of "managing and being a member" of the Mau Mau Society. The Mau Mau Society was a radical anti-colonial movement engaged in the Mau Mau Rebellion. The accused were known as the Kapenguria Six. The trial lasted five months: Rawson Macharia, the main prosecution witness, turned out to have perjured himself; the judge, who had only recently been awarded an unusually large pension, and who maintained secret contact with the then colonial Governor of Kenya, Evelyn Baring, during the trial, was openly hostile to the defendants' cause. The defense, led by British Lawyer Dennis Pritt, argued that the White settlers were trying to scapegoat Kenyatta and that there was no evidence tying him to the Mau Mau. The court sentenced Kenyatta on April 8, 1953 to seven years imprisonment with hard labor and indefinite restriction thereafter. The subsequent appeal was refused by the British Privy Council in 1954. Kenyatta remained in prison until 1959, after which he was detained in Lodwar, a remote part of Kenya. The state of emergency was lifted in December of 1959. On February 28, 1960, a public meeting of 25,000 in Nairobi demanded his release. On April 15, 1960, over a million signatures for a plea to release him were presented to the Governor. On May 14, 1960, Kenyata was elected Kenya African National Union (KANU) President *in absentia*. On March 23, 1961, Kenyan leaders, including Daniel arap Moi, later his long-time Vice President and successor as president, visited him at Lodwar. On Apr 11, 1961, Kenyata was moved to Maralal with his daughter, Margaret, where he met world press for the first time in eight years. On Aug 14, 1961, he was released and brought to Gatundu to a hero's welcome. While contemporary opinion linked Kenyatta with the Mau Mau, historians have questioned his alleged leadership of the radical movement. Kenyatta was in truth a political moderate. His marriage of colonial chiefs' daughters, his post-independence Kikuyu allies mainly being former colonial collaborators, and his short shrift treatment of former Mau Mau fighters after he came to power, all strongly suggest he had scant regard for the Mau Mau (Boddy-Evans, 2010).

Kenyata's policy was that of continuity and gradual Africanization of the government, keeping many colonial civil servants in their old jobs as they were gradually replaced by Kenyans. He asked for British troops' help against Somali rebels, *Shiftas,* in the northeast and in ending an army mutiny in Nairobi in January of 1964. In the 1969 elections, Kenyatta banned the only other party, KPU, formed and led by his former vice president, Jaramogi Oginga Odinga, who had been forced to quit KANU along with his left leaning allies, detained its leaders, and called elections in which only KANU was allowed to participate (Boddy-Evans, 2010).

Nelson Rolihlahla Mandela, President of South Africa from 1994 to 1999 and the first South African president to be elected in a fully representative democratic election, was an anti-apartheid activist and the leader of Umkhonto we Sizwe, the armed wing of the African National Congress (ANC). In 1962, he was arrested and convicted of sabotage and other charges, and sentenced to life in prison. Mandela served 27 years in prison, spending many of those years on Robben Island. Following his release from prison on February 11, 1990, Mandela led his party in the negotiations that led to multi-racial democracy in 1994. As President from 1994 to 1999, he frequently gave priority to reconciliation. In South Africa, Mandela is often known as *Madiba*, an honorary title adopted by elders of Mandela's clan.

In his speech titled "We Are Committed to Building a Single Nation in Our Country" prepared for and delivered at a rally in Durban, South Africa on February 25, 1990, Mandela stated that the past is a rich resource on which we can draw in order to make decisions for the future, but it does not dictate our choices. He urged that we look back at the past and select what is good, and leave behind what is bad. The issue of chiefship, he noted, is one such question. According to him, not only in Natal but throughout South Africa there have been chiefs who have been good and honest leaders, who have with great skill piloted their people through the dark days of the oppression of Blacks; these are the chiefs who have looked after the interests of their people and who enjoy the support of their people and, thus, should be saluted. Nonetheless, he pointed out, there have been many bad chiefs who had profited from apartheid and who had increased the burden of their people. These chiefs, he said, must be denounced (Hord and Lee, 1995:110).

On the issue of apartheid, Mandela sated that it is the real enemy of the people, as a great deal of energy had been wasted by people in violent actions across the towns and villages to fight the evil system. He added that Blacks have already waited for their freedom for far too long and, therefore, can no longer wait. He called upon Indians, coloreds, Africans, and freedom-loving Whites to join forces in order to give apartheid its final blow. He then urged that in the process, the people must develop an active democracy with democratic structures which will serve the people in every school, township, village, factory, and farm (Hord and Lee, 1995:114-115).

Mandela iterated his long-held position that the African National Congress (ANC) will offer a home to all who ascribe to the principles of a free, democratic, nonracial, and united South Africa. He declared that the ANC is committed to building a single nation, one that will include Blacks and Whites, Zulus and Afrikaners, and speakers of every other language. He then quoted ANC president-general Chief Luthuli who said that "I personally believe that here in South Africa, with all of our diversities of color and race, we will show the world a new pattern for democracy…I think that there is a challenge to us in South Africa, to set a new example for the world" (Hord and Lee, 1995:111).

The khęperu/Kubadilisha/Reformist Perspective

It can be gleaned from Table 1 that this group seems to encompass the second largest number of notable African/Black thinkers, albeit only very slightly larger than the *åtenu m'ţen/Mapinduzi ya Malazi*/Revolutionary-Accommodationist group. The *khęperu/Kubadilisha*/Reformist group's general position is that Africans/Blacks must advance their cause within the frameworks of other groups, including their oppressors. This group is also quick to claim that it is its willingness to work for change within the system, oppressive as it may be, that has brought the most gains to Blacks. But this perspective has been countered that it is the pressure brought to bear by Revolutionaries that forced the oppressors to listen to what the Reformists have to say as a way for the oppressors to claim that they have acquiesced to some demands made by Blacks. Sociologist Herbert H. Haines characterized this situation as a "positive radical flank effect" on political affairs. Haines' study of the relationship between Black Revolutionaries and Reformists indicated that the Black Power movement generated a crisis in political and social institutions which made the legislative agenda of "polite, realistic and businesslike mainstream organizations" more appealing to oppressors (cited in DeBurg, 1992:306). It can therefore be argued that the more strident and oppositional messages of Revolutionaries enhanced the bargaining position of the Reformists. In fact, Revolutionaries saw Reformists as the culprits for the slow pace of and marginal changes the oppressors have been willing to make. (For more on the debate between the Revolutionaries and the Reformists over the acquiescence of the oppressors to some demands by Blacks, see, for example, Hanes, Jr., 1972; Katznelson, 1973; Karnig and Welch, 1980; Preston et al., 1982; Bush, 1984.)

Tajudeen Abdul-Raheem, general secretary of the Pan-African Movement, director of Justice Africa, the Deputy Director of United Nations Millennium Campaign for Africa, as well as a writer for newspapers and journals across Africa, saw the transformation of Pan-Africanism as urgent when he wrote these words that call for the full unity of the peoples of Africa within a democratic dispensation:

> We also do so not just as defensive impulse against the more fashionable industry of Afro pessimism. Our optimism is based on the concrete reality of our lived experiences and the brutal reality of the condition of many Africans today both on the continent and in the Diaspora. These have made Pan-Africanism a precondition for our survival instead of it just being a dream. And some of us will even go further to assert that we need our dreams and we need to accelerate the process of their realisation because those who have no dreams to live for and work towards will suffer nightmares. And Africa has suffered enough nightmares (quoted by Campbell, 2009).

As Horace Campbell (2009) observed, Abdul-Raheem believed that the use of violence, both physical and social, against the people ensures that grassroots Pan-Africanists eschew all forms of armed struggle. He pointed to the experiences in the Democratic Republic of the Congo after the overthrow of Mobutu Sese Seko that cured his branch of the movement from all romanticism associated with armed struggles. He noted that Foday Sankoh, Jonas Savimbi, Charles Taylor, the butchers of Sudan, Congo and Somalia cured the movement. For a brief moment after the overthrow of Mobutu and the rot in society prevailed, he recalled how his section supported the armed uprising in the East. This proved to be a colossal error and Tajudeen saw this very early and retreated from any support for that form of struggle. He spoke openly on this question as one of the roads to healing. It was clear to him that there is no work that can be better than the work of political education, organization and mobilization. So when he saw in Nigeria the growth of a branch of a movement for emancipation and some sections of this movement for emancipation call for the bearing of arms for liberation, his branch of the Pan-African movement said: "This is not the way for peace, nor for a clean-up of the environment and reconstruction" (Campbell, 2009).

In her 1992 memoir, *A Taste of Power*, Brown wrote the following about her experience in the Black Panther Party: "A woman in the Black Power movement was considered, at best, irrelevant. A woman asserting herself was a pariah. If a black woman assumed a role of leadership, she was said to be eroding black manhood, to be hindering the progress of the black race. She was an enemy of the black people.... I knew I had to muster something mighty to manage the Black Panther Party" (Brown, 1992). During her leadership of the Black Panther Party, she focused on electoral politics and community service. In 1977, she managed Lionel Wilson's victorious campaign to become Oakland's first Black mayor. She also developed the Panther's Liberation School, which was recognized by the state of California as a model school. She stepped down from Chairwoman of the Black Panther Party less than a year after Huey Newton's return from Cuba in 1977 when he condoned the beating of Regina Davis, the administrator of the Panther Liberation School. This incident was the point at which, according to Brown, she could no longer tolerate the sexism and patriarchy of the Black Panther Party (Brown, 1992:444). She left the United States with her daughter, Erika, and entered psychotherapy to end her addiction to Thorazine, a long-time addiction she had developed due to the stress and difficulties she had encountered as a woman and a leader in the Black liberation movement (Brown, 1992).

Brown eventually returned to the struggle for Black liberation, especially espousing the need for radical prison reform. From 1980 to 1983, she attended Southwestern University School of Law in Los Angeles. From 1990 to 1996, she lived in France; and in 1996, she moved to Atlanta, Georgia and founded Fields of Flowers, Inc., a non-profit organization committed to providing educational opportunities for impoverished African American children. In 1998, she co-founded the grassroots group, Mothers Advocating Juvenile Justice, to advocate for children being prosecuted as adults in the state of Georgia. Around the same time, Brown continued her advocacy for incarcerated youth by founding and leading the Michael Lewis Legal Defense Committee. Michael Lewis, also known as "Little B," was sentenced to life in prison at the age of 14 for a murder that Brown believed he did not commit. She would eventually write a non-fiction novel, *The Condemnation of Little B*, which analyzed the prosecution of Michael Lewis as part of the greater problem of the increased imprisonment of Black youth (Brown, 1992 & 2002).

In her book, *Talking Back: Thinking Feminist, Thinking Black* (1989), Bell Hooks reminded us that we live in a world of crisis, a world governed by politics of domination, one in which the belief in a superior and inferior and its concomitant ideology, that the superior should rule over the inferior, affects the lives of all people everywhere, whether poor or privileged, literate or illiterate. Systematic dehumanization, world wide famine, ecological devastation, industrial contamination, and the possibility of nuclear destruction, she argued, are realities which remind us daily that we are in crisis. She pointed out that contemporary feminist thinkers often cite sexual politics as the origin of this crisis, they point to the insistence on difference as that factor which becomes the occasion for separation and domination, and they suggest that differentiation of status between females and males globally is an indication that patriarchal domination of the planet is the root of the crisis. She argued that such a view in turn fosters the notion that elimination of sexist oppression would necessarily lead to the eradication of all forms of domination. It is an argument, she posited, that has led influential Western White women to feel that feminist movement should be *the* key political agenda for females globally. Ideologically, she maintained, thinking in this direction enables Western women, especially privileged White women, to suggest that racism and class exploitation are merely the offspring of the parent system: i.e. patriarchy. She observed that within feminist movement in the West, this thinking has led to the assumption that resisting patriarchal domination is a more legitimate feminist action than resisting racism and other forms of domination. Such thinking, she argued, prevails despite radical critiques made by Black women and other women of color who question this proposition. She added that to speculate that an oppositional division between men and women existed in early human communities is to impose on the past, on non-White groups, a worldview that fits all too neatly within contemporary feminist paradigms that name men as the enemy and women as the victim (Hord and Lee, 1995:329).

Martin Luther King, Jr., African American clergyman, activist, and prominent leader in the African American Civil Rights Movement, is best known for being an iconic figure in the advancement of civil rights in the United States and around the world. He was an important figure in the history of classic American liberalism, albeit in recent years his core beliefs, such as a society based on color blindness, the necessity of faith-based association and self-government based on fixed moral law, in addition to his embrace of the American founding, have made him a popular figure in modern American conservatism. A Baptist minister, King became a civil rights activist early in his career. He led the 1955 Montgomery Bus Boycott and helped found the Southern Christian Leadership Conference (SCLC) in 1957, serving as its first president. King's efforts led to the 1963 March on Washington, where King delivered his "I Have a Dream" speech. There, he expanded American values to include the vision of a color blind society and established his reputation as one of the great orators in American history. In 1964, King became the youngest person to receive the Nobel Peace Prize for his work to end racial segregation and racial discrimination through civil disobedience and other non-violent means. By the time of his death in 1968, he had refocused his efforts on ending poverty and stopping the Vietnam War. King was assassinated on April 4, 1968, in Memphis, Tennessee. He was posthumously awarded the Presidential Medal of Freedom in 1977 and the Congressional Gold Medal in 2004; Martin Luther King, Jr. Day was established as an American national holiday in 1986.

In his 1967 essay titled "Black Power," King declared that Black Power had become part of the nomenclature of the national community. He pointed out that the slogan is abhorrent to some, dynamic to others, repugnant to some, exhilarating to others, destructive to some, and useful to others. He argued that since Black Power means different things to different people, it is impossible to attribute its ultimate meaning to any single individual or organization. He therefore suggested that one must look beyond personal styles, verbal flourishes, and the hysteria of the mass media to assess its values, its assets and liabilities honestly (Hord and Lee, 1995:285).

King urged that it was necessary to understand Black Power as a cry of disappointment, it did not spring full grown from the head of some philosophical Zeus; instead, it was born from the wounds of despair and disappointment. For centuries, he noted, African Americans had been caught in the tentacles of White power. The frustration of Blacks, he pointed out, was further fed by the fact that even when Blacks and Whites die together in the cause of justice, the death of the White person gets more attention and concern than the death of the Black person. Consequently, he noted, many African Americans had given up faith in the White majority because "white power" with total control had left them empty-handed. So, in reality, he added, the call for Black Power is a reaction to the failure of white power (Hord and Lee, 285-286).

King further noted that African Americans are descendants of enslaved Africans; the offspring of men and women who were kidnapped from their native land and chained in ships like beasts; heirs of a great and exploited continent known as Africa; and the heirs of a past of rape, fire, and murder. He declared that he was not ashamed of this past and his shame was for those who became so inhuman that they could inflict such torture upon Africans on the continent and in the Diaspora. He then asserted that African Americans are also Americans; abused and scorned though they may be, their destiny is tied up with the destiny of America. He argued that in spite of the psychological appeals of identification with Africa, African Americans must face the fact that America is now their home, a home that they helped to build through blood, sweat, and tears. He added that as Americans, African Americans must not seek to build a separate Black nation within a nation, but to find that creative minority of the concerned from the oftentimes apathetic majority, and together move toward that colorless power that we all need for security and justice.

Julius Kambarage Nyerere, Tanzanian politician who served as the first President of Tanzania and previously Tanganyika, from the country's founding in 1961 until his retirement in 1985, was born in Tanganyika to Nyerere Burito (1860–1942), Chief of the Zanaki. Nyerere was known by the Swahili name *Mwalimu* or "teacher," his profession prior to politics. He was also referred to as *Baba wa Taifa,* meaning "Father of the Nation." Nyerere received his higher education at Makerere University in Kampala, Uganda and the University of Edinburgh, United Kingdom. After he returned to Tanganyika, he worked as a teacher. In 1954, he helped form the Tanganyika African National Union (TANU). In 1961, he was elected Tanganyika's first Prime Minister; following independence, in 1962, he was elected the country's first President. In 1964, Tanganyika became politically united with Zanzibar and was renamed Tanzania. In 1965, a one-party election returned Nyerere to power. Two years later, he issued the Arusha Declaration, which outlined his socialist vision of Ujamaa that came to dominate his policies. Nyerere retired in 1985, while remaining the chairman of the Chama Cha Mapinduzi. He died of leukaemia in London in 1999. In 2009, the United Nations General Assembly named Nyerere World Hero of Social Justice.

In his now widely cited and famous 1962 essay, "Ujamaa—The Basis of African Socialism," Nyerere outlined the way forward for us Africans to regain our power. The first step, he insisted, is to re-educate ourselves, to regain our former attitude of mind. He noted that in traditional African society, we were individuals within a community; we took care of the community, and the community took care of us; we neither needed nor wished to exploit our fellow man. He therefore urged us to reject the capitalist attitude of mind which colonialism brought into Africa and also reject the capitalist methods which go with it. One of these methods, he pointed out, is the individual ownership of land because to us Africans, land was always recognized belonging to the community. Each individual within our society, he pointed out, had a right to the use of land, because otherwise he could not earn his living, and one cannot have the right to life without also having the right to some means of maintaining life. But the African's right to land, he added, was simply the right to use it; he had no other right to it, nor did it occur to him to try and claim one. All this changed, according to Nyerere, when the foreigner introduced a completely different concept of land as a marketable commodity; a person could claim a piece of land as his own private property whether or not he intends to use it (Hord and Lee, 1995:68-69).

Nyerere then called for the rebuilding of the foundation and objective of African socialism which is based on the extended family. He insisted that the true African socialist does not look on one class of men as his brethren and another as his natural enemies; he should not form an alliance with the "brethren" for the extermination of the "non-brethren." Instead, he suggested, man should regard all men as his brethren, as members of his ever extending family. He urged that the recognition of the family to which we all belong must be extended further—beyond the ethnic group, the community, the nation, or even the continent—to embrace the whole society of mankind. For him, this is the only logical conclusion for true socialism (Hord and Lee, 1995:72).

Léopold Sédar Senghor, Senegalese poet, politician, and cultural theorist, served as the first President of Senegal (1960–1980). He was the first African to sit as a member of the Académie Française. He was also the founder of the political party called the Senegalese Democratic Bloc, and he is regarded by many as one of the most important African intellectuals of the 20th Century.

Senghor, in his now famous rebuttal 1966 essay, "Negritude: A Humanism of the Twentieth Century," argued that contrary to critics, especially among English-speaking critics, who characterize Negritude as racialism and self-negation, Negritude is none of those. He also argued that it is not just affirmation; instead, it is rooting oneself in oneself and self-confirmation; confirmation of one's *being*. Negritude, Senghor posited, is nothing more or less that what some English-speaking Africans have called the *African personality*; it is no different from the "black personality" discovered and proclaimed by the American New Negro movement. He nonetheless admitted that perhaps the only weakness of the proponents of Negritude, since it was the West Indian poet Aimé Césaire who coined the word Negritude, is to have attempted to define the concept a little more closely; to have developed it as a weapon, as an instrument of liberation, and as a contribution to the humanism of the 20th Century. He then went on to define Negritude as *"the sum of the cultural values of the black world;* that is, a certain active presence in the world, or better, in the universe." He added that it is essentially relations with others, an opening out to the world, contact and participation with others. Because of what it is, he posited, Negritude is necessary in the world, as it is humanism of the 20th Century (Hord and Lee, 1995:45-46).

Senghor went on to point out that ethnologists have often praised the unity, the balance, and the harmony of African civilization, of Black society, which was based both on the *community* and on the *person*, and in which, because it was founded on dialogues and reciprocity, the group had priority over the individual without crushing him, but allowing him to blossom as a person. Thus, he emphasized how much these characteristics of negritude enable it to find its place in contemporary humanism, thereby permitting Black Africa to make its contribution to the "Civilization of the Universal" which is so necessary in our divided but interdependent world. He noted that it will be a contribution to international cooperation, which must be and which shall be the cornerstone of that civilization. It is through these virtues of Negritude, he argued, that decolonization has been accomplished without too much bloodshed or hatred and that was a positive form of cooperation based on dialogues, and reciprocity has been established between former colonizers and colonized. It is through these virtues, he added, that there has been a new spirit at the United Nations, where the "no" and the bang of the fist on the table are no longer signs of strength. It is through these virtues, he further opined, that peace through cooperation could extend to South Africa, Rhodesia (now Zimbabwe), and the Portuguese colonies, if only the dualistic spirit of the Whites would open itself to dialogues (Hord and Lee, 1995:50).

Conclusion

Indeed, contrary to popular belief, Africans/Blacks are not a minority and they are not powerless; in addition to their abundant human and other natural resources, Africans/Blacks are the majority on the world scene. As J. D. Jackson/Hawk (2006) pointed out, totaling over one billion people worldwide, they are arguably, to paraphrase the late world-renown Black scholar-activist and historian John Henrik Clarke, the most widely-dispersed people on the face of the globe. Geographically, that means that there are over 250 million African/Black people in the Western Hemisphere (40-50 million plus in North America, roughly 160 million plus in South America, with over 60 million of them alone residing in Brazil, not to mention the other million or so Africans/Blacks who live within and around the Caribbean area); nearly 800 million or more Africans/Blacks in Africa; in excess of 250 million Black people in India known as the Black Untouchables; countless millions of Blacks throughout Europe (Spain and Portugal, France and Germany, among other countries there), the so-called Middle East (especially Saudi Arabia, Iran, and Iraq), the rest of Asia (Russia and China, Cambodia and Korea, Vietnam and the Philippines, and, say some experts, even Japan), and the Pacific Islands, most especially Melanesia ("the Black Islands"), which include the Fiji and the Solomon Islands. Another 100,000 plus Blacks, commonly known as the aboriginal ("the original") Australians, still live in their native land of Australia, although under many horrible conditions. Of course, these numbers do not include by any means the untold millions of Blacks globally who are "passing" for either European (White) or Asian (Yellow) or Hispanic (Brown and which is not a race but which describes, in general, a Spanish-speaking person or someone who comes from a Spanish-speaking country) or anything other than African/Black.

And, as Ali A. Mazurui (1986) has pointed out, geographically speaking, three definitions have dominated the discourse on where Africa is. He then offered a fourth definition that captures the natural geographical boundaries of Africa based on sound empirical evidence—recent findings by geneticists and paleontologists are in line with Mazrui's definition (see, for example, the report by Gray, 2009). The first definition of Africa is the racial one that restricted identity to the Black populated parts of the continent and its Diaspora. The second definition of Africa is the continental one and is the principle upon which the Organization of African Unity (OAU) was and now its successor, the African Union (AU), is based: i.e. Africa is a continent as a whole. The third definition is the power one that excluded those parts of Africa that were under "non-African" control—a definition that is now obsolete. The fourth definition Mazrui offered pushes Africa's boundaries not only across the Sahara but even across the Red Sea. Restating the details provided by Mazrui for his definition will take many pages; thus, the interested reader is urged to consult his book. Two other good books on this topic are Alan B. Mountjoy and David Hilling's *Africa: Geography and Development* (1988) and Samuel Kasule's *The History Atlas of Africa: From the First Humans to the Emergence of a New South Africa* (1998). But as Mazrui himself conceded, although decidedly under protest, we are stuck with the geopolitical definition of Africa being mainly west of the Red Sea and both north and south of the Sahara: i.e. the continental one.

So, continentally defined, Africa is indeed a very large area. It is the world's second largest continent after Asia. Its land area is 11.6 million square miles stretching nearly 5,000 miles from Cape Town, South Africa to Cairo, Egypt and more than 3,000 miles from Dakar, Senegal to Mogadishu, Somalia. The African continent is nearly three and one-half times the size of the continental United States. Africa's political geography consists of more than 50 modern nations, including island republics off its coasts. Details on the richness of the African continent's location, rivers, lakes, seas, surrounding oceans, valleys, mountains, hills, swamps, waterfalls, weather, etc. can be found in Vincent B. Khapoya's *The African Experience: An Introduction*, 2nd ed. (1998:2-8), among numerous other sources, of course.

A Pan-African Union will be geopolitically very well endowed. A geographical cluster that coordinates the various geopolitical facets will make it possible for Africans to benefit from their strategic geographical locations and endowments, particularly from major powers seeking such access. Nonetheless, Africans must not give up on the idea of pushing Africa's boundaries not only across the Sahara but even across the Red Sea because, as Mazrui correctly stated, we live in an age when a people's perception of themselves can be deeply influenced by which continent or region they associate themselves. What is the basis for such hope? Mazrui's observation is instructive:

> Until the 1950s the official policy of the government of Emperor Haile Selassie was to emphasise that Ethiopia was part of the Middle East rather than part of Africa. Yet it was the Emperor himself who initiated the policy of re-Africanising Ethiopia as the rest of Africa approached independence, fearing to be outflanked by the radicalism of (Gamal Abdel) Nasser of Egypt and (Kwame) Nkrumah of Ghana. In particular, Nasser's strong support for continental Pan-Africanism and active support for anti-colonial liberation struggles both north and south of the Sahara encouraged Haile Selassie to emphasise that Ethiopia, too, was part of Africa. Yet cultural similarities between Ethiopia and the rest of Black Africa are not any greater than cultural similarities between north Africa and the Arabian peninsula. Nevertheless, a European decision to make Africa end at the Red Sea has decisively dis-Africanised the Arabian peninsula, and made the natives there see themselves as West Asians rather than as north Africans (1986:37-38).

Mazrui continued:

> The most difficult people to convince of a greater territorial Africa may well turn out to be the inhabitants of the Arabian peninsula. They have grown to be proud of being the 'Arabs of Asia' rather than the 'Arabs of Africa'....Yet if Emperor Haile Selassie could initiate the re-Africanisation of Ethiopia, and Gamal Abdel Nasser could inaugurate the re-Africanisation of Egypt, prospects for reconsideration of the identity of the Arabian peninsula may not be entirely bleak. At the moment the re-Africanisation of the Arabian peninsula is only an idea in the head of a scholar. It may never become a cause in the hearts of men. But its advocacy may help to keep alive the issue of where Africa ends and Asia begins, and encourage other individuals on either side of the Red Sea to re-examine the validity of Africa's north-eastern boundaries and question the arbitrariness of this boundary (1986:38).

Without a doubt, earlier Western prejudices against Arabs exacerbated by the backlash after the terrorist attacks on the World Trade Center in New York City and the Pentagon in Washington, DC on September 11, 2001 has prompted many Arabs to reexamine their cultural connections. The appointment of Sheikh Adil Kalbani as the first Black Imam at the Grand Mosque in Mecca (Worth, 2009), Islam's holiest city whose guardian is the Saudi Arabian King, and the election of Jean Gregoire Sagbo to a political office in Novozavidovo, Russia (Narizhnaya, 2010) are hopeful signs.

References

Abu-Jamal, Mumia. February 07, 2003. Questions for Mumia: Tell me about your name. Retrieved on August 17, 2010 from http://www.prisonradio.org/maj/maj_2_7_name.html

Abu-Jamal, Mumia. 1996. *Live from Death Row*. New York, NY: Harper Perennial.

Adeleke, Tunde. 2005. Gloracialization: The response of Pan-Blackists to globalization. *Globalization*. Retrieved on July 28, 2010 from http://globalization.icaap.org/content/v5.1/adeleke.html

African American Literary Book Club. 2010. Haki R. Madhubuti. Retrieved on August 23, 2010 from http://aalbc.com/authors/haki.htm

Alexander, Amy. September 18, 2006. Tavis Smiley's *Covenant, The Nation*.

Ammons, Elizabeth. 2010. Anna Julia Haywood Cooper. Retrieved on August 27, 2010 from http://www.answers.com/topic/anna-julia-haywood-cooper

Ani, Marimba. 1994. *Yurugu: An African-Centered Critique of European Cultural Thought and Behavior*. Trenton, NJ: Africa World Press.

Antoine, Jacques C. 1981. Jean Price-Mars and Haiti. Washington, DC: The Three Continents Press.

Asante, Molefi Kete. 1990. *Kemet, Afrocentricity and Knowledge*. Trenton, NJ: Africa World Press.

Asante, Molefi Kete. 1988. *Afrocentricity*. Trenton, NJ: Africa World Press.

Asante, Molefi Kete. 1987. *The Afrocentric Idea*. Philadelphia, PA: Temple University Press.

Bagley, Mark. 2010. Seale, Robert George (Bobby). Retrieved on August 28, 2010 from http://www.pabook.libraries.psu.edu/palitmap/bios/seale__bobby.html

Bangura, Abdul Karim. In press. *African-centered Research Methodologies from Ancient Times to the Present*. Lanham, MD: Rowman and Littlefield Group.

Bangura, Abdul Karim. 2006. Paul Robeson's linguistics breakthrough. *Journal of Pan-African Studies.* 1, 5:42-47.

Bangura, Abdul Karim and Erin McCandless. 2007. *Peace Research for Africa: Critical Essays on Methodology.* Geneva, Switzerland: United Nations University for Peace Press.

bell hooks. 1989. *Talking Back: Thinking Feminist, Thinking Black.* Boston, MA: South End Press.

Bekerie, Ayele. 1997. *Ethiopic: An African Writing System.* Trenton, NJ: Red Sea Press.

ben-Jochannan, Yosef A. A. 1970. *African Origins of the Major "Western Religions": The Black Man's Religion.* Baltimore, MD: Black Classic Press.

Boddy-Evans, Alistair. 2010. Jomo Kenyata. *About.com: African History.* Retrieved on August 27, 2010 from http://africanhistory.about.com/od/biography/a/bio-Kenyatta01.htm

Brown, Elaine. 2002. *The Condemnation of Little B: New Age Racism in America.* Boston, MA: Beacon.

Brown, Elaine. 1992. *A Taste of Power: A Black Woman's Story.* New York, NY: Doubleday.

Brown, Gillian and George Yule. 1983. *Discourse Analysis.* (Cambridge, UK: Cambridge University Press.

Budge, E. A. Wallis. 1978. *An Egyptian Hieroglyphic Dictionary* 2 vols. New York, NY: Dover Publications, Inc.

Burroughs, Todd Stevens. 2004. *Ready to Party: Mumia Abu-Jamal and the Black Panther Party.* Ewing, NJ: The College of New Jersey. Retrieved on August 17, 2010 from http://www.tcnj.edu/~kpearson/Mumia/index.htm

Bush, Rod. (ed.). 1984. *The New Black Vote: Politics and Power in Four American Cities.* San Francisco, CA: Synthesis Publications.

Campbell, Horace. 2009. Tajudeen Abdul-Raheem and the tasks of Pan-Africanists. *Pan-African Postcard.* Issue 442, July 16, 2009. Retrieved on July 28, 2010 from http://pambazuka.org/category/panafrica/57755

Carew, Jan. 1994. *Ghosts in Our Blood with Malcolm in Africa, England, and the Caribbean.* Chicago, IL: Lawrence Hill Books.

Carmichael, Stokely and Charles V. Hamilton. 1967. *Black Power: The Politics of Liberation in America*. New York, NY: Vintage Books.

Center for Islamic Pluralism. 2008. Black America, prisons, and radical Islam. Retrieved on August 17, 2010 from http://www.islamicpluralism.org/documents/black-america-prisons-radical-islam.pdf

Chabal, Patrick. 1983. *Amilcar Cabral: Revolutionary Leadership and People's War*. New York, NY and Cambridge, UK: Cambridge University Press.

Crystal, David. 1992. *An Encyclopedic Dictionary of Language and Languages*. Cambridge, MA: Blackwell Publishers.

Davis, Angela Yvonne. 1989. *Angela Davis: An Autobiography*. New York, NY: International Publishers.

Digital Library of the Caribbean. 2010. Collections: Eric E. Williams. Retrieved on August 30, 2010 from http://www.dloc.com/ufdc/?m=hiteew

Diop, Cheikh Anta. 1974a. *The African Origin of Civilization: Myth and Reality*. Chicago, IL: Lawrence Hill (Africa World Press edition).

Diop, Cheikh Anta. 1974a. *Black Africa: The Economic Basis for a Federated State*. Chicago, IL: Lawrence Hill (Africa World Press edition).

Duberman, Martin. 1995. *Paul Robeson*. New York, NY: New Press.

E-blackstudies.org. 2010. Introduction to Afro-American Studies: A Peoples College Primer. Retrieved on August 28, 2010 from http://www.eblackstudies.org/intro/chapter13.htm

Encyclopedia Britanica. 2010. Ahmed Sékou Touré. Retrieved on August 25, 2010 from http://www.britannica.com/EBchecked/topic/600761/Sekou-Toure

First World Conference. 2006. Featured speakers. Retrieved on August 26, 2010 from http://www.sankofaworldpublishers.com/sankofawponline/sankofawp-featured%20speakers.htm#Oba%20T%27Shaka%20photo

Florence, Namulundah. 1998. *bell hooks's Engaged Pedagogy*. Westport, CT: Bergin and Garvey.

Frankfort-Nachmias, Chava and David Nachmias. 1886. *Research Methods in the Social Sciences* 5th ed. New York, NY: St. Martin's Press.

Gray, Richard. May 09, 2009. African tribe populated rest of the world. *Telegraph*. Retrieved on May 10, 2009 from http://www.telegrapgh.co.uk

GuyanaCaribbeanPolitics.com. 2010. Walter Rodney: A biography. Retrieved on August 25, 2010 from http://www.africanholocaust.net/news_ah/capitalismsocialism.html

Hanes, Jr., Walton. 1972. *Black Politics*. Philadelphia, PA: J. B. Lippincot.

Hilliard, David et al. 2006. *Huey: The Spirit of the Panther*. New York, NY: Thunder's Mouth Press.

HistoryMakers. November 05, 2006. Yosef Ben-Jochannan biography. Retrieved on August 19, 2010 from http://www.thehistorymakers.com/biography/biography.asp?bioindex=1369&category=Educationmakers

Hoover, Kenneth and Todd Donovan. 2004. *The Elements of Social Scientific Thinking*. Belmont, CA: Wadsworth.

Hoppers, C. Odora. 2002. *Indigenous Knowledge and the Integration of Knowledge Systems: Towards an Articulation*. Claremont, South Africa: New African Books (Pvt.) Ltd.

Hord, Fred Lee (Mzee Lasana Okpara) and Jonathan Scott Lee. (eds.). 1995. *I Am Because We Are: Readings in Black Philosophy*. Amherst, MA: University of Massachusetts Press.

Jackson, J. D. 2006. The hawk's nest: The African world family—Part 1. *Black Commentator*. December 21, Issue 211. Retrieved on July 23, 2010 from

James, C. L. R. 1967. Black Power (talk given by C. L. R. James in London in 1967). Retrieved on August 06, 2010 from http://www.marxists.org/archive/james-clr/works/1967/black-power.htm

Joseph, Paniel E. 2006. *Waiting 'til the Midnight Hour: A Narrative History of Black Power in America* New York, NY: Henry Holt and Company.

Karnig, Albert and Susan Welch. 1980. *Black Representation and Urban Policy*. Chicago, IL: The University of Chicago Press.

Kasule, Samuel. 1998. *The History Atlas of Africa: From the First Humans to the Emergence of a New South Africa*. New York, NY: Macmillan.

Katznelson, Ira. 1973. *Black Men, White Cities*. New York, NY: Oxford University Press.

Khapoya, Vincent B. 1998. *The African Experience: An Introduction*, 2nd ed. Upper Saddle River, NJ: Prentice Hall.

Liukkonen, Petri. 2008. Aimé Césaire (1913-2008). Retrieved on August 19, 2010 from http://www.kirjasto.sci.fi/cesaire.htm

Liukkonen, Petri. 2008. Richard (Nathaniel) Wright (1908-1960). *Kaupunginkirjasto*. Retrieved on August 26, 2010 from http://www.kirjasto.sci.fi/rwright.htm

Ludwig, Samuel. December 18, 2002. Ishmael Reed. *The Literary Encyclopedia*. Retrieved on August 30, 010 from http://www.litencyc.com/php/speople.php?rec=true&UID=3731

Lyons, John. 1977. *Semantics* vol. 1. Cambridge, UK: Cambridge University Press.

Malcolm X. 1967. *On Afro-American History*. New York, NY: Pathfinder Press.

Marable, Manning and Leith Mullings. 2003. *Let Nobody Turn Us Around: Voices of Resistance, Reform, and Renewal: An African American Anthology*. Lanham, MD: Rowman & Littlefield.

Mazrui, Ali Al'amin and Ricardo Rene Laremont. 1992. *Africanity Redefined: Collected Essays of Ali A. Mazrui*. Trenton, NJ: Africa World Press.

Mazrui, Ali Al'amin. 1986. *The Africans: A Triple Heritage*. Boston, MA: Little, Brown and Company.

Mazrui, Ali Al'amin. 1986. The Africans: A triple heritage. BBC and PBS: Video Series in Eight Parts.

Mazrui, Ali Al'amin. 1977. *Africa's International Relations: The Diplomacy of Dependency & Change*. Boulder, CO: Westview Press.

Mountjoy, Alan B. and David Hilling. 1988. *Africa: Geography and Development*. London: Hutchinson Education.

Muslim Alliance in North America. October 29, 2009. The FBI raid and shooting death of Imam Luqman. Retrieved on August 08, 2010 from http://www.mana-net.org/pages.php?ID=&MUM=1165

Mustafaa, 2010. My walk with Farrakhan. Retrieved on August 20, 2010 from http://brothermustafaa.com/

Mybanglaspace. 2009. Baby Naznin. Retrieved on July 24, 2010 from

http://www.mybanglaspace.com/mytunes/view/artist_496/name_baby-naznin-_mbs_/

Nabudere, Dani Wadada. 2002. The epistemological and methodological foundations for an all-inclusive research paradigm in the search for global knowledge (Occasional Paper Series, Volume 6, Number 1, published by the African Association of Political Science, Pretoria, South Africa.

Nabudere, Dani Wadada. 2001. The African Renaissance in the age of globalization. *African Journal of Political Science* 6, 2:11-27.

Narizhnaya, Kristina. July 25, 2010. A Russian milestone: 1st Black elected to office. *Associated Press*. Retrieved on July 27, 2010 from http://news.yahoo.com/s/ap/20100725/ap_on_re_eu/eu_rusia_black_politician

National Association of Black Journalists. December 02, 2005. Moments in journalism. Retrieved on August 17, 2010 from http://www.nabj.org/30/moments/thirty/v-print/story/31591p-46158c.php

NobelPrize.org. 1986. Wole Soyinka—Biography. Retrieved on August 25, 2010 from http://nobelprize.org/nobel_prizes/literature/laureates/1986/soyinka-bio.html

Ogbar, Jeffrey Ogbonna Green. 2005. *Black Power: Radical Politics and African American Identity.* Baltimore, MD: Johns Hopkins University Press.

Oji, Chima. 2007. Neo-Black Movement Worldwide: A brief history. Retrieved on August 23, 2010 from http://nbmarena.org/history.html

Oxaal, Ivar. 1968. *Black Intellectuals Come to Power: The Rise of Creole nationalism in Trinidad and Tobago.* Cambridge, MA: Schenkman Publishing Company, Inc.

Pearson, Hugh. 1994. *Shadow of the Panther: Huey P. Newton and the Price of Black Power in America.* Upper Saddle River, NJ: Addison-Wesley (Pearson).

Pement, Eric. 1999. Louis Farrakhan and the Nation of Islam. *Connerstone Magazine*. Retrieved on August 20, 2010 from http://www.cornerstonemag.com/features/iss111/islam1.htm

Pinsky, Stefan/Emory University English Department. Fall 1996. Merle Hodge. Retrieved on August 21, 2010 from http://english.emory.edu/Bahri/Hodge.html

Pragmatism Cybrary. 2010. Cornel West, prophetic pragmatist. Retrieved on August 30, 2010 from http://www.pragmatism.org/west.htm

Preston, Michael et al. (eds.). 1982. *The New Black Politics.* New York, NY: Longman.

Public Broadcasting Service (PBS). January 20, 2003. Brother outsider: The life of Bayard Rustin. *Documentaries with a Point of View (POV)*. Retrieved on August 30, 2010 from http://www.pbs.org/pov/brotheroutsider/

Rashidi, Runoko. 2010. *The Global African Presence* (comprising 341 essays). Available at http://www.cwo.com/~lucumi/runoko.html

Rashidi, Runoko. 2010. **The African presence in Asia: Introduction and overview.** *People of Africa and America Magazine.* Retrieved on July 24, 2010 from http://ipoaa.com/african_presence_in_asia.htm

Rashidi, Runoko. 2002. Dr. Chancellor James Williams. *The Global African Community.* Retrieved on August 26, 2010 from http://www.cwo.com/~lucumi/williams-ref.html

Rashidi, Runoko. 1998. Dr. Chancellor James Williams and the reconstruction of African civilization. *The Global African Community.* Retrieved on August 26, 2010 from http://www.cwo.com/~lucumi/williams.html

Rashidi, Runoko. 1976. West Papua New Guinea: Interview with Foreign Minister Ben Tanggahma. *The Global African Community History Notes. Black Books Bulletin* 4,2 (Summer 1976). Retrieved on July 25, 2010 from *http://www.cwo.com/~lucumi/nguinea.html*

Richards, Dona M. 1994. *Let the Circle be Unbroken: The Implications of African Spirituality in the Diaspora.* Trenton, NJ: The Read Sea Press.

Riesberg, Chris K. and Roger Schank. 1978. Comprehension by computer: Expectation-based analysis of sentences in context. In W. J. M. Levelt and G. B. Flores d'Arcais (eds.). *Studies in the Perception of Language.* New York, NY: Wiley.

Rodriguez, Dylan. 2006. *Forced Passage: Imprisoned Radical Intellectuals and the U.S. Prison Regime.* Minneapolis, MN: University of Minnesota Press.

Rosengarten, Frank. 2007. *Urbane Revolutionary: C. L. R. James and the Struggle for a New Society.* Jackson, MS: University of Mississippi Press.

Salaam, Kalamu ya. 2010. Black Arts Movement (originally published in *The Oxford Companion to African American Literature* (New York, NY: Oxford University Press, 1997). Retrieved on August 30, 2010 from http://aalbc.com/authors/blackartsmovement.htm

Sales, Jr., William W. 1994. *From Civil Rights to Black Liberation: Malcolm X and the Organization of Afro- American Unity.* Boston, MA: South End Press.

Schank, Roger C. 1973a. Identification of conceptualizations underlying natural language. In R. C. Schank and K. M. Colby (eds.). *Computer Models of Thought and Language.* San Francisco, CA: Freeman.

Schank, Roger C. 1973b. Conceptual dependency: A theory of natural language understanding. *Cognitive Psychology* 3:552-631.

Schomburg Center. 2009. John Henrik Clarke, Legacy Exhibit online, New York Public Library Schomburg Center for the Study of Black Culture. Retrieved on August 20, 2010 from http://legacy.www.nypl.org/research/sc/WEBEXHIB/legacy/imgins15.htm

Scott, Joseph W. 1976. *The Black Revolts: Racial Stratification in the USA: The Politics of Estate, Caste, Class, and Class in American Society.* Cambridge, MA: Schenkmen Publishers.

Seale, Bobby. 1970. *Seize the Time: The Story of the Black Panther and Huey P. Newton.* New York, NY: Random House.

Shaw, Theodore M. et al. July 27, 2007. Brief of *amicus curiae*. *Mumia Abu-Jamal v. Martin Horn, Pennsylvania Director of Corrections et al.* Retrieved on August 17, 2010 from http://www.naacpldf.org/content/pdf/jury/Abu-Jamal_v_Horn_amicus_brief.pdf

Shapiro, Fred R. (ed.). 2006. *Yale Book of Quotations*. New Haven, CT: Yale University Press.

Smith, Laura. October 27, 2007. I spend my days preparing for life, not for death. *The Guardian*. Retrieved on August 17, 2010 from http://www.guardian.co.uk/usa/story/0,,219855700.html

Spartacus Educational. 2010. Booby Seale. Retrieved on August 28, 2010 from http://www.spartacus.schoolnet.co.uk/USAseale.htm

Stanford University Martin Luther King, Jr. Research and Education Institute. 2010. Stokely Carmichael, *King Encyclopedia*. Retrieved on August 28, 2010 from http://mlk-kpp01.stanford.edu/

Stevenson, Lisbeth Gant. 1992. *African-American History: Heroes in Hardship*. Cambridge, MA: Cambridgeport Press.

The Final Call (online edition). June 06-11, 2002. From exile with love. Retrieved on August 08, 2010 from http://www.finalcall.com/international/asata_shakur06-11-2002.htm

The Global African Community. 2010. Runoko Rashidi. Retrieved on August 24, 2010 from http://www.cwo.com/~lucumi/bio.html

The Organization Us. 1999. The chair's message. Retrieved on August 22, 2010 from http://www.us-organization.org/

The Philadelphia Inquirer. December 10, 1981. The suspect—one who realized his voice. Retrieved on August 17, 2010 from http://fortunecity.com/meltingpot/botswana/509/inqarticles/12-10a.htm

Touré, Ahmed Sékou. 1989. A dialectical approach to culture. In R. Chrisman and N. Hare, eds. *Contemporary Black Thought.* Indianapolis, IN and New York, NY: The Bobbs-Merrill Co, Inc./MacMillan Press.

T'Shaka, Oba.1995. *Return to the African Mother: Principles of Male and Female Equality*. Oakland, CA: Pan-Afrikan Publishers.

Tyson, Timothy B. 2001. *Radio Free Dixie: Robert F. Williams and the Roots of Black Power*. Chapel Hill, NC: The University of North Carolina Press.

Van DeBurg, William L. 1992. *New Day in Babylon: The Black Power Movement and American Culture, 1965-1975*. Chicago, IL: The University of Chicago Press.

Walton, Jr., Hanes. 1972. *The Poetry of Black Politics*. London, UK and New York, NY: Regency Press.

17

Ali A. Mazrui's meditation about Global Africa:
From Otto Von Bismarck to Barack Obama

Darryl C. Thomas

Introduction

In recent years there has been a new wave of scholarly studies focusing on Global Africa, the Black (African) Diaspora, and Black internationalism drawing attention to the interrelationships, interconnections, and linkages between Africa and its diasporas including the diaspora of enslavement – both the Eastern and the Black Atlantic and the diaspora of colonialism. Scholars are paying more attention to how African Americans and their counterparts in Africa, the Americas and Europe sought to influence international affairs, drawing attention to the plight of Africans during the Congress of Berlin/Scramble for Africa, as well as Haiti, Ethiopia, India and other colonial areas during and after both the First and Second World Wars.

Moreover, the election and recent re-election of Barack Obama as the first American President of African descent (2008 and 2012 respectively), the growing importance of the African continent in the scramble for oil, minerals, and other vital commodities between the East (China, India, Russia and others) and the West (the United States, European Union and Japan), and the pursuit of African land for farming by food production companies from the Middle East and Asia places an enormous importance on Africans and their descendants as critical actors in the contemporary phase of global economic and political restructuring. In addition, the new scholarship is establishing the evidence of the dynamic roles of Africans and people of African descent in the development of American, European and global civilization, and history. For a long while, the Cold War conflict cast a seductive spell over the world as well as the production of knowledge or regime of knowledge rendering the Black (African) diaspora and Black internationalism, and the global African phenomenon a façade of invisibility. The demise of the Cold War conflict and the rise of a new wave of globalization have spawned new approaches to the production of knowledge. The role of African Studies, Africana Studies, Black Studies and Black (African) Diaspora Studies, and the Global African phenomenon has been critical to this new discourse. Ali A. Mazrui has been one of the unsung trailblazers in this arena. What will follow is a critical examination of his work in this arena.

Students of world politics and international relations are often concerned with the distribution of power in the world system, that is, to what extent is the international system characterize by bipolar, multipolar or unipolar system? What is the distribution of power and where is this power concentrated? How does the distribution of power in the international system influence the policies and actions of the weaker states in the world system? Students of the Third World have been concerned with similar issues as they seek to understand how the power distribution in the system how its impact on states with less power and capabilities. How did the global power equation influence the global South's response to the Cold War conflict? How does the distribution of power in the international system influence North-South relations? The end of the Cold War conflict between the United States and the Soviet Union led Ali A. Mazrui to address the impact on North-South relations and critical examine cultural forces in world politics.

Introduction

Ali A. Mazrui had a perennial concern for the linkages between social conflict and identity and this interest was very pronounced in several public addresses and a couple of papers that revolve around this theme, including, 'From Bismarck to Obama'. Mazrui was interested in the paradox of how Otto von Bismarck played a key role in the unification of Germany in the nineteenth century and initiated the partition of Africa that resulted in some of the most vulnerable societies in the contemporary era. He also noted how Germany was divided again in the middle of the twentieth century as a result of the ideological conflict that permeated the Cold War era – communist East Germany and a capitalist Federal Republic of Germany. He observes that the re-unification of Germany at the end of the twentieth century was almost a celebration of the centenary of Otto von Bismarck's final years as effective leader of German Empire. There were three European wars in the nineteenth were responsible for Germany's unification. These included Germany's wars with Denmark in 1864; with Austria in 1866; and with France in 1871. At this juncture he was appointed Chancellor of German Empire in 1871 – preceded to govern Germans from that year until 1890. He became the most influential Western statesmen of his day.[1]

Mazrui died before the end of Obama's second term. But in his writings, Mazrui described the influential statesmanship of Obama as one that was predicated on the power of the United States rather than as a result of his own personal performance. It is not clear if Mazrui would have evaluated Obama's performance differently after his presidency. Mazrui draws attention to the dialectic of Obama being a descendant of Africa which Bismarck partition. Both Germany and the USA emerged as major players in the capitalist game and played a much minor role in the colonial one. Neither country built a large territorial colonial empire. The United States was limited to the Philippines and a few islands here and there. Germany acquired a larger empire but did not succeed in keeping them long. Mazrui's second dialectic focus is connected to the fact that Bismarck hosted a conference that officially launched the partition of Africa. The United States, on the other hand, produced citizens who launched the ideology of unity of Africa. Bismarck hosted the Berlin Conference of 1884-85, which brought together approximately sixteen Western powers. These states established the ground rules for the European scramble for Africa (Mazrui 2009:11). Nevertheless, the United States was present at the conference but did not compete for African territory. However, the United States racial policies at home began to produce a cadre of African Americans who were for the unification of the Black World as a whole. W. E. B. Du Bois was born in February 1869 in Massachusetts. Before the end of the nineteenth century he was active in an organization of what became the first Pan-African Congress of 1900. Du Bois played midwife to the ideology of African unity. Mazrui draws attention to how a divided Africa managed to father a Black President of the United States and the potential ramification for this president challenging Africa's fragmentation and resolving outstanding conflicts.[2] Let us explore the cultural forces paradigm as articulated by Mazrui.

Mazrui observed that the central divide between East and West since World War II has of course been ideological – communism versus capitalism. He also noted that the central divide between the North and South in the same period has been *technological* – the industrialized states versus the developing societies. East-West tensions have resulted in *military* rivalries. The North-South tensions have been linked to economic disparities. Furthermore, the East and West have competed for new skills of *destruction*. When he examines the North-South conflict he concludes that different levels of production were the primary driving force behind this conflict. Mazrui contends that cultural change needed for technological progress is more complex than cultural change needed for ideological revisionism Ali A. Mazrui 1990:1). These observations were made during the initial period when the USA and USSR were winding down the Cold War conflict and Gorbachev was pursuing perestroika, that is, the prelude to the fall of the Soviet Empire and the emergence of unipolar world order with a lone superpower.

Ali A. Mazrui and Cultural Forces in World Politics

In 1990, *Cultural Forces in World Politics* was published extending Mazrui theoretical meditation on the impact of perestroika on North-South relations providing a provocative cultural sweep of history in the late 20th century. Mazrui was concerned with how the thawing of the Cold War conflict between the United States and the Soviet Union might expand the technological distance between the North and the South and reduce foreign aid as a critical factor in the Eastern and Western bloc and this led Mazrui to ponder the cultural cost. Foreign aid to the Third World was partly a consequence of the competition between both superpowers to recruit newly independent states from the global South into their ideological /strategic camps. Both Washington and Moscow considered foreign aid critical tool of diplomacy and influence with the Third World. To American policymakers, foreign aid was a strategic concept related to national security. Soviets operated on the premise that foreign aid was also related to their strategic interests. Most of American foreign aid was directed toward the Israel, while the most of Soviet aid went to Cuba.

In his evaluation of perestroika, Mazrui declared that foreign aid would decline in importance as the ideological contest between the two superpowers began to decline in the 1990s and become one of the first cost or casualties of perestroika. Hence, there would be a mark reduction in the transfer of resources from the North to the South. He expected a dramatic drop in resource transfers from the Soviet Union to the Third World as the for Moscow sought entrance into international economic and financial organizations associated with the capitalist world and gain access to the technological innovations in the western world. Mazrui also drew attention to the probable decline on military expenditure as the Soviets began to focus on consumer goods the technological gap between the North and South would also intensify by leaps and bounds. Thus, the northern hemisphere would become even more advanced outstripping the global South even more and some of the cost of restructuring or perestroika in the second world of socialism would be born by the Third World of underdevelopment.

Basically, Mazrui adopted the traditional international relations conception of the First, Second, and Third Worlds. The First World comprises the industrialized North America, Western Europe, and Japan. The Second World of industrialized socialism included the Soviet Union and its European allies. The Third World encompasses most of Africa, Asia, the Caribbean, and Latin America. He observes that the cultural divide between the East and West is much more narrow than the cultural divide between the North and the South and this is the basic theme of this text. Will Western businessmen be so tempted and mesmerized by the potential new markets and customers in the eastern bloc that there will be an inevitable flight of Western capital from the Third World toward the Soviet Union and its allies in Eastern and Central Europe? He also contends that could be one more cost of perestroika between the East and the West. He was also concerned with the Soviet bloc departure from anti-systemic conflicts in the global South. As the Soviets sought entrance into capitalist circles Moscow might also depart from supporting armed struggles in Southern Africa and elsewhere in the Third World.[3]

In the early 1980s, the Soviet Union stood by its commitments to defend anti-systemic movements in the global South, ranging from Cuba and Nicaragua in the Americas to Angola, Ethiopia, and Mozambique on the African continent, to Afghanistan and Vietnam in the Far East and South Asia. The Soviets supported the antiapartheid movements in the Republic of South Africa and the anti-colonial movement in Namibia as well as the anti-systemic movement in El Salvador. At the twenty-sixth Party Congress in 1991, neither commitment to détente nor Soviet support of radical Third World states was questioned. Brezhnev committed Moscow to combating the new counterrevolution being launched by the Reagan administration. During the interim between Brezhnev's death in 1982 and the election of Gorbachev in February 1985, Soviet leadership was rethinking Moscow's role in Third World-oriented conflicts. President Yuri V. Andropov announced some initial steps toward reducing Moscow's exposure to Third World regional conflicts; however, he died before a number of these policy initiatives were implemented. With Gorbachev rise to power in 1985, Soviet's Third World policies underwent a dramatic transformation.

During the first Reagan administration the conflict between the two superpowers in the Third World was so intense that it was virtually impossible to schedule any summits between these two antagonistic blocs. Since the mid-1980s there has been several such gatherings between Washington and Moscow. In July 1991, the Soviets participated in the Group of Seven meeting for the first time. This momentous event came as a result of meetings between President Bush and President Gorbachev. At these gatherings, Washington and Moscow laid the groundwork for a massive reduction in the arms race, conflict resolution with reference to Third World regional militarized disputes, and a comprehensive Middle East conference in the wake of the Gulf War of 1991. This new approach toward Third World regional conflict became known as *international glasnost*.[4]

International glasnost involved a broad rejection of Soviet commitment to support anti-systemic movements in the Third World that were supporting the cause of socialism. In the Soviet's new view, Third World regions constituted zones of instability and crisis where superpower confrontation had the potential of escalating into full-blown nuclear war, threatening the very survival of spaceship earth. Therefore, the greatest cost of Third World regional conflict was military rather than economic, although socialist regimes were becoming a fiscal burden by the mid-1980s. At this juncture, the Soviets entered a number of discussion through the United Nations that eventually led to the Soviet withdrawal from Afghanistan: a negotiated settlement among Angola's Marxist-Leninist government, UNITA, South Africa, and the United States; the Cuban departure from Southern Africa; and the independence of Namibia. Similar discussions took place over the civil war in Cambodia and other hot spots in the Third World. Washington and Moscow began reducing their arms transfers to the Third World with the exception of the Middle East.[5]

Mazrui observes that before the East-West rapprochement Africans used to emphasize that side of their ancestral heritage which affirmed *'when two elephants fight, it is the grass which suffers.'* The hostility between East and West, the two elephants, hurt the grass of the Third World – Korea, Vietnam, Afghanistan, and Latin America have been hurt even more directly than Africa by the enmity between the superpowers. However, with the new rapprochement between East and West, the Third World is wondering whether not it is equally true *that when two elephants make love, it is also the grass that suffers.* Another side of Africa's proverbial wisdom is asserting its contemporary relevance. The embraces of the superpowers in amorous mutual discovery can be costly to the grass of the Third World as the original rivalry of the cold war. Although rapprochement was good news in the field of disarmament and reduce the danger of conflict between the East and the West, it may be bad news from the point of view of economic justice and technological fairness between the North and South.[6]

Mazrui on the Black Struggle & Transition from Black Power to Barack Power

Barack Obama was born in the 1960s, which were the glory days of the Black Power movement and Civil Rights activism. For the United States, the 1960s was a decade of diverse radicalizing forces. At the same time, the Vietnam War morphed into a seismic Cold War conflict, triggering the launch of the anti-war movement, which later convinced President Johnson not to seek re-election. Similarly, the civil rights movement had set off racial skirmishes, and the assassination of Malcolm X and Martin L. King, Jr., (the murder of Robert Kennedy was precipitated by the Arab-Israeli conflict rather than the civil rights movement in the United States). The 1960s also witnessed students' protest movement, whose demands also included greater campus democracy and Black Studies academic units across the nation. At this juncture a proliferation of academic publications on "Black Power" and racial politics materialized. Mazrui contends that these divergent radicalizing factors contributed to the earlier stages of deracialization of America in both the North and South.[7]

President Lyndon B. Johnson's inaugurated his "Great Society" vision, and succeeded in getting legislation passed expanding the voting rights for people of color. At this critical juncture, the US Supreme Court struck down in 1967 long-standing laws against inter-racial mating and inter-racial marriages. The case was *Virginia vs. Loving* that declared anti-miscegenation laws unconstitutional.

Next, affirmative action policies at the federal, state, and local levels attempted to expand educational, economic, and professional opportunities for Black people and women. Such policies directly and indirectly benefited Barack Obama get quality education at Occidental College, Columbia University, and at Harvard Law School. Later in 1984 and again in 1988, there were two attempts by Jesse Jackson to run for President of the United States. At this critical juncture, the country was not quite ready for a black president but the atmosphere had become congenial enough for a serious attempt to be made for the nomination to be made for the Democratic Party.[8]

The second half of the twentieth century also saw the election of the first two Black senators of the United States since Reconstruction – Edward Brooks of Massachusetts and Carole Moseley Braun of Illinois. The election of Barack Hussein Obama in 2004 provided the fifth Black senator of the United States in history (two were during the Reconstruction era). When Barack Obama resigned from the Senate after being elected president in 2008, Roland Burris of Illinois succeeded him – the sixth Black senator since the institution was first created.[9] Because Barack Obama was a product of an inter-racial marriage, he had for a while, white identity problems. He knew he was half Kenyan but he was not sure for a while if he was an African

American culturally. Later, he became ideologically liberal and Democratic by party-affiliation – quite early because of his mother. Through his growing knowledge of African American history, he realized that the early Black response to racial inequality was to struggle for education and economic opportunities rather than fight for political rights. Indeed, this was the Booker T. Washington model (1856-1915) who rose from slavery to become the most distinguished educator of his time. He also served as political leader and spokesman for the African American community from 1895-1915.

Later, another approach to Black inequality was launched by W. E. B. Du Bois (1868-1963). He believed in a highly educated Black elite ("the Talented Tenth") who would then be the vanguard of the Black struggles for rights and opportunities. W. E. B. Du Bois was himself the first Black person to get a Ph.D. in Sociology from Harvard University in Cambridge, Massachusetts (in 1895). Side by side with the model of Du Bois' "Talented Tenth" model was the model of Marcus Garvey (1887-1940). Garvey was an immigrant from Jamaica who politically inspired more than a million African Americans. Garvey's solution was racial separatism. Garvey's answer to racial inequality in the United States was to Garvey a "Back to Africa movement," a kind of Black Zionism, seeking wholesale African American migration back to the ancestral continent. Eventually U.S. authorities arrested Garvey for using the mail to defraud the public and this led to his deportation from the United States. Marcus Garvey spent his last years in London where he died poor and in obscurity. Mazrui observes that he did not fully realize his enormous influence on the history of Black consciousness, combined with Black dignity.

Closer to the time of Barack Obama was the mode championed by Martin L. King, Jr., (1929-1968) and Jesse Jackson (born in 1941). Both Reverend King and Reverend Jackson struggled for the integration of Black Americans into the wider American society without the renunciation of their own unique separate identity. Jesse Jackson called for a combination of a "rainbow coalition" indicating that the ultimate goal was not *non-racism* but *multiracialism*.

Nevertheless, the ideal for both Dr. King and Reverend Jackson was not the pursuit of a *post-racial* America but the creation of a *post-racism* society. Mazrui declares that a post-racial America would seek to minimize race consciousness and discouraged racial pride in favor of the broader national identity. Hence, a post-racism society would maintain racial consciousness and racial pride in each race, but eradicate negative racial prejudice towards others and seek to end antagonism between the races. Mazrui asserts that the relevant metaphor in this case is neither a cocktail mixture nor still a mosaic, but precisely what Reverend Jackson had in mind a "rainbow coalition", indicating that the ultimate goal was not *non-racialism* but *multiracialism*.[10]

Next, Barack Hussein Obama enters the national and global stages. Mazrui contends that for Obama the quest was not Booker T. Washington's pursuit of *skills without necessarily rights*; nor Du Bois's *Talented Tenth* pursuing racial equality; nor Garvey's clarion call for a *return to Africa*; nor Dr. King's and Reverend Jackson's quest for a multiracial America. For Barack Obama the ideal was not merely to end racism but to minimize race consciousness and the utopia of racial balance. Obama's dream is for a non-racial rather than multiracial America. His ultimate pursuit is for a post-racial age. Mazrui contends that the election of Barack Obama as the first African American U.S. president has resulted in the creation of the most powerful single Black person in history of civilization (although Mazrui does acknowledge that there are constraints on his power by both the U.S. Congress and the Supreme Court). However, he notes that on the global stage and in the context of world history, Obama is far more powerful than Shaka Zulu was in South Africa's history, or Menelik II was in Ethiopia's historical experience, or Ramses II was in the annals of ancient Egypt, or Julius Nyerere was in post-colonial Tanzania. Mazrui ponders that equipped and endowed with both hard and soft dimension of power including economic, military, and diplomatic power of the United States of America, Obama is more powerful than all those African makers of history added together.

Huntington, Cultural Forces and the Clash of Civilization

At the beginning of the 20th century W. E. B. Du Bois, already considered as a seminal African American thinker and leader, predicted that the principal problematic of the twentieth century was going to be the *problem of the color line*. Du Bois forecast the century engulfed by racism, lynching, and the white man's burden and what came to be known as Apartheid. Refugees on the run from racially and nationalistically instigated conflict overwhelmed the 20th century.

Mazrui states now that we are in the twenty-first century, the question has arisen whether the central problem of the twenty-first was going to be the *problem of the culture line*. Has the transition occurred between the clash of identities (such as races) to the clash of values (such as cultural norms in conflict)? Are refugees of the 21st century already disproportionately *cultural* refugees? Samuel Huntington contend that now the Cold War is over, future conflicts in the world would be less and less between states and ideological blocs and more between civilizations and cultural blocs. Huntington launched this debate in his article in *Foreigh Affairs*, New York, 1996, in an article that echoed around the world.

At this juncture, Samuel Huntington entered the fray revolving around cultural forces in world politics as a post-Cold War phenomenon emphasizing what he called: "the clash of civilizations," in a provocative article in *Foreign Affairs* in 1993,[11] and then his full-length book published in 1996: *The Clash of Civilizations and the Remaking of World Order* that ideologically codified and gave power and consent to post-Cold War consensus around the threat posed by Islam and Muslims in the Third World. Huntington observes that conflict between states in the post-Cold War era will converge along cultural lines where religion, history, and ethnic differences may generate political violence. Hence, new battle lines are emerging in the Middle East, Central Asia, and elsewhere in the Third World. Huntington asserts that most people in Third World nations desire both economic development and modernization. However, their longing for economic development and modernization does not necessarily lead to broad acceptance of Western values. In the post-Cold War era, Huntington hypothesizes a world in which conflict erupts between the global North and the global South especially the worlds of Islam and Confucianism. Huntington contends that, precisely because of economic modernization and social change throughout the world, people are being unglued or alienated from their established identities, while at the same time the nation-state is weakened as a source of identity.[12] Religions move in to fill the vacuum left by the decline of the nation as a source for identity. Huntington urges American policymakers to forge new alliances with likeminded and culturally similar states, meaning the Northeast and the Northwest. He urges these same policymakers to be willing to compromise with and confront these alien civilizations. Hence, the clash of civilizations symbolically represents the new zone of conflict between the global North and the global South.[13] Civilization, according to Huntington is the highest cultural alliance or consortium of people and the broadest level of cultural identity people have short of that which distinguishes humans from other species. It is defined both by the common impartial features, such as language, history, religion, customs, and institutions, and by the subjective self-identification of people.[14]

Huntington's clash of civilizations thesis resonates with the work of George Kennan', who is often celebrated as the "father of the containment policy" for America's Cold War and whose famous anonymous piece: "The Source of Soviet Conduct," in the 1947 issue of *Foreign Affairs*, heavily influence Truman, Eisenhower, and the architects of American anticommunist policy in the Third World.[15] Huntington had high expectations that this clash would intensify between the West and Islam. Huntington laid the groundwork for the linkages and interconnections between the "Red Scare" and the "Green Menace" but also the deeply held existential need and desire for a narrative of threat that could give coherence to U.S. national identity and the West. Consequently, Huntington's thesis, while privileging civilizations over nations – in the case of the West over Islamic or Sinitic (Chinese) nations – ultimately suggests that the United States, though a nation could act as a substitute as the epitome of the West to protect not only its own ideas but also those of the countries of Europe and their allies the world over:

> The world is a dangerous place, in which a large number of people resent our wealth, power, and culture, and vigorously opposed our efforts to persuade or coerce them to accept our values of human rights, democracy and capitalism. In this world America must learn to distinguish among our true friends who will be with us and we with them through the thick and thin… and unrelenting enemies who will try to destroy us unless we destroy them first.[16]

Sohail Daulatzai observes that Huntington's ideas gain credence and legitimacy because they absolve the global North (the West) of any responsibility in creating the contemporary world order in which massive inequality, wars, and poverty exist. Consistent with the triumphalism that sought to re-etch or re-carve American Exceptionalism, Huntington saw poverty, war, and massive inequality as the results of intrinsically different – and even deficient – civilizations and their values. Nevertheless, his ideas have become an uncritical confirmation of power and the status quo, because he declined to acknowledge the heterogeneity or diversity within and among groups and completely disregarded Edward Said thesis concerning "the bewildering interdependence" of humans, ideas, and the march of history.[17]

Recall that one of the underlying themes of Mazrui's *Cultural Forces in World Politics* was his concerned emergent of the unipolar moment with the United States as the lone superpower and this momentous event intensified the power gap between the global North and the global South. Mazrui's recitation on America and the Third World focus on the one-way communication and how Uncle Sam's earplug was turned off or dysfunctional thus acerbating the North –South divide. Huntington's clash of civilization mantra with Muslims and the Chinese being conceptualize as the new enemies in the post-Cold War era reinforced these concerns.

Mazrui notes that since the end of the Cold War and the collapse of apartheid, far more Muslims than Blacks have died in conflicts with white folks. At this juncture, the natural enemy of the white man is now perceived to be less and less a person with a different skin color, and more and more a person with a different religion and values. For him, the salience of culture continues to rise. Barack Obama's prospects for the United States presidency were threatened less by his being black (which is apparent) than by the pervasive rumors that he is a Muslim in subterfuge. His African name is less of a handicap than his middle Muslim name, Hussein.

In addition, inter-racial military conflicts of Blacks versus whites are waning or have almost disappeared. But inter-cultural and inter-religious wars are rampant in Iraq, Sudan, Afghanistan, Kosovo, Pakistan, Chechnya, between Israelis and Palestinians – between Al- Qaida, ISIS, and their enemies in Syria and surrounding Middle Eastern countries, Africa and the world. These conflicts are producing what Mazrui calls cultural refugees – rather than racial asylum seekers. The European Union is contemplating temporarily bringing to a halt the free movement of people between member-states for at least two years in response to Muslim refugees from the Syrian civil war. Furthermore, the worst terrorist acts in sub-Saharan Africa in recent years have not been between races, but between civilizations. These include the 1998 bombing of the U.S. Embassies in Nairobi in and Dar es Salaam and the 2002 suicide bombing of the Israeli-owned hotel in Mombasa, Kenya. Mazrui asserts that in confrontations between antagonistic cultures, many cultural bystanders are often annihilated by default.

Starting in the 1980s the U.S. prison population increased more than 500 percent. Although its' population is less than 5 percent of the world's population, the United States holds roughly a quarter of its prisoners: approximately more than 2.3 million people, including 1.6 m in state and federal prisons and over 700,000 in local jails and immigration detention centers. Per head, the incarceration rates in the United States has risen sevenfold since the 1970s, and is five times Britain's, nine times Germany's and 14 times Japan. At any one time, one American adult in 35 is in prison, on parole, or probation. Approximately one-third of African American men and one in six Hispanic men can expect to be locked up at some point in their lives, and one in nine black children has a parent behind bars (*The Economist,* June 20th-26th, 2015: 11).[18] No country imprisons as many people as the United States does or for so long. The American criminal justice system is particularly punishing toward Blacks and Latinos, who are imprisoned at six times and twice the rates of whites respectively. According to a report in a recent *Economist* report, the system is riddle with drugs, abuse, and violence.

This past year alone, policing of black and brown communities ended in a significant civil rights violation that gained national attention. On April 25, 2015, a twenty-five-year-old African American male was stopped on the streets of Baltimore, forcibly taken into custody, and thrown, screaming in pain, into a police van. Later, he arrived at the University of Maryland R. Adam Crowley Shock Trauma Center in a coma from which he was never revived. He died one week later from a fatal spine injury after also experiencing complete cardiopulmonary arrest. His spine was 80% severed at the neck. As Jeffrey C. Isaac has observed: Freddie Gray never made it to prison. His incarceration began and ended in the back of the police van. The Freddie Gray death at the hands of Baltimore police officers came only months after the controversial August 14 fatal shooting of Michael Brown, an unarmed African American teenager in Ferguson, Missouri; the September 2014 fatal police shooting of Tamir Rice, a twelve year-old African American child, in Cleveland, Ohio; days after April 5, 2015 fatal police shooting of Walter Scott, an unarmed African American man with a broken taillight, in North Charleston, South Carolina; and the list goes on. The number of African American males as well as females who have been shot dead by the police has increased with regularity and the language of justice and injustice has become part of the discourse revolving around human rights and democratic legitimacy (Jeffrey C. Isaac 2015:609). The American high incarceration rates and the increase in police killings of unarmed African American suspects raised questions about the United States *Exceptionism*. Taking a trip back in time reminds us of the role of infamous National Advisory Commission on Civil Disorders (The Kerner Report); and the 971 Attica Prison Riot in New York; and the early 1970's revelation of the FBI's COINTELPRO initiative (Counterintelligence Program) and the so-called seamy-side of democracy.

Ta-Neshisi Coates notes that from the mid-1970s to the mid-1980s, incarceration rates in the United States doubled, from 150 people per 100,000 to about 300 per 100,000. From the mid-1980s to the mid-1990s, it doubled again. By 2007, it had reached a historic high of 767 people per 100,000, before reaching a modest decline to 707 people per 100,000 in 2012. In absolute terms, America's prison and jail population from 1970 until today has rose sevenfold, from 300,000 people to 2.2 million. Currently, the U.S. incarceration rate – which accounts for people in prisons and jails – is roughly 12 times the rate in Sweden, eight times the rate in Italy, seven times the rate in Canada, five times the rate in Australia, and four times the rate in Poland. America's nearest competitor is Russia – and with autocratic Vladimir Putin locking up about 450 people per 100,000. At the same time, China has about four times the American population, however, American jails and prison houses about half a million more people. According to an authoritative 2014 report by the National Research Council – current American rate of incarceration rate is unprecedented by historical and comparative standards.[19]

The policies associated with the practice of extraordinary rendition by which the United States sends terrorists suspects for interrogation in countries with a history of torture, unfortunately many of those receiving countries are in Africa – both north of the Sahara and in the Horn of Africa. Obama has only just begun to correct these injustices. African countries with both Muslims and Christian citizens are still reportedly performing America's dirty work. Good relations between Africa's Christians and Muslims are endangered by the policy of extraordinary rendition.

Recall that Du Bois argued that American foreign policy and approach to world politics is a mirror image of its domestic policy…challenging the idea of "American Exceptionalism" as a benevolent force for good in the international system. Du Bois contends that a nation whose white citizens could not treat with equity, justice and equality, their Black neighbors and citizens living in the same nation…could not develop a foreign policy involving relationships reflecting equality and justice with two-thirds of the people of the world who are people of color.[20] The problem of the color line that Du Bois spent most of his academic and professional career in efforts to resolve and explain, has remained the center of American and global life since the seventeenth century.

As Dr. King expanded his notion of the American dream and as he moved toward Malcolm X's position of linking the black struggles in the U.S. with Third World struggles against colonialism, imperialism, and white supremacy, he also began to question racial capitalism.

> We've got to begin to ask questions about the whole society. We are called upon to help the discouraged beggars in life's marketplace. But one day we must come to see that an edifice, which produces beggars, needs restructuring. It means that questions must be raised. "Who owns the oil?"…"Who owns the iron ore?"…. "Why is it that people have to pay water bills in a world that is two-thirds water?

Mazrui has tapped into a deep well of black internationalism that challenges the global racial/cultural hierarchy, globalization, neoliberalism, and structural adjustment policies. Mazrui questions the reliance on the cash nexus link to market forces and globalization. He also questions the ideas that there are no alternatives to neoliberalism and globalization that also emerges from Huntington's clash of civilization thesis and Fukuyama's mantra that we have reached the "end of history." Mazrui taps into the black archives of black internationalism to articulate alternative futures as outline by Malcolm, Martin, and others.

Mazrui also focuses on the importance of Nelson Mandela in deracialization of the African continent, while Barack Obama is redefining the racial history of the world. The late Nelson Mandela is the most distinguished of the citizens from the African continent. During his time in prison Mandela united the Black world through his martyrdom. Mandela became globally famous because of decades of suffering and because he stuck to his principles. Mandela is one of architects of the post-racism age. He provided a positive model for Barack Obama. Obama is helping to foster what Mazrui calls a post-racial condition. He goes on to state that a world without racism is not necessarily a world without race consciousness. The African continent is still suffering from the consequences of Otto von Bismarck's Berlin Conference of 1884-85.

Notes

1. Ali A. Mazrui, *Barack Obama in Comparative Perspective: McCain to Mandela; Othello to Pushkin.* May 2009 Draft
2. Ali A. Mazrui, op. cit. p.11
3. Ali A. Mazrui, eds., *Cultural Forces in World Politics*, p. 2
4. Darryl C. Thomas, eds., *The Theory and Practice of Third World Solidarity.* Westport and London: Praeger Publishers, 2001, p. 209
5. Darryl C. Thomas, *The Theory and Practice of Third World Solidarity,* p. 210
6. Ali A. Mazrui, *Cultural Forces in World Politics*, p.4
7. See Penial E. Joseph, *Waiting 'Til The Midnight Hour: A narrative of Black Power in America.* New York: Henry Holt and Company, 2006; Dayo F. Gore, Jeane Theoharris, and Komozi Woodard, *Want to Start A Revolution: Radical Women in Black Freedom Movement,* New York and London: New York University Press, 2009; Martin Biondi, *The Black Revolution On Campus*, Berkeley, Los Angeles and London: University of California Press, 2012
8. Manning Marable, *The Great Wells of Democracy: The Meaning of Race in American Life,* New York: Basic Books, 2002 pp. 76-80
9. Ali A. Mazrui, op. cit, p.34
10. Ali A. Mazrui, op. cit., p.35
11. S.P. Huntington, "The Clash of Civilizations?" *Foreign Affairs* 72, no.3 (1993): pp. 22-49
12. Ankie Hoogvelt, *Globalization and the Postcolonial* World, p. 198
13. Darryl C. Thomas, *The Theory and Practice of Third World Solidarity*, p.16
14. S.P. Huntington, op. cit., p. 24
15. Sohail Daulatzai, eds. *Black Star/Crescent Moon: The Muslim International and Black Freedom Beyond America.* Minneapolis and London: University of Minnesota Press, 2012, pp. 155-156
16. Sohail Daulatzai, *Black Star/Crescent Moon,* p. 156
17. Sohail Daulatzai, *Black Star/Crescent Moon,* p. 157
18. *The Economist* June 20th-26th, 2015, p. 11
19. Ta-Neshisi Coates, "The Black Family in the Age of Mass Incarceration," *The Atlantic/TheAtlantic.com* 2015 p. 64
20. Mark Ledwidge, eds. *Race and US Foreign Policy: The African American Foreign Policy Affairs Network,* London and New York: Routledge, 2012, p. 6

Notes on Contributors

Abdul Karim Bangura, Ph.D, is a professor of Research Methodology and Political Science at Howard University. He is also a researcher-in-residence of Abrahamic Connections and Islamic Peace Studies at the Center for Global Peace in the School of International Service at American University. He holds five PhDs in Political Science, Development Economics, Linguistics, Computer Science, and in Mathematics. He is the author of 86 books and more than 600 scholarly articles. The winner of more that 50 prestigious scholarly and community service awards, Prof. Bangura serves as a Special Envoy of the African Union Peace and Security Council.

Adekeye Adebajo, Ph.D, is the director of the institute for Pan-African Thought and Conversation at the university of Johannesburg. He served as Executive Director of the Centre for Conflict Resolution (CCR) in Cape Town between 2003 and 2017. He is the author of four books on Africa's international relations, including *The Curse of Berlin: Africa After the Cold War* (Columbia University Press, 2010); and co-editor or editor of eight books, including *Africa's Peacemakers: Nobel Peace Laureates of African Descent* (Zed, 2014).

Alamin Mazrui, Ph.D, is Professor at Rutgers University. He teaches Political Sociology of Language in Africa and the African Diaspora; African literature in English and Swahili; Politics of cultural production in East Africa; Cultural discourses on human rights in Africa; Islam and Identity in Africa and the African Diaspora. He has written several books, book chapters and numerous journal articles. Some of his special interests include human rights and civil liberties and have written policy reports on these subjects

Darryl Thomas, Ph.D., is an associate professor of African American Studies. He received his B.A. in African American History and U.S. History from Florida A & M University and his MA and Ph.D. from the Department of Political Science at the University of Michigan. He has published widely on the International Politics of the Third World, African and Africana Studies, Globalization, Global Africa/African Diaspora and the USA/China Contention over Africa and the Global South. He is a member of the Chinese in Africa/Africans in China Research Network, and the Black Curriculum Development Project. Dr. Thomas is currently completing a text that is entitled: *Global Africa and the Challenge of the 21st Century* and is co-editing *Global Africa, Black Internationalism and the Shifting Boundaries of Freedom*.

Etwin Anwar, Ph.D., is Associate Professor and the chair of Religious Studies at Hobart and William Smith Colleges, Geneva, New York. She teaches introductory classes on Islam, gender, and comparative ethics. She is the author of Gender and Self in Islam. She edited Mazrui's The Politics of Gender and the Culture of Sexuality: Western, Islamic, and African Perspectives. She has also published several articles on Ibn Sina, Meister Eckhart, Ibn Arabi, and the women's movements in Indonesia in various journals including Islamic Studies, Islam and Christian-Muslim Relations, and Hawwa. She is a contributor to Encyclopedia of Islam and the Muslim World, on "The Public Role of Women" and "Harem."

Henry Chakava is the Chairman of East African Educational Publishers Ltd., and is one of the leading voices in the publishing industry in Africa. A recipient of several awards, Chakava has published and promoted some of the leading African writers and has enormously contributed to the growth of the education sector in Africa. He is the author of *"Publishing in Africa: A one Man's Perspective." "Coming of Age: Strides in African Publishing"* is a collection of essays by various key scholars to mark Chakava's 70th birthday.

Macharia Munene, Ph. D., is Professor of History and International Relations, United States International University in Nairobi, since 1997; Collaborating International Faculty, Universitat Jaume-1, Castellon, Spain, since June-July 2000; Professorial Affiliate of the National Defence College, Karen, Nairobi, Kenya. He has also taught at the University of Nairobi, Kenyatta University, Moi University, The Ohio State University, and Kentucky State University. He has served as a resource person to many institutions. He has written and edited many books, book chapters and journal articles. Munene serves as an issue analyst for various radio, TV and newspapers in Kenya and internationally.

Maurice Nyamanga Amutabi, PhD., is the Vice Chancellor of Lukenya University. He has served as the Deputy Vice Chancellor for Academic and

Student Affairs (ASA) at Kisii University, Kenya, and as Director of Research at the Catholic University of Eastern Africa (CUEA). Prof. Amutabi taught at Central Washington University, USA (2005-2010) where he was in charge of African and Middle East Studies. Between 1992 and 2000, he taught at Moi University. He holds a PhD in African Studies from the University of Illinois at Urbana-Champaign, USA. He is the author of *The NGO Factor in Africa: The Case of Arrested Development in Kenya*, and co-author of *Nationalism and Democracy for People-Centered Development in Africa*, and *Foundations of Adult Education in Africa*.

Micere Githae Mugo, Ph.D. is Emeritus Meredith Professor for Teaching Excellence Department of African American Studies, Syracuse University. She is a renowned a playwright, author, activist, poet and literary critic. Her publications include several books, book chapters, monographs, journal articles, and collections of poems. Micere is an active community organizer and a strong advocate of orature as a site of knowledge production.

Michael O. West, Ph.D., is professor of Sociology, Africana Studies and History at Binghamton University. He has published broadly in the fields of African studies, African diaspora studies, African American studies, pan-Africanism, history and historical sociology. His current research centers on the Black Power movement in global perspectives. His works include the following authored and co-edited books: *The Rise of an African Middle Class: Colonial Zimbabwe, 1890-1965*; *Out of One, Many Africas: Reconstructing the Study and Meaning of Africa*; *From Toussaint to Tupac: The Black International Since the Age of Revolution*.

Ndirangu Wachanga, Ph.D., is Associate Professor of media studies and information science, University of Wisconsin. He is the authorized documentary biographer of Prof. Ali A. Mazrui, Prof. Ngũgĩ wa Thiong'o, and Prof. Micere Mugo. His documentary, *Ali Mazrui: A Walking Triple Heritage*, won the 2015 New York African Studies Book Award. He is the editor of *Cultural Identity and New Communication Technologies: Political, Ethnic and Ideological Implications*, and has published widely in different peer reviewed journals. Wachanga has written for media in different continents and regularly appears on the British Broadcasting Corporation and Voice of America. His research interests include memory, global media and information ethics.

N'Drie Assie Lumumba, Ph.D., is a Professor of African and Diaspora education, comparative and international education, social institutions, African social history, and the study of gender in the Africana Studies and Research Center at Cornell University. She is a Fellow of the World Academy of Art and Science. She has served as Director of the Cornell Program on Gender and Global Change (GGC) and as Director of Graduate Studies (DGS) of the Africana Studies. She is also a member of four other Cornell graduate fields: Education; Global Development, and the Cornell Institute of Public Affairs (CIPA). She is a leading scholar and policy analyst who has published numerous articles in peer-reviewed/referred journals and chapters in books carried by prestigious publishers and major published and unpublished peer-reviewed reports.

Ngũgĩ wa Thiong'o is Distinguished Professor of English and Comparative Literature at the University of California, Irvine. He is a leading African intellectual and cultural and political activist. His work includes several novels, plays, short stories, and essays, ranging from literary and social criticism to children's literature. He is the founder and editor of the Gikuyu-language journal Mutiiri.

Oscar Gakuo Mwangi, Ph.D., is Associate Professor of Political Science at the Department of Political and Administrative Studies, National University of Lesotho. His research interests are in comparative politics especially in the areas of democratization and governance, conflict and security, and environmental politics in eastern and southern Africa. His teaching areas are in the fields of Comparative Politics, International Relations, Political Economy and Political Theory.

Tukumbi Lumumba-Kasongo, Ph. D., is Professor of Political Science and Chair of the Department of International Studies at Wells College; He is a Visiting Scholar in the Department of City and Regional Planning at Cornell University. He is also currently Diaspora Fellow in the Center for International Affairs and Diplomacy at the University of Ghana, Legon. He has taught political science in many universities and colleges, including the University of Liberia where he was the Chair of the Department of political science. His research interests include: world politics; international political economy; South-south relations; peace, conflict, security and development studies; Africa-Asia. He has published many books and over hundred book chapters, monographs, and peer-reviewed articles. He is the Editor-in-Chief of African and Asian Studies and Co-Editor of the African Journal of International Affairs.

Wanjala S. Nasong'o, Ph.D. is the Stanley J. Buckman Professor of International Studies and Chair of the Department of International Studies at Rhodes College in Memphis, Tennessee. He has previously taught at the University of Nairobi and Kenyatta University in Nairobi, Kenya; and at the University of Tennessee, Knoxville. Prof. Nasong'o's latest publications include three edited and coedited volumes: *The Roots of Ethnic Conflict in Africa* (Palgrave Macmillan, 2015), *Gendering African Social Spaces* (Carolina Academic Press, 2015), and *Contentious Politics in Africa* (Carolina Academic Press, 2016). Among Prof. Nasong'o's honors are the Rhodes College's Clarence Day Award for Excellence in Research and Creative Activity (2012) and the University of Texas at Austin's Ali A. Mazrui Award for Excellence in Research and Scholarship.

Index

A

A Walking Triple Heritage 40, 45, 167, 313

Abacha, Sani 112

Abiola, Moshood 166

Achebe, Chinua v, xii–xiii, 39–43, 60, 64, 97, 106, 184

Adebajo, Adekeye v, xv, 109, 311

Adoko, Akena 51–52

Afghanistan 62, 212, 299–300, 306

Afrabia 162, 167

African Diaspora 117, 132, 162, 179, 262, 311, 313

African Union 56, 71, 109, 150, 197, 236, 248, 252, 273, 284, 311

Africanity xiii–xiv, 56, 138, 155, 158, 167, 176, 222, 252, 290

African National Congress 275–276

African Liberalism 56, 61

African Writers Of English Expression 41

Afro-Pessimism 277

Algeria 106, 110–111, 113–114, 149, 249

Ali, Mohammed v–vii, ix–xvi, 1, 15, 20–21, 23, 25, 29–37, 39–40, 42, 45–46, 48, 51, 53–54, 63–69, 73, 77–86, 88–91, 93, 95–102, 104–105, 107, 109, 115, 117, 120–121, 124–125, 133–135, 137–138, 145, 152–153, 155–169, 171–172, 174–176, 181–199, 201, 204, 216, 219, 227, 230–231, 233, 236, 251–252, 284, 290, 295–296, 298, 309, 313, 315

Aidoo, Ama Ata 124–126, 136

Amin, Idi vi, xiv, 25, 37, 48, 50, 56–57, 67, 82–83, 89–93, 96, 110, 137–138, 157, 166, 175, 187, 189, 233, 241–242, 251, 290

Amutabi, Maurice vi, xiii, 183, 188–189, 195, 198–199, 312

Annan, Kofi 111, 139, 150

Anti-Terrorism Legislation 209–210

Anwar, Etin vi, xiii, 16, 153, 219, 312

Apartheid 57–58, 61, 80, 95–96, 133, 148, 159, 269, 275–276, 303, 305

Arabic 3, 14, 54, 67, 100, 149, 204, 206, 213, 234, 241

Arusha Declaration 281

Assie-Lumumba, Ndri xvi

B

Bangura, Abdul Karim vi, xiii–xiv, 192, 233, 239, 243, 256–257, 286–287, 310–311

Bokassa, Jean-Bedel 112

Black Atlantic 295

Black Power vi, xiii, 119–120, 133, 233–234, 236, 238–239, 243–244, 247, 250–251, 257–258, 265, 276, 278, 280, 288–289, 291, 294, 300–301, 309, 313

Brazil 114, 196, 283

British 5–7, 10, 13–15, 19, 22, 50, 57–58, 66–67, 69–82, 85, 98–99, 101, 105, 117, 121, 134, 138–139, 151, 160–161, 166, 172–173, 184, 193, 241, 251, 255, 273–275, 313

British Broadcasting Corporation 15, 57, 138, 151, 166, 172, 184, 313

Biafra 41–42, 60, 183

Bush, George W. 209–211, 277, 287, 300

C

Cameroon 110

Capitalism 54, 56, 87–88, 98, 105, 119, 133, 175, 222, 263, 270, 297, 305, 308

Chakava, Henry v, 25, 312

Citizens 110–112, 114, 210, 297, 308–309

Colonialism 56, 62, 70, 77–78, 80–81, 87, 89, 92, 96, 105–106, 117, 119, 121, 133, 135, 144, 146–148, 162, 176, 178, 186, 250, 252, 254, 256, 262–263, 274, 281, 295, 308

Cold War 74, 91, 110–111, 113, 115, 128, 145, 186, 296, 298, 300–301, 303–305, 311

Corruption 111, 204, 227

Counter-Terrorism xi, 199, 215

D

Dakar 21–22, 90, 109, 182, 284

Decolonization 55, 62, 82, 117, 176, 249, 283

Democracy xv, 75, 93, 110, 165, 188, 192, 198, 200, 212, 216, 227, 229, 275–276, 301, 305, 307, 309, 313

Development 2, 22, 75, 80–82, 84, 87, 107, 110, 139–145, 148–150, 169–171, 173, 175, 179–180, 182, 185, 198, 216–217, 239, 243, 246–248, 265, 269–270, 284, 290, 296, 304, 311, 313–314

Diop, Cheikh Anta vi, xiv, 106, 147, 181, 184, 187, 233, 239, 247–248, 288

Djibouti 113, 162

Doe, Samuel 110

Drayton, Arthur 41

Dubois, W.E.B. 105

E

East African Community 148

Ecomog 149–150

Education vi, xi, xiv–xvi, 6–8, 12–15, 19, 48–49, 54, 62, 67, 69–73, 77, 94, 99, 102–103, 114, 137–138, 155–157, 161, 166–167, 169–180, 183, 216, 226, 239, 241, 261, 267, 277, 281, 290, 293, 301–302, 312–314

Index

Eden 53, 138, 144, 147

Egalitarianism 253

Egypt 16, 48, 95, 106, 110–111, 129–130, 135, 146–147, 149, 239, 245, 247, 270, 284–285, 303

Engels, Friedrich 139–142, 152

Ethics 3, 52, 93, 163, 207, 215, 312–313

Evangelism 54

F

Falola, Toyin ix–x, 184, 187

Fanon, Frantz 106, 187, 249, 251

Fascism 122, 255

Federal Bureau Of Investigation (FBI) 210, 242, 255

Fort Jesus 31, 67, 194

G

Gaddafi, Muamar 48, 192, 250

Gambia 110

Ghana vii, xiii, 66, 84, 86, 95, 106, 110–111, 117–123, 125, 127, 129–130, 133–135, 144–145, 148, 252, 262, 270, 273, 285, 314

Gikandi, Simon 60, 64

Gikuyu 106, 157, 314

Global African 23, 47, 66, 68, 73, 84, 97, 99, 120, 161, 181, 292–293, 296

Guinea 114, 118, 120, 148, 245, 260–262, 270, 292

H

Hausa 222

Hegemony 227, 229, 238

Higher Education vi, xiv–xv, 6, 19, 155–156, 161, 166–167, 177, 179–180, 261, 281

Home Guards 94

Houphouet-Boigny, Felix 180

Hughes, Langston 41

Humanitarian 93, 150, 263

Hutu 222

I

Ideology xv–xvi, 134, 136, 161, 163, 174, 199, 201, 203–205, 207, 214–216, 219, 228, 237, 253, 259, 278, 297

Imperial 7–8, 96, 165, 222

Indian Ocean 7, 30, 56, 131

Indigenous Languages 149

Islam xii–xiii, xv, 3, 5, 12, 17–19, 54–56, 60–61, 67, 107, 131, 136, 138, 144, 149, 153, 155, 158, 160–161, 165, 167, 170, 172, 176, 184, 193–194, 199, 203–206, 208–209, 211–216, 221, 224, 228–230, 242, 249–250, 286, 288, 291, 304–305, 311–312

Islamophobia 60

Israel 61, 197, 213, 298

Israel-Palestine 61

J

Jackson, Jesse 162, 230, 266, 283, 289, 292, 301–303

Jamal 50, 138, 240–241, 286–287, 293

Jamaica 167, 196, 302

Jesus 31, 67, 155, 194

Jews 17, 58, 159, 199, 245

Jihad 54, 112, 213

Juhad-Salafists 205, 208

Judeo-Christian 214

K

Kaunda, Kenneth 187

Kenya v, viii, xii, xiv–xv, 2, 4, 6–8, 13–14, 19, 22–23, 30, 40, 48–50, 57, 60–61, 63, 65–67, 69–71, 73–77, 79–81, 83, 85, 87–88, 90–95, 100–103, 105, 110, 112, 127, 131, 137–138, 149, 151, 153, 157, 173, 183, 186–195, 197–198, 200, 205–206, 210, 216, 222, 241, 251, 272–274, 306, 312–313, 315

Kenyatta, Jomo 21–22, 49, 57, 70–71, 73, 83, 85, 87–88, 90, 92–93, 103–105, 173, 183, 187–188, 190–191, 195, 273–275, 312, 315

Kadhi xii, 4, 48, 67, 90, 137, 156

King, Martin Luther, Jr vii, 48, 106, 112–113, 162, 279–280, 286, 293, 301–303, 308

Kiswahili 13, 60, 73, 149, 172, 180, 234

L

Lamu 67

Lenin, Vladimir Ilyich 84, 118–119, 122, 133, 139, 144, 152, 261–262

Liberia 110–111, 150, 314

Liberation 61, 90, 104–105, 112, 148, 150, 177–178, 229, 239, 244–245, 249, 251, 254–255, 258, 261, 265, 269–270, 277–278, 282, 285, 288, 292

Libya 99, 112–113, 149, 250

Lumumba-Kasongo, Tukumbi vi, xiv, xvi, 314

Luo 76, 83, 222

M

Maasai 60

Makerere University College vii, xiv, 6, 49–50, 84, 118, 137

Malcom X 48, 138, 235, 241, 251, 262, 268–270, 290, 292, 301, 308

Mali 111–113, 148, 262

Mandela, Nelson 23, 48, 66, 192, 275–276, 308–309

Maputo 109

Marx, Karl 139–141, 143, 152–153, 261

Marxism 56, 80, 153, 175, 262, 272

Marrakesh 109

Mau Mau 69, 73–74, 79–80, 99, 274–275

Mazrui, Ali v–xvi, 1, 5, 15, 18, 20–23, 25–27, 29–34, 36–37, 39–43, 45–69, 73, 76–86, 88–107, 109–115, 117–139, 143–153, 155–201, 203–216, 219–231, 233, 236–237, 251–252, 284–285, 290, 295–303, 305–306, 308–309, 311–313, 315

Mazrui, Alamin v–xvi, 1, 5, 15, 18, 20–23, 25–27, 29–34, 36–37, 39–43, 45–69, 73, 76–86, 88–107, 109–115, 117–139, 143–153, 155–201, 203–216, 219–231, 233, 236–237, 251–252, 284–285, 290, 295–303, 305–306, 308–309, 311–313, 315

Mbeki, Thabo 112

Mbiti, John 59, 83, 85, 97, 106

Mboya, Tom 74–75, 79, 83, 87–88, 90, 237

Index

Modisane, Bloke 41

Moi, Daniel 22, 61, 85, 91–95, 100, 102–104, 187–190, 274, 312–313

Mombasa xii, 2–3, 5–8, 10, 12–14, 19, 29, 31–34, 36, 48–49, 54, 63, 65–69, 73, 77, 104, 131, 137, 155, 173, 205–206, 251, 273, 306

Mozambique 149, 162, 299

Mphahlele, Es'kia 41

Morrison, Tony 162, 244

Mugo, Micere vii, xi, 70–71, 313

Munene, Macharia v, xiv, 65, 70, 73–74, 79, 84–85, 87, 90–91, 93–94, 105, 312

Mutunga, Willy v, viii, 61, 63, 86, 93, 96, 100, 102, 147, 153, 200, 230–231

Museveni, Yoweri 187, 190

Mwalimu v, vii, xi, xiv, 29–37, 39, 60, 62–63, 96, 106, 109, 115, 190–192, 197, 281

Mwangi, Oscar vi, xv, 70, 201–203, 216, 314

N

Nationalism 26, 55, 94, 104, 134, 146, 176–177, 233, 253, 269, 291, 313

Nasser, Gamal Abdel 129–131, 135, 285

Negritude 146–147, 253, 259, 282–283

New York Times, The 57–58, 64, 75, 98–99, 107, 151–153, 230

Nigeria xv, 41, 57, 66, 90, 95, 110, 112–114, 127, 138, 143–144, 153, 166, 173, 185–186, 192, 198, 222, 252, 258–259, 277

Nkrumah, Kwame vi–vii, xiii, 41, 46, 48, 52, 63, 84, 86, 106, 110, 117–136, 144–145, 148, 153, 158, 173, 175, 184, 252–253, 262, 270, 273, 285

Nkosi, Lewis 41–42

Nyerere, Julius vii, 41, 48, 54, 90, 96, 106, 110, 132, 187, 270, 281–282, 303

O

Obama, Barack vi, xv, 75, 82, 86–88, 113, 192, 211, 213–214, 221, 230, 295–297, 301–303, 306, 308–309

Obasanjo, Olesegun 110

Obote, Milton vii, 41, 51, 54, 56, 82–83, 89, 91–92, 135, 159, 187

Okigbo, Christopher 21, 26, 41–43, 60, 64, 109, 183, 199

Orature v, xi, 29, 32, 313

Organization Of African Unity (OAU) 236, 252, 284

P

Padmore, George 134, 237, 273

Pan-Africanism 22, 61, 105, 115, 120–122, 129–130, 134, 145–146, 148–150, 153, 179, 182, 236–237, 240, 252, 265, 277, 285, 313

Pakistan 227, 306

Pax-Africana xv–xvi, 195

Plato 139

Post-Colonial xiii, 51, 76, 82, 97, 101, 105–106, 150, 171, 176, 216, 249, 303

Post-Racial 302–303, 309

public intellectual vi–vii, xiii, 47, 109,

129, 180, 183–187, 189, 195, 197–198, 252

Q

Queen Of England 101

Qur'an 3, 5, 223, 230

R

Redding, Saunders 41

Resistance 36, 112, 204, 208, 252, 254, 272, 290

Rhodesia 80–81, 283

Rodney, Walter 89, 91, 98, 106, 187, 257–258, 289

Rome 268

Rushdie, Salman 160

Russia Revolution 118

Rwanda 111, 149–150, 166, 222

S

Said, Edward 9, 11, 15, 21, 34, 40, 46–47, 58–59, 99, 105, 107, 119, 127, 134, 138–139, 141, 151, 184, 192–194, 196, 205, 211, 221, 234, 238, 249, 254, 257, 266, 273, 275–278, 305

Satanic Verses, The 160

Seko, Sese Mobutu 112, 192, 277

Senghor, Leopold Sedar 19, 21, 110, 147, 246, 282

Senegal 21–22, 110, 147, 282, 284

Selassie, Haile 285

Shari'a 206

Shiite 204

Sierra Leone 110–111, 150, 166, 233

Slaves 98, 124, 186, 196, 268

Social Construction 201, 203, 215, 217

Socialism 84, 87–88, 121, 175, 255–256, 270, 272, 281–282, 298–300

Socrates 139

Somalia 8, 16, 110, 112–113, 149–150, 193, 211, 215–216, 252, 277, 284

South Africa 23, 41, 57–58, 60, 71, 80, 96, 112–114, 126, 143–144, 148–149, 153, 185–186, 192, 198, 269, 272, 275–276, 283–284, 289–290, 299–300, 303

Soyinka, Wole 40–41, 45–46, 52, 61, 63, 77, 97, 100–101, 107, 112, 184, 187, 193–194, 258–259, 291

Structural Adjustment Programs 308

Sunni 204, 213

T

Terrorism vi, xi, xv, 84, 94, 133, 199, 201, 203, 205–217, 228

Thiong'o, Ngugi Wa v, vii, xi–xii, 21, 39, 60, 64, 66, 72, 88, 90, 92–93, 106, 126, 184, 194, 313–314

Third World 16, 87, 91, 95–96, 98, 163, 192, 215–216, 223, 227, 229, 244, 248, 266, 269–270, 296, 298–300, 304–305, 308–309, 311

Thomas, Darryl vi, xv, 105, 158, 167, 175, 295, 309, 311–312

Trans-Atlantic 167, 171, 236

Trial Of Christopher Okigbo, The 21, 26, 42, 60, 64, 109, 183, 199

Trinidad And Tobago 212, 233, 291

Triple Heritage vi, x–xiii, 16, 19, 26, 40, 42, 45–46, 56–57, 60, 62, 64,

77, 84, 95, 97–100, 107, 118, 131, 133–136, 138, 151, 153, 155–156, 160–161, 165, 167, 176, 181, 184, 186, 196–197, 199, 206, 219–220, 290, 313

Truman, Harry 214, 304

Tutsi 166, 222

U

Ujamaa vii, 106, 281

Uganda vii, 6, 8, 25, 51, 54, 56–57, 63, 66, 81–83, 89–92, 110, 112–113, 118, 149, 157, 159, 164, 166, 173, 187, 222, 281

Uhuru 84, 158, 167, 175, 181, 190

University Of Michigan 57, 59, 90, 138, 157, 162–163, 173, 311

United Nations 50, 52, 63, 71, 111, 113, 139, 150, 258, 277, 281, 283, 287, 300

V

Vietnam 91, 131, 135, 260, 269, 280, 283, 299–301

Villain 111–113

Virginia 70, 165, 301

Village 18, 20, 97, 99, 241, 259–260, 276

W

Wachanga, Ndirangu v, xvi, 21, 27, 40, 45, 64, 313

West, Michael vi, xiii, 2, 23, 40–41, 48, 52, 55–56, 58, 82, 84, 96, 98–101, 113, 117, 128, 144–145, 148–150, 165, 167, 175, 177–179, 185–186, 190, 192–193, 196, 198, 206, 211, 236–237, 242, 250, 260, 266, 270, 279, 282, 284–285, 291–292, 295, 297, 299–300, 305, 313

World Bank 113, 156

World War II 10, 13, 68, 105, 117, 145, 210, 213, 255, 273, 297

X

Xenophobia 60

Y

Yeats 40

Yemen 162

Yugoslavia 50, 79

Yoruba 42, 60, 222

Z

Zaire 112, 149

Zambia 52, 110, 187

Zanzibar 2, 5–8, 10, 12–13, 32, 49, 68, 162, 166, 281

Zimbabwe 16, 91, 110, 146, 252, 269, 283, 313

Zionism 159, 302

Zulu 105, 126, 146, 303